Frontispiece: Baalbec. From *The Holy Land*, Volume II, by David Roberts (1843). F. G. Moon, London.

The Collapse of Complex Societies

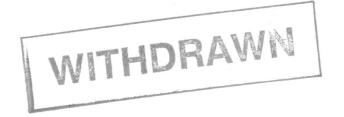

NEW STUDIES IN ARCHAEOLOGY

Series editors
Colin Renfrew, *University of Cambridge*
Jeremy Sabloff, *University of Pittsburgh*

Other titles in the series include

Dean E. Arnold: *Ceramic Theory and Cultural Process*
Graeme Barker: *Prehistoric Farming in Europe*
Richard E.G. Blanton, Stephen A. Kowalewski, Gary M. Feinman and Jill Appel: *Ancient Mesoamerica*
Peter Bogucki: *Forest Farmers and Stockherders*
Graham Connah: *Three Thousand Years in Africa*
Geoffrey Conrad and Arthur Demarest: *Religion and Empire: The Dynamics of Aztec and Inca Expansionism*
John Fox: *Maya Postclassic State Formation*
Bo Gräslund: *The Birth of Prehistoric Chronology*
Ian Hodder and Clive Orton: *Spatial Analysis in Archaeology*
Rosalind L. Hunter-Anderson: *Prehistoric Adaptation in the American Southwest*
Patrick Vinton Kirch: *The Evolution of the Polynesian Chiefdoms*
Daniel Miller: *Artefacts as Categories*
Olivier de Montmollin: *The Archaeology of Political Structure: Settlement Analysis in a Classic Maya Polity*
Ian Morris: *Burial and Ancient Society: The Rise of the Greek City State*
Keith Muckelroy: *Maritime Archaeology*
Stephen Plog: *Stylistic Variation in Prehistoric Ceramics*
Joseph Tainter: *The Collapse of Complex Societies*
Michael Shanks and Christopher Tilley: *Re-Constructing Archaeology*
Robin Torrence: *Production and Exchange of Stone Tools*
Peter Wells: *Culture Contact and Culture Change*
Alasdair Whittle: *Problems in Neolithic Archaeology*

JOSEPH A. TAINTER

The Collapse of
Complex Societies

CAMBRIDGE
UNIVERSITY PRESS

PUBLISHED BY THE PRESS SYNDICATE OF THE UNIVERSITY OF CAMBRIDGE
The Pitt Building, Trumpington Street, Cambridge, United Kingdom

CAMBRIDGE UNIVERSITY PRESS
The Edinburgh Building, Cambridge CB2 2RU, UK
40 West 20th Street, New York, NY 10011–4211, USA
477 Williamstown Road, Port Melbourne, VIC 3207, Australia
Ruiz de Alarcón 13, 28014 Madrid, Spain
Dock House, The Waterfront, Cape Town 8001, South Africa

http://www.cambridge.org

First published 1988
Reprinted 1989
First paperback edition 1990
Fourteenth printing 2005

Printed in the United Kingdom at the University Press, Cambridge

British Library Cataloguing in Publication data
Tainter, Joseph A.
The collapse of complex societies. –
(New studies in archaeology)
1. History, Ancient   2. Civilization
I. Title   II. Series
930 D57

Library of Congress Cataloguing in Publication data
Tainter, Joseph A.
The collapse of complex societies.
(New studies in archaeology)
Includes index.
1. Civilization, Ancient
2. Comparative civilization   3. Civilization – Philosophy.
I. Title.   II. Series.
CB311.T245 1987   930   86–33432

ISBN 0 521 38673 X paperback

For Bonnie and Emmet

CONTENTS

FIGURES

TABLES

ACKNOWLEDGEMENTS

Edward Hallett Carr once suggested that Toynbee's cyclical theory of history was the characteristic view of a society in crisis (1961: 37), and others have noted that there is often a concern with collapse at times of distress. While doubtlessly this is true, the present work reflects an interest that has lain unfulfilled since my first exposure to this topic. Its fruition owes much to two persons. Foremost is my wife, Bonnie Bagley Tainter, who encouraged me to transform my interest in collapse, and my dissatisfaction with the state of its study, into this book. Where I had in mind perhaps a few papers, she saw that only a longer treatment would suffice, and the work owes a great deal to her foresight. It was in the course of many conversations with Bonnie that the ideas presented here reached their final form. Both she and our son, Emmet, tolerated the disruption that such a work entails, for the nearly two years needed for research and writing, without wavering in their support. Finally, Bonnie's sharp editorial eye helped smooth the first draft into a more readable document.

Thomas King has for several years been dissatisfied with the archaeological research done in the United States under the mandate of historic preservation. To formulate a program of improvement, he organized a symposium for the 1982 Annual Meeting of the Society for American Archaeology on the subject of 'National Archaeological Research Topics,' and invited me to make a presentation. The short paper that resulted was my first attempt to articulate what previously had been vague misgivings about the study of collapse. What is presented in these pages is an outgrowth of that paper, and of Tom's encouragement to undertake it.

A number of colleagues with whom I corresponded expressed interest in the work, and responded readily to my requests for references and papers. These were George Cowgill, T. Patrick Culbert, Michael Parker-Pearson, John Pfeiffer, Robert Sharer, Stephen Whittington, Robert Wenke, and most especially, Norman Yoffee.

Emily Garber and Carol Raish gave generously of time and effort to help obtain bibliographic materials. I am grateful to Larry Nordby of the U.S. National Park Service, and to various authors and publishers as noted in the text, who gave permission to reproduce illustrations. Sherry Holtke capably prepared Fig. 19, and Scott Shermer developed several computer-generated illustrations.

Several colleagues also, upon request, reviewed either the 1982 paper or drafts of the present work, and made welcome suggestions. These include Arthur Ireland, Christopher Peebles, Michael Schiffer, H. Wolcott Toll, Henry Wright and Norman Yoffee.

I must especially mention Colin Renfrew and Jeremy Sabloff, series editors for the

New Studies in Archaeology, whose interest in the work brought it to its present form, and whose comments led to material improvements. Peter Richards, archaeology editor for Cambridge University Press, and Iain White, who meticulously prepared the typescript for printing, deserve special thanks.

To all – family, colleagues, and editors – I offer my great appreciation for your help.

Joseph A. Tainter

1

Introduction to collapse

Much of the central floodplain of the ancient Euphrates now lies beyond the frontiers of cultivation, a region of empty desolation. Tangled dunes, long disused canal levees, and the rubble-strewn mounds of former settlement contribute only low, featureless relief. Vegetation is sparse, and in many areas it is almost wholly absent. Rough, wind-eroded land surfaces and periodically flooded depressions form an irregular patchwork in all directions, discouraging any but the most committed traveler. To suggest the immediate impact of human life there is only a rare tent... Yet at one time here lay the core, the heartland, the oldest urban, literate civilization in the world.

Robert McC. Adams
(1981: xvii)

We ascended by large stone steps, in some places perfect, and in others thrown down by trees which had grown up between the crevices...we followed our guide...through the thick forest, among half-buried fragments, to fourteen monuments...one displaced from its pedestal by enormous roots; another locked in the close embrace of branches of trees, and almost lifted out of the earth; another hurled to the ground, and bound down by huge vines and creepers; and one standing, with its altar before it, in a grove of trees which grew around it, seeming to shade and shroud it as a sacred thing... The only sounds that disturbed the quiet of this buried city were the noise of monkeys...

John L. Stephens
(1850: 102-3)

The image of lost civilizations is compelling: cities buried by drifting sands or tangled jungle, ruin and desolation where once there were people and abundance. Surely few persons can read such descriptions and not sense awe and mystery. Invariably we are spellbound, and want to know more. Who were these people and, particularly, what happened to them? How could flourishing civilizations have existed in what are now such devastated circumstances? Did the people degrade their environment, did the climate change, or did civil conflict lead to collapse? Did foreign invaders put these cities to an end? Or is there some mysterious, internal dynamic to the rise and fall of civilizations? Some of us are so fascinated by these questions that we devote our lives to studying them. Most people encounter the dilemma of fallen empires and devastated cities in casual reading, or in a school course. The image is troublesome to all, not only for the vast human endeavors that have mysteriously failed, but also for the enduring implication of these failures.

The implication is clear: civilizations are fragile, impermanent things. This fact inevitably captures our attention, and however we might wish otherwise, prompts disturbing questions. Are modern societies similarly vulnerable? Is it likely, as Ortega

1

asserts, that 'The possibility that a civilization should die doubles our own mortality' (quoted in Mazzarino [1966: 171])? Many of course prefer to believe that modern civilization, with its scientific and technological capacity, its energy resources, and its knowledge of economics and history, should be able to survive whatever crises ancient and simpler societies found insurmountable. But how firm is this belief? Many persons who have some awareness of history no doubt harbor the suspicion, as Wilamowitz voiced regarding the Roman Empire, that 'Civilization can die, because it has already died once' (quoted in Mazzarino [1966: 174]).

To some historians of the early twentieth century the twilight of Rome seemed almost a page of contemporary history (Mazzarino 1966: 173; Casson 1937: 183). This analogy has become deeply rooted in popular thought, and certainly persists today. It is even reflected in the writings of some modern competent authorities (e.g., Isaac 1971). The irresistible allusion to ancient Rome has dominated the thinking of large numbers of people for one and one-half millennia (Mazzarino 1966). Were it not for this well-documented example of a powerful empire disintegrating, to which every Western schoolchild is exposed, the fear of collapse would certainly be less widespread. As it is, those who are concerned about the future of industrial society, about its economic direction, its ecological basis, and its political superstructure, have an irrefutable illustration of the contention that civilizations, even powerful ones, are vulnerable.

Why study collapse? Many social scientists might agree with Isaac: 'It goes without saying that the collapse of ancient civilization is the most outstanding event in its history...' (1971: xi). Yet beyond scientific interest there is an additional reason: collapse is a topic of the most widespread concern and the highest social significance. The reason why complex societies disintegrate is of vital importance to every member of one, and today that includes nearly the entire world population. Whether or not collapse was the most outstanding event of ancient history, few would care for it to become the most significant event of the present era. Even if one believes that modern societies are less vulnerable to collapse than ancient ones, the possibility that they may not be so remains troubling. In the absence of a systematic, scientific treatment of collapse such concerns range untethered to any firm, reliable base.

Disintegration of the social order has been a recurrent concern in Western history, and has often been expressed in a religious idiom. In the last few decades this concern has seemingly become rampant, and has achieved expression through a more secular form. A review of a recent exhibit of Mayan artifacts expressed popular thinking well:

> ...some of the fascination of the Maya...may lie in the legendary 'collapse' of their culture several centuries before the Spanish conquest. Every thoughtful person who ponders the bureaucratic and technological pressures on ordinary life today must wonder whether it is possible for a society to strangle on its own complexities... Sensing that our own collective future is in jeopardy...we are hungry for historical analysis to help us imagine the direction events might take (Baker 1986: 12).

This concern crosses the social and intellectual spectrum, from the responsible scientists and business leaders who make up the Club of Rome, to the more extreme fringes of the 'survivalist' movement. In between one finds a variety of serious, well-meaning persons: environmentalists, no-growth advocates, nuclear-freeze proponents, and others. All fear, for one reason or another, that industrial civilization is in danger. Such fears are frequently based on historical analogy with past civilizations that have disappeared (and indeed it is sometimes suggested that we are about to go the way of the dinosaurs).

Contemporary thinkers foresee collapse from such catastrophes as nuclear war, resource depletion, economic decline, ecological crises, or sociopolitical disintegration (e.g., Meadows et al. 1972; Catton 1980; Turco et al. 1984). Only recently have such fears become widespread. As Dawson has noted:

> Of all the changes that the twentieth century has brought, none goes deeper
> than the disappearance of that unquestioning faith in the future and the absolute
> value of our civilization which was the dominant note of the nineteenth century
> (1956: 54).

Although collapse has been of interest for as long as societies have proven vulnerable, it has been a difficult mystery for historians and social scientists. Perhaps because of this, the development of political complexity has attracted more scholarly attention than collapse, its antithesis. Human history as a whole has been characterized by a seemingly inexorable trend toward higher levels of complexity, specialization, and sociopolitical control, processing of greater quantities of energy and information, formation of ever larger settlements, and development of more complex and capable technologies. This persistent aspect of our history has rightfully received an overwhelming amount of research, so that today we are beginning to understand how this came about. Yet the instances when this almost universal trend has been disrupted by collapse have not received a corresponding level of attention. To be sure, innumerable writers have produced myriad explanations of collapse; but even so, understanding disintegration has remained a distinctly minor concern in the social sciences. Explanations of collapse have tended to be *ad hoc*, pertaining only to one or a few societies, so that a general understanding remains elusive. At the same time, as will be shown, such theories have suffered in common from a number of conceptual and logical failings. When this study was begun there was no reliable, universal explanation of collapse, no theory that would help us to understand most or all of its occurrences. It was indeed this state of affairs that prompted the present undertaking. The objective of this work then is to develop a general explanation of collapse, applicable in a variety of contexts, and with implications for current conditions. This is a work of archaeology and history, but more basically of social theory.

The approach is to first introduce and exemplify collapse, and then in Chapter 2 to briefly examine the nature of complex societies. Chapter 3 discusses and evaluates existing approaches to understanding collapse. A general explanation is developed in Chapter 4, and evaluated by case studies in Chapter 5. A concluding chapter further discusses the proposed explanation, synthesizes the work, and raises some implications for the contemporary scene.

What is collapse?

'Collapse' is a broad term that can cover many kinds of processes. It means different things to different people. Some see collapse as a thing that could happen only to societies organized at the most complex level. To them, the notion of tribal societies or village horticulturalists collapsing will seem odd. Others view collapse in terms of economic disintegration, of which the predicted end of industrial society is the ultimate expression. Still others question the very utility of the concept, pointing out that art styles and literary traditions often survive political decentralization.

Collapse, as viewed in the present work, is a *political* process. It may, and often does, have consequences in such areas as economics, art, and literature, but it is fundamentally a matter of the sociopolitical sphere. *A society has collapsed when it displays a rapid, significant loss of an established level of sociopolitical complexity.* The term 'established level' is important. To qualify as an instance of collapse a society must have been at, or developing toward, a level of complexity for more than one or two generations. The demise of the Carolingian Empire, thus, is not a case of collapse – merely an unsuccessful attempt at empire building. The collapse, in turn, must be rapid – taking no more than a few decades – and must entail a substantial loss of sociopolitical structure. Losses that are less severe, or take longer to occur, are to be considered cases of weakness and decline.

Collapse is manifest in such things as:

> a lower degree of stratification and social differentiation;
> less economic and occupational specialization, of individuals, groups, and terri-
> > tories;
> less centralized control; that is, less regulation and integration of diverse econo-
> > mic and political groups by elites;
> less behavioral control and regimentation;
> less investment in the epiphenomena of complexity, those elements that define
> > the concept of 'civilization': monumental architecture, artistic and literary
> > achievements, and the like;
> less flow of information between individuals, between political and economic
> > groups, and between a center and its periphery;
> less sharing, trading, and redistribution of resources;
> less overall coordination and organization of individuals and groups;
> a smaller territory integrated within a single political unit.

Not all collapsing societies, to be sure, will be equally characterized by each item on this list, and the list is by no means complete. Some societies that come under this definition have not possessed all of these features, and indeed one or two that will be introduced had few of them. This list, however, provides a fairly concise description of what happened in most of the better known cases of collapse.

Collapse is a general process that is not restricted to any type of society or level of complexity. Complexity in human societies, as discussed in greater detail in Chapter 2, is not an all-or-nothing proposition. Societies vary in complexity along a continuous scale, and any society that increases or decreases in complexity does so along the progression of this scale. There is no point on such a scale at which complexity can be said to emerge. Hunting bands and tribal cultivators experience changes in complexity, either increases or decreases, just as surely as do large nations. Collapse, involving as it does a sudden, major loss of an established level of complexity, must be considered relative to the size of the society in which it occurs. Simple societies can lose an established level of complexity just as do great empires. Sedentary horticulturalists may become mobile foragers, and lose the sociopolitical trappings of village life. A region organized under central chiefly administration may lose this hierarchical umbrella and revert to independent, feuding villages. A group of foragers may be so distressed by environmental deterioration that sharing and societal organization are largely abandoned. These are cases of collapse, no less so than the end of Rome, and no less significant for their respective populations. To the extent, moreover, that the collapses of simpler societies can be understood by general principles, they are no less illuminating than the fall of nations and empires. Any explanation of collapse that purports to have general potential should help us to understand the full spectrum of its manifestations, from the simplest to the most complex. This, indeed, is one of the central points and goals of the work.

These points made, it should be cautioned that in fact defining collapse is no easy matter. The present discussion may serve to introduce the orientation, but the definition will have to be added to as the work progresses.

Collapse in history

The fall of the Roman Empire is, in the West, the most widely known instance of collapse, the one which comes most readily to popular thought. Yet it is only one case, if a particularly dramatic one, of a fairly common process. Collapse is a recurrent feature of human societies, and indeed it is this fact that makes it worthwhile to explore a general explanation. The following pages give a brief overview of some cases of collapse. This overview is intended to illustrate common elements to the phenomenon, and also to portray the range of societies that are susceptible. In accord with the discussion of the previous section, the reader will find in the following pages a spectrum of societies from simple to powerful and complex. The discussion is arranged by major geographical areas, and then chronologically. The picture that emerges is of a process recurrent in history and prehistory, and global in its distribution.

This is by no means a complete list. Further cases were no longer sought when it seemed that redundancy would result. There have been, in addition, no doubt many hundreds or thousands of collapses among centralized societies that were not organized at a sufficient level of complexity to produce written records. Some of these are known archaeologically, but probably only a small minority. To the extent that collapse is a general process, such cases are fully pertinent to understanding it, and should be studied whenever found.

The Western Chou Empire

The Chou dynasty succeeded the corrupt Shang in the mastery of China by 1122 B.C. A reign was subsequently established that later Chinese looked back on as a golden age. The Chou ruled through a feudal system, but within a few centuries their control began to slip. The royal house began to lose power as early as 934 B.C. Barbarian invasions increased in frequency through the ninth and eighth centuries, and regional lords began to ignore their obligations to the Chou court. In 771 B.C. the last Western Chou ruler was killed in battle and the capital city, Hao, overrun and sacked by northerners.

Following this disaster, the Chou capital was moved east to Loyang, where the Eastern Chou dynasty resided from 770 to 256 B.C. The Eastern Chou, however, were powerless figureheads: Chinese unity effectively collapsed with the Western Chou. Through the Spring and Autumn (770-464 B.C.) and Warring States (463-222 B.C.) periods, disintegration and endless conflict were the norms. Powerful regional states emerged which contended endlessly for hegemony, forging and breaking alliances, engaging in wars, and manipulating barbarian groups. Through time, as conflict intensified, smaller states were continuously absorbed. The contending states became fewer but larger, until finally the Ch'in reunified China in 221 B.C.

The period of disintegration and conflict produced some of China's major philosophical, literary, and scientific achievements. Confucius wrote during, and in reaction to, this era. Contending schools of philosophy (the 'Hundred Schools') proliferated and flourished between 500 and 250 B.C. In addition to many technical and economic developments, Chinese political thought in its classical form emerged during the worst of the breakdown (Creel 1953, 1970; Needham 1965; Levenson and Schurman 1969; Hucker 1975).

The Harappan Civilization

The Harappan, or Indus Valley, Civilization existed in northwestern India perhaps as early as 2400 B.C. It was apparently dominated by two major cities, Mohenjo-Daro in the central Indus Valley, and Harappa upstream. Both were established according to similar designs: a fortified citadel on the western side, with civic and religious buildings, and a lower urban zone, with gridded, standardized streets, and systems of drainage and refuse disposal. There were many smaller centers, some with the same basic layout. Seaports controlled the coastline above and below the Indus. This literate civilization shows a striking degree of uniformity through time and space in pottery, ornaments, bricks, weapons, implements of bronze and stone, seals, and civic planning. Both major sites had massive granaries. The impression is of a highly centralized society in which the state controlled many facets of daily living – milling grain, manufacturing bricks and mass producing pottery, obtaining firewood, and building residences.

Yet by roughly 1750 B.C. this regional uniformity and centralized control had broken down. In urban centers the standardization of street frontages declined, brickwork was less careful, bricks from older buildings were reused in new, expedient ones, and older buildings were subdivided. Pottery kilns came for the first time to be built within city walls. Expressive art became simpler. Hoards of jewelry were stashed away. Groups of unburied corpses were left lying in the streets. At some centers, the Harappan occupation was followed by people who lived among the ruins in flimsy huts, seemingly after the complete breakdown of civil authority. Eventually these, too, passed into history (Piggott 1950; Raikes 1964; Dales 1966; Thapar 1966; Wheeler 1966, 1968; Allchin and Allchin 1968; Gupta 1982).

Mesopotamia

Mesopotamia is characteristically seen as the heartland, the center of origin of civilization and urban society. It displays a history of political rises and declines that furnishes many examples of collapse.

From the competing city-states of the early third millennium B.C., Sargon of Akkad developed the first Mesopotamian empire (ca. 2350-2150 B.C.). Its fall some 200 years following establishment was presaged by a series of rebellions in the subject city-states. A period of decentralization followed in southern Mesopotamia. The next period of regional hegemony was established by the Third Dynasty of Ur (ca. 2100-2000 B.C.), which set up a vast regional bureaucracy to collect taxes and tribute. The Third Dynasty of Ur encouraged expansion of the irrigation system, and growth of population and settlement. This attempt to maximize economic and political power led to a rapid collapse, with disastrous consequences for southern Mesopotamia. Over the next millennium or so there was a 40 percent reduction in the number of settlements, and a 77 percent reduction in settled area.

Political power shifted to the north, to Babylon. The empire established by Hammurabi (ca. 1792-1750 B.C.) did not survive the death of his son, Samsuiluna (died ca. 1712 B.C.). Four succeeding kings ruled a greatly reduced realm, until the dynasty was terminated by the Hittites. Partly coterminously, the Assyrians in the period between 1920 and 1780 B.C. established widespread trade routes, and then collapsed. The Assyrians enjoyed a political resurgence in the 14th century B.C., and then again from the ninth to the seventh centuries. In this latter era they held a vast empire over much of the Near East, only to lose most of these dependencies and suffer defeat by the Medes in 614 B.C. Assyrian social and political institutions disappeared thereafter.

After a brief resurgence by Babylon, brought to an end by Cyrus the Great, Mesopotamia was incorporated into successive Near Eastern empires of varying size and durability - Achaemenian, Seleucid, Parthian, Sassanian, and Islamic. There was an irregular but largely sustained increase in the scale and complexity of the agricultural regime, in population density, and in city building.

Sometime in the seventh through tenth centuries A.D., however, there was a major collapse in the Mesopotamian alluvium. By the eleventh or twelfth centuries A.D. the total occupied area had shrunk to only about six percent of its level 500 years earlier. Population dropped to the lowest point in five millennia. State resources declined precipitously. In many strategic and formerly prosperous areas, there were tax revenue losses of 90 percent or more in less than a single lifetime. People rebelled and the countryside became ungovernable. By the early tenth century irrigation weirs were nearly all confined to the vicinity of Baghdad. As described in the quote that heads this chapter, the basis for urban life in perhaps 10,000 square kilometers of the Mesopotamian heartland was eliminated for centuries. Until the modern era the region was claimed primarily by nomads (R. McC. Adams 1978, 1981; Jacobsen and Adams 1958; Waines 1977; Yoffee 1979, 1982).

The Egyptian Old Kingdom

The unification of Upper and Lower Egypt is usually traced to the First Dynasty, ca. 3100 B.C. This event has always been regarded as a milestone in political history. The Egyptian Old Kingdom was a highly centralized political system headed by a leader with qualified supernatural authority. The government was based on a literate, hierarchically organized bureaucracy. It enjoyed substantial permanent income from the crown lands, commanded large labor pools, and virtually monopolized some vital materials and imported luxuries. This government in turn enhanced productive capabilities, provided administration and outward expansion, and maintained supernatural relations.

As the Old Kingdom developed, however, it became difficult to ensure effective control of the provinces, which began to show strong feudal characteristics. The political authority of the ruler seems to have declined, while the power of provincial officials and the wealth of the administrative nobility rose. Crown lands were subdivided. The establishment of tax-exempt funerary endowments diminished royal resources. And yet these developments coincided with immense construction at royal expense. The last ruler of the Sixth Dynasty, Phiops II, built a magnificent funerary monument even as the declining power of the royal family was felt sharply at the close of his reign.

With the end of the Sixth Dynasty in 2181 B.C. the Old Kingdom collapsed. Beginning with the Seventh Dynasty there was a period of strife, one of the darkest episodes in Egyptian history. In the First Intermediate Period national centralization collapsed, and was replaced by a number of independent and semi-independent polities. There were many rulers and generally short reigns. Royal tombs became less elaborate.

Contemporary records are few, but those that exist indicate a breakdown of order. There was strife between districts; looting, killing, revolutions, and social anarchy; and incursions into the Delta. Tombs were plundered, royal women were clothed in rags, and officials were insulted; peasants carried shields as they tilled their fields. Foreign trade dropped, famines recurred, and life expectancy declined. With the Eleventh Dynasty, beginning in 2131 B.C., order and unity began to be restored. The Middle Kingdom was established. Yet local and regional independence was not fully suppressed until ca. 1870 B.C. (Smith 1971; Bell 1971; O'Connor 1974).

The Hittite Empire

The Hittites are a little known people of Anatolia, whose political history begins about 1792 B.C. with the conquests of Anitta. Throughout the succeeding centuries Hittite fortunes rose and fell. Episodes of conquest and expansion were interspersed with periods of defense and disintegration. During the latter times Hittite armies suffered reverses, provinces were lost, and the Kaska tribes raided and burned the cities of the homeland. Even the Hittite capital, Khattusha, fell to the Kaska. The great ruler

Shuppululiumash restored the Hittite position after his accession to the throne ca. 1380 B.C. In this and succeeding reigns the empire was firmly established in Anatolia and Syria. In Syria the Hittites contested successfully for domination with Egypt, concluding a treaty with Rameses in 1284 B.C.

In the early thirteenth century B.C. the Hittites were at the height of their power. Their empire included most of Anatolia, Syria, and Cyprus. The Hittites and the Egyptians were the two major powers in the region. Yet the resources of this empire were strained. Although relations with Egypt remained peaceful, the Hittites encountered troubles in nearly all directions, including the Assyrians to the southeast, the Kaska tribes to the east, and little known peoples in western Asia Minor and Cyprus. Toward the end of the thirteenth century B.C. their written records decline and finally cease altogether.

As the Hittite Empire collapsed a catastrophe of major magnitude but uncertain form overtook the region. Excavated sites across Anatolia and Syria are consistently found to have burned about this time. Hittite Civilization collapsed with the Empire. The life of the central Anatolian Plateau, after about 1204 B.C., was disrupted for a century or more. The area ceased to sustain urban settlements, and seems to have been thinly populated or used by nomads. When a new empire emerged in the region between the twelfth and ninth centuries B.C. it was Phrygian, and totally unrelated to that of the Hittites (Gurney 1973a, 1973b; Goetze 1975a, 1975b, 1975c; Hogarth 1926; Akurgal 1962; Barnett 1975b).

Minoan Civilization

The Minoan Civilization of Crete was the first in Europe. The earliest palaces on the island were built soon after 2000 B.C. They were thereafter repeatedly destroyed by earthquakes, and up to the final collapse were each time rebuilt more splendidly than before. The Minoans possessed advanced knowledge of architecture, engineering, drainage, and hydraulics. The palace of Knossos after 1700 B.C. was more luxurious than the contemporary palaces of Egypt and the Near East. It contained water-flushing latrines and a drainage system. Rich frescoes adorned many walls. There were craft production rooms for potters, weavers, metal workers, and lapidaries. Palaces functioned as administrative centers, as warehouses, and as controlling nodes in the economy. They contained large numbers of storerooms and storage vessels, Knossos alone having the capacity to hold more than 240,000 gallons of olive oil. There was administrative writing: records included the contents of armories, and indicate that goods were directed to the palace, and from there redistributed. The Phaistos Disk is the oldest known example of printing, being made from movable type impressed into the clay.

The Minoans traded widely about the Mediterranean, particularly the eastern half. They were most likely the major sea power of the time. For most of Minoan history Crete seems to have been peaceful, for the palaces were unfortified and the scenes on the frescoes peaceful. About 1500 B.C., however, a powerful earthquake caused widespread destruction, and thereafter there were major changes. An earlier script, undeciphered but known as Linear A, was replaced by the Greek Linear B. New methods of warfare were introduced, involving new kinds of arms and the horse. The Mycenaean civilization of mainland Greece became a serious trade competitor. Security declined as militarism increased. The central and eastern parts of Crete, and possibly the whole island, may have come under the domination of Knossos. Many palaces were devastated. At places like Phaistos the local governor had to report agricultural and industrial production in detail to Knossos. About 1380 B.C. the Cretan palaces were finally destroyed; most were not rebuilt. Minoan Civilization collapsed. Political, economic, and administrative centralization declined. A late, reduced administration at Knossos and some other sites finally ended about 1200 B.C. (Matz 1973a, 1973b; Willetts 1977; Stubbings 1975b; Hooker 1976; Chadwick 1976).

Mycenaean Civilization

Mycenaean Civilization of Mainland Greece began to develop about 1650 B.C. It reached the height of its power and prosperity after 1400 B.C., following the Minoan collapse. Throughout central and southern Greece there developed a great deal of homogeneity in such things as art, architecture, and political organization. This region was divided among a number of independent states which were each centered on a fortified palace/citadel complex headed by a single ruler. Mycenae itself is the most famous of these, and was probably the most powerful. Nobles made up the royal court and administration; major land holders (lesser nobles) administered estates in the countryside. The Linear B tablets from Pylos indicate that this kingdom was divided into 16 administrative districts, each controlled by a governor and deputy. Mycenaean palaces, like their Cretan counterparts, served as controlling economic centers at which goods and foodstuffs were stored and redistributed. Much of the Linear B writing was devoted to the accounting needs created thereby.

The art and architecture of Mycenaean Civilization are widely known. Major structures were built with massive, 'cyclopean' walls. Palaces contained frescoes and bathrooms. Gem cutting, metalwork, and pottery making were carried out by skilled artisans, as was inlay and work in ivory, glass, and faience. Very often these artisans worked under the close supervision of a palace authority. Roads, viaducts, and aqueducts were built. Mycenaean wares were traded widely about the Mediterranean.

After about 1200 B.C. disaster struck. Palace after palace was destroyed. There followed a period of more than 100 years of unstable conditions, repeated catastrophes afflicting many centers, and movement of population. The uniform Mycenaean style of pottery gave way to local styles that were less well executed. Metalwork became simpler. Writing disappeared. The craftsmen and artisans seem to have everywhere vanished. Fortifications were built across the Isthmus of Corinth and at other places. At Mycenae, Tiryns, and Athens water sources were developed within the citadel, cut through solid rock at great labor. The rock-cut well at Athens, at least, seems to date to the time of the troubles. Trade dropped off, and one author has suggested that the subsequent preference for iron implements was due to a sharp decline in copper and tin trade.

The number of occupied settlements dropped precipitously, from 320 in the thirteenth century B.C., to 130 in the twelfth, and 40 in the eleventh. In some areas, such as the southwest Peloponnese, settlement increased at this time, and it seems that some of the people of the devastated regions may have migrated to less troubled areas. Yet only a small part of the population loss can be accounted for in this way. Estimates of the magnitude of overall population decline range from 75 to 90 percent. Even areas that escaped devastation, such as Athens, suffered ultimate political collapse. By 1050 B.C. Mycenaean Civilization, despite brief local resurgences, was everywhere gone, and the Greek Dark Ages had begun (Stubbings 1975a, 1975b; Hooker 1976; Chadwick 1976; Desborough 1972, 1975; Betancourt 1976; Snodgrass 1971; Mylonas 1966; Taylour 1964).

The Western Roman Empire

The Roman Empire is the prime example of collapse; it is the one case above all others that inspires fascination to this day. A vast empire with supreme military power and seemingly unlimited resources, its vulnerability has always carried the message that civilizations are fleeting things. If the Roman Empire, dominant in its world, was subject to the impersonal forces of history, then it is no wonder that so many fear for the future of contemporary civilization.

Rome in the last few centuries B.C. extended its domination first over Italy, then over the Mediterranean and its fringing lands, and finally into northwestern Europe. A combination of stresses at home, dangers abroad, and irresistible opportunities made expansion a workable policy until Augustus (27 B.C.-14 A.D.) effectively capped the size of the empire. Additions thereafter tended to be of minor importance. Despite Rome's spectacular rise, the *Pax Romana* did not endure long. As early as the second century A.D. barbarian invasions and plague at home combined to weaken the empire. In the third century the empire nearly disintegrated, as civil wars and economic crises were added to more barbarian incursions and another outbreak of plague. By the end of the third and the beginning of the fourth centuries, Diocletian and Constantine restored order for a time. In 395 A.D. the Roman Empire was permanently divided into western and eastern halves. The West began a precipitous decline as provinces were increasingly lost to barbarians. Finally, the last Roman Emperor of the West was deposed in 476 A.D. (Gibbon 1776-88; A. Jones 1964, 1974).

The Olmec

Mexico's oldest civilization, the Olmec, developed in the humid swamps of coastal Veracruz toward the end of the first millennium B.C. Olmec art influenced much of Mesoamerica, and many subsequent civilizations. A succession of Olmec political centers emerged and disappeared in the jungle before the final collapse of Olmec Civilization. This latter event is poorly dated, but seems to have occurred sometime in the last few centuries B.C.

The Olmec are best known from the archaeological remains of their political centers. Perhaps the earliest of these was San Lorenzo Tenochtitlan (ca. 1150-900 B.C.). It consists in part of a major, formally arranged mound complex on a primarily artificial plateau. Groups of long, low mounds flank courts, with large pyramids at one or both ends. A stone aqueduct was built, and pools were lined with bentonite. Exotic obsidians were imported from the Mesoamerican Highlands, and there were workshops for obsidian, brown flint, and serpentine. Basalt monuments weighing more than 20 tons were brought from mountains some 50 kilometers away, and then lifted a vertical distance of 50 meters.

The site of La Venta (ca. 800-400 B.C.) may have been the political successor to San Lorenzo. It too consists of mounds, platforms, and a pyramid. Basalt columns weighing several tons in aggregate form a court that may never have been finished. A large jaguar mask mosaic was built of serpentine and then buried. After the demise of La Venta power may have shifted to Tres Zapotes, a site about which little is known.

At some Olmec sites, including San Lorenzo, there is evidence of violence at the end. At a cost of great effort, basalt monuments were deliberately and systematically mutilated and destroyed, and subsequently buried (Drucker, Heizer, and Squier 1959; Coe 1981; Soustelle 1984).

The Lowland Classic Maya

One of the most famous of civilizations that have collapsed, the Maya of the southern Peten lowlands have left a legacy of temples, palaces, entire cities lying abandoned in the jungle. This creates a powerful image. No doubt the rain forest has much to do with this. In popular thought, civilization is what stands between humanity and the chaos of nature. The picture of cities that have been overcome by this chaos compels us to morbid fascination.

Elements of the complex of features called Mayan Civilization can be traced far into the first millennium B.C. By the last few centuries B.C. complex political organization and massive public architecture were emerging in many areas. Throughout most of the first millennium A.D. Mayan cities grew in size and power. Vast public works were undertaken, temples and palaces were built and decorated, the arts flourished, and the landscape was modified and claimed for planting. These patterns intensified in the first half of the eighth century A.D. Thereafter, with a swiftness that is shocking, the Mayan cities began one-by-one to collapse. By about 900 A.D. political and ceremonial activity on the previous level came to an end, although some remnant populations tried to carry on city life. A major part of the southern Lowlands population was correspondingly lost, either to increased mortality, or to emigration from the newly deserted centers (J. Thompson 1966; Culbert n.d.).

The Mesoamerican Highlands

A number of powerful states rose to regional prominence and subsequently collapsed in the prehistory of the Mesoamerican Highlands. These include Teotihuacan in the northern part of the Valley of Mexico, Tula to the northwest of the Valley, and Monte Alban in Oaxaca.

Teotihuacan was the largest native city in the New World (and in 600 A.D. the sixth largest in the world), with a peak population estimated at roughly 125,000. Its central feature, the Street of the Dead, contains more than two kilometers of monumental construction. There are more than 75 temples, including the Pyramids of the Sun and the Moon. The former is the largest structure in pre-Columbian America, measuring 210 meters along each axis and 64 meters in height, with an estimated 1,000,000 cubic meters of material. At the south end of this street was the Ciudadela, with twin palaces. The city contained more than 2000 residential compounds, and hundreds of craft workshops in obsidian, pottery, jade, onyx, and shell. There were hundreds of painted murals. Networks of drains carried off rainwater.

Teotihuacan exerted a major influence throughout Mesoamerica. The city leaders had the ability to mobilize labor at an unprecedented level. The population and resources of the Valley of Mexico and beyond were economically reorganized. Tens of thousands of people were relocated to Teotihuacan and its vicinity. For 600 years or more, 85 to 90 percent of the population of the eastern and northern Valley of Mexico lived in or near the city. Materials such as shell, mica, and cinnabar were imported from locations up to hundreds of kilometers away.

In the later phase of Teotihuacan's dominance military themes became prominent in art. The flow of some goods into the city was reduced. About 700 A.D. Teotihuacan abruptly collapsed. The politically and ceremonially symbolic center of the city, the Street of the Dead and its monuments, was systematically, ritually burned. The population dropped within 50 years to no more than a fourth of its peak level. This remnant population sealed off doorways, and partitioned large rooms into smaller ones. A period of political fragmentation followed.

To the south, in Oaxaca, the center of Monte Alban was roughly coeval with Teotihuacan. Monte Alban is located on a mountaintop. A large section of this was leveled to build a center of monumental architecture and a community. The population of perhaps 24,000 created pyramids, temples, ballcourts, stelae, and frescoes. Defensive walls were built, and there was craft production in obsidian, shell, and other commodities. Monte Alban experienced its major growth between 200 and 600 A.D. Sometime in the seventh century it collapsed as the political center of the Valley, and a series of autonomous petty states formed. Within a few generations population at Monte Alban had declined to about 18 percent of its peak level, and more defensive walls were built.

Tula is generally regarded as the center of the semi-mythical Toltecs of Mesoamerican legend and history. Tula was a city of about 35,000 people with pyramids, ballcourts, and palaces. It reached its maximum size and importance between about 950 and 1150/1200 A.D. Craft specialists included obsidian workers, lapidaries, metalworkers, wood carvers, feather workers, scribes, potters, spinners, and weavers. Raw materials and finished goods were imported over long distances. Tula as a state was overwhelmingly concerned with militarism. Like Teotihuacan before, it attracted a major part of the Basin of Mexico population. The end of Tula came between about 1150 and 1200 A.D., and may have been accompanied by burning of its ceremonial center (Blanton 1978; Blanton and Kowalewski 1981; Davies 1977; Diehl 1981; Katz 1972; Millon 1981; Parsons 1968; Pfeiffer 1975; Sanders 1981b; Sanders et al. 1979; M. Weaver 1972; Willey 1966).

Casas Grandes

In northern Mexico, far north of Mesoamerica and a few kilometers south of the present U.S./Mexico border, a major center was built which displays both Mesoamerican and Southwestern trappings of centralized political integration.

Beginning about 1060 A.D., there was a major construction program at the regionally unique center of Casas Grandes. Various rebuildings took place until the site reached its zenith in the first half of the thirteenth century. At this time it formed a massive, multistoried apartment complex surrounded by a ring of ceremonial structures that included geometric mounds, effigy mounds, ballcourts, open plazas, a marketplace, and other specialized edifices. A city water system included a reservoir, underground stone-lined channels, and perhaps a sewage drain. These structures were clearly built in an economic system in which labor and building materials were hierarchically controlled.

Casas Grandes was surrounded by several thousand satellite villages. It was supported by a hydraulic agricultural system and by an extensive trade network. The site contained millions of marine shells representing over 60 species, plus ricolite, turquoise, salt, selenite, copper ore, and elaborate ceramic vessels. (These last have inspired a modern imitative renaissance that serves the tourist industry in the Southwestern United States.) Occupational specialists worked in shell, copper, and other materials.

Sometime about 1340 A.D. Casas Grandes political supremacy came to an end. The site fell into disrepair. Goods were still produced in large volume, but civil construction and public maintenance ceased. Public and ceremonial areas were altered for living quarters. The dead were buried in city water canals and plaza drains. As walls crumbled, ramps were built to reach the still usable upper rooms. Casas Grandes finally burned, at which time corpses were left unburied in public places, and altars were systematically destroyed (DiPeso 1974).

The Chacoans

The San Juan Basin is an arid, upland plateau located in northwestern New Mexico. Across this inhospitable landscape are found the remains of once-populous towns and villages, now utterly ruined and filled with windblown sand. The Chacoan towns, while not as widely known as the Mayan cities, present a similarly compelling picture. Instead of cities overtaken by jungle, the Chacoan image is of lost towns filled with drifting sands, and frequented only by desert fauna or occasional Navajo herders. The Chacoans were clearly masters of this desert, but somehow, disturbingly, they lost their mastery and the desert prevailed.

The Chacoans built a series of walled stone towns, called pueblos, across the San Juan Basin, and connected many of them by roads – roads that traverse the desert, ascend mesas, and cross ravines. Exotic goods were imported from as far away as northern Mexico and the Pacific Ocean. Trees to roof the towns were carried up to 50 kilometers across the desert to Chaco Canyon, the center of the Basin. From as early as 500 A.D. this regional society thrived. Sometime after 1050 A.D., however, something went wrong. Construction at towns ended, and some, then many, began to be abandoned. Trade networks declined, and the towns were scavenged for building materials. By 1300 A.D. the last sedentary peoples had either left, or reverted to a simple, mobile lifestyle.

The Chacoans were not alone among prehistoric Southwesterners in this experience. Peoples such as the Mimbres, the Jornada, and many others lived through their own episodes of collapse and abandonment of settled areas (Powers et al. 1983; Schelberg 1982; Tainter and Gillio 1980; Jelinek 1967; Stuart and Gauthier 1981; Upham 1984; Minnis 1985; Kelley 1952; Reed 1944).

The Hohokam

The Hohokam were dwellers of the southern Arizona desert, who before their collapse in the fifteenth century A.D. developed a complex cultural system characterized by extensive canal irrigation, public architecture, and an elaborate artifactual repertoire.

The Hohokam canal systems from the Salt and Gila rivers were large and sophisticated. Modern canals around the city of Phoenix parallel this ancient pattern. The population supported by this system invested in the construction of Mesoamerican-like symbols of political integration, such as ball courts and platform mounds. After ca. 1300 A.D. the Hohokam began to develop a new form of architecture, characterized by 'Great Houses' of above-ground, multi-storied, poured adobe. The Great House at Casa Grande was situated within a 26 hectare walled compound that included many residential structures. The site of Los Muertos extended over several square kilometers.

The contemporary Pima of southern Arizona appear to be the lineal descendants of the Hohokam, but at the time of European contact lacked the political centralization that was characteristic of their ancestors (Haury 1976; Doyel 1981; McGuire 1982; Martin and Plog 1973).

The Eastern Woodlands

There were at least two cases of region-wide sociopolitical collapse in the prehistory of the North American Eastern Woodlands: those of the Hopewell and Mississippian complexes.

The Hopewell complex developed in the last one or two centuries B.C. and the first four centuries A.D. in the Great Lakes-Riverine area of the Midwest. Hopewell is distinguished by such features as construction of large earthworks requiring mobilization and coordination of labor, complex systems of mortuary ritual, elaborate artifact forms, and importation of exotic raw materials and goods from across the eastern two-thirds of what is now the United States. Archaeological analysis reveals that Hopewell in many areas was characterized by complex, hierarchically organized societies in which segments of the economic system were controlled by elites of hereditary status. By perhaps 400 A.D., however, the regional constellation of localized Hopewellian societies had everywhere collapsed. The succeeding Late Woodland period (ca. 400-900 A.D.) is marked by a curtailment in trade, mortuary ceremonialism, public construction, and social complexity.

This hiatus was terminated by the Mississippian complex, with trade, ceremonialism, public architecture, and political centralization that exceeded by far the levels of Hopewell. The most complex, and best known, Mississippian polity was centered at Cahokia. Located at a confluence of major river systems in what is now East St Louis, Cahokia is the largest archaeological site north of Mesoamerica. Cahokia contained some 120 mounds spread across 8 square kilometers, and with its outlying settlements had a population of perhaps 40,000 persons. It contains Monks Mound, a 6 hectare, 600,000 cubic meter, 30 meter high earthwork that is the third largest pyramid in the Americas and one of the largest features ever built by prehistoric peoples. A timber stockade was built around the central part of Cahokia, including Monks Mound. Several circular astronomical observatories were built, considered by some to be wooden versions of England's famous Stonehenge (and misappropriately labeled 'woodhenges').

There is a planned pattern to Cahokia. It was built by a stratified society in which there was centralized control of resources. At least one member of the community elite was buried with human retainers and an array of imported luxury goods.

After 1250 A.D. activity at Cahokia declined, some areas were converted from public to private use, and over time this center lost its regional supremacy. Some Mississippian-like societies persisted in the southeastern U.S. until European contact, but no native societies in the Midwest achieved a comparable level of complexity (D. Cook 1981; Fowler 1975; Griffin 1967; Pfeiffer 1974; Struever 1964; Struever and Houart 1972; Tainter 1977, 1980, 1983; for another view see Braun [1977]).

The Huari and Tiahuanaco Empires

The period between 200 B.C. and 600 or 700 A.D. saw the development in Peru of extensive irrigation and agricultural terracing in conjunction with growth of population. True cities were built that were the capitals of regional states. These shared a common heritage of technology and ideology, but were divided by distinctive art styles, separate governments, and competition for food and land. Out of this competitive situation two empires emerged, those of Huari in the north and Tiahuanaco in the south.

At its height the Huari Empire dominated almost the entire central Andes and much of the adjacent coastal lowlands. This empire was controlled by the highland city of Huari. In a short time, Huari-derived ceramic styles (themselves influenced by Tiahuanaco wares) appeared in many regions. Early Huari ceramics (like the later Inca wares) tend to occur in politico-religious contexts: in ceremonial centers, in cities, and in other high-prestige sites. Molds were used for the mass production of pottery. As these wares spread, local styles began to lose importance.

The Huari Empire imposed economic, social, and cultural changes on the areas it dominated. Local cultures were disrupted. Major urban centers were established in each valley. Building complexes in the Huari architectural style (administrative structures, storehouses, or barracks) were constructed at various places. Cities rose and fell with the Huari Empire. Goods and information were exchanged across the central Andes on a scale never seen before. Various authors have suggested that urbanism and militarism, state distribution of foodstuffs, the Andean road system, and the spread of the Quechua language began with the Huari Empire.

Until recently, the case for a contemporaneous, or chronologically overlapping, Tiahuanaco Empire was less clear. Since the only detailed work had been at the city of Tiahuanaco itself, in the Lake Titicaca Basin, the argument for an empire was by comparison to Huari. Recent work, however, has shown that a large rural hinterland was transformed by the Tiahuanaco rulers into an artificial agricultural landscape. There were massive public reclamation and construction projects that required large, coordinated labor forces. Throughout the Lake Titicaca Basin state administrative structures were built near potentially arable land. The settlement pattern suggests political unification of the Basin, and the existence of an empire. Tiahuanaco itself may have held between 20,000 and 40,000 persons.

In both cases there was a major collapse by ca. 1000/1100 A.D. With the fall of the city of Huari, centers in various provinces were abandoned. Regional traditions re-emerged, as did local and regional political organizations. All cities of the southern highlands were abandoned, and their populations scattered to the countryside. The north coast must have been depopulated. With the fall of the Huari Empire an era of smaller, contending states emerged (Lanning 1967; Lumbreras 1974; Willey 1971; Kolata 1986).

The Kachin

The Kachin of Highland Burma are a classic people of anthropology. They are organized into three contrasting forms of society. These are the *gumlao*, or egalitarian, the *gumsa*, or stratified, and the *shan*, or feudal. Sociopolitical complexity and level of hierarchical authority increase through these social forms, in the order listed.

The noteworthy fact about the Kachin is that these forms are not static. Local groups may oscillate between *gumlao* and *shan*-like characteristics. *Gumsa* organization is a compromise between these contrasting poles. Some *gumsa* become *shan*, others revert back to *gumlao* organization. Yet equality of descent groups cannot be maintained, and eventually *gumsa* societies emerge from *gumlao*. What is most pertinent to the present topic is that stratified *gumsa* societies do not remain so. Through disaffection of their members, principles of hierarchy and associated complexity are periodically lost as such societies collapse to egalitarian organization (Leach 1954).

The Ik

The Ik are a people of northern Uganda who live at what must surely be the extreme of deprivation and disaster. A largely hunting and gathering people who have in recent times practiced some crop planting, the Ik are not classifiable as a complex society in the sense of Chapter 2. They are, nonetheless, a morbidly fascinating case of collapse in which a former, low level of social complexity has essentially disappeared.

Due to drought and disruption by national boundaries of the traditional cycle of movement, the Ik live in such a food- and water-scarce environment that there is absolutely no advantage to reciprocity and social sharing. The Ik, in consequence, display almost nothing of what could be considered societal organization. They are so highly fragmented that most activities, especially subsistence, are pursued individually. Each Ik will spend days or weeks on his or her own, searching for food and water. Sharing is virtually nonexistent. Two siblings or other kin can live side-by-side, one dying of starvation and the other well nourished, without the latter giving the slightest assistance to the other. The family as a social unit has become dysfunctional. Even conjugal pairs don't form a cooperative unit except for a few specific purposes. Their motivation for marriage or cohabitation is that one person can't build a house alone. The members of a conjugal pair forage alone, and do not share food. Indeed, their foraging is so independent that if both members happen to be at their residence together it is by accident.

Each conjugal compound is stockaded against the others. Several compounds together form a village, but this is a largely meaningless occurrence. Villages have no political functions or organization, not even a central meeting place.

Children are minimally cared for by their mothers until age three, and then are put out to fend for themselves. This separation is absolute. By age three they are expected to find their own food and shelter, and those that survive do provide for themselves. Children band into age-sets for protection, since adults will steal a child's food whenever possible. No food sharing occurs within an age-set. Groups of children will forage in agricultural fields, which scares off birds and baboons. This is often given as the reason for having children.

Although little is known about how the Ik got to their present situation, there are some indications of former organizational patterns. They possess clan names, although today these have no structural significance. They live in villages, but these no longer have any political meaning. The traditional authority structure of family, lineage, and clan leaders has been progressively weakened. It appears that a former level of organization has simply been abandoned by the Ik as unprofitable and unsuitable in their present distress (Turnbull 1978).

Remarks

Other cases that could be added to this list are the collapses of modern empires (such as the Spanish, French, and British). The demise of these empires clearly represents a retrenchment from a multi-national level of centralized organization that was global in extent. There are, however, differences from the majority of cases just discussed. Most notable is the fact that the loss of empire did not correspondingly entail collapse of the home administration. In this the modern cases appear like the Old Babylonian kingdom, where a short-lived empire was followed by a period of retrenchment, with no end to Babylon itself.

There are qualitative differences between ancient societies and modern ones in their susceptibility to collapse (although not for the reasons usually thought). This point will be addressed in the final chapter.

After collapse

Popular writers and film producers have developed a consistent image of what life will be like after the collapse of industrial society. With some variation, the picture that emerges is of a Hobbesian war-of-all-against-all, Ik-conditions extended globally. Only the strong survive; the weak are victimized, robbed, and killed. There is fighting for food and fuel. Whatever central authority remains lacks the resources to reimpose order. Bands of pitiful, maimed survivors scavenge among the ruins of grandeur. Grass grows in the streets. There is no higher goal than survival. Anyone who has read modern disaster literature, or seen it dramatized, will recognize this script. It has contributed substantially to current apprehensions about collapse.

Such a scenario, although clearly overdramatized, does contain many elements that are verifiable in past collapses. Consider, for example, Casson's account of the withdrawal of Roman power from Britain:

> From A.D. 100 to 400 all Britain except in the north was as pleasant and peaceful a countryside as it is to-day...But by 500 A.D. it had all vanished and the country had reverted to a condition which it had, perhaps, never seen before. There was no longer a trace of public safety, no houses of size, dwindling townships and all the villas and most of the Roman cities burnt, abandoned, looted and left the habitation of ghosts (1937: 164).

Casson was not following poetic license, for he witnessed the breakdown of order in Istanbul after the disintegration of Turkish authority in 1918:

> ...the Allied troops...found a city that was dead. The Turkish government had just ceased to function. The electrical supply had failed and was intermittent. Tramways did not work and abandoned trams littered the roads. There was no railway service, no street cleaning and a police force which had largely become bandit, living on blackmail from citizens in lieu of pay. Corpses lay at street corners and in side lanes, dead horses were everywhere, with no organisation to remove them. Drains did not work and water was unsafe. All this was the result of only about three weeks' abandonment by the civil authorities of their duties (1937: 217-18).

Based on the sketches of the preceding pages, and an excellent summary by Colin Renfrew (1979: 482-5), the characteristics of societies after collapse may be summarized as follows.

There is, first and foremost, a breakdown of authority and central control. Prior to collapse, revolts and provincial breakaways signal the weakening of the center. Revenues to the government often decline. Foreign challengers become increasingly successful. With lower revenues the military may become ineffective. The populace becomes more and more disaffected as the hierarchy seeks to mobilize resources to meet the challenge.

With disintegration, central direction is no longer possible. The former political center undergoes a significant loss of prominence and power. It is often ransacked and may ultimately be abandoned. Small, petty states emerge in the formerly unified territory, of which the previous capital may be one. Quite often these contend for domination, so that a period of perpetual conflict ensues.

The umbrella of law and protection erected over the populace is eliminated.

Lawlessness may prevail for a time, as in the Egyptian First Intermediate Period, but order will ultimately be restored. Monumental construction and publicly-supported art largely cease to exist. Literacy may be lost entirely, and otherwise declines so dramatically that a dark age follows.

What populations remain in urban or other political centers reuse existing architecture in a characteristic manner. There is little new construction, and that which is attempted concentrates on adapting existing buildings. Great rooms will be subdivided, flimsy façades are built, and public space will be converted to private. While some attempt may be made to carry on an attenuated version of previous ceremonialism, the former monuments are allowed to fall into decay. People may reside in upper-story rooms as lower ones deteriorate. Monuments are often mined as easy sources of building materials. When a building begins to collapse, the residents simply move to another.

Palaces and central storage facilities may be abandoned, along with centralized redistribution of goods and foodstuffs, or market exchange. Both long distance and local trade may be markedly reduced, and craft specialization end or decline. Subsistence and material needs come to be met largely on the basis of local self-sufficiency. Declining regional interaction leads to the establishment of local styles in items such as pottery that formerly had been widely circulated. Both portable and fixed technology (e.g., hydraulic engineering systems) revert to simpler forms that can be developed and maintained at the local level, without the assistance of a bureaucracy that no longer exists.

Whether as cause or as consequence, there is typically a marked, rapid reduction in population size and density. Not only do urban populations substantially decline, but so also do the support populations of the countryside. Many settlements are concurrently abandoned. The level of population and settlement may decline to that of centuries or even millennia previously.

Some simpler collapsing societies, like the Ik, clearly do not possess these features of complexity. Collapse for them entails loss of the common elements of band or tribal social structure – lineages and clans, reciprocity and other kin obligations, village political structure, relations of respect and authority, and constraints on non-sociable behavior. For such people collapse has surely led to a survival-of-the-fittest situation, although as Turnbull (1978) emphasizes, this is but a logical adjustment to their desperate circumstances.

In a complex society that has collapsed, it would thus appear, the overarching structure that provides support services to the population loses capability or disappears entirely. No longer can the populace rely upon external defense and internal order, maintenance of public works, or delivery of food and material goods. Organization reduces to the lowest level that is economically sustainable, so that a variety of contending polities exist where there had been peace and unity. Remaining populations must become locally self-sufficient to a degree not seen for several generations. Groups that had formerly been economic and political partners now become strangers, even threatening competitors. The world as seen from any locality perceptibly shrinks, and over the horizon lies the unknown.

Given this pattern, it is a small wonder that collapse is feared by so many people today. Even among those who decry the excesses of industrial society, the possible end of that society must surely be seen as catastrophic. Whether collapse is *universally* a catastrophe, though, is an uncertain matter. This point will be raised again in the concluding chapter.

2

The nature of complex societies

How wondrous this wall-stone, shattered by Fate;
Burg-places broken, the work of giants crumbled.
Ruined are the roofs, tumbled the towers,
Broken the barred gate: frost in the plaster,
Ceilings a-gaping, torn away, fallen,
Eaten by age...
Bright were the halls, lofty-gabled,
Many the bath-house; cheerful the clamour
In many a mead-hall, revelry rampant –
Until mighty Fate put paid to all that...

'The Ruin,' *Exeter Book* (an eighth-century A.D. Saxon poet, remarking on Roman ruins in Britain

[quoted in Magnusson 1980: 125])

Introduction

A study of why complex societies collapse should begin with a clear picture of what it is that does so. What, in other words, are complex societies? What are their defining characteristics? How do they differ from the simpler societies out of which they developed, and to which they often revert? Are complex societies a discrete type or a 'stage' in cultural evolution, or is there a continuum from simple to complex?

A related question is why complex societies develop. This, as noted, has been a question of perennial interest in the social sciences. Although much is now known about the evolution of complexity, there is no overall consensus about such things as why complexity emerges, why societies become stratified, why the small, independent groups of early human history have given way to the large, interdependent states of recent millennia. This is without doubt a fascinating topic, and one that offers a tempting diversion for the present work. It is a diversion that will largely have to be resisted. It cannot be wholly resisted, for collapse may not be understood except in the context of how complex societies function and operate, and that cannot be divorced from the question of how they have come into being. (As in any scientific endeavor, one question leads to another, one problem appears connected to all others, and one of the most difficult tasks is simply to draw boundaries to the inquiry.) To explain collapse it will be necessary to discuss, briefly, alternative general views of how complex societies have developed, and to evaluate the usefulness and relevance of these views to the problem at hand. The lively and interesting debate over what (if any) are the prime movers in the development of complexity is regrettably only partially pertinent. Accordingly, it will be treated in only a partial fashion.

In this chapter three topics will be addressed: (1) the nature of complexity; (2) the question of whether complexity is a continuum or is characterized by discrete stages; and (3) major views on the emergence of complex societies. The discussion that follows will be necessarily selective, focusing on those aspects of the evolution of complexity that are relevant to understanding collapse.

Complexity

Nature of complexity

Complexity is generally understood to refer to such things as the size of a society, the number and distinctiveness of its parts, the variety of specialized social roles that it incorporates, the number of distinct social personalities present, and the variety of mechanisms for organizing these into a coherent, functioning whole. Augmenting any of these dimensions increases the complexity of a society. Hunter-gatherer societies (by way of illustrating one contrast in complexity) contain no more than a few dozen distinct social personalities, while modern European censuses recognize 10,000 to 20,000 unique occupational roles, and industrial societies may contain overall more than 1,000,000 different kinds of social personalities (McGuire 1983: 115).

Two concepts important to understanding the nature of complexity are inequality and heterogeneity (Blau 1977; McGuire 1983). Inequality may be thought of as vertical differentiation, ranking, or unequal access to material and social resources. Heterogeneity is a subtler concept. It refers to the number of distinctive parts or components to a society, and at the same time to the ways in which a population is distributed among these parts (Blau 1977: 9; McGuire 1983: 93). A population that is divided equally among the occupations and roles of a society is homogeneously distributed; the converse brings increasing heterogeneity and complexity (see also Tainter 1977, 1978). A society with a great deal of heterogeneity, then, is one that is complex. Inequality and heterogeneity are interrelated, but in part respond to different processes, and are not always positively correlated in sociopolitical evolution (McGuire 1983: 93, 105). In early civilizations, for example, inequality tended to be initially high and heterogeneity low. Through time, inequality decreased and heterogeneity grew as multiple hierarchies would develop (McGuire 1983: 110-11). Johnson relates this process to growth in the amount of information that must be processed by a society, with greater quantity and variety of information requiring greater social complexity (1978: 91, 94).

Complex societies tend to be what Simon has called 'nearly decomposable systems' (1965: 70). That is, they are at least partly built up of social units that are themselves potentially stable and independent, and indeed at one time may have been so. Thus, a newly established state may include several formerly independent villages or ethnic groups, or an empire may incorporate previously established states. To the extent that these states, ethnic groups, or villages retain the potential for independence and stability, the collapse process may result in reversion (decomposition) to these 'building blocks' of complexity (cf. Simon 1965: 68).

Simpler societies

The citizens of modern complex societies usually do not realize that *we* are an anomaly of history. Throughout the several million years that recognizable humans are known to have lived, the common political unit was the small, autonomous community, acting independently, and largely self-sufficient. Robert Carneiro has estimated that 99.8 percent of human history has been dominated by these autonomous local communities (1978: 219). It has only been within the last 6000 years that something unusual has emerged: the hierarchical, organized, interdependent states that are the major reference for our contemporary political experience. Complex societies, once established, tend to expand and dominate, so that today they control most of the earth's lands and people, and are perpetually vexed by those still beyond their reach. A dilemma arises from this: we today are familiar mainly with political forms that are an oddity of history, we think of these as normal, and we view as alien the majority of the human experience. It is little surprise that collapse is viewed so fearfully.

The small, acephalous communities that have dominated our history were not homogeneous. The degree of variation among such societies is substantial. Although these societies would be characterized (in comparison to ourselves) as 'simple,' nevertheless they display variations in size, complexity, ranking, economic differentiation, and other factors. It is from this variation that many of our theories of cultural evolution have been developed.

Simpler societies are, of course, comparatively smaller. They number from a handful to a few thousand persons, who are united within sociopolitical units encompassing correspondingly small territories. Such societies tend to be organized on the basis of kinship, with status familial and centered on the individual. One can know most everyone in such a society, and can categorize each person individually in terms of position and distance in a web of kin relationships (Service 1962).

Leadership in the simplest societies tends to be minimal. It is personal and charismatic, and exists only for special purposes. Hierarchical control is not institutionalized, but is limited to definite spheres of activity at specific times, and rests substantially on persuasion (Service 1962; Fried 1967). Sahlins has captured the essence of petty chieftainship in these societies. The holder of such a position is a spokesman, a master of ceremonies, with otherwise little influence, few functions, and no privileges or coercive power. One word from such a leader, notes Sahlins, 'and everyone does as he pleases' (1968: 21).

Equality in these societies lies in direct, individual access to the resources that sustain life, in mobility and the option to simply withdraw from an untenable social situation, and in conventions that prevent economic accumulation and impose sharing. Leaders, where they exist, are constrained from exercising authority, amassing wealth, or acquiring excessive prestige. Where there are differences in control of economic resources these must be exercised generously (Gluckman 1965; Woodburn 1982).

Personal political ambition is either restrained from expression, or channeled to fulfill a public good. The route to an elevated social position is to acquire a surplus of subsistence resources, and to distribute these in such a way that one establishes prestige in the community, and creates a following and a faction (Service 1962; Gluckman 1965; Sahlins 1963, 1968). Where several ambitious individuals follow this course there is a constant competition and jockeying for position. The result is an unstable, fluctuating political environment in which ephemeral leaders rise and fall, and in which the death of a leader brings the demise of his faction and wholesale political regrouping.

Native Melanesians often refer to such an ambitious individual as a Big Man, a term that has achieved anthropological currency (e.g., Sahlins 1963). A Big Man strives to build a following, but is never permanently successful. Since his influence is limited to his faction, extending that influence means extending the size of the following. At the same time, the loyalty of his existing followers must be constantly renewed through generosity. Herein lies a tension: as resources are allocated to expanding a faction, those available to retain previous loyalties must decline. As a Big Man attempts to expand his sphere of influence, he is likely to lose the springboard that makes this possible. Big Man systems contain thus a built-in, structural limitation on their scope, extent, and durability (Sahlins 1963, 1968).

Other simple societies are organized at higher levels of political differentiation. There are true, permanent positions of rank in which authority resides in an office, rather than an individual, and to which inhere genuine powers of command. Chiefly rank is often hereditary, or nearly so. Inequality pervades such societies, which tend to be larger and more densely populated to a degree coordinate with their increased complexity.

In these centrally focused, chiefly societies, political organization extends beyond the community level. Accordingly, economic, political, and ceremonial life transcend purely local concerns. In the classic chiefdoms of Polynesia, entire islands would often be integrated into a single polity. There is a political economy in which rank conveys the authority to direct labor and economic surpluses. Labor may be mobilized to engage in public works (e.g., agricultural facilities, monuments) of an impressive scale. Economic specialization, exchange, and coordination are characteristic features.

Social statuses in these more complex societies, while still moored in kinship, tend to be more established and continuing, rather than variable from the perspective of different individuals. As complexity and number of members grow, individuals must increasingly be socially categorized, so that appropriate behavior between persons is prescribed more by the impersonal structure of society and less by kin relations. The epitome of this is the position of chief, which is now a true office extending beyond the lifetime of any individual holder.

The authority to command in such chiefdoms is not unrestrained. The ruler is limited in his or her actions by the moorings of kinship, and by possessing, not a monopoly of force, but only a marginal advantage. Claims of followers obligate a chief to respond positively to requests. Chiefly generosity is the basis of politics and economics: downward distribution of amassed resources ensures loyalty.

Chiefly ambitions, like those of Big Men, are thus structurally constrained. Too much allocation of resources to the chiefly apparatus, and too little return to the local level, engender resistance. The consequence is that chiefdoms tend to undergo cycles of centralization and decentralization, much like Big Man systems, but at a higher cut-off point (Service 1962; Fried 1967; Gluckman 1965; Leach 1954; Sahlins 1963, 1968).

Chiefdoms display many points of similarity to more complex, state-organized systems, but are still regarded by most anthropologists as firmly within the category of simple or 'primitive' societies. Chiefdoms are limited by the obligations of kinship and the lack of true coercive force. By the time human organizations emerged that today would be called a state, these limitations had been surpassed.

Anthropologists have had some difficulty defining the concept 'state.' It is something that seems clearly different from the simplest, acephalous human societies, but specifying or enumerating this difference has proven an elusive goal. Many anthropologists, despite this difficulty, insist that states are a qualitatively different kind of society, so that the transition from tribal to state societies represents the 'Great Divide' (Service 1975) of human history.

The emphasis on qualitative differences among societies, as illustrated above, leads some scholars to subdivide simpler societies into what are thought to be discrete types, or levels of complexity. Whether it is more profitable to view sociopolitical evolution as traversing a continuum of complexity, or as characterized by discrete stages or levels, is a matter pertinent to understanding collapse, and will be discussed later in this chapter.

States

States are, to begin with, territorially organized. That is to say, membership is at least partly determined by birth or residence in a territory, rather than by real or fictive kin relations. Illustrating this, as pointed out by Sir Henry Sumner Maine, was the transformation from the Merovingian title 'King of the Franks' to the Capetian 'King of France' (Sahlins 1968: 6). The territorial basis both reflects and influences the nature of statehood (Fortes and Evans-Pritchard 1940: 10; Claessen and Skalnik 1978a: 21).

States contrast with relatively complex tribal societies (e.g., chiefdoms) in a number of ways. In states, a ruling authority monopolizes sovereignty and delegates all power. The ruling class tends to be professional, and is largely divorced from the bonds of kinship. This ruling class supplies the personnel for government, which is a specialized decision-making organization with a monopoly of force, and with the power to draft for war or work, levy and collect taxes, and decree and enforce laws. The government is legitimately constituted, which is to say that a common, society-wide ideology exists that serves in part to validate the political organization of society. And states, of course, are in general larger and more populous than tribal societies, so that social categorization, stratification, and specialization are both possible and necessary (Carneiro 1981: 69; Claessen and Skalnik 1978a: 21; Flannery 1972: 403-4; Fortes and Evans-Pritchard 1940; Johnson 1973: 2-3; Sahlins 1968: 6).

States tend to be overwhelmingly concerned with maintaining their territorial integrity. This is, indeed, one of their primary characteristics. States are the only kind of human society that does not ordinarily undergo *short-term* cycles of formation and dissolution (cf. R. Cohen 1978: 4; Claessen and Skalnik 1978b: 632).

States are internally differentiated, as an illustration at the beginning of this chapter makes clear. Occupational specialization is a prime characteristic, and is often reflected in patterns of residence (Flannery 1972: 403). Emile Durkheim, in a classic work, recognized that the evolution from primitive to complex societies witnessed the transformation from groups organized on the basis of what he labeled 'mechanical solidarity' (homogeneity; lack of cultural and economic differentiation among the members of a society) to those based on 'organic solidarity' (heterogeneity; cultural and economic differentiation requiring interaction and greater cohesiveness). Organic solidarity has increased throughout history, and in states is the preponderant form of organization (Durkheim 1947).

By virtue of their territorial extensiveness, states are often differentiated, not only economically, but also culturally and ethnically. Both economic and cultural heterogeneity appear to be functionally related to the centralization and administration that are defining characteristics of states (Fortes and Evans-Pritchard 1940: 9).

Despite an institutionalized authority structure, an ideological basis, and a monopoly of force, the rulers of states share at least one thing with chiefs and Big Men: the need to establish and constantly reinforce legitimacy. In complex as well as simpler societies, leadership activities and societal resources must be continuously devoted to this purpose. Hierarchy and complexity, as noted, are rare in human history, and where present require constant reinforcement. No societal leader is ever far from the need to validate position and policy, and no hierarchical society can be organized without explicit provision for this need.

Legitimacy is the belief of the populace and the elites that rule is proper and valid, that the political world is as it should be. It pertains to individual rulers, to decisions, to broad policies, to parties, and to entire forms of government. The support that members are willing to extend to a political system is essential for its survival. Decline in support will not necessarily lead to the fall of a regime, for to a certain extent coercion can replace commitment to ensure compliance. Coercion, though, is a costly, ineffective strategy which can never be completely or permanently successful. Even with coercion, decline in popular support below some critical minimum leads infallibly to political failure (Easton 1965b: 220-4). Establishing moral validity is a less costly and more effective approach.

Complex societies are focused on a center, which may not be located physically where it is literally implied, but which is the symbolic source of the framework of society. It is not only the location of legal and governmental institutions, but is the source of order, and the symbol of moral authority and social continuity. The center partakes of the nature of the sacred. In this sense, every complex society has an official religion (Shils 1975: 3; Eisenstadt 1978: 37; Apter 1968: 218).

The moral authority and sacred aura of the center not only are essential in maintaining complex societies, but were crucial in their emergence. One critical impediment to the development of complexity in stateless societies was the need to integrate many localized, autonomous units, which would each have their own peculiar interests, feuds, and jealousies. A ruler drawn from any one of these units is automatically suspect by the others, who rightly fear favoritism toward his/her natal group and locality, particularly in dispute resolution (Netting 1972: 233-4). This problem has crippled many modern African nations (cf. Easton 1965b: 224).

The solution to this structural limitation was to explicitly link leadership in early complex societies to the supernatural. When a leader is imbued with an aura of sacred neutrality, his identification with natal group and territory can be superseded by ritually sanctioned authority which rises above purely local concerns. An early complex society is likely to have an avowedly sacred basis of legitimacy, in which disparate, formerly independent groups are united by an overarching level of shared ideology, symbols, and cosmology (Netting 1972: 233-4; Claessen 1978: 557; Skalnik 1978: 606).

Supernatural sanctions are then a response to the stresses of change from a kin-based society to a class-structured one. They may be necessitated in part by an ineffective concentration of coercive force in emerging complex societies (Webster 1976b: 826). Sacred legitimization provides a binding framework until real vehicles of power have been consolidated. Once this has been achieved the need for religious integration declines, and indeed conflict between secular and sacred authorities may thereafter ensue (see, e.g., Webb 1965). Yet as noted, the sacred aura of the center never disappears, not even in contemporary secular governments (Shils 1975: 3-6). Astute politicians have always exploited this fact. It is a critical element in the maintenance of legitimacy.

Despite the undoubted power of supernatural legitimization, support for leadership must also have a genuine material basis. Easton suggests that legitimacy declines mainly under conditions of what he calls 'output failure' (1965b: 230). Output failure occurs where authorities are unable to meet the demands of the support population, or do not take anticipatory actions to counter adversities. Outputs can be political (Eisenstadt 1963: 25) or material. Output expectations are continuous, and impose on leadership a never-ending need to mobilize resources to maintain support. The attainment and perpetuation of legitimacy thus require more than the manipulation of ideological symbols. They require the assessment and commitment of real resources, at satisfactory levels, and are a genuine cost that any complex society must bear. Legitimacy is a recurrent factor in the modern study of the nature of complex societies, and is pertinent to understanding their collapse.

Levels of complexity

Anthropologists who have studied the evolution of human organization have often found it convenient to develop typologies of simpler societies. The distinction between state and non-state is one example of such a classification, and is probably the one with which most anthropologists would feel comfortable. Some scholars (to be discussed below) have further divided states into subcategories of this class (e.g.,

Steward 1955; Claessen and Skalnik 1978a), while others have subdivided non-state societies into levels of complexity (e.g., Service 1962; Fried 1967). A consideration of these evolutionary typologies is pertinent to understanding collapse, indeed even to defining what the process is. Some anthropologists, for example, have suggested that drops in complexity within a level (such as the state level) are not instances of collapse, merely 'waxings and wanings of scale' (B. Price 1977: 218).

The details of such typologies (there are many of them, incompatible to varying degrees) are not pertinent to the present work, but the philosophy and assumptions underlying them are. One of the basic assumptions of the typological approach is that as societies increase in complexity, they do so by leaps from one structurally stable level to another (e.g., Segraves 1974). Thus, what are called 'chiefdoms' are thought to have arisen out of 'tribes,' which in turn developed from 'bands' (Service 1962). In another formulation, egalitarian societies are succeeded by ones that are ranked, then ones that are stratified, and finally (in a few instances) by the state (Fried 1967). The alternative view, which to some degree vitiates a typological approach, is that as societies increase in complexity they do so on a *continuous* scale, so that discrete, stable 'levels' will be difficult to define, and indeed may not exist.

Any good classifier knows that in the process of classification, information about variety is lost while information about similarities is gained. The utility of a classification must be judged (at least partially) by whether the quantity and quality of information gained outweighs that lost, and this depends largely on the purposes and needs of the analyst. In some respects, evolutionary typologies of human societies are useful in that they facilitate initial communication and comparison. When an anthropologist says that he or she is working with a society of type X (chiefdoms, say), most colleagues readily know, at least generally, what the characteristics of that society are likely to be. Yet in this example some of the weaknesses of the typological approach become apparent. The degree of variation *among* societies called 'chiefdoms' (e.g., Northwest Coast, Hawaii) is such that many feel uncomfortable with the concept (e.g., Tainter 1977; Cordy 1981). For many purposes, it may obscure more than it reveals. Solutions that focus on further subdividing the chiefdom category bring only the potential for endless debate, and unprofitable concentration on labels rather than on processes of stability and change (Tainter 1978: 117; McGuire 1983: 94-5).

The typological distinction of most interest here is that which exists between states and all other kinds of societies. This, as noted, is a classificatory distinction that most anthropologists seem to accept, and is often called the 'Great Divide' of history (Service 1975). Many of the characteristics of states appear to be so qualitatively different from tribal societies that a major distinction seems indicated (Webb 1975: 164-5). With the emergence of states human organization began an entirely different career. The features that set states apart, abstracting from the previous discussion, are: territorial organization, differentiation by class and occupation rather than by kinship, monopoly of force, authority to mobilize resources and personnel, and legal jurisdiction. Upon closer examination, though, it does not appear that there is always the discontinuity claimed between state and non-state societies for many of these characteristics.

Territoriality, and the capacity to mobilize labor and other resources, occur in varying degrees among non-state societies, depending on such things as population density, pressures from competing neighbors, degree of stratification, and requirements for centralized storage, redistribution, and public works. The presence of formal law in primitive societies, furthermore, has been a matter of anthropological debate for some time. Carneiro notes that not all so-called states have had a true monopoly of force (e.g., Anglo-Saxon England) (1981: 68).

Various authors, as noted, have felt the need to create classifications of early states. Webb, for example, uses the term *conditional state* to describe complex, fairly durable chiefdoms that are like states, but never achieve a true monopoly of force. Conditional states appear superficially to be similar to states, but never fully complete the transformation (Webb 1975: 163-4). (It must be observed that formulations like this, which comes from a strong proponent of the 'states are different' school, create serious doubts about the postulated distinctiveness of states.)

Claessen and Skalnik (1978a; see also Claessen [1978]) distinguish various types of early states. These are:

1. *The Inchoate Early State.* In this type, kinship, family, and community ties still dominate political relations; there is limited full-time specialization, *ad hoc* taxation, and reciprocity and direct contacts between ruler and ruled.
2. *The Typical Early State.* Kinship, in this variety, is balanced by ties to locality, competition and appointment counterbalance heredity, leading administrative roles are allocated to non-kinsmen, and redistribution and reciprocity dominate relations between strata.
3. *The Transitional Early State.* Kinship in this final category affects only marginal aspects of government. The administrative apparatus is dominated by appointed officials, and market economies and overtly antagonistic social classes develop with the emergence of private ownership of the means of production.

There are aspects to this subdivision that are both intriguing and disturbing. Just as Webb's identification of conditional states makes us doubt whether monopoly of force really is a criterion of statehood, so the concept of Inchoate and Typical Early States raises questions about the subordination of kinship as a characteristic of states. We have been told that states are distinctive because, among other things, they are based on class rather than kinship, and enjoy a monopoly of force. Now we learn that some states do indeed have these characteristics, but some states only partially have them. It begins to sound as if state formation is not such a Great Divide after all. There are apparently continuities in the transition from tribal to state societies, continuities even in those characteristics thought to be most peculiar to states. Cohen is correct in noting that state formation is a continuous phenomenon: there is no clear-cut state/non-state dividing line (R. Cohen 1978: 4).

While asserting that there is indeed a structural rift between tribal and state societies, Webb lists the facts that contradict this view. He notes, of chiefdoms and states, that

> On a day-to-day basis the two social types do much the same sort of thing and, in the short run, can produce the same kinds of results in terms of the establishment of public order, dispute resolution, defense against external enemies, monumental erection, public works, record keeping, the provision of luxury goods, and the support of marked distinctions of rank... (Webb 1975: 159).

The difference between chiefdoms and states, notes Webb, is that in regard to such things as size and complexity, chiefdoms peak where states begin (1975: 161).

It was noted in the first chapter that to define collapse is actually quite a complex matter, and that such a definition would be developed throughout the work, but not completed until the final chapter. The foregoing discussion leads to installment number two.

As the development of complexity is a continuous variable, so is its reverse. Collapse is a process of decline in complexity. Although collapse is usually thought of as something that afflicts states, in fact it is not limited to any 'type' of society or 'level' of complexity. It occurs any time established complexity rapidly, noticeably, and significantly declines. Collapse is not merely the fall of empires or the expiration of states. It is not limited either to such phenomena as the decentralizations of chiefdoms. Collapse may also manifest itself in a transformation from larger to smaller states, from more to less complex chiefdoms, or in the abandonment of settled village life for mobile foraging (where this is accompanied by a drop in complexity).

The typological approach has the flaw of obscuring social variation and change within a typological level, so that only social change between levels can be recognized and addressed. Abandonment of the typological approach admits a whole range of interesting and significant social transformations. A prime example is the development of complex chiefdoms, and periodic reversions to smaller chiefdoms, as in the islands of Polynesia (Sahlins 1963, 1968). The collapse of a society that was not organized as a state (the Chacoans) will be one of the major examples discussed in Chapter 5.

The evolution of complexity

The factors that lead to complexity are pertinent to understanding collapse, for the emergence of complex social institutions, and their failure, are inevitably intertwined. Unfortunately, despite the great advances that have been made in recent years in understanding complex societies, much about their origins remains controversial. Elman Service has hit upon one of the main reasons for this. He notes that long-standing states have acquired in their later history so many functions and features that their *original* functions are often obscured (Service 1975: 20). This is an important point. The behavior of states at the point where they come to be studied by social scientists may have little relation to the reasons for their emergence. Furthermore, the evolution of states subsequent to their development may respond to a variety of new factors, including both internal and external political situations (R. Cohen 1978: 8). Service is correct that these factors may make it difficult to ascertain the nature of early, emerging states. Some modern theories have not taken this into account to the extent desirable. Similarly, though, many theories of state origins do not account for the persistence of this form once established (Kurtz 1978: 169).

A number of authors have synthesized the different theories formulated to account for the origin of the state (e.g., Flannery 1972; Wright 1977a; Claessen and Skalnik 1978c; R. Cohen 1978; Service 1975, 1978; Haas 1982). The major lines of thought (after Wright 1977a) seem to be (in no particular order):

1. *Managerial.* As societies come under stress, or as populations increase in numbers, integrative requirements may arise that can be resolved by the emergence of managerial hierarchies. Examples of this approach include: (a) Wittfogel's (1955, 1957) argument that the need to mobilize labor forces for construction of irrigation works, and the need to manage established water control facilities, necessitates authoritarian government; (b) Wright's and Johnson's suggestion (Wright 1969; Johnson 1973, 1978) that increasing need to process information, arising from more and more information sources, selects for both vertical differentiation and horizontal specialization; (c) Isbell's (1978) elaboration of the classic argument (e.g., Sahlins 1958) that economic differentiation within a society requires centralized, hierarchically managed storage and redistribution of goods and produce; and (d) Rathje's (1971) proposal that management of external trade, and critical imports, leads to complexity.
2. *Internal Conflict.* Theories within this school postulate that class conflict is the prime mover behind complexity. Fried (1967), along with Marxist writers to be discussed later, maintains that the state emerged to protect the privilege of a limited few with preferential access to resources. Childe's views were similar (1951: 181-2).
3. *External Conflict.* Carneiro (1970) argues that in circumscribed environments (bounded environments from which emigration is infeasible) stresses lead to conflict, while success at war necessitates the development of institutions to administer conquered groups. Webster (1975) has a different emphasis. He suggests that effective domination is impossible in chiefdoms, and that warfare in any event can offer only a short-term advantage. But a constant state of tension places a value on stable leadership and dampening of within-group competition. At the same time, acquisition of land, through conquest, that is outside the traditional system, gives elites a capital resource that can be used to create new kinds of patron-client relations.
4. *Synthetic.* Several interrelated processes generate complexity and state institutions. Colin Renfrew, for example, cites the influence of agriculture on social organization, of social factors on craft production, and so forth (1972: 27).

These theories pertain to the emergence of pristine or primary states, those that arose independently in various parts of the world. States are dominating, expansive organizations, and they have a competitive advantage over less complex social forms.

They tend thus to either spread, or to stimulate like developments among their neighbors. The emergence of complexity among the competitors and trade partners of states yields the process of 'secondary state' formation. So far as is known, there have been only six instances of primary state formation. These are: Mesopotamia, Egypt (ca. 3500-3000 B.C.), China, Indus River Valley (ca. 2500 B.C.), and Mexico and Peru (ca. 0 A.D.) (Service 1975: 5). Some experts challenge the degree of independence of several of these developments, but that matter need not concern us here.

Despite this variety of theories about the origin of the state, there seem to be, as several authors have recognized (e.g., Lenski 1966; R. Cohen 1978; Service 1975, 1978; Haas 1982), two main schools of thought. These are conveniently labeled the *conflict* and *integration* theories (Lenski [1966] prefers the terms *conflict* and *functionalist*). These contrasting views are more than scholarly theories of political evolution: they are philosophies of politics and society whose ramifications extend far beyond academic concerns. As such, they may be nearly as old as civil society itself. Service (1975: 23), for example, traces the conflict school to Ibn Khaldun, whose *Introduction to History* was begun in 1377. Haas (1982: 21-4) extends the dichotomy even further, recognizing conflict and integration views in the political philosophies of ancient Greece and Confucian-era China. There is thus a remarkable, continuous history to basic theories of the state. This fact is interesting in several ways, as will be seen in Chapter 4.

The European Enlightenment produced a florescence of thought and writing on the subject. The names of Jean Bodin, Thomas Hobbes, David Hume, Adam Ferguson, and Jean-Jacques Rousseau are associated with various approaches to the purpose and nature of civil society; these approaches have occasionally managed to integrate the two contending schemes. In more recent times, the major contributions to the conflict school have been by Morgan, Marx, Engels, Childe, White, and Fried, and to the integration view by Spencer, Sumner, Durkheim, Moret, Davy, and Service (Service 1975, 1978; Haas 1982).

In essence, conflict theory asserts that the state emerged out of the needs and desires of individuals and subgroups of a society. The state, in this view, is based on divided interests, on domination and exploitation, on coercion, and is primarily a stage for power struggles (Lenski 1966: 16-17). More specifically, the governing institutions of the state were developed as coercive mechanisms to resolve intra-societal conflicts arising out of economic stratification (Fried 1967; Haas 1982: 20). The state serves, thus, to maintain the privileged position of a ruling class that is largely based on the exploitation and economic degradation of the masses (Childe 1951: 181-2).

Conflict theory has reached its clearest expression in the writings of the Marxist school. Friedrich Engels, in his 1884 essay *Origins of the Family, Private Property, and the State* (Engels 1972), argued that the differential acquisition of wealth led to hereditary nobility, monarchy, slavery, and wars for pillage. To secure the new sources of wealth against older, communistic traditions, and resulting class antagonisms, the state was developed.

The state, according to one leading conflict theorist (Krader 1978), is the product of society divided into two classes: those directly engaged in social production, and those not. The surplus produced is appropriated by and for the non-producers. The state is the organization of society for regulating relations within and between these classes. The direct producers have no immediate interest in the formation of the state, the agencies of which act in the interest of the non-producers. The state, says Krader, is the formal organization of class-composed and class-opposed human society (1978: 96).

In the basic Marxist view, the production and reproduction of subsistence constitute the basis of society. The determinants of sociopolitical organization are the technical and social relations of production, which are equivalent to the relations of appropriation between classes (O'Laughlin 1975: 349, 351). Human life is defined by its social character, while a society's structural and superstructural elements specify the uses to be made of an environment, population densities to be maintained, and the like. Since material conditions are, therefore, always culturally mediated, Marxists reject integrationist theories that focus on such things as population pressure and subsistence stress (O'Laughlin 1975: 346; Wenke 1981: 93-8).

Integrationist or functionalist theories suggest that complexity, stratification, and the state arose, not out of the ambitions of individuals or subgroups, but out of the needs of society. The major elements of this approach are: (a) shared, rather than divided, social interests; (b) common advantages instead of dominance and exploitation; (c) consensus, not coercion; and (d) societies as integrated systems rather than as stages for power struggles (Lenski 1966: 15-17). The governing institutions of the state developed to centralize, coordinate, and direct the disparate parts of complex societies.

Integrationists argue that complexity and stratification arose because of stresses impinging on human populations, and were positive responses to those stresses. Complexity then serves population-wide needs, rather than responding to the selfish ambitions of a few. Complexity seen thus might be a response to: (a) circumscription and warfare in a limited, stressed environment (e.g., Carneiro 1970; Webster 1975); (b) the need to process increasing amounts of information coming from ever more sources (e.g., Wright 1969; Johnson 1973, 1978); (c) the need to mobilize labor forces for socially useful public works and to manage critical resources (e.g., Wittfogel 1955, 1957); (d) the need for regional integration of specialized or unreliable local economies (e.g., Sahlins 1958; Sanders and Price 1968; Renfrew 1972; Isbell 1978); (e) the need to import critical commodities (e.g., Rathje 1971); or (f) some combination of these. Integration, in this view, is socially useful, and if differential rewards accrue to high status administrators that is a cost that must be borne to realize the benefits of centralization.

Either school, standing alone, has both strong and weak points. I will begin with conflict theory. A conflict interpretation of human society is easy to adopt, and certainly comes readily to mind for many citizens of contemporary societies who are not in the economic upper strata. Since greed, oppression, exploitation, and class conflict obviously *are* characteristics of complex societies, it is tempting to see these as both the source of complexity and its dominant nature. Such a view is not without validity, and any theory of society must take this fact into account. But conflict theory is not completely adequate to explain how complex societies came into existence. Eisenstadt, for example, has pointed out that the failures of the Carolingian and Mongolian empires reflect the fact that such entities must be based on necessary conditions, and not solely on political goals (1963: 29).

Conflict theory suffers from a problem of psychological reductionism. That is, the emergence of the state is explained by reference to the wishes, intentions, needs, and/or desires of a small, privileged segment of society. How this segment comes to hold these needs and desires is not specified, but presumably arises from some universal human tendency toward ambition and self-aggrandizement. The expression of this tendency on the part of those who are economically more successful leads to class conflict and the development of repressive governing institutions.

Psychological explanations of social phenomena are laced with pitfalls. If social patterns arise from the wishes or needs of individuals, where in turn do these wishes and needs come from? To the extent that the origin of these cannot be explained, the social phenomenon is also unexplained. To the extent that these are *universal*, social *variation* is unexplained. If ambition and self-aggrandizement are universal, and lead to the state, why then did pristine states emerge no more than six times in human history? How did the human species survive roughly 99 percent of its history without the state? Why is the state such a recent oddity? Why were there no states in the Pleistocene?

Conflict theorists point to the existence of a surplus as a necessary condition for the expression of this universal tendency (e.g., Engels 1972; Childe 1951; Friedman 1974: 462), but a contradiction arises here. Marxists view material conditions as socially and culturally mediated (Wenke 1981: 94). If so, then surpluses could supposedly be concocted whenever desired. The fact that they are not always concocted (Sahlins 1971) points to a *lacuna* in conflict theory: the emergence of surpluses, the supposed basis of stratification and the state, remains unexplained. Cancian makes the observation that the potential for production of a surplus exists even among hunters and gatherers, but is usually not realized (1976: 228-9). This is an important point. If ambition and self-aggrandizement are universal human characteristics, then why don't foragers ordinarily produce surpluses, wealth differentials, class conflict, and the state? Could it be that either ambition, or its expression, is not universal? If ambition is not universal, then for reasons just discussed the Marxist explanation of the state is incomplete in its failure to specify the origins of ambition. If it is universal, but its expression is suppressed in certain kinds of societies, then obviously there is more to sociopolitical evolution than self-aggrandizement. We cannot fully explain the emergence of social institutions by a psychological feature that is itself conditioned by social institutions.

As briefly discussed earlier in this chapter, there is indeed a tendency toward social leveling in simpler societies. Richard Lee (1969) has given a delightful illustration of this from his work among the Bushman foragers of the Kalahari Desert in southern Africa. One year at Christmas he bought an ox for a Bushman group. Rather than the praise he expected, Lee encountered criticism of his gift. This criticism, that the animal was thin and old, continued right up to the Christmas feast. At this time the ox was eaten with obvious enjoyment. Bushmen questioned on the matter explained that they simply could not allow arrogance, or let anyone think of himself as a chief or a big man. Superior outside hunters are treated similarly. Thus the egalitarian ethic is reinforced.

Where egalitarian cooperation is essential for survival, hoarding and self-aggrandizement are simply not tolerated. It is only in societies already following a trajectory of developing complexity that such tendencies are allowed expression. Why is this? Can it be that the fulfillment of individual ambition, in certain contexts, has society-wide benefits, just as its suppression does in other settings (such as the Bushmen)? While the answer to that fascinating question is far beyond the scope of this work, it does lead to a consideration of integration theory, and must indeed be a central assumption of that theory.

In integration theory, the differential benefits accruing to those who fulfill society-wide administrative roles are seen as compensation for performing the socially most important functions (Davis 1949: 366-8). The costs of stratification are a necessary evil which must be borne to realize its integrative benefits. In basing the development of complexity on real, observable, physical needs (defense, public works, resource sharing, etc.) integration theory avoids the psychological reductionism that cripples Marxism. Human tendencies toward self-aggrandizement are seen as controlled in a sociopolitical matrix, so that they are expressed in situations of benefit, and suppressed elsewhere. Expression of ambition is a dependent social variable, rather than an independent psychological constant.

This view, however appealing to many social theorists (as well as the elites thereby defended), is clearly oversimplified. It seems obvious, for example, that the costs and benefits of stratification are not always as balanced as integration theory might imply. Compensation of elites does not always match their contribution to society, and throughout their history, elites have probably been overcompensated relative to performance more often than the reverse. Coercion, and authoritarian, exploitative regimes, are undeniable facts of history.

Haas (1982: 82-3) has made an important point overlooked by many integration theorists: a governing body that provides goods or services has coercive authority therein. The threat of withholding benefits can be a powerful inducement to compliance. As Haas has stated '...coercive force is an inevitable covariable of an essential benefit...' (1982: 83). Granting the logic of this, it seems clear that there must be more to sociopolitical evolution than the Panglossian view that integration theory implies.

Legitimacy is a matter that touches both views. As long as elites must rely on force to ensure compliance, much of their profit will be consumed by the costs of coercion (Lenski 1966: 51-2). Even conflict theorists must, therefore, acknowledge the role of legitimizing activities in maintaining a governing elite. Indeed, one Marxist anthropologist has argued that

> ...classes could only have grown up in societies *legitimately* – or, at least...the process of transformation must have been slow and the legitimacy of their

transformation must long have weighed more heavily in the balance than such factors as violence, usurpations, betrayals, etc. (Godelier 1977: 767 [emphasis in original]).

All official ideologies incorporate the thesis that the structure of government serves the common good. Conflict theorists may smirk at this 'opiate of the masses,' but in fact it binds the rulers as well as the ruled. Some delivery on this promise is essential (Lenski 1966: 180-1). Legitimizing activities must include real outputs (Easton 1965b) as well as manipulation of symbols, and where they don't, costly and unprofitable investments must be made in coercive sanctions (Haas 1982: 211). Claessen makes the point that, in order to secure loyalty, rulers need return as gifts to the populace only a fraction of what has been secured in taxes or tribute (1978: 563).

Conflict and integration theory seem, then, to be individually inadequate to account for both the origin and the persistence of the state. This fact has led some to call for their combination (e.g., Lerski 1966; R. Cohen 1978; Haas 1982). Governmental institutions both result from unequal access to resources, and also create benefits for their citizenry (R. Cohen 1978: 8). There are definitely beneficial integrative advantages in the concentration of power and authority (Haas 1982: 128); once established, however, the political realm becomes an increasingly important determinant of change in economy, society, and culture (R. Cohen 1978: 8). Integration theory is better able to account for distribution of the necessities of life, and conflict theory for surpluses (Lenski 1966: 442).

The reader may have discerned that, while accepting the suggestion that a synthesis is necessary to understand both the emergence and continuation of states, the view followed here leans toward the integration side. The psychological reductionism of conflict theory is an insurmountable flaw. Self-aggrandizement cannot account for the development of states, but it certainly does help in understanding their subsequent history. There is, however, a very important point that conflict and integration theory have in common. In both views, states are problem-solving organizations. Both theories see the state as arising out of changed circumstances, and as being a response to those circumstances. In conflict theory the state develops to solve problems of class conflict that emerge from differential economic success. In integration theory governing institutions arise to secure the well-being of the total populace. While the purposes of the state are seen as different, on this level the state of conflict theorists and the state of integrationists are the same kind of institution.

As will be seen in subsequent chapters, the nature of complex societies as problem-solving organizations has much to do with understanding why they collapse. In this regard, while conflict theorists will be disappointed by these views on the nature and emergence of complexity, they will still find utility in the explanation of collapse.

Summary and implications

Complex societies are problem-solving organizations, in which more parts, different kinds of parts, more social differentiation, more inequality, and more kinds of centralization and control emerge as circumstances require. Growth of complexity has involved a change from small, internally homogeneous, minimally differentiated groups characterized by equal access to resources, shifting, ephemeral leadership, and unstable political formations, to large, heterogeneous, internally differentiated, class structured, controlled societies in which the resources that sustain life are not equally available to all. This latter kind of society, with which we today are most familiar, is an anomaly of history, and where present requires constant legitimization and reinforcement.

The process of collapse, as discussed in the previous chapter, is a matter of rapid, substantial decline in an established level of complexity. A society that has collapsed is suddenly smaller, less differentiated and heterogeneous, and characterized by fewer specialized parts; it displays less social differentiation; and it is able to exercise less control over the behavior of its members. It is able at the same time to command smaller surpluses, to offer fewer benefits and inducements to membership; and it is less capable of providing subsistence and defensive security for a regional population. It may decompose to some of the constituent building blocks (e.g., states, ethnic groups, villages) out of which it was created.

The loss of complexity, like its emergence, is a continuous variable. Collapse may involve a drop between the major levels of complexity envisioned by many anthropologists (e.g., state to chiefdom), or it may equally well involve a drop within a level (larger to smaller, or Transitional to Typical or Inchoate states). Collapse offers an interesting perspective for the typological approach. It is a process of major, rapid change from one structurally stable level to another. This is the type of change that evolutionary typologies imply, but in the reverse direction.

3

The study of collapse

I see no reason to suppose that the Roman and the Megatherium were not struck down by similar causes.

Ronald Ross
(1907: 2)

Introduction

It is not for lack of effort that collapse is still a little understood process. The research devoted in the historical and social sciences to explaining collapse is substantial, and has produced a literature which clearly reflects the significance of the topic. Among literate societies the attempt to understand the disintegration of states can be traced nearly as far as the phenomenon itself.

The fall of the Western Roman Empire must surely be the most wrenching event of European history. It figured prominently in the writings of the late Empire itself, of the Middle Ages, and up to recent times (Mazzarino 1966). The collapses of the Chou Dynasty in China (Creel 1953, 1970; Needham 1965; Fairbank et al. 1973) and of the Mauryan Empire (ca. 300-100 B.C.) in India (Nehru 1959; Thapar 1966) hold similar significance for those areas. Quite often the fall of such early empires acquires for later peoples the status of a paradise lost, a golden age of good government, wise rule, harmony, and peace, when all was right with the world. This is clearly evident in the writings of, for example, Gibbon (1776-88) on the Antonine period of the Roman Empire, of the 'Hundred Schools' on Chou China (Creel 1970; Needham 1965; Fairbank et al. 1973), or of Nehru on Mauryan India (1959). The attempt to understand the loss of paradise is at the same time a grasping to comprehend current conditions and a philosophy of how a political society should be. Here then is another dimension to the study of collapse: it is not only a scholarly attempt to understand the past and a practical attempt to ascertain the future, but also, in many minds, a statement of current political philosophy (see, for example, Isaac [1971]). This last aspect will not figure highly in the present work, but does account for much of the perennial concern with collapse.

What collapses? More on definitions

Ancient and medieval writers saw collapse in a way that is largely congruent with the perspective of the present work, that is, as the fall of specific *political* entities. With the formal development of the social sciences in the last two centuries, however, a new conception has emerged: the transformation of civilizations as *cultural* forms. Many of the most prominent twentieth-century scholars, such as Spengler (1962), Toynbee

(1962), Kroeber (1944, 1957), Coulborn (1954, 1966), and Gray (1958), and most of those who are read by popular audiences, have written in this vein.

This school sees the end of a civilization as a transformation of the features or behaviors that characterize a cultural entity. These features are typically those that form the popular notion of 'civilization': specific styles of art and public architecture, traditions of literature and music, and philosophies of life and politics. Examples include Toynbee's 'Syriac,' or Spengler's 'Magian' (Arabian) and 'Faustian' (Western) civilizations. To such authors it is the end of these civilizations (that is, their transformation into some other civilization, defined as new traditions in art, literature, music, and philosophy) that is of concern. Each civilization may typically contain a number of individual political entities that themselves rise and fall, but the longevity of the civilization itself usually transcends such short-term fluctuations. In some cases, though, a civilization can be weakened when such polities conflict. So to Toynbee, the end of his 'Orthodox Christian' civilization lies in the decimation of the manpower of the Byzantine Empire in the Romano-Bulgarian war of A.D. 977-1019. The overexploitation of the Empire's Anatolian recruiting grounds for this campaign led to the disastrous loss to the Seljuk Turks at the Battle of Manzikert in 1071, and to the subsequently easy conversion of Anatolia to Islam and the Turkish language (Toynbee 1962 (IV): 371-2, 392, 398). Yet in the main, the rise and fall of civilizations does not correspond (to such authors) nearly so closely to specific polities or events.

There are major difficulties with this view, and specific reasons why it is not fruitful. The reader will have noticed that, while the fall of civilizations was discussed by way of introductory material in the first chapter, that term has since been avoided, and for the most part will continue to be. There are two reasons for this: first, the definition of what constitutes a 'civilization' tends to be vague and intuitive, and secondly, there is an almost unavoidable element of unscientific value judgement in the very concept.

Pitirim Sorokin is particularly noted for criticism of the 'death of civilizations' idea (e.g., 1950, 1957). He correctly points out that at any point where such a death is postulated, there is nonetheless much continuity in cultural behavior from the dying civilization to the emerging one. Moreover, specific parts of cultural systems change continuously, so that qualitative transformation to a new civilization is difficult to pinpoint. He asserts as well that human cultures are not unified in any event, merely chance amalgamations of features, so that by definition they cannot cease to exist. On this last point most current social scientists would disagree with Sorokin, but that matter leads away from the discussion.

The question of value judgements is equally serious. What distinguishes 'civilized' from 'uncivilized' societies? Anthropologists have long recognized that the very terms are value-laden: in popular thought civilized societies are superior. How do we recognize a civilized society? By such things as refined art styles, monumental architecture, and literary and philosophical traditions that seem akin to our own experiences. Civilizations display artistic, architectural, and literary styles that are similar in structure (if not in form and content) to our own; hence civilized societies are those like us. Many authors (supposed scientists) are blatant about their value judgements to the point of embarrassment. Gray, for example, characterized the Greek Archaic period as 'crude' (1958: 19). Clough defined civilization as achievement in aesthetic and intellectual pursuits, and success in controlling the physical environment. A more civilized people is more successful in these (Clough 1951: 3). Kroeber, one of the masters of this field, made reference to '...higher cultural values and forms' (1944: 8), assigned to ancient Egypt '...a fairly high idea system' (1944: 664), and referred to cultural patterns '...which we adjudge as of high quality' (1944: 763). In *A Study of History* Toynbee asserted that '...civilizations are in their nature progressive movements' (1962 (III): 128). Spengler was curiously different. To him, civilizations are undesirable, even evil.

> They are a conclusion...death following life, rigidity following expansion...
> They are an end, irrevocable, yet by inward necessity reached again and again
> (1962: 24).

Such biases have no place in objective social science, and a concept that is so laden with this problem is better abandoned or rethought.

Not all have approached the concept so uselessly. Melko (1969: 8) characterizes civilizations as large, complex cultures, and is echoed in this by Flannery (1972: 400) and Coulborn (1966: 404). Somewhat refined, such a definition will more clearly fit the present study. A civilization is the cultural system of a complex society. The features that popularly define a civilized society – such as great traditions of art and writing – are epiphenomena or covariables of social, political, and economic complexity. Complexity calls these traditions into being, for such art and literature serve social and economic purposes and classes that exist only in complex settings. Civilization emerges with complexity, exists because of it, and disappears when complexity does. Complexity is the base of civilization, and civilization, by definition here, can disappear only when complexity vanishes (see also Clark [1979: 9-12]). It may be true that specific polities can rise and fall within a civilization, but political complexity itself must disintegrate for civilization to disappear. For this reason the study of rising and falling complexity serves as a monitor of the phenomenon termed civilization, a monitor that is at once measurable and specifiable, and so less subject to the biases and value judgements of other approaches. The concept of civilization is thus obviated for present purposes.

Does this mean that the work of the cultural school is not pertinent to the study of collapse? Surely the popularity of this school would itself argue against this supposition. But there are other reasons for considering the works of Spengler, Toynbee, Kroeber, and others, and indeed, considering these in some detail. The inextricable link between complexity and civilization, even if denied or unrecognized by this school, indicates that a discussion of why civilizations disappear will be pertinent to understanding why polities do. More basically, though, the approach to selecting works to consider in this chapter dictates their inclusion. Some of the work to be discussed pertains, for example, to societies that never did collapse (as defined here), such as the Byzantine and Ottoman empires. Such cases are included, along with the theories of the cultural school, because of the importance not only of political collapse, but also of circumstances that *could* lead to this condition. Thus, theories of the end of civilizations and discussions of political weakness will receive prominent treatment.

Classification of theories

In conducting the research for this chapter it became tempting at times to rephrase an old joke, and suggest that there are two or three theories of collapse for every society that has experienced it. While greater scientific attention has been devoted to the development of complexity than to collapse, the literature on the latter subject is still voluminous, and the diversity of ideas impressive. True, these range from respectable and scholarly to some that provide only comic relief. Yet the popularity of some views that scholars value little requires that all receive some treatment.

This diversity of views dictates a need to impose order. Theories of collapse fall into a limited number of recurrent explanatory themes. These themes by and large persist through time. The authors whose works are here assigned to each theme are characterized by overriding similarities in framework, assumptions, and approach. Within each theme, of course, a great deal of diversity still exists, so that some level of individual discussion is necessary for many authors.

It should be noted that any such classification of theories is to some degree arbitrary, and indeed, many approaches to classification would be possible. It is common in the social sciences to write of internal *vs.* external causes of social change, and the study of collapse can be similarly dichotomized (e.g., Sabloff 1973a: 36). (There is nothing new here: Polybius made the same observation in the second century B.C. [1979: 350].) Similarly, just as one can write of conflict *vs.* integration theories of change (see Chapter 2), so such theories have been advanced to account for collapse. Again, this is an ancient development (contrast, for example, Plato's *Laws* with Flannery [1972]). Neither dichotomy is useful for this work, although both are certainly valid and will be discussed in the final chapter.

There appear to be eleven major themes in the explanation of collapse. These are:

1. Depletion or cessation of a vital resource or resources on which the society depends.
2. The establishment of a new resource base.
3. The occurrence of some insurmountable catastrophe.
4. Insufficient response to circumstances.
5. Other complex societies.
6. Intruders.
7. Class conflict, societal contradictions, elite mismanagement or misbehavior.
8. Social dysfunction.
9. Mystical factors.
10. Chance concatenation of events.
11. Economic factors.

As simple as it is to present this classification, there are still ambiguities. There is much overlap in the categories listed, while some themes could be subdivided further. The assignment of authors to themes adds another level of uncertainty, for many fall easily into more than one class. Other investigators, including the authors so classi-fied, might legitimately assign writers to different themes, or even devise an alterna-tive classification. The present classification is based on an assessment of the *major* approaches and assumptions in an author's work. While other classifications are clearly possible, the evaluation of individual studies would not in any event be altered.

Framework of discussion

The goal of this study throughout is to understand collapse as a general phenomenon, to gain an understanding not limited to specific cases, but applicable across time, space, and type of society. Most explanations of collapse focus on a particular society or civilization, rather than approach the global process. Thus there are far more explanations of the fall of Rome or of the Maya than there are comparisons of these. Some authors do make comparisons of two or three cases of collapse, but desist from further generalization. This situation, indeed, is no more than characteristic of history and the social sciences, which have always been overwhelmingly particularistic.

One outcome of explaining individual collapses is that criticisms of these attempts have been primarily factual. While a critique of an author's explanation for the demise of society X might discuss the logic of the argument, it seems easier for such critics to focus on factual matters: to show that the historical and/or archaeological records of society X don't fit the proposed explanation. Thus, when scholars postulate climatic deterioration for the fall of Mycenaean Civilization, or invaders for the collapse of the Maya, critics will generally assert that factual evidence for climatic fluctuations or invaders is either lacking, or contradictory to the proposal. Subsequent debate tends to turn about the factual contest: there is/is not evidence for the climatic fluctuation, for the invaders, and the like. Rarely do authors question the logic of the original proposition. How does or how can climatic fluctuations, invaders, and so forth lead to collapse? Can the postulated cause really account for the outcome? Is the explanation adequate? While some critics do raise such questions, this is rarely done on a general basis. The factual debate remains prominent.

The premise of the present approach is that if the logic of an argument is faulty, a discussion of factual matters is largely unnecessary. If the climatic shift or the intruders could not have caused the society to collapse, then all the evidence for or against these is interesting, but immaterial. Hence in what follows the major focus will be on the logic of proposed explanations. Factual matters will from time to time be discussed, but these are never of major importance.

The stimulus to undertake this study was the perception that existing explanations of collapse logically cannot account for it. This chapter will detail the reservations about previous approaches, and show where these approaches fail. The tone is necessarily critical, but it is worth noting that for all this the existing literature does have much to offer in understanding collapse. It simply cannot offer all that might be presently wished. After these pages of skepticism, the chapter will conclude with some hopeful comments.

Resource depletion

Two major explanations for collapse are subsumed under this theme: the gradual deterioration or depletion of a resource base (usually agriculture), often due to human mismanagement, and the more rapid loss of resources due to an environmental fluctuation or climatic shift. Both are thought to cause collapse through depletion of the resources on which a complex society depends.

Although the causal chain from economic deterioration to collapse is a recent theory, the linkage between the two was a source of speculation to many who experienced the Roman breakdown. Among some ancient writers, though, the causal chain was reversed from theories of today. The decline in agricultural yields in Italy in the first century B.C., for example, was thought by some to be a result of moral decadence (Mazzarino 1966: 21, 32-3). Writers of the second and third centuries A.D. are often reminiscent of nineteenth- and twentieth-century climatological theorists, although usually the decline of agriculture and mining was seen by the Romans as a covariable rather than as a cause of political weakness. The world as a whole, to these observers, was aging and losing vigor (Mazzarino 1966: 40-2). The Christian writer Cyprian, in *Ad Demetrianum* (third century A.D.), asserted

> ...that the age is now senile...the World itself...testifies to its own decline by
> giving manifold concrete evidences of the process of decay. There is a diminu-
> tion in the winter rains that give nourishment to the seeds in the earth, and in
> the summer heats that ripen the harvests. The springs have less freshness and
> the autumns less fecundity. The mountains, disembowelled and worn out, yield
> a lower output of marble; the mines, exhausted, furnish a smaller stock of the
> precious metals: the veins are impoverished, and they shrink daily. There is a
> decrease and deficiency of farmers in the field, of sailors on the sea, of soldiers in
> the barracks, of honesty in the marketplace, of justice in court, of concord in
> friendship, of skill in technique, of strictness in morals...Anything that is near
> its end, and is verging towards its decline and fall is bound to dwindle...This is
> the sentence that has been passed upon the World...this loss of strength and loss
> of stature must end, at last, in annihilation (quoted in Toynbee [1962 (IV): 8]).

The present link between climate and resource depletion, and the rise and fall of civilizations, owes much to the work of Ellsworth Huntington (1915, 1917), and to more recent theorists such as Winkless and Browning (1975), J. Hughes (1975), and Butzer (1976, 1980, 1984). Huntington espoused a biological model that few anthropologists today could endorse: 'The nature of a people's culture...depends primarily upon racial inheritance...' (1915: 1). But beyond biology, Huntington argued that civilization is affected by climate, that many of the great nations of the past rose and fell with favorable and unfavorable climatic conditions. During '...times of favorable climate in countries such as Egypt and Greece the people were apparently filled with a virile energy, which they do not now possess' (1915: 6). With aridity in Greece there came economic distress, famine, and lawlessness. To Huntington, high frequencies of cyclonic storms 'energized' populations to create civilizations, and when a climate became unfit, no people could retain the energy and 'progressiveness' that he believed was necessary for civilization (1915: 9, 257). The fall of Rome was explained by adverse climatic conditions after the early third century A.D. (Huntington 1917: 194-6).

Winkless and Browning provide an updated climatic theory, but with a curious reversal of some of Huntington's reasoning. To them, changing physical factors (e.g., increased volcanism) lead to changing climates, which lead to changing food supplies, and thus to changing human behavior (wars, migrations, economic upheavals, changing ethics, etc.) (Winkless and Browning 1975: 15). Whereas Huntington saw civilizations flourishing in stimulating climates, Winkless and Browning ascribe civilization to benign climatic conditions, and collapse conversely. They suggest that when climate changes, marginal areas are affected first. Buffer states begin to abandon the characteristics of civilization, return to nomadism and raiding, and ultimately topple the weakened centers of power. These authors further postulate an 800 year climatically-induced cycle to human affairs, superimposed on shorter cyclic patterns (1975: 147-9, 185).

An alternative resource depletion argument has been offered by Ekholm (1980), who ascribes collapse to loss of trade networks, external resources, and imported goods. An economic system becomes fragile when it comes to depend on external exchange over which it has little control. Since civilizations are always dependent on access to foreign markets, they are intrinsically vulnerable in this regard. Ekholm accounts in this manner for the collapses of the Third Dynasty of Ur and of Mycenaean civilization, for regional instability in the Near East and the eastern Mediterranean ca. 2300-2200 B.C., and for recent political upheavals in Madagasgar.

Similarly, Robert Briffault in 1938 predicted the demise of the British Empire for reasons of unfavorable trade. Hodges and Whitehouse, in their critique of the Pirenne thesis (1983), ascribe the post-Carolingian dark age to disruption of trade between Europe and the Near East, following the economic collapse of the Abbasids. Cipolla argues that the economic decline of Italy in recent centuries has resulted from unsuccessful competition in foreign trade (1970b).

Resource depletion arguments are perennial favorites in collapse studies. They have been prevalent for some time in Mesoamerican and Southwestern studies, but have also begun to gain prominence in eastern North America, Europe, and the Near East. The possibility of resource depletion is, of course, a major concern to contemporary forecasters (e.g., Catton 1980).

Mesoamerica

The spectacular collapse of Mayan civilization in the Southern Lowlands has frequently led scholars to focus on resource depletion. C. W. Cooke proposed in 1931 that collapse here was caused by soil erosion and land scarcity, encroachment of grasses, silting of lakes with consequent destruction of water transportation, a decline of water supply in dry years, and an increase in mosquito populations along with increase or introduction of malaria. Thirty years later, Sanders (1962, 1963) conducted an extensive study of Lowland ecology, and reached nearly the same conclusions. He argued that swidden agriculture in this region leads to soil nutrient depletion, weed competition, and savanna formation. In later writings, Sanders continues to favor an environmental deterioration argument, but supplements it by suggesting that political competition between Mayan centers, favoring resource intensification, was also a factor (Sanders and Webster 1978: 291-5). Haas argues similarly, that the Mayan collapse was due to weakening of the power base of subsistence resources and trade goods by environmental deterioration and external events (1982: 212). Rathje (1973) and Sharer (1982) both indict loss of trade in the Mayan collapse.

Such ideas have been applied elsewhere in Mesoamerica. S. Cook argued that soil exhaustion was responsible for both the Olmec and Highland collapses (1947). Weaver sees the destruction of Tula as largely due to a climatic change that caused the desiccation of north-central Mexico, forcing peripheral northern populations to push south and overthrow the city (1972: 213). Sanders et al. (1979: 137) and Hirth and Swezey (1976: 11, 15) suggest that the collapse of Teotihuacan was due to loss of control over vital trade networks.

Peru

Moseley (1983) indicts tectonic uplift in the agricultural collapse of Chimu, post-1000 A.D. Due to tectonic underthrust, the Pacific watershed tends to tilt and rise, causing rivers to downcut, and leading to lower groundwater levels and less runoff. The entire Chimu hydrological regime constricted, with consequences for surface vegetation. Canal intakes had to be repositioned upstream, which was less efficient. As water tables dropped in the Chimu case, farmers concentrated more on sunken gardens. But both sunken gardens and canals contracted through time back toward the river, and downslope toward the sea. Moseley does not single out tectonic movement as the sole source of collapse (see also Kus [1984]). He suggests that it provides the background conditions that make intelligible such things as revolt, conquest, soil depletion, and so forth. He does, however, implicate uplift in agricultural collapses elsewhere, such as the Near East, the Mayan Lowlands, and the Mesoamerican Cordillera.

The American Southwest

Climatic change is the most common explanation for the collapse of horticultural settlements, and of social complexity, in various areas of the Southwest. Agricultural mismanagement is occasionally added to the picture. The most frequent resource depletion arguments postulate such things as drought, erosion, shifts in rainfall seasonality, lower temperatures, overhunting of game, and depletion or increasing alkalinity of cultivable soils (summarized in Martin and Plog [1973: 322-5] and Martin, Quimby, and Collier [1947: 147]). Throughout the Southwest uplands, drought and arroyo cutting have long been the dominant explanations of regional abandonment (Reed 1944; Kelley 1952; Wenke 1981: 110).

Climatic explanations are common in the Hohokam region of southern Arizona (e.g., Doyel 1981), but here the results of agricultural malpractice are often added, such as waterlogging and/or salt build-up in soils (Haury 1976: 355). D. Adams notes that there are signs of malnutrition in some late Hohokam skeletons, and links these signs to agricultural problems (1983: 37). Weaver has developed the most complete argument along these lines. He suggests that after 1275 A.D., drought and salt accumulation in tilled fields led to a decline of the complex Hohokam social, political, and ritual systems, especially in outlying areas. Then ca. 1325 a period of abnormally high moisture with heavy spring runoff damaged or destroyed many canal heads and brush dams. This led to continued declines in crop yield, lower population, and increased dependence on wild foods. The economic stress led to sociopolitical collapse. When normal climatic conditions returned after ca. 1475 a variety of factors prevented the reemergence of Hohokam complexity (D. Weaver 1972: 49).

Eastern North America

Over the last two decades or more climatic explanations have gained currency in Midwestern archaeology. This is due largely to the work of James B. Griffin (1960, 1961). The collapse of northern Hopewell was ascribed by Griffin to a slightly cooler climatic phase in the upper Mississippi Valley. He has made similar assertions regarding the shift from the agricultural Mississippian Old Village Tradition to the foraging Oneota pattern, which occurred ca. 1200-1400 A.D. Vickery (1970) supports the argument, as in large part do Barreis, Bryson, and Kutzbach (1976; see also Barreis and Bryson [1965]). Melvin Fowler has developed a contrasting interpretation for the collapse of the Mississippian center of Cahokia, arguing for exhaustion of local resources (timber, game, fertile soil), and the rise of competitive political centers (1975: 100-1).

Egypt

Karl Butzer has argued in a number of studies (1976, 1980, 1984) that the collapse of the Old Kingdom, and other political catastrophes of Egyptian history, can be traced at least in part to variations in Nile flood levels, and thus to precipitation patterns in the interior of Africa. High Nile floods are damaging in that they favor soil crop parasites; destroy dikes, ditches, settlements, food stores, and livestock; and delay harvesting into the dry season. Low floods also reduce yields (Butzer 1976: 52, 1984: 105). Butzer cites Nile failure as a definite factor in the end of the New Kingdom (1570-1070 B.C.), and as a likely factor in the Old Kingdom disintegration between 2760 and 2225 B.C. This was the most prominent element in the failure of the Second Dynasty (2970-2760 B.C.), and of the Middle Kingdom (2035-1668 B.C.) (Butzer 1980: 522).

Butzer's argument is by no means a simple climatic one. He notes that ca. 1720 B.C. Egyptian unity was threatened by the establishment of petty principalities in the Delta, well before the Hyksos invasion of 1668 B.C. This in turn followed a period from 1840 to 1770 B.C. in which one-third of Nile floods were destructive enough to ruin the entire irrigation system. He also suggests that in the Old Kingdom collapse, political weakness preceded any Nile-related disasters, but these in turn may have triggered social unrest (1980: 520, 1984: 109, 110). Butzer thus sees Nile fluctuations as a contributory rather than causal agent, acting in concert with political weakness, poor leadership, overtaxation, and a top-heavy social pyramid to bring about episodes of disintegration (1980: 522, 1984: 112).

Butzer's views are reinforced by O'Connor (1974), who believes the Old Kingdom collapsed from consistently lower Nile inundations and consequent famines. Barbara Bell's thesis (1971) is more encompassing. She argues that the widespread, eastern Mediterranean and Near Eastern regional dark ages of ca. 2200-2000 and 1200-900 B.C. can *both* be accounted for by widespread droughts, each lasting several decades. In the Old Kingdom case, Bell argues, the failure of the Egyptian king to maintain proper flood levels through ritual intervention led to reduced legitimacy of, and confidence in, the central government at a time when the power of regional nobles was increasing (1971: 21-2).

The Harappan Civilization

There are a variety of resource depletion arguments for the end of the Indus Valley, or Harappan, civilization. Both Thapar (1982) and Sharer (1982) implicate declining foreign trade in this collapse. Dales suggests that '...massive extrusions of mud, aided by the pressure of accumulated gases,' caused damming of the Indus River 90 miles downstream from Mohenjo-Daro, and formation of a large lake (1966: 95, 96). Raikes (1964) argues for the same outcome, but with flooding resulting from coastal uplift. By either mechanism (perhaps in conjunction with earthquakes) commerce, agriculture, and communications were disrupted (Raikes 1964: 296; Wheeler 1966: 83). Mortimer Wheeler (1966, 1968) and Dales (1966) prefer an argument with a more mystical tone: that the morale of the population was simply worn down by centuries of fighting mud, that the '...Harappan spirit mired in an unrelenting sequence of invading water and engulfing silt' (Dales 1966: 98).

Mesopotamia

One of the best explanations of collapse has been developed by Jacobsen and Adams (1958) and R. McC. Adams (1981) for episodic political catastrophes in the Mesopotamian alluvium. Like Butzer, they recognize that resource depletion arguments can only partially account for any instance of collapse, that political and economic factors frequently influence production systems to create favorable or unfavorable conditions.

In this area, agricultural intensification and excessive irrigation lead to short-term above-normal harvests, with increasing prosperity, security, and stability. Within a few years, though, the rise of saline groundwater erodes or destroys agricultural productivity, and thus stability. When powerful regimes (such as the Third Dynasty of Ur, the late Sassanians, and in the early Islamic period) pursued policies of maximizing resource production, complex irrigation systems were developed that were beyond local abilities to manage and repair. State control was required. When the political realm proved unstable, dangers of salinity increased and the possibility loomed for sudden, catastrophic fluctuations.

In the Sassanian and Islamic periods, both population and the state's fiscal demands increased, more marginal land was cultivated regardless of declining returns, and for many there was a catastrophic drop in living standards. Impressive accomplishments were built on an unstable political base, and at the expense of increasing ecological fragility. Decline was inevitable, and became precipitate in the late ninth century A.D. While revenues dropped the costs of agricultural management remained stable or increased. Harsh taxation alienated the support population, leading to revolts and destruction of irrigation facilities. With reduced government power, repair was impossible. The perimeter of government jurisdiction contracted to the area around Baghdad, and any chance for a solution to the agricultural problems was lost. The result was the devastation and abandonment of much of the region, as Adams (1981: xvii) has described so well in the quote that heads this work (see also Waines [1977]).

Mycenaean Civilization
In 1966 Rhys Carpenter developed an elegantly written argument for the collapse of Mycenaean civilization: that it, and other thirteenth-century B.C. upheavals in the Mediterranean, were due to climatic change leading to famine, depopulation, and migration. What appears to be a Mycenaean collapse in the Peloponnese is actually a drought-induced evacuation to other areas, including Attica. The climatologist Reid Bryson and his colleagues support Carpenter's interpretation of this climatic fluctuation (Bryson et al. 1974: 47-50).

The Roman Empire
Both Huntington (1915: 6) and Winkless and Browning (1975: 179-82) argued that climatic change, leading to resource insufficiencies, stimulated the barbarian migrations that so disastrously affected the Roman Empire, but disagree on causal mechanisms. Huntington ascribed the matter to desiccation in Asia, Winkless and Browning to the end of a cool period.

In a study of pollen diagrams from northern Europe, Waateringe (1983) noted a disastrous change toward the end of the Empire. There was a major decline in pollens of cereals, arable plants, and pasture weeds, and an increase in tree pollen. Woodland apparently encroached on land formerly cultivated. Waateringe believes this was brought about by intensification of production for market distribution. Large markets, the *Pax Romana*, road networks, and centralized administration created a situation in early Roman times where local food shortages could be alleviated to a greater degree than previously. The subsequent opportunities to profit from agriculture led to intensification and surplus production. Population consequently increased, leading to still greater demands for food and then to agricultural exhaustion. Agricultural collapse ensued both within and adjacent to the Empire.

Hughes indicts the Roman failure to adapt their society and economy harmoniously to the natural environment. This failure was then a major cause of collapse. Deforestation led to erosion, the most readily accessible minerals were mined, lands were overgrazed, and agriculture declined. Food shortages and population decline sapped the Empire's strength (J. Hughes 1975). In focusing on agricultural decline, Hughes echoes the opinions of both ancient and recent writers (e.g., Simkhovitch 1916; Finley 1973).

Another explanation of the Roman collapse concentrates on lack of *human* re-sources. Gilfallen, in a well-known argument (1970), indicts lead poisoning for debilitating the human population on which Roman strength depended.

Assessment

Resource depletion arguments, to judge from the number advanced, are perpetually attractive. There is something to such arguments, for no society can maintain complexity when its resource base is depleted beyond a certain point. Yet long before that point is reached a whole range of responses may be undertaken. Here is the first of several problems which make one uneasy at the resource depletion theory.

The resource depletion argument, at base, ascribes collapse to economic weakness, often suddenly induced. Most investigators would assume at the outset that economically weakened societies are indeed prone to collapse, so this point may be taken as a warranted assumption. One supposition of this view must be that these societies sit by and watch the encroaching weakness without taking corrective actions. Here is a major difficulty. Complex societies are characterized by centralized decision making, high information flow, great coordination of parts, formal channels of command, and pooling of resources. Much of this structure seems to have the capability, if not the designed purpose, of countering fluctuations and deficiencies in productivity. With their administrative structure, and capacity to allocate both labor and resources, dealing with adverse environmental conditions may be one of the things that complex societies do best (see, for example, Isbell [1978]). It is curious that they would collapse when faced with precisely those conditions they are equipped to circumvent.

It is entirely possible, of course, that environmental fluctuations or deterioration may occur that existing production systems and social arrangements cannot overcome. Resource depletion theorists, indeed, would have to make just such an argument. Several kinds of information are needed, though, to truly demonstrate that such conditions can cause collapse. The data in question would include climate, population, crop or other resource yields, yearly requirements of the population and of the sociopolitical system, and the adaptive capabilities of the society in question. Such data have not been systematically sought in the study of collapse.

As it becomes apparent to the members or administrators of a complex society that a resource base is deteriorating, it seems most reasonable to assume that some rational steps are taken toward a resolution. The alternative assumption – of idleness in the face of disaster – requires a leap of faith at which we may rightly hesitate. If the former assumption may be admitted, then new variables enter whose mere existence indicates that the resource depletion argument is inadequate.

If a society cannot deal with resource depletion (which all societies are to some degree designed to do) then the truly interesting questions revolve around the society, not the resource. What structural, political, ideological, or economic factors in a society prevented an appropriate response? This is no idle question, however simple it may seem, for the literature on resource depletion contains some disturbing ambiguities. One study of the Hohokam of the American Southwest, for example, asserts that environmental deterioration caused collapse in one instance (Sacaton to Soho phases), but increased complexity in another (Soho to Civano phases) (Doyel 1981). Elsewhere, J. Hughes (1975) cites deforestation as a cause of the Roman collapse. Yet Wilkinson (1973) has shown how in late- and post-Medieval England, deforestation spurred economic development and, far from leading to collapse, was at least partly responsible for the Industrial Revolution. Clearly the major factor in understanding these episodes is not that a resource was depleted, but that the respective societies responded in different ways. Why would resource stress lead to collapse in some instances, and to increased complexity and economic intensification in others? Citing resource depletion does no more than scratch the surface of an enormously complex matter.

Butzer and R. McC. Adams, in awareness of such problems, present scenarios in which environmental, social, and political factors intertwine. Both have developed plausible explanations of collapse in the specific cases they have studied. Yet while the incorporation of political factors in Butzer's and Adams' studies is a strength of their individual efforts, it also betrays a weakness in the broader approach. To the extent that elite mismanagement or miscalculation figures in, for example, the Mesopotamian cases, we are left with a major explanatory *lacuna*. To suggest that societies collapse because elites act unwisely explains little. Are there conditions under which elites act wisely or unwisely, or is this a random variable? Is it even a definable and measurable factor? At this point we anticipate a later section in which such matters are more appropriately considered.

As always, empirical questions can be raised about specific resource depletion explanations. In the Hohokam case, Haury points to an ambiguity in the waterlogging/salt concentration argument: settlements that were not dependent on canal irrigation were simultaneously abandoned (1976: 355). In criticism of Carpenter's drought theory of the Mycenaean collapse, Chadwick points out that Attica, the supposed refuge for desiccated Messenia, has only about half the rainfall of the latter region (1976: 192). Such questions add to the theoretical problems.

New resources

This theme, decidedly a minority view, presents a reversal of the resource depletion theory. Here the suggestion is that new, bountiful resources lead to collapse. This argument derives squarely from the integration school, which sees complexity as a response to stress conditions, including resource inequities. When such inequities are alleviated, the need for ranking and social control may break down, leading to collapse to a lower level of complexity (Harner 1970: 69). A variation on this is presented by Martin (1969), who argues that South American foragers dropped in complexity following the depopulation attendant upon European contact. Although Martin is vague about causal mechanisms, one route could be alleviation of pressure on resources, leading to the situation Harner envisions.

Jelinek (1967) argues similarly, that along the Pecos River in New Mexico sedentary horticultural villages were abandoned for mobile bison-hunting when increased moisture between 1250 and 1350 A.D. led to the spread of grasslands, and increased local availability of bison.

Childe (1942) and Needham (1965) followed a variant explanation. Childe suggested that with the introduction of iron, cheaper and easier to acquire than bronze, peasants and barbarians could obtain weapons that allowed them to challenge the armies of civilized states. The Mycenaean and Hittite collapses accordingly followed (Childe 1942: 177-8, 191-3). Needham (1965: 93) suggests that in China, the spread of iron in the middle Chou period led to the disintegration of Chou feudalism and the rise of independent states (although he is less clear than Childe about specific causal mechanisms).

Assessment

To an integration theorist, Harner's (1970) stress-alleviation argument has some appeal, but much less to a conflict theorist. In any event it is mainly restricted to simpler societies. It has no power to explain the fall of Rome, much less many other cases.

Catastrophes

Single-event catastrophes, such things as hurricanes, volcanic eruptions, earthquakes, or major disease epidemics, are enduring favorites for explaining collapse (e.g., Easton 1965a: 82-3). There is something so appealing in simple solutions to complex processes that it is not likely such ideas will ever go out of fashion. (It is interesting to note that students of paleontology are as attracted to simple catastrophe theories to explain the disappearance of the dinosaurs, or other life forms, as social scientists are for understanding collapse [e.g., Gould 1983: 320-4].) There is no clear-cut dividing point between catastrophe and resource depletion arguments, only a subtle difference in emphasis.

Catastrophe scenarios are old. Plato's *Critias* and *Timaeus* characterize the demise of the mythical Atlantis in such terms. The Biblical flood, and similar stories, fall into this theme.

Mesoamerica

Earthquakes, hurricanes, and disease epidemics figure occasionally in studies of the Mayan collapse (summarized in R. E. W. Adams [1973a] and Sabloff [1973a]). Spinden (1928), for example, suspected that the sudden appearance of yellow fever was involved. Mackie (1961) argued that signs of structural collapse at Benque Viejo indicate an earthquake, followed by social upheaval. More recently, Brewbaker (1979) has indicted maize mosaic virus, which he brings to the Maya Lowlands from the eastern Caribbean by hurricane, subsequently causing repeated crop failures. He cites by comparison the 1845 potato blight in Ireland, which led to the death or emigration of half the island's 4,000,000 inhabitants.

Earthquakes and plagues have also been implicated in the collapse of Teotihuacan (discussed in Katz [1972: 77]).

Minoan Civilization

A well-known explanation for the Minoan collapse was advanced by Marinatos (1939): that it was caused by the immense volcanic eruption of the nearby island of Thera. The effect on Crete was supposedly disastrous, including ash, mud, and tsunamis, while earthquakes before and after the eruption destroyed the inland palaces. Crete received an '...irreparable blow, and from then onwards gradually declined and sank into decadence, losing its prosperity and power' (Marinatos 1939: 437).

Variations on this proposal have followed. Carpenter argues that the eruption devastated Crete, which was prevented from recovering by aggressive Greek mainlanders, who invaded and established control at Knossos (1966: 32-3). Chadwick brings in no invaders, but proposes that a tsunami following the eruption struck Crete, destroying the Minoan fleet, while ash made eastern Crete barren (1976). Pomerance extends this devastation to the entire eastern Mediterranean (1970).

The Roman Empire

Malaria has been implicated in the decline of the Roman state. W. Jones (1907) argued that the devastation of Italy by Hannibal's invasion (218-204 B.C.), and ensuing agricultural desertion of large areas, led to the establishment of malaria. Italians, and those who settled in Italy, became infected, and this helped bring down the Empire. The development of extravagance, cruelty, and lack of self-control in the Roman character of the first century A.D. was, under this argument, due to malaria. McNeill, in a more modern theory (1976), indicts the weakening effect of plagues in the Roman collapse.

Assessment

As obvious and favored as catastrophe scenarios are, they are among the weakest explanations of collapse. The fundamental problem is that complex societies routinely withstand catastrophes without collapsing. Thus, catastrophe arguments present an incomplete causal chain: the basic assumption, rarely explicated, must be that the catastrophes in question somehow exceeded the abilities of the societies to absorb and recover from disaster. At this point some of the criticisms raised in regard to the resource depletion argument become pertinent: if the assumption is correct, then the interesting factor is no longer the catastrophe but the society.

As a matter of practicality, though, catastrophe explanations are too simple to accommodate the complexities of human societies and the collapse process. Human societies encounter catastrophes all the time. They are an expectable aspect of life, and are routinely provided for through social, managerial, and economic arrangements. It is doubtful if any large society has ever succumbed to a single-event catastrophe. And the cause of understanding is not advanced by the suggestion that collapse is caused by accidents. 'Accidents,' notes R. M. Adams, 'happen to all societies at all stages of their history...' (1983: 5). Too many societies encounter accidents without collapsing.

The analogies that catastrophe theorists advance to support their arguments actually weaken them. The eruption of Thera, for example, is often compared to the late-nineteenth-century eruption of Krakatoa in the South Pacific. To my knowledge, though, no complex society collapsed under Krakatoa's onslaught. Similarly, Brewbaker (1979) cites the effect of the potato blight in Ireland to bolster his argument that maize mosaic virus could have caused the Mayan collapse. He fails, though, to point out to his readers that Ireland suffered no cessation of sociopolitical complexity as a result of this disaster.

Empirically, the Thera-eruption argument for the devastation of Crete falters on a dating problem. This eruption is currently dated toward the end of the Late Minoan IA period (ca. 1500 B.C.), whereas the widespread destruction on Crete occurred at the end of Late Minoan IB (ca. 1450 B.C.) (Doumas 1983: 139, 142). The Cretans of ca. 1500 B.C. most likely stopped to watch the eruption of Thera, made whatever preparations were called for, and when it was all over went about their business. And while I am not a geomorphologist, the argument that ash made east Crete barren seems odd compared with the effects of ash in northeastern Arizona, where the prehistoric eruption of Sunset Crater significantly improved local agriculture (Martin and Plog 1973: 143).

It should be pointed out that catastrophe explanations, as discussed here, differ from Catastrophe Theory as applied by Renfrew (1979) to modeling the collapse process. The latter is an abstract mathematical theory that specifies no causal mechanisms.

Insufficient response to circumstances

The basic factor that unites the rather disparate arguments under this theme is the notion that fundamental limitations of social, political, and economic systems prevent an appropriate response to circumstances, and this makes collapse inevitable. Two of the major views considered here, well known in the history of anthropology, are those of Betty Meggers (1954) regarding environmental limitations to civilization, and Elman Service (1960, 1975) on the 'Law of Evolutionary Potential.' Toynbee's 'Challenge and Response' theory is not included at this point.

Meggers' argument was simple: more productive environments can produce more complex societies. More specifically, '...the level to which a culture can develop is dependent upon the agricultural potentiality of the environment it occupies.' As this potentiality improves '...culture will advance' (Meggers 1954: 815). Classifying tropical rainforest as inadequate in this regard, Meggers encountered the problem of the Maya. Her solution: Mayan civilization must have been introduced from elsewhere, and the history of Mayan occupation should represent decline or disintegration. Introduce a civilization into an environment that is inappropriate, and ultimately the environment will win. Mayan society could not respond appropriately to its circumstances.

Despite serious criticism, this argument continues to find expression (occasionally, one suspects, by authors who are unaware of their intellectual linkage to Meggers). Both Sabloff (1971, 1973a) and Webb (1973: 403) present up-to-date variations, linking the Mayan environment with events elsewhere in Mesoamerica as sources of collapse. (These prominent Mayan scholars are, of course, fully aware of Meggers' theory and of recent ideas derived from it.) Stuart and Gauthier (1981: 40) argue similarly for the Chacoan collapse: that the height of Chacoan complexity was impossible to sustain in an arid environment.

A similar view argues (sometimes implicitly) that complex societies are unstable, not just in certain kinds of environments, but inherently. Kent Flannery (1972) and Roy Rappaport (1977) are the best known proponents of this line of reasoning. These authors suggest that more complex societies are more closely interlinked, with greater mutual influences among parts. Self-sufficiency and autonomy of local systems are reduced as specialization increases. As special-purpose subsystems become increasingly differentiated, stability declines. Disruptions occurring anywhere will be spread everywhere, whereas in less complex settings a society would be cushioned against disruptions by less specialization, less interlinkage among parts, and greater time delays between cause and ultimate outcome. Civilization itself (i.e., great complexity), to Rappaport, may be maladaptive: 'Civilisation has emerged only recently – in the past six thousand or so years – and it may yet prove to be an unsuccessful experiment' (Rappaport 1977: 65).

An intriguing variation on this last theme has been developed by Phillips (1979). In a statement reminiscent of Gibbon's views on the Roman Empire, Phillips suggests that 'In a sense, the problem is not that states collapse (for this happens constantly), but rather that some states last so long...' (1979: 138). Phillips' argument is that it takes time for a newly dominant state to use all its resources efficiently, which he defines as '...high output or return per unit investment' (1979: 140). Efficiency (so defined), though, leads to inflexibility in resource allocation. The mechanism is this: a newly dominant state controls a large territorial base, but has not yet developed (or come to depend on) complex institutions that will derive a significant return for this resource base. In such situations, a large proportion of the new resources will always be used in non-critical or low return ways (such as monumental architecture). This has the consequence of creating a hidden resource reserve that can be used for emergencies, for such non-critical activities are suspendable in a crisis.

But through time social and political institutions emerge that use this resource base more fully (in Phillips' terminology, 'efficiently'). Eventually, most resources are allocated to support of 'efficient' institutions (political offices and the like), leaving no reserves or flexibility in resource allocation. The dominant center is then left susceptible to disruptions, so that '...historical accident alone is sufficient to touch off major failures' (Phillips 1979: 142). A crisis like a revolt, which a newly dominant state would easily control, becomes an insurmountable problem for a more 'efficient' society that lacks reserves. Although formulated in regard to Mesoamerica, this argument has applicability elsewhere. The later Roman Empire, for example, succumbed to catastrophes the like of which had been overcome by the early Republic.

This argument is strongly reminiscent of that of Shephard Clough, who suggested that weakness and collapse can be caused by diverting resources from investment in capital to expenditures on art and knowledge. As more resources are devoted to artistic achievement, the share available for creating economic well-being diminishes, as does the society's strength. Thus the elements that define 'civilization' lead to its demise. The collapses of Egypt in the First Intermediate Period, and of Rome, are explained accordingly (Clough 1951: 3-7, 52-3, 143-59, 261). Thus to Clough and Phillips complex societies are not initially unstable, but eventually become so.

Elman Service's 'Law of Evolutionary Potential' (1960; 1975) has an intellectual history similar to Meggers' ideas: lack of initial acceptance, with occasional later usage, sometimes by authors who either do not recognize or do not note this precursor to their work. The Law states as follows: 'The more specialized and adapted a form in a given evolutionary stage, the smaller its potential for passing to the next stage' (Service 1960: 97). Specific evolutionary 'progress' is inversely related to general evolutionary 'potential' (Service 1960: 97). Within this view, success at adaptation breeds conservatism; dominant polities are less able to accommodate change (see also Cipolla [1970a: 9]). Successful complex societies become locked into their adaptations, and are easily bypassed by those less specialized. So by having greater flexibility, less complex border states gain an increasing competitive advantage, and are thus able ultimately to topple older, established states (Service 1960: 107, 1975: 254, 312-14). Service uses this principle to account for the success of barbarians along China's northern frontier, in Mesopotamia, and in Mesoamerica, and for discontinuities in political developments in Peru (1975: 315-19). In each case, he suggests, newly civilized peripheral populations adopt some competitive advantage (an organizational feature, weapon, tactic, or the like) that the old center is too conservative to adopt, and thereby rise to dominance (Service 1975: 319-20). R. N. Adams follows similar reasoning, and believes this rigidity and conservatism result from investment in controlling major energy sources (1975: 200).

Many investigators see competition with less complex neighbors as one of only a number of factors leading to collapse. Service's Law can perhaps be expanded into a more general 'failure to adapt' argument. Several authors make such an argument: that complex societies disappear because of some inability to bring forth an appropriate response to circumstances. Melko (1969), for one, argues (like Service) that once established a civilization's capacities for change become limited. Collapse results from sociopolitical ossification, bureaucratic inefficiency, or inability to deal with internal or external problems. Ho attributes the decline of Ming China to such matters (1970).

Writing as a sociologist, Buckley argues that rigidity in any social institution must lead to internal upheaval or to ineffectiveness against external challenge (1968: 495). Gregory Bateson suggested that civilizations expire by loss of flexibility, and that flexibility is lost automatically if it is not exercised (1972: 502-13).

Norman Yoffee has argued that with the loss of provinces in the Old Babylonian period, the revenues needed for public building, waterworks, and the military declined, but the attempt to sustain these did not. To maintain expenditures, the Crown became so oppressive that the empire quickly decomposed to its constituent elements (1977: 143-9). 'Without a drastic change in the idea of government on the part of the crown,' writes Yoffee, 'the power of the Babylonian state, subject to these negative feedback mechanisms, could only weaken further over time' (1977: 149). In short, a failure to make the correct response to circumstances engendered collapse.

Gregory Johnson argues that in the Susiana region, administrative breakdown and state fission occurred when administrative demands exceeded capacity in the Middle

Uruk period (1973: 153). Again, the basic notion is of an inability to bring about an appropriate response, which in this case would mean increasing administrative capacity.

Randall McGuire (1983) proposes a structural model to account for collapse. Following Blau (1977: 122) he argues that societies organized concentrically inhibit structural change, compared with societies organized by intersection of independent parameters. *Concentric* organization extends outward from the individual to ever wider social spheres: family, descent group, village, tribe, etc. *Intersection* refers to social dimensions that cross-cut concentric categories (such as sodality membership or occupation). Concentric organization tends to characterize simpler societies, and vice versa. In concentrically-organized societies, elites impose intergroup connections from above. Groups are played off against each other, rather than integrated into a coherent whole. Since change is rarely in the best interests of the ruling group, and there is lack of cohesion and common interest between groups, no mechanism exists for gradual adjustment to changing circumstances. Pressures then lead to collapse rather than to structural change (McGuire 1983: 117-22).

In the Mayan area, a 'failure to adapt' argument is offered by Willey and Shimkin (1971a, 1971b, 1973: 491). Despite internal stresses and external pressures, they argue, Classic Maya society could bring forth no appropriate organizational or technological response. The bureaucracy was simply unable to deal with an increasingly complex and unstable social situation, and so the society collapsed. Willey also argues, in another context (1978: 335), that the Maya collapsed because they did not '...proceed far enough on the ceremonial-center-to-true-city continuum.'

Accounting for the collapse of Teotihuacan, Pfeiffer proposes that this polity had simply reached its maximum integrative capacity without animal transport or wheeled vehicles (1975: 93). Diehl argues similarly for the fall of Tula (1981: 293). For Cahokia, Pfeiffer suggests population pressure on a technology unable to feed both the populace and the bureaucracy (1974: 62).

Dhavalikar argues that the Chalcolithic cultures of India 'died' because they did not have the technology to cultivate adequately the black cotton soil (1984: 155). Minnis suggests that the Mimbres culture of the American Southwest collapsed following a failure to attempt economic intensification (1985: 156).

Various economic explanations for the collapse of the Roman Empire border on the 'failure to adapt' theory (e.g., M. Hammond 1946). These studies postulate deficiencies in Roman social structure and economy, such as: (a) economic stagnation and lack of lower- or middle-class incentives; (b) the formation of large estates using slave or serf labor; (c) lack of regional economic integration; (d) overtaxation and the cost of government; (e) a weak financial system limited by minimal credit arrangements and by the supply of precious metals; and (f) the end of geographical expansion. The Empire, in short, was unable to bring forth the changes necessary for its continued existence.

In regard to contemporary nations, Deutsch (1969: 28-30) suggests that collapse may occur where a government is unable to satisfy its population's demands for public services. Since about 1890 these demands have accelerated far faster than governments' income or ability to respond, leading to increasing dissatisfaction, political bankruptcy, and revolution.

Other scholars implicate a positive feedback loop in collapse, from which escape is impossible. Colin Renfrew (1979: 488) argues that under stress complex societies lack the option to diversify, to become less specialized. By doing more of what may have caused the problem in the first place, the breakdown of the system is made inevitable.

Guglielmo Ferrero (1914), comparing Rome and America, indicted excessive urbanization as the cause of the Roman collapse. A rapid increase in wealth and commerce associated with the Roman expansion led to the development of prosperous middle-class families who migrated to the cities and, once there, spent lavishly on them. As the countryside was taxed and exploited to sustain urban living, and as the government established a public dole in many centers, the cities increasingly attracted the very peasantry upon whose labors in the countryside they depended. In the second and third centuries A.D. the expenditures of the cities outdistanced the fertility of the countryside, which became increasingly depopulated. With rural depopulation it became harder to find farm labor and army recruits, so that these occupations were finally made hereditary. A situation developed in which the problems of cities were treated with a dose of the very remedy sure to aggravate things: further expenditures on the cities and more taxes on agriculture. Ultimately this system exceeded its tolerance and collapsed. All of this was stimulated by competitive display, between cities, provinces, districts, sects, professions, classes, families, and individuals (see also Widney [1937: 16-21]).

Robert Sharer (1977) argues that in the Mayan Late Classic both population size and sociopolitical complexity formed an intertwined upward spiral. State control over the economy led to greater efficiency in the production and distribution of food. This then led to larger populations, which in turn required more managerial control. But as population grew, measures taken to increase food production stretched environmental resources to the breaking point. New production systems were vulnerable to climatic shifts, natural disasters, disease/pest problems, and soil exhaustion. The elites compounded the crisis by increasing investment in monumental architecture, thus diverting time and labor from food production. Crop losses due to pests, soil exhaustion, climatic shifts, or some natural disaster, combined with an invasion by non-Mayan neighbors, led to collapse.

Conrad and Demarest have presented (1984) an important discussion of political and economic weakness in the Aztec and Inca empires. They argue that ideological factors which were beneficial early in the histories of these empires became maladaptive later. For the Aztecs, the cult of Huitzilopochtli demanded human sacrifice to maintain the world, and this spurred militaristic expansion to secure the necessary victims. Among the Inca, property was not inherited by a new emperor. Each ruler continued to be served by his court and retinue, even after death, and to command the lands and resources held during life. Since a new ruler thus ascended to the throne without an endowment, continued conquests were necessary to avoid royal poverty. Both ideologies led to expansion, but became maladaptive when the number of profitable conquests declined. When the ideological system proved difficult to change, civil conflict inevitably followed.

Friedman and Rowlands (1977) propose a model in which competitive feasting in tribal societies gives an incentive for surplus production. By the acquisition of captive external slaves and internal debt slaves, a conical clan forms in which one descent group promotes itself to chiefly rank. The expanding chiefdom, practicing perhaps swidden agriculture, will inevitably collapse due to declining productivity in an economy demanding accelerating surpluses.

Assessment

By and large, these 'failure to adapt' arguments are superior in one respect to many considered up until this point. Recognizing that an understanding of collapse often depends more on the characteristics of the society than of its stresses, these authors postulate causal mechanisms – such as environmental insufficiency and the Law of Evolutionary Potential – to explain why adaptive responses are not made. This is a significant step. Yet as intriguing as some of these explanations are, they seem as a lot to rely on certain assumptions about the nature of complex societies, assumptions that the authors leave implicit. If these assumptions are made explicit, we will find that they give us cause for hesitation. The assumptions seem to revolve around three models of complex societies. For lack of more elegant terms, I will call them the *Dinosaur* model, the *Runaway Train* model, and the *House of Cards* model.

In the Dinosaur model, a complex society is seen as a lumbering colossus, fixed in its morphology, and incapable of rapid change. Locked into an evolutionary dead end, it represents an investment in structure, size, and complexity that is awesome and admirable, yet highly maladaptive. When stresses arise, such a society cannot adapt, and so must expire. Complex societies seen thus present a spectacle of power that evokes both wonder and pity. In colloquial terms, they are all pitiful, helpless giants, and are inevitably outcompeted by newer, leaner, more aggressive societies.

The Dinosaur model, as characterized, is coincident with the Law of Evolutionary Potential, as well as with derivative and similar theories. The argument of this 'Law' is that all societies, complex or otherwise, run the risk of adapting so well to existing circumstances that change becomes impossible. Among complex societies this tendency becomes fatal when newer societies acquire capabilities that the lumbering colossus is incapable of adopting.

The Runaway Train model may be a variant of the Dinosaur model, but it has its own distinct characteristics. A complex society is seen as impelled along a path of increasing complexity, unable to switch directions, regress, or remain static. When obstacles impinge, it can continue in only the direction it is headed, so that catastrophe ultimately results.

The variety of studies that cite positive feedback mechanisms make precisely this assumption about complex societies. Ferrero's arguments about urbanization in the Roman Empire, Sharer's views about social and economic intensification among the Maya, and Conrad and Demarest's account of the Aztecs and the Inca, all assume that some factor in these societies made it impossible to deviate from their catastrophic paths.

The House of Cards model differs from the previous two. It suggests that complex societies, either as a rule or in certain kinds of environments, are *inherently* fragile, operating on low margins of reserve, so that their collapse is inevitable. Betty Meggers' environmental limitation theory, and Flannery's and Rappaport's maladaptation arguments, fall under this model.

There is much to give one pause in these models. Our present knowledge of complex societies does not allow us to either conclude or assume that they are inherently fragile, or static, or incapable of shifting directions, or that they cannot respond to productivity fluctuations, catastrophes, or other ailments. Indeed, it is not hard to point to societies that have done some or all of these things (e.g., the Roman resurgence and reorganization following the crises of the third century A.D.; population movements and societal reorganization at various times in Southwestern prehistory; the Late Classic Mayan renaissance following the Hiatus [all to be discussed in Chapter 5]; and various political cycles in ancient China). In other words, our knowledge of complex societies will not support the assumptions such studies make. Complex societies are not simply intractable fossils. Where they do appear incapable of change, that is a matter to be explained. By itself it explains nothing.

The Runaway Train model, as formulated in the cases of the Aztecs and the Inca, is belied by available data. In both cases, late rulers apparently perceived that further conquest was unprofitable, and took steps to change the political and ideological systems that generated expansion. Conrad and Demarest (1984) interpret Aztec and Inca resistance to these changes as a failure of the attempt, but this cannot be known with confidence. The Spanish conquest prematurely terminated the process of change. The attempted reforms of Moctezuma II (Aztec) and Huascar (Inca) can easily be seen as appropriate first steps to curtail abusive systems. Certainly Webb's (1965) account of the overthrow of the *kapu* system in Hawaii by Kamehameha II indicates that ideologies, even entrenched ones, can be changed when necessary.

A few additional comments are in order. When Willey argues that the Maya collapsed because they did not '...proceed far enough on the ceremonial-center-to-true-city continuum' (1978: 335) some confusion results. Other scholars have seemed to argue that the Maya may have been *too far* along this continuum, or at least too far for their environmental setting (e.g., Meggers, Sabloff, Sharer). Mayanists cannot be expected to be more unified in their views than any other archaeologists, but some clarification of this point would be useful. Were the Maya too complex or not complex enough? And how can collapse result from both?

Phillips' (1979) use of the term 'efficiency' carries a whole series of ambiguities. He argues (1979: 140) that societies using resources efficiently (i.e., fully) experience inflexibility in resource allocation, since with more benefits a particular activity becomes harder to abandon. Here he assumes that activities performed efficiently by a complex society are necessarily beneficial. Conflict theorists will disagree – and we might all wonder. Indeed, the very notion that complexity is required to use resources efficiently is debatable. David Stuart argues the opposite: that complex societies use resources inefficiently, and that this is one of their weaknesses (Stuart and Gauthier 1981: 10-13). Finally, Phillips' assumption, that allocatable reserves decrease with increasing complexity, denies to complex societies any flexibility, and to their leaders any capacity for rational action. Phillips assumes that the levying of resources by a state (a) remains at a constant level, and (b) is not geared to needs. The possibility of increasing resource flow – by increasing taxes and/or by intensification – is ignored.

Other complex societies

In some scenarios, competition with other complex societies is a cause of collapse, through various causal mechanisms. Lanning (1967: 140), for instance, suggests that competition between empires may have led to the demise of Huari and Tiahuanaco. R. E. W. Adams (1977b: 220) pursues a similar argument for Teotihuacan. Blanton (1978, 1983) follows a different tack. He suggests that political centralization at Monte Alban, in the Valley of Oaxaca, was a competitive response to the threat from Teotihuacan. With the collapse of the latter this need vanished. At the same time, growth of population would have led to filling of agricultural land and thus to increased disputes over this resource. The result would be a strain on the adjudicative authorities, including Monte Alban. With declining surpluses for supporting this political center, and its decreasing effectiveness at administration, the population became unwilling to support a political hierarchy that had lost its military role.

Assessment

Although there may be too many unverifiable factors in Blanton's argument (land disputes, willingness of a population to support a political center), it will have a certain appeal to integration theorists, although little or none to conflict theorists. Lanning's arguments about competition between empires raises matters that will be discussed in more depth in the final chapter. At this point it will suffice to say that conflict between empires more often leads to expansion of the victor than to the collapse of both. Major instances of collapse, such as that of Rome, cannot be explained by this principle.

Intruders

One of the most common explanations for collapse ascribes it to the effects of intruding populations, typically at a lower level of complexity than the society on which they impinge. Such scenarios are common in Europe, the Near East, and China, where literary traditions often refer to barbarian migrations. Intruder explanations are also to be found in the New World (with limited literary allusion), more often in some areas than in others.

North and South America

In a major review of theories of the Mayan collapse (as these stood in the early 1960s), George Cowgill (1964: 153) listed destruction of reservoirs by intruders as a possible contributor. Jeremy Sabloff, Gordon Willey, and Richard E. W. Adams, based on work in the Rio Pasion region, have constructed a scenario of invasion through this sector as a major factor in the collapse (Sabloff and Willey 1967; Sabloff 1973b; R. E. W. Adams 1971, 1973b). The archaeological characteristics of sites in this area suggest to these authors an occupation by non-Classic Mayan peoples, possibly from the Gulf Coast region. Sabloff, Willey, and Adams have over time modified their ideas about the relationship of this event to the collapse. Sabloff and Willey (1967) initially argued that these invaders sent raiding parties throughout the Peten, were successful against the Maya because of superior weapons (atlatl and spear), and caused regional collapse within 100 years of their arrival. More recent statements downplay the invaders' role (e.g., Willey and Shimkin 1973; Hosler, Sabloff, and Runge 1977). R. E. W. Adams assigns to the invaders a supplementary role in the collapse: that throughout the Lowlands the news of their presence led to loss of morale and to civil wars. With raiding and local production disasters, collapse ensued (R. E. W. Adams 1971: 164, 197, 1973b: 152). Bove (1981) has studied spatial trends in the cessation of stela (stone monument) construction across the Lowlands. He does find some west to east trend (the direction of the postulated invasion), but it is only a weak tendency.

Writing of the Mesoamerican Highlands, Willey ascribes the collapse of the High-land city of Teotihuacan to northern barbarians who acculturated to Teotihuacan civilization, and then destroyed it (1966: 116). Rene Millon, who has conducted the major study of the city, notes that the monumental architecture of the Street of the Dead (temples, pyramids, etc.) was burned in a ritualistic manner, and that in later Mesoamerican history such an act signified political subjugation. He suggests that the city center was destroyed by invaders, with subsequent local uprisings (Millon 1981: 236-8).

With support from literary traditions (which significantly postdate the twelfth-century event), the collapse of Tula is often ascribed to invading northern barbarians (M. Weaver 1972: 213; Davies 1977: 364-5).

Farther to the north, the Anasazi abandonment of the Colorado Plateau is sometimes attributed to an early invasion by Athabaskan peoples (summarized in Reed [1944: 69], Martin, Quimby, and Collier [1947: 146], and Martin and Plog [1973: 323]). Similar notions have been advanced regarding the end of Hopewell in the Midwest (discussed in Braun [1977: 37]).

In South America, the collapses of the Huari and Tiahuanaco empires are sometimes blamed on invading barbarians (Lanning 1967: 140).

The Harappan Civilization

Based on the traditions of the *Rigveda*, the downfall of the Harappan Civilization is frequently attributed to invading Aryans, who toppled this urban society by virtue of superior military technology (war chariots) (Piggott 1950; Wheeler 1968; Allchin and Allchin 1968). To Piggott, the invaders found a society already crumbling: '...[C]ivilization...was already effete and on the wane when the raiders came...' (1950: 239).

Mesopotamia

Less complex societies are frequently implicated in the fall of various Mesopotamian polities, often in Mesopotamian literary accounts. The downfall of Sargon of Akkad, for instance, is attributed to Gutian invaders from the eastern mountains (discussed in Oates [1979: 37]), while the fall of Ur is ascribed to Amorites and Elamites (Diakonoff 1969: 197).

The Hittite Empire

The collapse of the Hittite Empire, ca. 1200 B.C., is frequently seen as the action of migratory 'Sea Peoples,' who engulfed the Aegean and the eastern Mediterranean, and who were stopped only at the gates of Egypt. Some see the collapse as due to a combination of these invaders and the Hittites' traditional enemies, the barbarian Kaskas. Egyptian records speak of the Hittites as having fallen before such invaders (Hogarth 1926; Akurgal 1962; Barnett 1975a, 1975b; Goetze 1975c). An inscription of Rameses III reads in part 'The isles were restless, disturbed among themselves. No land stood before their weapons, from Khatti [the Hittites], Qode, Carchemish, Arzawa and Alishiya on' (quoted in Carpenter [1966: 43]).

Minoan Civilization

Various authors assign the Minoan collapse to invading Mycenaean Greeks, themselves only recently the recipients of Minoan Civilization (Carpenter 1966: 32-3; Matz 1973b: 580-1; Chadwick 1976: 10-12; Willetts 1977: 136). Usually, some factor is invoked – the eruption of Thera or a great earthquake ca. 1500 B.C. – that weakened Cretan power and opened the door to mainland invasion.

Mycenaean Civilization

The destruction of Mycenaean Civilization by Dorian Greek invaders is the classic example of an intruder theory, and is endorsed by a variety of current scholars (e.g., Taylour 1964; Vermeule 1964; Mylonas 1966; Desborough 1972, 1975; Stubbings 1975b; Chadwick 1976).

The Roman Empire

The role of barbarians in the fall of the Roman Empire has been a subject of debate since the invasions themselves (Mazzarino 1966). It is a topic so well known that there is no need to discuss it in any depth here.

China

The susceptibility of the northern frontier to barbarian incursions is a constant theme of Chinese history, and has been well treated by Lattimore (1940).

Assessment

Barbarian invasions have a clear attraction to collapse theorists, somewhat like catastrophe explanations. They provide a clean, simple resolution to a distressingly convoluted problem. As a *deus ex machina*, invasions are an old favorite in archaeological studies, where sudden episodes of cultural change may otherwise be difficult to explain. They have a similar attraction in the study of collapse. In some cases, fear of 'uncivilized' peoples has served to legitimize existing political arrangements, as well as taxation, military expenditures, and behavioral regimentation.

Invasion explanations do not offer global coverage, being irrelevant in such cases as the Ik and Highland Burma. They are unsatisfactory in that a recurrent process – collapse – is explained by a random variable, by historical accident. But the fundamental problem with intruder theories is that they do not clarify much. The overthrow of a dominant state by a weaker, tribally-organized people is an event greatly in need of explanation. It is, standing alone, an acceptable explanation of nothing. Notwithstanding Service's 'Law of Evolutionary Potential,' complex societies are not dinosaurs, they do not fossilize, and they do not succumb to smaller states due to inertia. The later Roman Empire, as an example, brought forth technical innovations, new applications for old technologies, and effective leaders like Constantine, Julian, and Stilicho (Mazzarino 1966: 186). The assumptions required by the intruder theory are simply unacceptable.

There are so many factual debates regarding intruder theories that it is necessary to discuss only one: the Dorian invasion of Mycenaean Greece. Quite simply, for a people who wrought such devastation, the Dorians have left curiously little archaeological trace (Taylour 1964: 176; Mylonas 1966: 228; Desborough 1975: 660, 662). Only two artifacts were introduced at this time (the cut-and-thrust sword and the violin-bow fibula), and both were used by the Mycenaeans, not by invaders (Desborough 1975: 660, 662). Desborough suggests that perhaps the invaders completed their work and then withdrew (1972: 22) (which notion leaves the historic linguistic distribution unexplained). Rhys Carpenter, in his ever-delightful prose, characterizes the dilemma well:

> All in all, an extraordinary and paradoxical situation, in which there is no sign of the presence of any hostile invader, for whom no route of entry and no passage can be found; yet the native population is deserting its established habitations as though driven by some invisible and nameless terror, 'like ghosts from an enchanter fleeing' (1966: 40).

Desborough's suggestion of destruction and withdrawal raises a point of uncertainty in regard to the Harappan, Mycenaean, and Mayan collapses: if these areas were so worth invading, why then destroy those things that would repay conquest? This and the other ambiguities in the intruder theory tempt one to rename it the *Poltergeist* model: collapse is caused by mysterious troublemakers, whose behavior is inexplicable, and whose very presence is difficult to show.

Conflict/contradictions/mismanagement

Judging by the number of authors whose work falls under this theme, it may be the most popular approach to understanding collapse. There is some variety in the approaches lumped herein – class conflict, Marxian contradictions, and elite mis-behavior or mismanagement – but the common underlying theme is antagonism and conflicting goals between social classes. Collapse is thought to result from such conflicts through withdrawal of support and outright revolt by peasant populations, and by elite self-serving and political mismanagement. There are a variety of both general and area-specific applications of these ideas.

General

Conflict theories date at least to the time of Plato, who believed proper government to be a balance of democracy and despotism, with an excess of either leading to decay (*Laws*), and Aristotle, who suggested that arrogance and self-aggrandizement in office engender factional conflicts, revolutions, and the destruction of regimes (*Politics*). Polybius (1979) relied heavily on class conflict in his cyclical theory of political evolution.

The great Arab historian Ibn Khaldun, in the fourteenth century, developed a cyclical theory of history that falls under this theme (1958 [original 1377-81]). He argued that dynasties run their course from accession to fall in three to four generations: the founder, who had the personal qualities needed to gain paramount power; his son, who had personal contact with the founder and learned his qualities; the third generation heir, who never knew the founder and must be content with imitation and reliance on tradition; and the fourth, who is inferior in every respect and even despises good qualities. Dynasties thus have a natural life span like individuals. In the course of this progression rulers become ever more addicted to luxuries and security. Taxes are raised to pay for these. Whereas at the beginning of a dynasty large revenues are received from small assessments, at the end of a dynasty this situation is reversed. When taxes are low, the population is more productive and the tax yield is greater. Yet as the dynasty evolves, increased spending on luxury leads to higher taxes. Eventually taxes become so burdensome that productivity first declines, then is stifled. As more taxes are enacted to counter this, the point is finally reached where the polity is destroyed.

In the early eighteenth century Giambattista Vico postulated a cyclical theory of history which proceeded from First Barbarian Times to Civil Societies, and back to Returned Barbarian Times. The factors responsible are changing relations of dominance between elites and the populace, class conflict, and pursuit of self-interest. In a civil society, discord fanned by demagoguery leads to the abandonment of civic responsibilities for the pursuit of individual goals. This in turn leads to barbarism: '…through obstinate factions and desperate civil wars, they shall turn their cities into forests and the forests into dens and lairs of men' (Bergin and Fisch 1948: 381).

This theme was seconded later in the eighteenth century by C. F. Volney, who was spurred by seeing the ruins of Palmyra to consider why empires decline. His conclusion was that greed and despotism lead to degradation of the populace, and this weakens societies and brings on collapse. In ancient states, as a result of greed and class conflict,

> …a holy indolence spread over the political world; the fields were deserted, empires depopulated, monuments neglected and deserts multiplied; ignorance, superstition and fanaticism combining their operations, overwhelmed the earth with devastation and ruin (Volney 1793: 51).

Volney's concerns were not solely for the disasters of antiquity, but also for the possibility that a similar fate might befall his own world:

> Who knows if on the banks of the Seine, the Thames, or the Zuyder-Zee...some traveller, like myself, shall not one day sit on their silent ruins and weep in solitude over the ashes of their inhabitants, and the memory of their greatness? (1793: 25).

In more recent times, Casson suggested that civilization in his day had already collapsed, and that the responsible factor was increased factional conflict (1937: 202). Julian Steward ascribed the collapses of ancient civilizations to a causal sequence in which empires, irrigation works, and population all grew in concert, but where overexploitation of the population led to rebellion, reversion to smaller states, and dark ages (1955: 204). Karl Wittfogel, discussing hydraulic societies, suggested that decay occurs when elites arrogate to themselves an increasing portion of the national surplus (1955, 1957: 171).

Among less complex societies, excessive demands and abuse by paramount individuals are known to lead to withdrawal of support (Fortes and Evans-Pritchard 1940: 11; Leach 1954: 204; Sahlins 1963, 1968). Friedman (1975) offers a generalized model in which competitive feasting between lineages leads to differential ranking. Accelerating demands for surpluses lead in turn to ecological degradation, weakening the hierarchical structure. Friedman's model has been applied by Pearson (1984) to account for cyclical collapses in the Iron Age of Jutland, and for the Anglo-Saxon migration to Britain.

Erwin suggests that civilizations gain '...stamina according to how widely they diffuse operational responsibility' (1966: 1193). The Indus Civilization concentrated power in a few, and crumbled.

Claessen and Skalnik (1978b: 634) argue that in the evolution of early states a point is reached where the state organization becomes an instrument in the hands of members of a landed class which has monopolistic control over the means of production. At this point, which marks the end of the early state, it may no longer be possible to prevent fission. Haas suggests that investment in police forces for social control is costly and destabilizes a regime (1982: 211-12). Service implicates quarrels between levels of a hierarchy as leading to centrifugal tendencies (1975: 300-1).

Political scientists have made similar points, most especially through the major work of Eisenstadt (1963, 1978). He notes that the major difficulties in empires have tended to be: (a) pressure on resources caused by the extravagance of the elites; (b) faulty administration in dealing with concrete problems; (c) the distribution of power among groups and regions; and (d) crises in relations of rulers and elites, or competition between elites (Eisenstadt 1963: 237). Rulers have often pursued policies favoring immediate fiscal and personnel needs, to the detriment of long-term economic development, and at the cost of depleting or alienating the support population (Eisenstadt 1963: 318). As resources come to be depleted and peasantry alienated, taxes are often increased, and power delegated to local authorities. Feudal systems emerge that undermine central authority. Societies in such conditions are susceptible to collapse (Eisenstadt 1963: 318-19, 327, 343, 349-50, 1978: 96). The driving factor throughout is the leadership's pursuit of costly political goals.

Mancur Olson's (1982) thesis is that, in complex societies, special interest groups promote their own welfare above that of the state. The resulting damage leads to national economic weakness.

Mesoamerica

Conflict theories have a distinguished history in Mesoamerican research, especially in the Mayan area, where 'peasant revolt' models (and variations thereon) have enjoyed long currency (e.g., Morley 1956: 68-9). Sir Eric Thompson is most closely associated with this view, having argued that increased demands for services, construction, and food led to a peasant revolt that toppled Mayan civilization (1966: 105). Hamblin and Pitcher argue that intensive cultivation resulted in the displacement of peasants from their land, turning them into an agricultural proletariat (1980: 251). They cite graphic representations of elites dominating peasants, and the post-Classic mutilation of elite sculpted faces (but not those of commoners), in support of the peasant revolt scenario.

More recent studies have concentrated on managerial theories, such as Willey and Shimkin's ideas about inadequate bureaucratic response to the Late Classic stresses (1973: 491), ideas which are followed by other scholars (e.g., Hosler, Sabloff, and Runge 1977). Webb cites the resource strains attendant upon elite attempts to participate in long-distance trade (1973). Cowgill implicates Late Classic militarism and inter-polity competition, which led to population growth, overtaxation, and destructive wars (1979: 61). Lowe argues that agricultural degradation weakened the population at the same time that elite demands intensified (1985: 187-8, 231).

Katz involves internal unrest in the external overthrow of Teotihuacan (1972: 78-9). Millon, as noted, also invokes internal discord (1981). Blanton's (1983) idea of Oaxacan dissatisfaction with the Monte Alban administration has already been discussed. Cowgill (1977: 189-90) compares the breakdown of Teotihuacan to the Chinese dynastic cycle, with larger and more inefficient bureaucracies allocating resources to themselves, leading to lower state revenues, exploitation of peasantry, and ultimately fall and restoration.

Beyond the northern Mesoamerican frontier, DiPeso assigns the destruction of the center of Casas Grandes to local revolt against foreign rulers (1974 (2): 320-1).

Peru

Lanning (1967: 140) and Katz (1972: 247) both suggest peasant revolt for the collapse of the Huari Empire.

China

Chinese political thought (seconded to a great extent by current historical research) has long seen conflict and mismanagement as the sources of dynastic collapse (i.e., since at least the Warring States period and the Confucian era) (Lattimore 1940: 45; Creel 1953, 1970; Fairbank et al. 1973: 72-3). All great dynasties began with initial prosperity and peace, as land was brought back into production. Palaces, roads, canals, and walls would be built, and costly defensive lines maintained. But as imperial relatives, nobility, and the bureaucracy increased in numbers and grew used to luxury, more resources were allocated to the ruling class, and less to administration. Because of increased expenditures, and often a slightly declining income, each dynasty experienced serious financial difficulties within a century of its founding. Official self-serving and corruption would worsen, administrative efficiency would decline, and there would be more factional quarrels at court. Potential rivals of the imperial family became more independent. Burdens on the peasantry were increased at the same time that dikes and canals were allowed to fall into disrepair. Famines that previously would have been met from government granaries now would lead to starvation, banditry, and peasant uprisings. Inadequately maintained frontier defenses crumbled. Provincial officials and their armies began to defect. The resulting wars would clear the slate for a new dynasty (Fairbank et al. 1973: 72-3; Lattimore 1940: 531).

Within this broader process, Lattimore has implicated a social system that emphasized large families while the economic system provided no activities for surplus labor. Agrarian depression was the inevitable result (Lattimore 1940: 45). Boserup argues the contrary view, that there was insufficient labor to maintain irrigation systems, peasants were consequently overworked, and upkeep of investments was thus neglected (1981: 87).

Mesopotamia

Norman Yoffee (1979) argues that in the Old Babylonian period, losses of conquered territories and revenues were met by intensification within the remaining territories, and by proliferation of new offices and ranks. This may have been an attempt to administer the crown lands more intensively, but only aggravated the problem. Yoffee suggests that collapse was due to a failure to integrate '...traditional, locally autonomous controls within and among city-states within the larger sociopolitical organization' (1979: 14).

Struve (1969) and Tyumenev (1969) argue that the development of slave economies in Mesopotamia led to economic weakness, and made societies like Akkad, Ur, and Babylon susceptible to collapse. Diakonoff suggests that the Gutian invasion of Akkad led to a popular rising, but that the Gutians themselves ultimately developed a burdensome rule (1969: 193).

Jankowska (1969) constructs a scenario where trade within the neo-Assyrian Empire (ca. eighth century B.C.) and tribute imposed on subject countries brought advantage only to Assyria: any goods bought from subject countries were purchased with their own tribute. The subject countries then had to seek alternative trade routes, avoiding Assyrian commercial centers. Increasing economic differentiation of regions was in 'contradiction' to the predatory policy of the Assyrian Empire. As this contradiction grew there came to be more traffic along new trade routes, and less along old ones. Jankowska concludes:

> It seems that the explanation of the law of inverse ratio between the dimensions

of political entities of the type of the Assyrian Empire and their stability is to be sought in the steadily growing aggravation of this contradiction (1969: 276).

Jacobsen and Adams' (1958; R. McC. Adams 1974, 1978, 1981) arguments regarding political intensification, mismanagement, and agricultural disaster on the Mesopotamian alluvium have been summarized previously (see also Gibson [1974] and Waines [1977]).

The Roman Empire

Interpretations of conflict and mismanagement abound in Roman studies (e.g., Wason 1973; Westermann 1915; Bernardi 1970; Guha 1981: 64-7), and can be traced to the later Empire itself. Ammianus Marcellinus, for example, attributed Roman decadence to growth of the bureaucracy, and to excessive taxation (Mazzarino 1966: 54). Gibbon, although he cited a variety of causes for the Roman collapse in his classic work (Christianity, decline of martial spirit, ignorance of dangers), indicted poor leadership as frequently as any other factor (1776-88).

Frank ascribed the Roman failure to lack of vision on the part of the landed gentry: the willingness during the Republic to betray the peasantry for large slave estates, and to accept the monarchy for personal safety (1940: 304). Caudwell indicted soil impoverishment by large estates and the general demoralization of the exploited class (1971: 55). Boak and Sinnigen single out the fact that

> Rome failed to develop an economic system that could give to the working
> classes of the Empire living conditions sufficiently advantageous to encourage
> them to support it devotedly and to reproduce in adequate numbers (1965: 522).

Dill also cited the economic weakness of the Roman class system, but believed that collapse was due to the ruin of the middle class and of the municipalities (1899: 245).

Childe noted a contradiction of Hellenistic and Roman economy – the lack of adequate development or extension of productive forces, leaving the peasantry static or declining. The resulting low standard of living restricted internal markets, and when the economy could no longer grow by spatial expansion, it began to decline. By A.D. 250 prosperity was gone and the Empire was economically dead (Childe 1942: 280-5; see also Heitland [1962]).

Isaac (1971) suggested that multiple factors were responsible for the Empire's demise, but like Gibbon he seemed regularly to focus on poor management. West (1933: 103) cited a number of factors he believed were responsible for the collapse of the Empire. Most are economic in nature, but seem to involve mismanagement: (a) slavery; (b) introduction of barbarians into the Empire; (c) waste of precious metals and capital in domestic luxuries; (d) export of precious metals to pay for imported luxuries; (e) increasing state authoritarianism; and (f) increasing taxation and expenditures. Brown suggests a novel idea: that the Senatorial aristocracy and the Catholic Church in the West had disassociated themselves from the army, and unwittingly sapped its strength (1971: 119). C. Northcote Parkinson, true to the theme of his other writings, blamed overtaxation (1963: 121).

In one of the fundamental works of Marxist theory, Engels singled out Roman exploitation of the provinces as bringing on impoverishment, declines in commerce and population, the decay of towns, and lower agricultural activity (1972: 208-9).

Rostovtzeff (1926) developed one of the most unusual class conflict explanations, especially of the crisis of the third century A.D. The peasant army, to Rostovtzeff, was resentful of the privileged in cities. The power of the military led to increased pay and ruinous costs under the Severan dynasty (early third century A.D.). These emperors militarized the government, staffed it with peasants, and eliminated the traditional upper classes from the army and the administration. Civil strife between military contenders weakened defenses and allowed barbarian incursions. This in turn led to the regimentation of the population, and to the rigid system of Diocletian and Constantine. There came to be little inducement to betterment, for then one would merely be forced to work for the state. When the state was threatened, it named itself the prime economic beneficiary (Rostovtzeff 1926: 208).

A different interpretation of the role of the military has been offered by writers who blamed decline on the end of compulsory service, and consequent employment of barbarians (e.g., Piganiol 1962; Salmon 1970).

An alternative class conflict view has been offered by Ste. Croix (1981), who believes that the wealthy classes depressed the political and legal status of almost all others to the slave level. Many were exploited for the benefit of a few, and increasingly so through time. Conflicts and tensions between classes amounted to societal contradictions. By the Severan period the legal rights of the poorer classes were practically gone. With nothing to restrain the greed and ambition of the propertied class except the Emperor, the support base for the Empire was ruined (see also Walbank [1969, 1970]).

Toynbee's (1965) views were along similar lines, although not so overstated, and relied on a different mechanism. Toynbee argued that the destruction of the Italian countryside and peasantry during the Hannibalic war led to decline of subsistence production and the formation of large estates producing for market sale. The subsequent expansion of Rome brought ruin to the peasantry, power and wealth to the elites. A professional army replaced that formerly composed of peasants. The consequences overall were far-reaching, and condemned the Roman Empire, in advance, to be short-lived (Toynbee 1965: 9).

The Byzantine Empire

Charanis (1953) argued that the eleventh-century decline of the Byzantine Empire resulted from the triumph of the landed military aristocracy, and the decline of the soldier-peasantry. As great landowners absorbed small holdings, free peasant proprietors began to disappear. Conflict between emperors and the rising aristocracy brought on civil wars. Manpower and resources were drained at a time when new enemies appeared. A mercenary army was adopted, while overtaxed, alienated peasants lost all concern for the welfare of the state.

Spain

Economic weakness, managerial ineptitude, and a lack of inclination to economic development are routinely cited in explaining the Spanish imperial decline (e.g., Vives 1970; Elliott 1970). '[T]he state,' claims Vives, 'neglected to develop the country's interests and trampled on the ethic which should have ruled its relations with its subjects' (1970: 166).

The Netherlands

High taxes are implicated by many writers as among the factors that led to the eighteenth-century Dutch economic decline (e.g., Wilson 1969: 116-22; Boxer 1970).

The Harappans

If the Harappans were not after all done in by mud, there is no end to ingenious explanations of their collapse. Miller believes there was a contradiction between a Harappan ideology that refused to acknowledge change and human aspirations, and an inevitable tendency toward individual and group aggrandizement, heresy, and innovation. This contradiction could only manifest itself in the revolutionary overthrow of the state (Miller 1985: 64).

Easter Island

The great statue-carving period on Easter Island, writes Englert (1970), ended when two population segments came into conflict over agricultural development. With the subsequent political disintegration, conditions became everywhere unsafe.

Assessment

Conflict explanations achieve one remarkable thing: they appeal to the spectrum from Marxists to capitalists. The former's view has been treated in the preceding pages. The latter's is exemplified in the following quote:

> In a word, the poor and the army [of Rome] had eaten up the capital of the thrifty, and the western half of Europe sank into the dark ages, from which it did not emerge until the thrifty and energetic could again safely use their abilities in wealth-producing activities (West 1933: 106).

Few explanatory themes are so flexible in application.

The basic objections to conflict explanations of decreasing complexity largely mirror those given in Chapter 2 to conflict theories of increasing complexity. There are, however, additional considerations. Attention here will be on general considerations, and on the two major themes of elite mismanagement and exploitation, and disaffection/revolt among the populace.

Class conflict theories must at some point make the argument that complex societies come ultimately to violate one of the tenets of their existence. One consequence of the administrative capacity to control labor and allocate resources is the ability to deal with natural and social adversities. Since both the population and the administrators of a complex society benefit from this capability, it must achieve some recognition in both integration and conflict theory. Conflict theorists, in particular, will have to acknowledge that any rational dominant class, however oppressive, must make some provision for the welfare of the populace on which they rely. Any suggestion that complex societies fail because of a characteristic – control of labor and resources – that is both intrinsic to their nature and crucial to their survival, simply leaves too many questions unanswered. Not the least of these is why some complex societies fail as a result of overtaxing their populations, and some don't.

Since elementary self-interest will dictate that a dominant elite look after their support population (as they would any vital resource), the few instances where this may not have happened (later Roman Empire, later phases of Chinese dynastic cycles) urgently require explanation. Failure to resolve this matter when citing elite misbehavior as a cause of collapse ultimately reduces the explanation to a dichotomous psychological variable: some elites behave rationally and some don't. It need hardly be pointed out that this dichotomy is not illuminating. Until some theory is developed concerning the expression of elite rationality *vs.* collective suicide, we may confidently dismiss the elite mismanagement argument as unproductive.

In a similar vein, the use of greed and self-aggrandizement (e.g., among landed gentry or entrenched bureaucrats) as explanations for economic weakness and collapse really take us nowhere. Both are psychological factors whose expression, to the extent that it is variable, needs explanation. We cannot cite collapse as a function of greed if greed itself is not fully understood. To the extent that elite self-aggrandizement is controlled by social, political, and economic factors (as in the later phases of Chinese dynasties), then it is these social, political, and economic factors that are relevant to understanding collapse. Greed and self-aggrandizement are symptoms and contributors, but not final causes. Many conflict theorists, fortunately, are well aware of this point, but perhaps even more of those reviewed herein show no indication that they are. Too many authors begin their arguments under the assumption that self-aggrandizement is an independent, controlling factor.

Two points are in order regarding elite exploitation and mismanagement. These are:

1. exploitation is a *normal* cost of stratification; and
2. bad government is a *normal* cost of government.

Clearly these points cannot be regarded without controversy. The argument is that these things occur with such expectable regularity, and are so difficult to predict, that a society finding it necessary to invest in stratification and/or government must expect exploitation and/or misgovernment as a normal cost of that investment. It seems difficult, from the experience of history, to argue otherwise (see, e.g., Tuchman 1984).

If exploitation and misadministration are normal aspects of hierarchy, then it is difficult to see these as sources for the collapse of hierarchies. Moreover, if these are regular and recurrent, then by themselves they cannot easily account for collapse, which is an occasional event. If the Roman elite class, for example, was corrupt and exploitative by the first century B.C. (as many argue), and if this led to the collapse, why then did the Western Empire survive until the fifth century A.D.? As Guha has noted, social conflict '...is the price of the existence of society itself; and since man cannot survive without society, it is hardly something that can be described on balance as dysfunctional' (1981: 11).

Additional considerations apply to the 'peasant revolt' scenario. Peasants are frequently disaffected, but they rarely revolt. They are usually passive spectators of political struggles. Peasants often harbor a sense of injustice, but this needs to be given shape and expression. Thus peasant wars are generally initiated by a fusion of disaffected intellectuals or military leaders, and rural supporters. Moreover, peasantry will rarely join an uprising until the superior military forces of the rulers have been neutralized (Wolf 1969). More often the chief weapons of peasants are to turn to large landowners for protection, and/or to increase their passivity and indifference to the success of a regime (Eisenstadt 1963: 209), both of which happened in the later Roman Empire. Revolutions usually aim at a transformation of regime, or at restoration with modification (Kann 1968), not at sociopolitical collapse. A new hierarchy is always implicit in the alliance between intellectuals and peasants.

These brief notes indicate that the archaeological reliance on the peasant revolt explanation of collapse, which is so favored in some areas, greatly requires more attention to the known dimensions of peasant political action.

It is appropriate to close this section by noting that not all misadministration is exploitative. Certainly there are cases where problem-solving is well meaning but inept. The popular media, for example, recently carried an article suggesting that a large Southwestern pueblo was abandoned because the populace devoted excessive energy to ritual control of the environment, and too little time to actual farming (Brovsky 1985). This idea seems most appropriately characterized as the *Neronian* model: the Anasazi prayed while the corn was spurned.

Social dysfunction

This is a vague theme that requires little discussion. Its essence is that societies collapse due to mysterious internal processes whose nature cannot be specified. Martin, Quimby, and Collier, for example, listed integrative deficiencies of Puebloan social organization as one source of collapse and abandonment in the American Southwest (1947: 147). Melikishvili proposes that societies fall due to (a) violation of systemic connections in the economic core, and (b) external influences (1976-7: 32). Friedman argues that 'If social forms fail, it is because they have laws of their own whose purpose is other than making optimal use of their techno-environments' (1974: 466).

Assessment

Popular writers like to think in terms of social dysfunction, and often expound vaguely about unraveling of the fabric of society. This clearly should be known (as suggested to me by Bonnie Bagley Tainter) as the *Warp and Woof* model of collapse.

In a more serious vein, these studies alike offer neither sources of stress nor causal mechanisms that can be analyzed in any objective manner. They are thus unsatisfactory as explanations for collapse.

Mystical factors

Mystical explanations are second in popularity to those that postulate class conflict (an interesting fact in this age supposedly dominated by rational science). Their essence is that they contain no reference to empirically knowable processes, and often make value judgements about particular societies. Mystical explanations rely on concepts like 'decadence,' 'vigor,' or 'senility'; societies are ranked according to these subjective factors, and collapse is explained accordingly. 'Decadent' societies, in this view, are seen negatively, and are axiomatically liable to disintegrate. Many, many such theories have been developed, of great diversity, indeed often of diametrically opposite views. They are united in their lack of concern with empirically knowable or observable factors, and in their reliance on an author's subjective assessment of individual societies.

In contrast to the themes discussed to this point, mystical explanations are presented more often as universal theories than as case-specific scenarios. There are plenty of the latter to be sure, but for once they need not dominate the discussion. The best known of such accounts are those of Spengler and Toynbee, but these authors are merely the most prominent of a crowded field, a field with a long history indeed.

Mesopotamian historiography contains what must surely be one of the oldest explanations of collapse. In considering the fall of Sargon of Akkad and of the Third Dynasty of Ur, the decline of empires was ascribed by Mesopotamian writers to the impiousness of rulers, and to marauding enemies sent by the gods as punishment. Cities flourish under good kings, but suffer under impious ones (discussed in Yoffee [1982]).

Plato observed that in his day thousands of states had come into existence and perished (*Laws*). He asserted a biological analogy that has never disappeared from collapse studies: '...since all created things must decay, even a social order...cannot last for ever, but will decline' (Plato 1955: 315). The controlling dynamic, to Plato, was that there is a right and a wrong time for human reproduction. If the right time is not met, '...the children will be begotten amiss' (Plato 1955: 316). The appropriate time is controlled by a mystical numerology. The frequency with which it is missed leads to poor leadership, to war, hatred, and strife, and to conflict between those interested in either profit or virtue. Class oppression results.

Polybius, in a remarkable second-century B.C. anticipation of the Roman collapse some six centuries later, continued the biological analogy: 'Every organism, every state and every activity passes through a natural cycle, first of growth, then of maturity and finally of decay...' (1979: 345). The victory of Rome over Carthage was accounted for by the fact that Rome was ascending this cycle, and Carthage declining, at the time of their conflict. Rome was then at its zenith, but changes for the worse were sure to follow. 'This state,' wrote Polybius, '...will pass through a natural cycle to its decay' (1979: 310).

The decline of Rome was a source of speculation from the second century B.C. until the final collapse (Mazzarino 1966). Sallust ascribed Roman 'decadence' to loss of virtue and the biological cycle: '...everything that is born dies' (in Mazzarino [1966: 27]). To Seneca the Elder the decline of Italian agriculture was a sign of sociocultural age (Mazzarino 1966: 32-3).

Such thinking became commonplace with the onset of true crisis in the third century A.D. Cyprian's views on the matter have been quoted earlier in this chapter. To Ammianus Marcellinus in the fourth century, Rome had gone through a phase of childhood, with wars in her immediate vicinity, adulthood, when she crossed the Alps and the sea, youth and manhood, the time of great triumphs, and was now declining into old age (1939: 37). Ambrose, Bishop of Milan, and Vegetius, both contemporaries of Ammianus Marcellinus, seconded the theme of decadence (Mazzarino 1966: 53, 55).

To pagans of the era the blame for Rome's troubles was to be placed on Christians, and to Christians, the barbarians and other troubles were the judgements of God for Roman sins and transgressions (Mazzarino 1966: 56, 58, 65). Saint Augustine wrote his *City of God* in response to the pagan charges (completed 426 A.D.). Augustine's theory was that there were two kinds of persons, the good inhabitants of the City of God, who would be purified and improved by the troubles, and the evil, who loved worldly things, and would be overwhelmed.

In the fourteenth century Petrarch explained the fall of Rome by the disappearance of great men. Later, what was apparently the first 'decline and fall' was written by Flavio Biondo (1392-1463). His *Historiarum ab Inclinatione Romanorum Imperii Decades Tres* (1453) covers the years 412-1441 (R. M. Adams 1983: 19). To Flavio Biondo the collapse was attributable to the persecution of the Christians, the deterioration of moral life, and the arrival of inferior types of humanity. Leonardo Bruni Aretino (1441) was similar on this last point: the government was transferred into the worst hands, and so fell (Mazzarino 1966: 77-84).

To Antonio Agostino, a fifteenth-century Bishop of Lerida, and to most Renaissance thinkers, the Roman decline was due to abandonment of ancient manners. Machiavelli (*Discourses on Livy*) argued that the Romans won their early wars by their virtue, but when later this virtue was lacking and the armies had lost their ancient valor, the Western Empire was destroyed. Rome came to this condition when it was corrupted by its colonies. A great power becomes dependent on its colonies, and thus a colony itself (Mansfield 1979: 211-12, 215).

Interesting diversions from this tradition were provided by Rheticus and Jean Bodin. Rheticus, a disciple of Copernicus, proposed (1540-3) a Copernican explanation of collapse: the rise and fall of monarchies was tied to the terrestrial orbit and the sun's eccentricities. To Jean Bodin (1566) the birth and death of states was deterministically regulated by the perfect number 496 (Mazzarino 1966: 90). Bodin's tradition has been continued into recent times by at least two authors. Quetelet wrote in 1848 that five ancient empires each lasted an average of 1461 years, which in Egyptian numerology is the life span of the phoenix (in Kroeber 1957: 111). Lawler (1970) believes that history is cyclic, following a 1470-year rise and fall pattern. Each such pattern contains 2 sub-patterns of 735 years, in turn broken down into 10 phases. The collapse of the United States is predicted by 2040 (Lawler 1970: 249).

Montesquieu's major work on the rise and fall of Rome continued the morality argument. Roman power derived from Roman virtue, and when this declined the Romans weakened. Under the emperors the populace became a vile mob. Campaigning beyond Italy led to a decline in civic spirit among the soldiers. Epicureanism undermined the moral order. Rome gradually declined until collapse came under the emperors Arcadius and Honorius (ca. 400 A.D.) (Montesquieu 1968).

Gibbon (1776-88) cited a number of factors in the Roman collapse, including relaxation of military discipline, Christianity, ignorance of dangers, bad emperors, and the decline of martial spirit with prosperity.

Herder (1968 [original 1784-91]) believed that all human structures are transitory, and become oppressive within a few generations. Rome would in the end have been destroyed by class conflict or the military, but the proximate cause was the importation of luxuries leading to depraved, indolent living, vices, divorce, slavery, and tyranny toward the best persons. The population declined in numbers, stature, and 'vital energy' (Herder 1968: 250).

Hegel's *Philosophy of History* (1956) originated as a series of lectures in 1830 and 1831. Hegel believed that a polity is well constituted when the private interests of the citizens are one with the common interests of the state. But since material cravings, instincts, and self-interest present themselves first, some time is needed to achieve this point. A nation is moral and virtuous while pursuing its grand objects, but once these are realized, once opposition vanishes, the supreme interest also vanishes, and the spirit of the people disappears. A nation lives the same kind of life as an individual, passing from maturity to an old age in which there is satisfaction at accomplishment. This customary life brings on natural death, and a people then perish.

Curious perspectives on disintegration were offered by the Adams brothers, Brooks and Henry (distinguished historians and descendants of American presidents). Brooks Adams (1896) believed that the properties of the mind are strongly hereditary. Human societies vary in respect to how nature has endowed them with 'energetic material' (B. Adams 1896: ix). When a race is so richly endowed with energetic material that not all is expended in the daily struggle, the surplus may be stored in the form of wealth. Capitalism may result therefrom, as well as emphasis on economic and scientific intellect. Class stratification is inevitable, and can lead to collapse. In Rome, a martial, energetic race was exterminated by the usurers and landowners. The Romans were '...ill-fitted to endure the strain of the unrestricted economic competition of a centralized society' (B. Adams 1896: 1). The energy of such a race becomes exhausted, and the survivors must await the infusion of barbarian blood.

Henry Adams' thesis (1919) was that human thought has passed through a series of phases. Thought is analogous to an electric current, and obeys laws of inertia. Phases of thought accelerate through time at a rate equal to the square root of the time of the previous phase. The evolution of thought has now passed its apex, and is in retrograde. Thought, he predicted, would reach the limits of its possibilities in 1921, or barring that, in 2025.

Otto von Seek's theory of the Roman collapse was a biological one: massacres of the residents of Italy in the last centuries of the Republic led to elimination of the best parts of the population, and subsequent governance by the remainder (characterized in Woodward [1916: 96-7] and Mazzarino [1966: 123]; for a revival of dysgenic thinking see Shockley [1972: 303]). Georg Hansen in 1889 developed a similar theory based on Roman marriage patterns (in Mazzarino [1966: 124-30]). Tenney Frank believed that racial change in Italy brought a people lacking energy, enterprise, foresight, and common sense (1970). Burckhardt (1949 [original 1852]) threw his weight behind the senescence-and-corruption explanation of the Roman collapse.

Elliot Mills, writing anonymously in 1905, predicted the demise of the British Empire based on the prevalence of urban life and a consequent decline in agriculture, literary and dramatic taste, and intellectual and religious life (see also R. M. Adams [1983: 111]).

The Egyptologist Sir Flinders Petrie also entered this field (1911). The '...real nature of human progress,' argued Petrie (1911: 105), is expansion followed by collapse. Democracy is a regular feature of decaying civilizations. Moreover, 'The phase of civilization is inherent in the people, and is not due to the circumstances of their position' (Petrie 1911: 113). When a democracy is established, the destitute consume the capital of the wealthy, and the civilization must then decay until invasion destroys it. Petrie suggested, in curious anticipation of Toynbee, that 'There is no advance without strife,' and that 'The harder a nation strives the more capable it will be' (1911: 125).

This perusal of the history of the mystical theme, in its various forms, brings us to its flowering in the late nineteenth and twentieth centuries. Although the names of Spengler and Toynbee are most readily identifiable in this flowering, there are any number of other theorists, and at least one precursor, whose works merit attention.

Spengler is most surprisingly anticipated by the Russian Nikolai Danilevsky, whose *Russia and Europe* was published in 1869, but apparently not read by Spengler until his *Decline of the West* was finished (H. Hughes 1952: 53). There is a remarkably fortuitous convergence in their thinking. Danilevsky was a biologist, and a promoter of Slavic nationalism. His model of civilization was a distinctly organic one:

> The course of development of historico-cultural types is similar to the life-course of those perennials whose period of growth lasts indefinitely, but whose period of blossoming and fruit bearing is relatively short and then exhausts them once and for all (quoted in Sorokin [1950: 60]).

Each civilization emerges, goes through a fixed span of childhood, youth, maturity, and old age, and then passes away. Civilization is the last phase of a culture-historical type, and ends because '...every people is eventually worn out and exhausted creative-ly...' (quoted in Sorokin [1950: 57]). Danilevsky anticipated in this vision the decline of Western European civilization, and the rise of a Slavic one.

We come at last to Spengler, whose *Decline* (1962 [original 1918, 1922]) is one of the truly significant works of the twentieth century. For Spengler, as for so many others, '...the notions of birth, death, youth, age, lifetime, are fundamentals...' in the understanding of history (1962: 3). Spengler had a supremely mystical view of human cultures: each has '...*its own* idea; *its own* passions; *its own* life, will and feeling, *its own* death...its own new possibilities of self-expression which arise, ripen, decay, and never return' (1962: 16-17 [emphases in original]). Cultures are '...sublimated life essences [which] grow with the same superb aimlessness as the flowers of the field' (1962: 17). Civilization, in turn, is the inevitable destiny of a culture, the 'organico-logical sequel, fulfillment and finale...' (1962: 24). This civilizational phase is undesirable: 'Civilizations are the most external and artificial states of which a species of developed humanity is capable' (1962: 24). Civilizations are dominated by intellect, and '...as a historical process, consist in a progressive exhaustion of forms that have become inorganic or dead' (1962: 25). Cities are a symptom of this state, with their populace that is '...parasitical...traditionless, utterly matter-of-fact, religionless, clever, unfruitful...' (1962: 25). The Classical world of the fourth century A.D., and the Western of the nineteenth, exemplify this phase (hence the title of his work). For the latter, Spengler saw the symptoms of decline everywhere: in urban life, in art, in mathematics. 'What is practiced as art today,' he asserted, '...is impotence and falsehood' (Spengler 1962: 157-8).

Spengler's poetic imagery is renowned, and one passage in particular summarizes both his theory and his mysticism.

> A Culture is born in the moment when a great soul awakens out of the proto-spirituality of ever-childish humanity, and detaches itself, a form from the formless, a bounded and mortal thing from the boundless and enduring. It blooms on the soil of an exactly definable landscape, to which plant-wise it remains bound. It dies when this soul has actualized the full sum of its possibilities in the shape of peoples, languages, dogmas, arts, states, sciences, and reverts into the proto-soul. But its living existence, that sequence of great epochs which define and display the stages of fulfillment, is an inner passionate struggle to maintain the Idea against the powers of Chaos without and the unconscious muttering deep down within...The aim once attained – the idea, the entire content of inner possibilities, fulfilled and made externally actual – the Culture suddenly hardens, it mortifies, its blood congeals, its force breaks down, and it becomes *civilization*, the thing which we feel and understand in the words Egypticism, Byzantinism, Mandarinism. As such it may, like a worn-out giant of the primeval forest, thrust decaying branches towards the sky for hundreds or thousands of years, as we see in China, in India, in the Islamic world...
>
> This – the inward and outward fulfillment, the finality, that awaits every living Culture – is the purport of all the historic 'declines,' amongst them that decline of the Classical which we know so well and fully, and another decline, entirely comparable to it in course and duration, which will occupy the first centuries of the coming millennium but is heralded already and sensible in and around us

today – the decline of the West. Every Culture passes through the age-phases of the individual man. Each has its childhood, youth, manhood and old age. It is a young and trembling soul, heavy with misgivings, that reveals itself in the morning of Romanesque and Gothic... Childhood speaks to us also – and in the same tones – out of early-Homeric Doric, out of early-Christian (which is really early Arabian) art and out of the works of the Old Kingdom in Egypt that began with the Fourth Dynasty. A mythic world-consciousness is fighting like a harassed debtor against all the dark and daemonic in itself and in Nature, while slowly ripening itself for the pure, day-bright expression of the existence that it will at last achieve and know. The more nearly a Culture approaches the noon culmination of its being, the more virile, austere, controlled, intense the form-language it has secured for itself, the more assured its sense of its own power, the clearer its lineaments. We find every individual trait of expression deliberate, strict, measured, marvelous in its ease and self-confidence, and everywhere, at moments, the coming fulfillment suggested. Still later, tender to the point of fragility, fragrant with the sweetness of late October days, come the Cnidian Aphrodite and the Hall of the Maidens in the Erechtheum, the arabesques on Saracen horseshoe-arches, the Zwinger of Dresden, Watteau, Mozart. At last, in the grey dawn of Civilization, the fire in the soul dies down. The dwindling powers rise to one more, half-successful effort of creation, and produce the Classicism that is common to all dying Cultures. The soul thinks once again, and in Romanticism looks back piteously to its childhood; then finally, weary, reluctant, cold, it loses its desire to be, and, as in Imperial Rome, wishes itself out of the overlong daylight and back in the darkness of proto-mysticism, in the womb of the mother, in the grave (Spengler 1962: 73-5 [emphasis in original]).

One is reminded by such imagery of Hughes' assessment: 'In Germany, a book that is not hard to read is scarcely considered worth reading' (H. Hughes 1952: 66).

Although often lumped with Spengler's *Decline*, Toynbee's *A Study of History* (1962) is of a very different nature, and indeed Toynbee was critical of Spengler therein. In twelve volumes, the *Study* is a life-work (1939-61), and shows expectable evolution and change in the author's views. Yet some basic premises and assumptions are present throughout. Toynbee's view of the development of civilization was his famous 'challenge and response': a society encounters a succession of problems, each a challenge to undergo an ordeal (e.g., the challenge of the Nile swamps to the early Egyptians). A challenge leads to economic development: '...ease is inimical to civilization' (1962 (II): 31). By surmounting such challenges civilizations develop. The collapse of a civilization in turn entails a loss of 'creative power,' a 'failure of vitality' (Toynbee 1962 (I): 336). So the Maya collapsed, while Egypt didn't, because later generations of Mayans had ceased the exertions needed to maintain mastery over nature (1962 (II): 3-4).

In contrast to Spengler, Toynbee saw civilization as a '...fresh dynamic movement...' (1962 (IV): 128) that might be '...full of...meaning...' (1962 (V): 3). Its expansion '...is to be commended for being slow but sure' (1962 (V): 200). An accumulation of unmet challenges, though, can be the beginning of cultural collapse. This is an internal process: '...the ultimate criterion and the fundamental cause of the breakdown of civilizations is an outbreak of internal discord through which they forfeit their faculty of self-determination' (1962 (V): 17). Such an outbreak leads to conflicts between geographically segregated communities, and to schisms between socially segregated classes. The result is a division of society into three opposed classes: a 'dominant minority,' who develop philosophies and establish 'universal states' (i.e., empires), an 'internal proletariat' who establish a 'universal church,' and an 'external proletariat,' who become barbarian war bands (1962 (V): 17-21, (VI): 321-2). Thus went the Roman Empire, the universal state of Hellenic society. Horizontal schisms represent '...an increasing disintegration of the soul' (1962 (V): 21).

The breakdowns of civilizations '...are failures in an audacious attempt to ascend from the level of Primitive Humanity, being the life of a social animal, to the height of some superhuman kind of being in a Communion of Saints...' (1962 (VI): 5). This involves, as noted, a '...loss of creative power in the souls of the creative individuals, or the creative minorities...' (1962 (IV): 5). These compensate for the loss of creativity by resorting to coercion, which leads to the establishment of an imperial universal state. In civilizations, '...geographical expansion and spiritual growth' vary inversely (1962 (III): 141). Major geographical expansion is then a sign of 'social disintegration' (1962 (IV): 4). And yet

> In this conflict between a proletariat and a dominant minority...we can discern one of those drastic spiritual encounters which renew the work of creation by carrying the life of the Universe out of the stagnation of autumn through the pains of winter into the ferment of spring (Toynbee 1962 (I): 336).

Toynbee's emphasis on moral and spiritual values found prior expression in the work of Albert Schweitzer (1923). Schweitzer argued that if an ethical foundation is lacking, a civilization collapses. Civilization exists in the effort to perfect humanity, and originates when a population is inspired to attain progress and to serve. Schweitzer characterized Western civilization of the early 1920s as showing signs of collapse.

A volume published in the same year as Schweitzer's shows one peculiar extreme of thought. It should be read only by persons who have a firm sense of the historical relativity of knowledge. To Towner, civilization has a basis in pliable biology: with civilization, 'The nervous system is augmented, the intellect develops, the spiritual stature increases' (1923: 9). Towner never clearly defined what he meant by 'augmented nervous organization,' but it figured prominently in his theory. Whatever it is, he equated it with sexual frigidity, and suggested that women who have such 'nervous organizations' tend to produce geniuses. As such women in civilizations are less often forced into maternity, the proportion of genius progressively declines, and civilizations wither away.

Christopher Dawson's work (1956 [original 1921-55]) was considerably less bizarre, if also less unified in its perspective. He cited several factors in the weakness and collapse of civilizations. Increasing complexity and centralization present perils:

Hellenic civilization suffered the degradation of the 'Greek type'; in Rome, a material revolution broke down '...the organic constitution of society'; European civilization is currently weak because it '...no longer possesses vital rhythm and balance' (Dawson 1956: 56, 59-60, 63-4, 66).

Writing during imprisonment in Ahmadnagar Fort in 1944, Jawaharlal Nehru proposed that India's decline had been due to internal decay, that in the twelfth century '...India was drying up and losing her creative genius and vitality' (1959: 125).

Franz Borkenau was a contemporary of Spengler and Toynbee, and like them believed that civilizations rise and fall. He sided with Toynbee in regard to the precedence of spiritual and religious over material factors in history, but demurred from Toynbee's view that some wickedness or sin causes civilizations to fall (pointing out that terrible crimes repeatedly occur among developing civilizations) (Borkenau 1981).

Civilizations, to Paul Valéry, are inherently fragile (1962: 23). Moral qualities are intrinsically related to this. He likened Europe after World War I, with its intellectual and moral confusion, to the ages of Trajan or the Ptolemies. The global domination of Europe was accounted for by superior characteristics of the European population (which he identified as drive, curiosity, logic, skepticism, and mysticism). Yet the seeds of destruction are contained in this imbalance. Mass production today makes commodities universally available, so that in the future population and geographical size will become the major determinants of power, and Europe will consequently suffer.

The third of the major twentieth-century theorists of rise and decline was Alfred Kroeber (1944, 1957). Kroeber had a definite attitude about cultural phenomena. He wrote of 'higher cultural values and forms' (1944: 8), and of 'climaxes.' Egyptian civilization rose and fell four times '...before it exhausted itself' (1944: 663). It further had '...a fairly high idea-system' (1944: 700). Cultural patterns can be of 'high value' or of 'lower-grade' (1944: 763). Within the context of such evaluations, Kroeber analyzed cycles of creativity in such areas as art, science, and philosophy. All seem to show a common pattern: centuries of rising development, then long ages of repetition, imitation, and decline.

Two anthropologists following in Kroeber's tradition were Coulborn (1954, 1966) and Gray (1958). Coulborn extended Kroeber's concept of exhaustion in art and philosophy to any activity. The rise and fall of a civilization is characterized by a process of rise, elaboration, and exhaustion of a pattern. After the Roman collapse, '...the entire culture fell very low' (Coulborn 1954: 213). Any society passes through the cycle of an Age of Faith, an Age of Reason, and finally an Age of Fulfillment. In this latter state there may be decline '...from the very special excellence reached in every civil society' (Coulborn 1966: 415). Religion may be the source of decline, for a society maintains its strength while its religion is vigorous, and loses it when religious commitment weakens (1966: 430).

Charles Gray (1958) saw Classical history as a series of superimposed cycles. The major cycle is Formative, Developed, Florescent, and Degenerate. Each of these phases had its own creative and degenerate periods. Superimposed on this were two great epochs: city-states and super-states. Gray is not bashful about evaluating cultural periods: the Formative Archaic was 'crude,' the Roman period 'degenerate' (1958: 14,19). Degeneracy leads to political decay, while the '...higher the degree of civilization...' attained in any period, the more rapid its transit (Gray 1958: 22).

Pitirim Sorokin was a sociologist, and a scholar of Kroeber's stature. His *Social and Cultural Dynamics* (1957 [original 1937-41]) is a landmark. In it he defined two cultural modes: the Ideational culture, wherein reality is perceived as nonmaterial, and the Sensate culture, where reality is only as presented to sensory organs. The shift between the two in any society is intrinsic. Since each alone is incomplete, populations swing from one to the other. Totalitarian states rise and fall with Sensate culture. Sensatism increased in Rome after the second century B.C., and the state became totalitarian. Yet in the fifth century A.D. the Ideational culture of Christianity became dominant, and the Roman state disintegrated.

Finally there is David Ormsby-Gore (1966), who follows Toynbee, and is largely concerned about the fate of Western Civilization. His chief causes of decline or collapse are internal decay, manifesting itself in internecine warfare, exposure to '...a superior form of society,' military stagnation, and economic or demographic inferiority (Ormsby-Gore 1966: 41). The rise and the fall of civilizations are directly attributable to the making of right or wrong decisions, collectively by large numbers of people. He concludes that the West need not decline.

Specific applications of mystical themes span a segment of the intellectual spectrum that matches the more general formulations. Dennis Puleston (1979) argued that the Maya were done in by believing in their own cyclical calendar. When one point in this cycle witnessed a great volcanic eruption, and the next return of the same point experienced the vague event archaeologists call the Hiatus, Mayan prophecy foresaw doom for the third occurrence. As it approached, panic turned the affair into a self-fulfilling prophecy.

Writing of the American Southwest, but with reference to complex societies in general, David Stuart argues that as complex societies increase in size, rates of production, and rates of energy expenditure, they are impelled to the point where they simply 'burn out' (Stuart and Gauthier 1981: 10). Cultural systems are likened in this way to locust swarms (Stuart and Gauthier 1981: 11). And in a strictly Kroeberian formulation, James Griffin once suggested that the decline of Ohio Hopewell could be ascribed to 'cultural fatigue' (1952: 361).

Melko (1969) reflects Kroeber's view that once established a civilization's capacities for cultural change are limited, and so development continues until the 'pattern' culminates. Collapse follows from ossification, bureaucratic inefficiency, and the inability to deal with internal or external problems. In apparent echo of Sorokin, Melko projects the end of Western Civilization due to loss of interest in technological problem-solving, and change to a spiritual world outlook (1969: 164).

Assessment

Although complex societies are not really like plagues of locusts, it sometimes seems as if theories of their collapse may be. To make any sense out of the foregoing it is necessary to focus on a few basic themes. The reader will be spared major attention to ideas that clearly do not merit serious consideration. There will thus be little discussion of mystical numerology, or of reproductive patterns, or of theories that compare complex societies to swarms of insects or to lumps of coal. It is well to point out, though, that what separates these theories from those that will be discussed is only a matter of degree.

The works of Spengler and Toynbee have been reviewed for so long and so thoroughly (e.g., H. Hughes 1952; Montagu 1956), that little can be added that is really new. This will make the present assessment (compared with the overview just completed) mercifully short. It is nonetheless necessary to cover certain points to round out my critique of collapse studies, and this I shall do without concern for whether my objections are novel. In all, I find the work of Spengler's and Toynbee's critics much to the point, and will use it as a springboard.

The mysticism and value-laden nature of Spengler's writing fully validate Hughes' estimate of it as '...a massive stumbling-block in the path of true knowledge' (H. Hughes 1952: 1). Hughes echoed the feelings of many who have read Spengler: '...the *Decline* reeks with unpardonable exaggerations, delivered in a tone of dogmatic certainty' (1952: 53). 'Spengler's metaphysical passages...achieve the not unusual combination of being murky and superficial in the same breath' (1952: 155). Spengler's prejudices are '...narrow and hateful' (1952: 156). '...[A]ll cyclical theorists...play the role of intuitive seers' (Hughes 1952: 162).

Toynbee's critics have been scarcely kinder:

> [Toynbee metes] out rewards and punishments like a divine schoolmaster, a silver cup to Primitive Christianity, consolation prizes to the churches, and six with the cane to contemporary western agnostic and materialist civilisation (Stone 1956: 112).

> [Toynbee has the] inability to distinguish unverifiable presuppositions and subjective value-judgements from empirical deductions from the facts... (Stone 1956: 112).

> He compares himself with the prophet Ezekiel; and certainly, at times, he is just as unintelligible (Trevor-Roper 1956: 122).

> For Mr. Toynbee, history and the techniques for studying it are a curious blend of science and fiction (K. Thompson 1956: 201).

> Toynbee, like Jeremiah, is sure of his ground (Boer 1956: 240).

> [Toynbee's subjectivism is] a normative system based on a very private interpretation of the course of human destiny (Altree 1956: 271).

Despite the differences in approach between Spengler and Toynbee, these quotes could be interchangeably used for either author.

It seems almost unsporting to treat Spengler and Toynbee so severely, but these quotations introduce most of the problems in mystical explanations. These problems are: (a) reliance on a biological growth analogy; (b) reliance on value judgements; and (c) explanation by reference to intangibles.

The biological growth and decay analogy, as has been seen, is an ancient one (and it continues in use to this day [e.g., Haussig 1971: 13, 14]). Its essence has been stated in the previous pages: complex societies mimic organisms in a path of birth, growth, decay, and death. Organisms, though, follow such a path through a scientifically knowable process that involves such things as genetic coding, biological clocks, solar cycles, and the progression of the seasons. For human societies, as most social scientists recognize, the biological analogy can identify no such controlling mechanisms. It is necessary then to fall back on arguments that are openly vitalistic – that some mysterious, internal, dynamic force leads to the 'flowering and decay' of civilizations. Vitalistic arguments of this form are indefensible, for any such internal force is inherently unknowable, unspecifiable, unmeasurable, and unexplainable. This analogy, like so many of the explanatory themes discussed previously, does not advance the cause of understanding. It explains a mystery by reference to a mystery, and so explains nothing.

Alfred Kroeber, a master of the growth and senescence analogy, objected to such criticisms (1958: 33). His point was that it is not false to speak of cultures 'growing,' that the term is a metaphor. One is forced to use it due to limitations of language. Granting Kroeber this insight, one still has reservations, for it is not at all clear that many others perceive the matter as he did. Too many of the authors reviewed here seem to believe that cultures really do sprout, flower, wither, and die.

Value judgements are another matter altogether. A scholar trained in anthropology learns early on that such valuations are scientifically inadmissible, detrimental to the cause of understanding, intellectually indefensible, and simply unfair. A student of other cultures acquires a deep-seated aversion to statements indicating that various cultural phenomena are good/bad, better/worse, superior/inferior. One is either an impartial social scientist or a social critic, and the latter should not masquerade as the former. Cultural relativity may be one of the most important contributions anthropology can make to the social and historical sciences, and to the public at large. One would like to think that historians, sociologists, political scientists, economists, and others who study collapse could learn from anthropology in this regard. But then along come Kroeber, Coulborn, and Gray, anthropologists all and among the worst offenders.

The works reviewed under the mystical theme revert to value judgements to such an extent that they must be a necessary part of this approach. One could argue that this is so: since biological analogies cannot specify any measurable dimensions of change, it is necessary to fall back on subjective evaluations. This the mystical theorists do with zest. Thus Spengler wrote of cultures hardening and mortifying, of art forms that are false, of cities with inhabitants that are parasitical. Toynbee, as a previous critical quotation points out, sat like the great judge of civilizations and cultural phases, approving some, dismissing others. Toynbee's civilizations are fresh and dynamic, are to be commended, make audacious attempts, but their creative minorities ultimately lose such powers. Kroeber was perhaps the most unblushing in the subjective evaluations he dished out. Egypt had a high idea-system, France a high cultural luster. Cultural patterns in general could be of high value or lower-grade. Coulborn continued this tradition: post-Roman culture fell very low, civil society possessed special excellence. Gray was not at all behind his colleagues: cultures are occasionally crude or degenerate, but there may also be high degrees of civilization. Many other authors could be indicted on this count.

Terms that are commonplace in mystical explanations further the aura of subjectivism. 'Decadence' is a notable one, frequently applied to the Roman Empire. Even seemingly innocuous words like 'rise,' 'fall,' 'decline,' and 'vigor' imply value judgements: we all approve of things that have vigor, and conversely. As discussed earlier, the term 'civilization' itself falls into this trap.

Values, of course, vary culturally, socially, and individually, Herein lies the problem, so obvious that one feels embarrassed for authors who overlook it. What one individual, society, or culture values highly another does not, so that subjective ratings of cultural phenomena can never be scientifically standardized. Most of us approve, in general, of that which culturally is most like or most pleasing, or at least most intelligible, to us. The result is a global bedlam of idiosyncratic value systems, each claiming exclusive possession of 'truth.' No scientific theory can be raised on such a foundation, for the attempt will lead only to confusion and contradiction. Thus while most authors seem to approve of civilizations, Spengler detested them (as may Rappaport). Where Toynbee disapproved of empires, Kroeber counted Egyptian expansion as a period of success (Kroeber 1944: 664). Reliance on subjective value judgements is not only logically inadmissible, it can produce no consistent results.

The 'decadence' concept seems particularly detrimental. Although enjoying a patina of long use (Mazzarino 1966), it is notoriously difficult to define. Decadent behavior is that which differs from one's own moral code, particularly if the offender at some former time behaved in a manner of which one approves. There is no clear causal link between the morality of behavior and political fortunes. With the so-called decline of Roman virtues, for example, it is not clear (Polybius notwithstanding) that lack of such virtues early on would have forestalled Roman expansion, nor that their presence later would have held the barbarians at bay. R. M. Adams has phrased the problem well: '...each society known to history will be able to display a healthy proportion of decadent individuals' (1983: 11). Furthermore,

> ...we cannot seriously suppose that major political structures disintegrate from anyone's indulgence in excessive food, drink, or sex. No, the mechanisms of social disintegration have to be somehow proportionate to the dimensions of the resulting downfall (R. M. Adams 1983: 149-50).

Explanation by reference to intangibles is the third problem with mystical explanations. It is closely linked with the first two. Mystical explanations simply fail to identify any isolatable, observable, measurable factor controlling cultural change. In the few instances where this is attempted (e.g., by reference to human biology) it is not clear how the controlling mechanism leads to the observed outcome. The Adams brothers' theories are perhaps worst in this regard, but they are not atypical. Thus,

Brooks Adams cited biological 'energetic material,' while Henry likened thought to an electric current. Towner was not far behind when he ascribed the rise and fall of civilizations to 'augmented nervous organizations' and sexual frigidity. Yet while these may be the most audacious, they grade into more respectable views. Spengler believed cultures could have ideas, passions, and will, that they are 'sublimated life essences.' Civilizations to Toynbee were communions of saints and might possess souls. Dawson decried European civilization because it no longer possesses vital rhythm and balance. Sorokin conceived of Sensate *vs.* Ideational value systems, Puleston believed the Maya frightened themselves to death, Stuart likens complex societies to insect swarms, and Griffin blamed cultural fatigue. None has isolated a causal mechanism that provides any grounds for building a scientific theory. This problem is inherent in mystical theories, and indeed is the single criterion that readily identifies an explanation as mystical.

Chance concatenation of events

The great Classical historian J. B. Bury (1923 (I)) argued that there was no general explanation for the fall of Rome, that it resulted from a series of contingent events. The irruption of the Huns drove the Visigoths into the Illyrian provinces. The Roman government mismanaged this problem, and so lost the disastrous battle of Hadrianople (A.D. 378). Federate barbarian nations were then settled within the empire, a bad precedent. A series of weak emperors ascended to the throne in the West. Germans were elevated to high positions in the Empire. There was the treachery of Stilicho, and dependence on barbarians to man the army (Bury 1923 (I): 311-12).

Other authors bring chance concatenations into more general explanations. Willey and Shimkin on the Maya (1973), and Butzer on Egypt (1980, 1984), emphasize concurrent outbreaks of clusters of problems and weaknesses in their respective cases. Charles Diehl argued that a combination of events led to the decay of Byzantium: loss of agricultural lands, the formation of large estates, and unsuccessful economic competition with the Venetians (1970).

Assessment

Chance concatenation arguments by definition provide no basis for generalization, and so fail to satisfy the need for a global understanding of a recurrent process. Explanation by reference to historical accident furthermore has some logical failings. It is argued by some that *all* history is a chance concatenation of events. This argument goes too far, but there is some validity to the notion that random factors influence all processes. To the extent that random factors occur with some statistical regularity over time, they cannot account for a phenomenon far more limited in its occurrence.

Economic explanations

Economic explanations are the last to be considered. They occur in a variety of forms, but consistently exhibit a limited number of themes. Among these are: (a) declining advantages of complexity; (b) increasing disadvantages of complexity; or (c) increasing costliness of complexity.

A scenario that illustrates these points has been developed by Lewis (1958) to account for the decline of the Ottoman Empire. The Ottomans in the sixteenth century reached the limits of their geographical expansion, and thereafter began to fall behind in military science, in the professional standards of their army, in administration, in manpower and revenue, and in resources. With global European expansion the eastern Mediterranean quickly became a backwater. As trade routes bypassed it, the region was increasingly impoverished. When Europe was flooded with Spanish-American gold the Ottoman economy was ruined. Used to currency shortages, the leadership dealt with abundance by the same strategies: devaluation, coin-clipping, and debasement.

Against this backdrop of economic weakness the government had to embark on a great expansion in its salaried personnel and expenditures in coin. In previous monetary crises the government had lowered the number of paid soldiers and increased the proportion of cavalry. Cavalrymen were rewarded with fiefs rather than with coin. But in the sixteenth and seventeenth centuries changes in warfare made this impossible. The greatly increased use of firearms and artillery required a larger paid army, and reduced the importance of cavalry.

The price of this was staggering. Increasing expenditures had to be based on a depreciating currency. Civil, religious, and military personnel had a harder time making ends meet, with inevitable effects on honesty, prestige, and recruitment. With the disappearance of the cavalryman the Ottoman agrarian system collapsed. Cavalrymen had resided on or near their fiefs. Now fiefs were acquired by palace favorites and speculators. As the bureaucracy became more inefficient and venal, the effectiveness of the tax system declined. Tax farmers were employed, but these tended to intercept revenue, which added to the number of neglected estates. So the shrinking economy of the Empire had to support an increasingly costly and cumbersome superstructure. Lewis characterized the palace, bureaucracy, and religious hierarchy, the army, and the class of absentee landlords and tax farmers as more costly than any hierarchy medieval states or even the Roman Empire had tried to support, and based on an agricultural system that was no more productive. Traders, bankers, and merchants tended to be non-Moslems and so second-class citizens. Political and ideological factors thus militated against conditions favorable to commerce, or to a solid structure of banking and credit.

Lattimore (1940: 45-6) characterized the Chinese dynastic cycle as one of rising and falling returns. A new dynasty would increase returns by concentrating people in favorable areas in order to organize for water control and agriculture on a large scale. As production reached its peak, the economy provided no support for surplus population. Agrarian depression contrasted intolerably with the life of the rulers and bureaucrats, and led to uprisings that destroyed a dynasty.

Johnson argues, in a general vein, that processes that facilitate or inhibit cost-benefit efficiency in political organization lead to social continuity or collapse (1978: 98-9). This seems similar to the approach taken by R. McC. Adams (1981) in his discussion of the weaknesses induced by Sassanian intensification and expansion into marginal agricultural lands. Culbert (n.d.) adapts this model to an account of the Mayan collapse.

Blanton and Kowalewski (1981), as discussed earlier, ascribe collapse in the Valley of Oaxaca to declining benefits in supporting a hierarchy. Turnbull, in a discussion of the Ik (1978), and Laughlin and Brady in a more general discussion (1978), produce arguments that are similar to Blanton and Kowalewski's, but apply to less complex societies. To these authors, prolonged deprivation in tribal societies leads to a situation where the advantages to cooperation decline, and social institutions of cooperation and reciprocity accordingly disappear. In a reverse situation of abundant resources, Harner's (1970) model of collapse is logically similar.

Assessment

There are many historians and social scientists who are not enamored of economic explanations. Yet even for such skeptics there are aspects to the structure and logic (if not the full content) of these explanations that makes them superior to those considered before. Among these aspects are the following:

1. The discussion of some previous explanations (e.g., Resource Depletion, Catastrophes, Intruders, Insufficient Response) implicated characteristics of societies, rather than simply their environments, as instrumental in collapse. Why, it was asked, do societies not produce a sufficient response to circumstances? Debate can rage endlessly about whether the specific economic interpretations just discussed adequately account for weakness. They do, though, have one characteristic that makes them preferable: they recognize this need to identify internal factors of weakness, and set out to do so.
2. In contrast to some explanatory themes (e.g., Class Conflict, Social Dysfunction, Mystical), economic explanations identify a specific mechanism or event controlling change.
3. In contrast to several of the studies discussed, economic models identify a definite causal chain between the controlling mechanism and the observed outcome. Again, those causal chains can certainly be debated for the studies just discussed, but these are logically and structurally preferable because the causal chain is there.

These economic studies, of course, are not without weaknesses. None of these authors has attempted to generalize beyond an individual case, although there is great potential to do so. When Lewis cited religious and ethnic prejudice (1958: 122-3, 125-6) for the lack of Ottoman economic development, it is disappointing that he did not better account for Ottoman inflexibility in this matter. He simply stated that later Islam was not willing to learn from others, which clarifies nothing. R. McC. Adams' (1981) study of Mesopotamian intensification admirably outlines the processes that led to collapse, but does not fully account for elite mismanagement. And Lattimore can cite no reason for surplus labor in China, other than the needs of the elite. It is worth pointing out that the logical weaknesses to these explanations occur at precisely the point where the authors depart from an economic scenario.

Summary and discussion

The evaluations of the various approaches to explaining collapse can be summarized as follows:

1. *Resource depletion*. Dealing with resource uncertainties is a common activity of complex societies, and may be one of the things that they do best. Where this is not the case, research has to focus on the characteristics of the society that prevent an appropriate response, rather than exclusively on the characteristics of the depleted resource.

2. *New resources*. This theme has some attraction to integration theorists, but none to conflict theorists. Its usefulness is mainly restricted to simpler societies. societies.

3. *Catastrophes*. Complex societies regularly provide for catastrophes, and routinely experience them without collapsing. If the society cannot absorb a catastrophe, then in many cases the characteristics of the society will be of greater interest, obviating the catastrophe explanation.

4. *Insufficient response to circumstances*. The assumptions made in this theme about the nature of complex societies – that they are inherently fragile, or static, or incapable of shifting directions – simply cannot be supported. Where complex societies may display such characteristics, that is a matter to be explained.

5. *Other complex societies*. Major cases, such as the Roman one, cannot be accounted for by this theme. Conflict between states more often leads to cycles of expansion and contraction than to collapse.

6. *Intruders*. The overthrow of a dominant state by a weaker one is an event to be explained, not an explanation in itself. Empirically, intruders are often difficult to detect archaeologically where they have been postulated. It is difficult to understand why barbarians would destroy a civilization if it was worth invading in the first place.

7. *Conflict/contradictions/mismanagement*. The capacity to control labor and allocate resources is intrinsic and necessary in complex societies. Collapse cannot easily be explained by factors so vital to survival, at least not without raising many more questions than are answered. Elite mismanagement and self-aggrandizement, to the extent that these are detrimental to the survival of a society, are matters to be explained. Exploitation and misadministration are normal, regular aspects of complex societies, and by themselves cannot account for an occasional event, collapse. Peasants rarely revolt except when allied with other social strata, and their rebellions are not typically aimed at collapse.

8. *Social dysfunction*. These explanations offer neither sources of strain nor causal mechanisms that can be analyzed in any objective way.

9. *Mystical*. Mystical explanations fail totally to account scientifically for collapse.

They are crippled by reliance on a biological growth analogy, by value judgements, and by explanation by reference to intangibles.

10. *Chance concatenation of events*. This theme provides no basis for generalization. Collapse is not well explained by reference to random factors.

11. *Economic explanations*. These are structurally and logically superior to the others, at least as these others have been formulated to date. They identify characteristics of societies that make them liable to collapse, specify controlling mechanisms, and indicate causal chains between controlling mechanisms and observed outcome. While economic explanations are not universally accepted in the social and historical sciences, such scenarios remedy the logical deficiencies of the other approaches. Existing economic models often suffer from incomplete forays into political and social explanations, but this is not an *intrinsic* flaw. The major drawback to economic explanations, for present purposes, is failure to develop an explanatory framework that is globally applicable.

With the exception of mystical explanations, which are without scientific merit, none of these explanatory themes fails entirely. Indeed, the economic theme comes close to success – in logic, if not in specifics – but does not go quite far enough. Except for mystical explanations, these approaches are not necessarily wrong or misguided. They are simply inadequate as presently formulated. They require assumptions that cannot be unquestioningly accepted, and fail frequently in their logic. Yet they also point to relevant variables and processes. Societies do encounter resource shortages, class interests do conflict, catastrophes do happen, and not uncommonly the response does not resolve such problems. A general explanation of collapse should be able to take what is best in these themes and incorporate it. It should provide a framework under which these explanatory themes can be subsumed, so that one can account for what is worthwhile in each. A general explanation should make these themes clearer in application than each would be standing alone.

In the next chapter an explanation of collapse will be developed that follows the economic theme. After delineation and testing (Chapter 5), space will be devoted in Chapter 6 to showing how other explanatory themes can be subsumed under it.

4

Understanding collapse: the marginal productivity of sociopolitical change

It is provided in the essence of things that from any fruition of success, no matter what, shall come forth something to make a greater struggle necessary.

Walt Whitman
(quoted in Toynbee [1962 (III): 123])

Human societies and political organizations, like all living systems, are maintained by a continuous flow of energy. From the simplest familial unit to the most complex regional hierarchy, the institutions and patterned interactions that comprise a human society are dependent on energy. At the same time, the mechanisms by which human groups acquire and distribute basic resources are conditioned by, and integrated within, sociopolitical institutions. Energy flow and sociopolitical organization are opposite sides of an equation. Neither can exist, in a human group, without the other, nor can either undergo substantial change without altering both the opposite member and the balance of the equation. Energy flow and sociopolitical organization must evolve in harmony.

Not only is energy flow required to maintain a sociopolitical system, but the amount of energy must be sufficient for the complexity of that system. Leslie White observed a number of years ago that cultural evolution was intricately linked to the quantities of energy harvested by a human population (1949: 363-93). The amounts of energy required per capita to maintain the simplest human institutions are incredibly small compared with those needed by the most complex. White once estimated that a cultural system activated primarily by human energy could generate only about 1/20 horsepower per capita per year (1949: 369, 1959: 41-2). This contrasts sharply with the hundreds to thousands of horsepower at the command of the members of industrial societies. Cultural complexity varies accordingly. Julian Steward pointed out the quantitative difference between the 3,000 to 6,000 cultural elements early anthropologists documented for native populations of western North America, and the more than 500,000 artifact types that U.S. military forces landed at Casa Blanca in World War II (1955: 81).

More complex societies are more costly to maintain than simpler ones, requiring greater support levels per capita. As societies increase in complexity, more networks are created among individuals, more hierarchical controls are created to regulate these networks, more information is processed, there is more centralization of information flow, there is increasing need to support specialists not directly involved in resource production, and the like. All of this complexity is dependent upon energy flow at a scale vastly greater than that characterizing small groups of self-sufficient foragers or agriculturalists. The result is that as a society evolves toward greater complexity, the support costs levied on each individual will also rise, so that the population as a whole must allocate increasing portions of its energy budget to maintaining organizational institutions. This is an immutable fact of societal evolution, and is not mitigated by type of energy source.

Whether one endorses a conflict or an integration model of society, or some synthesis of these, it is necessary to inquire into the benefits that a population derives from its investment in complexity. Although in the previous chapter serious questions were raised about the view that complex societies collapse as a result of overtaxing their populations, nevertheless the question of benefits relative to investment merits a close look. This is so under either a conflict model, in which complexity is seen as a response to class competition and the needs of an elite to maintain privilege, or an integration model, in which complexity is viewed as a response to social needs. In either view, complexity is a solution to perceived problems, and its facility in resolving these problems is based in part on its ratio of benefits/investment. Where this ratio is unfavorable, complexity is not a very successful strategy. As with energy and organization, the benefits and costs of investment in complexity are opposite poles of an equation. Neither can be considered without the other, although regrettably they usually are.

It is the thesis of this chapter that return on investment in complexity varies, and that this variation follows a characteristic curve. More specifically, it is proposed that, *in many crucial spheres*, continued investment in sociopolitical complexity reaches a point where the benefits for such investment begin to decline, at first gradually, then with accelerated force. Thus, not only must a population allocate greater and greater amounts of resources to maintaining an evolving society, but after a certain point, higher amounts of this investment will yield smaller increments of return. Diminishing returns, it will be shown, are a recurrent aspect of sociopolitical evolution, and of investment in complexity.

The principle of diminishing returns is one of the few phenomena of such regularity and predictability that economists are willing to call it a 'law' (Hadar 1966: 30). In manufacturing, diminishing returns set in when investment in the form of additional inputs causes a decline in the rate of productivity. While this is not exactly analogous to the processes that cause diminishing returns in sociopolitical evolution, some of the terminology developed by economists will nevertheless be helpful in the discussion that follows.

Two concepts commonly used by economists are useful here. These are *average product* and *marginal product*. The average product of an economic activity is simply the output per unit of input. The marginal product of any input is the increase in the total output resulting from the input. Similarly, the average cost is the cost per unit of input, while the marginal cost is the increase or decrease in total cost resulting from one more (or less) unit of output (Hadar 1966; Hailstones 1976).

The law of diminishing returns refers to changes in average and marginal products and costs. Average product and average cost respond to, and ultimately follow, changes in marginal product and cost. Both are subject to this principle, which is also called the law of diminishing marginal productivity (Hailstones 1976). The relationship between marginal and average product is shown in Fig. 1.

For present purposes one term will be emphasized. The discussion will most often refer to the concept 'marginal return.' This may be taken to mean the same thing as marginal product, that is, return per increased unit of investment. The word 'return' is preferred to 'product' to emphasize the concern with whatever benefits a population obtains from its investment in complexity.

The proposition introduced above may now be rephrased in the terminology that will be used throughout the remainder of this work. It is suggested that the increased costs of sociopolitical evolution frequently reach a point of diminishing marginal returns. This is to say that the benefit/investment ratio of sociopolitical complexity follows the marginal product curve of Fig. 1. After a certain point, increased investments in complexity fail to yield proportionately increasing returns. Marginal returns decline and marginal costs rise. Complexity as a strategy becomes increasingly costly, and yields decreasing marginal benefits.

Four concepts discussed to this point can lead to an understanding of why complex societies collapse. These concepts are:

1. human societies are problem-solving organizations;
2. sociopolitical systems require energy for their maintenance;
3. increased complexity carries with it increased costs per capita; and
4. investment in sociopolitical complexity as a problem-solving response often reaches a point of declining marginal returns.

The remainder of this chapter will be devoted to showing how these factors are related to collapse. First, the proposition that investment in complexity breeds diminishing returns will be examined in some detail, for this proposition is crucial for explaining collapse. Next, the reasons for such declining marginal productivity will be examined. And finally, a synthetic explanation of collapse will be developed from these concepts.

The marginal productivity of increasing complexity
In this section it will be useful to break complexity down into several of its constituent parts, and examine these individually. The constituents include agriculture and resource production, information processing, sociopolitical control and specialization,

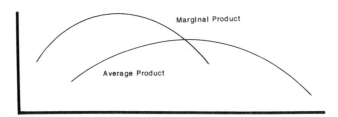

Fig. 1. Relationship of marginal and average product.

and overall economic productivity. In reality, of course, none of these is an independent entity. They form together an interdependent system that can be divided only
artificially. They are separated here solely for the purposes of analysis and illustration.
All of these spheres of activity represent investments by human populations in
stability and welfare.

The examples that follow are drawn from a variety of cases spanning the last several
hundred years. Many are drawn from recent history. It might be worthwhile to point
out that I do not imply by these illustrations that any of these societies is in immediate
danger of collapse. The examples merely show what are common problems faced by
all complex societies. The relationship of these problems to collapse varies with the
historical contexts of individual societies.

Agriculture and resource production

In 1965 the economist Ester Boserup put forward the radical thesis that increasing
intensity in agricultural use of land is brought about by labor investment that is
disproportionately greater than the returns received. Thus, although productivity per
unit of land increases under intensification, productivity per unit of labor actually
decreases.

Boserup developed an idealized (and as she recognized, somewhat arbitrary)
typology of agricultural land use. Her idealized types are as follows:

1. *Forest-fallow cultivation*. Also known as swidden, milpa, or slash-and-burn, this
   is a system in which plots of land are cleared in forest and planted for a number
   of years. As yields decline and weeds encroach, the plot is abandoned to forest
   succession and not used again until forest has become fully established. This
   fallow period may be as long as 25 years.
2. *Bush-fallow cultivation*. This system employs a shorter fallow of between six and
   ten years, so that no forest can grow.
3. *Short-fallow cultivation*. Fallow under this regime lasts only one or two years.
4. *Annual cropping*. This is not really a fallow system except that a period of a few
   months is left between one harvest and the next planting.
5. *Multi-cropping*. This is Boserup's most intensive system of land use, although it
   may be practiced in only a few favorable regions that do not have seasons of
   extreme cold (Boserup 1965: 15-16).

Boserup argues that through such factors as increasing land preparation,
fertilization, and irrigation, human labor per unit of agricultural output rises
throughout this sequence (cf. Boserup 1981: 45). She proposes that the factor
inducing agriculturalists to undertake such increased labor for diminishing marginal
returns is growth of population. Expanding population inevitably strains each
successive form of land use, forcing a shift to the next one, so that the productivity of
labor inevitably declines.

Boserup's framework is generalizable to other types of subsistence regimes. Asch,
Ford, and Asch, for example, have developed a compatible framework to explain
change in hunter-gatherer subsistence, from natural resources that are nutritious and

easily processed to ones that are less so (1972). Mark Cohen has argued that the transition from hunting and gathering to agriculture can be understood as an adaptation to population growth, with such growth ultimately requiring the development of a more intensive and more costly system of resource production – agriculture (1977). Hunter-gatherer foraging strategies are not immediately germane to the matter at hand, but these two studies do illustrate the universal nature of the economic process Boserup described.

Boserup's framework has been subject to some debate, particularly in the driving role of population growth. That debate will not be reviewed here, for it is not necessary to accept the demographic-stress argument to grasp the point of immediate relevance. This is that marginal returns on agriculture, in a subsistence economy, decline with increasing labor. That point can be amply illustrated. Clark and Haswell have shown that, *in subsistence regimes*, both the average and the marginal return on agriculture do indeed decline with increasing labor (1966: 83-4). This can be readily verified from Figs. 2, 3, 4, 5, 6, and 7. These illustrations, compiled by Clark and Haswell (1966), and Wilkinson (1973), provide the quantitative data lacking in Boserup's (1965) work, and needed to verify her proposition. It is clear from inspection that these data verify it substantially.

Animal husbandry follows the same pattern. The labor intensive nature and the costliness of animal husbandry is well known. Illustrating this point, the canals and steam railways that accompanied the development of industrialism in England were seen, at least in part, as a means of reducing the competition between people and horses for the produce of land (Wilkinson 1973: 124).

Fred Bateman (1969) has investigated changes in labor efficiency in the American dairy industry between 1850 and 1910. There was no major technological breakthrough in this interval, but other changes took place. One major shift was the widespread extension of dairying into the winter months. Another was improvements in feeding. Still a third was the addition of stricter sanitation requirements. All of these added to the labor requirements of dairying, although yields did not increase proportionately. The figures in Table 1 show that between 1850 and 1910 dairy output per unit of labor declined by 17.5 percent.

The investment that the human species as a whole makes in overall nutrition, moreover, reaches a point where further investment gives a declining marginal payoff in enhanced life expectancy. Fig. 8 shows that nutritional level varies nonlinearly with life expectancy, so that the productivity of nutritional investment for producing longer life declines as such investment increases.

Complex societies depend on the production of other resources besides agricultural crops. Energy and minerals production, as the modern industrial world is well aware, follows the same productivity curve as subsistence agriculture, and for a similar reason. The fuel resources used first by a rationally-acting human population, and the mineral deposits mined first, are typically those that are most economically exploited, that is, most abundant, most accessible, and most easily converted to the needs at hand (Rifkin with Howard 1980: 73). When it subsequently becomes necessary to use less economical resources marginal returns automatically decline.

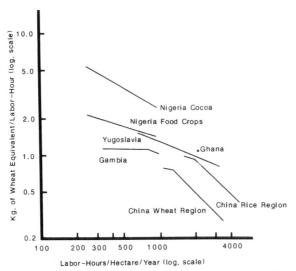

Fig. 2. Average returns of agriculture (after Clark and Haswell 1966: 83). Reproduced by permission of Macmillan Publishers Ltd., London and Basingstoke.

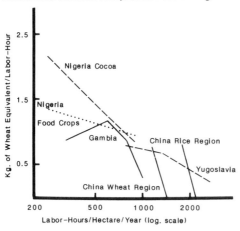

Fig. 3. Marginal returns of agriculture (after Clark and Haswell 1966: 84). Reproduced by permission of Macmillan Publishers Ltd., London and Basingstoke.

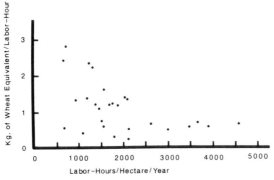

Fig. 4. Average returns of agriculture in Jamaica, 1954–5 (after Clark and Haswell 1966: 87). Reproduced by permission of Macmillan Publishers Ltd., London and Basingstoke.

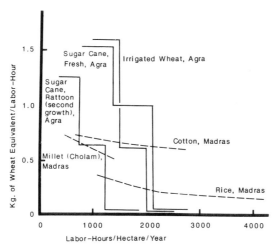

Fig. 5. Marginal returns of agriculture in India (after Clark and Haswell 1966: 88). Reproduced by permission of Macmillan Publishers Ltd., London and Basingstoke.

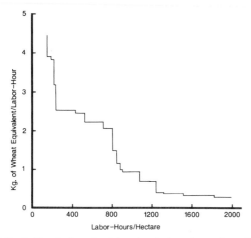

Fig. 6. Marginal productivity of agriculture in northern Greece (after Clark and Haswell 1966: 135). Reproduced by permission of Macmillan Publishers Ltd., London and Basingstoke.

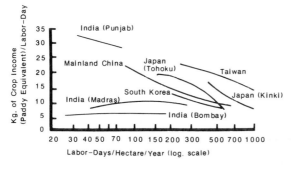

Fig. 7. Labor productivity in Asian agriculture (after Wilkinson 1973: 98). Reproduced by permission of Methuen & Co., London.

Table 1. *American dairy labor efficiency, 1850-1910[1]*

Year	Average annual yields per cow (lbs.)	Total annual labor time (hours)	Total labor per 100 lbs. milk (hours)	Milk output per labor hour (lbs.)
1850	2371	77.04	3.25	30.78
1910	3570	140. 60	3.94	25.39

[1]After Bateman (1969: 222).

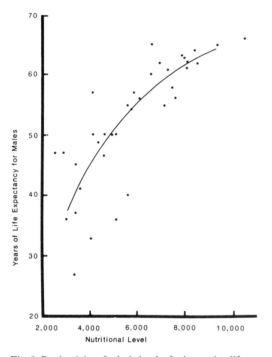

Fig. 8. Productivity of caloric intake for increasing life expectancy (after Cépède et al. 1964: 176).

The development of the coal-based economy in England is a case in point. Wilkinson (1973) has shown that major jumps in population, at around A.D. 1300, 1600, and in the late eighteenth century, each led to intensification in agriculture and industry (see also North and Thomas [1973]). As the land in the late Middle Ages was increasingly deforested to provide fuel and agricultural space for a growing population, basic heating, cooking, and manufacturing needs could no longer be met by burning wood. A shift to reliance on coal began, gradually and with apparent reluctance. Coal was definitely a fuel source of secondary desirability, being more costly to obtain and distribute than wood, as well as being dirty and polluting. Coal was more restricted in its spatial distribution than wood, so that a whole new, costly distribution system had to be developed. Mining of coal from the ground was more costly than obtaining a quantity of wood equivalent in heating value, and became even more costly as the most accessible reserves of this fuel were depleted. Mines had to be sunk ever deeper, until groundwater flooding became a serious problem. Ultimately the steam engine was developed, and employed to pump water out of mines. A similar historical course was followed with the depletion of the forests in the earliest settled parts of the United States (Wilkinson 1973).

The increased costliness per unit of thermal value in the initial shift from wood to coal is apparent, but unfortunately good quantitative data on returns to energy investment are usually not available before the recent period. Modern data not only illustrate the trend quantitatively, but indicate that the process of declining marginal returns is continuing. Adjusted for inflation, each dollar invested in energy production in 1960 yielded approximately 2,250,000 BTUs. By 1970 this had declined to 2,168,000 BTUs, while in 1976 the same dollar could produce only 1,845,000 BTUs (Rifkin with Howard 1980: 124). The world's consumers do not need to be shown such figures to know that energy and minerals production follows the classic curve of declining marginal returns.

Information processing

The processing of large quantities of information is an essential aspect of complex societies, and indeed the need for this processing is probably one of the reasons that such societies came into existence. Yet the costs of information processing, in many spheres, show a trend of declining marginal productivity.

Gregory Johnson (1982) has shown graphically that as the size of a social group increases, the communication load increases even faster. Information processing increases in response until capacity is reached. After this point, information processing performance deteriorates, so that greater costs are allocated to processing that is less efficient and reliable. At this point information processing hierarchies may be expected to develop (Johnson 1982: 394-5).

In the same vein, Moore has suggested that when the amount of information processed by a society is small, much can be collected at low cost. As the amount of information spreads, however, the marginal cost of useful information grows rapidly, in part because redundancy of information increases (1981: 212).

Complex societies engage in a large number of information-processing activities. Among those for which data could be gathered that would be pertinent to the present problem are: research and development, education, and development/maintenance of information channels. These are certainly not the only spheres of information processing in complex societies, but they are essential ones.

The marginal productivity of research and development (R&D) in the United States, and elsewhere, displays a disturbing trend. Fig. 9 shows clearly that as the number of scientists, engineers, and technicians in the United States rose between 1900 and 1954, their productivity, as reflected in patents issued, declined sharply. Furthermore, the number of patent applications relative to the population of the United States rose until about 1920, and then began to decline. Patent applications

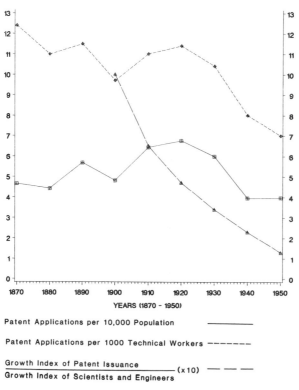

Fig. 9. Patent applications and issues in respect to population and scientific/technical personnel, 1870–1950 (data from Machlup 1962: 172).

filed between 1941 and 1960, relative to personnel and expenditures committed to research and development, declined noticeably (Fig. 10).

At first glance these charts seem to indicate declining marginal returns for investment in research and development. Some additional discussion is necessary, though, to demonstrate that this is so. Fritz Machlup, the source of these data, suggests that three factors may potentially account for them: (a) declining productivity of inventing; (b) decline in proportion of patentable inventions; and (c) decline in propensity to patent (1962: 174-5). Various economists have made similar suggestions (e.g., Schmookler 1966; Griliches 1984). Machlup suggests that the major part of the decline in patenting is due to the growth of military R&D, which does not usually yield patentable inventions.

Despite Machlup's caution, a number of factors suggest that the productivity of research and development has indeed declined. For one thing, the data in Fig. 9 show that patents have been declining in respect to population and number of technical workers since about 1920, well before the R&D effort of World War II and thereafter. Even more significantly, patenting relative to numbers of scientists and engineers has declined continuously since 1900. Jacob Schmookler has compiled figures showing that, *excluding* government-financed projects, the number of industrial research

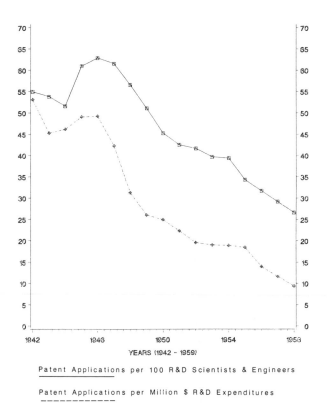

Fig. 10. Patent applications in respect to research inputs (data from Machlup 1962: 173).

personnel increased 5.6 times from 1930 to 1954, while the numbers of corporate patents rose between 1936-40 and 1956-60 by only 23 percent (1966: 28-9).

The problem, furthermore, is not restricted to the United States. In a survey of 50 countries (many of which do not invest heavily in military R&D), Evenson showed that inventions per scientist and engineer have declined in nearly all cases between the late 1960s and the late 1970s (1984: 89). In both the U.S. and Japan, between 1964 and 1979-80, the ratio of patents to productive inputs fell in almost all industries. In the U.S. between 1964 and 1978 R&D spending per scientist and engineer increased at an annual rate of .0047, while patenting declined at an annual rate of .0283. There has been a similar pattern in Japan (Evenson 1984: 107-8).

There are, moreover, other data suggesting declining productivity of inventing activity in the industrial world. Hornell Hart has demonstrated consistent patterns of increasing and then declining rates of patenting (logistic curves) in many fields that are partially or wholly unrelated to military R&D. These include airplanes, automobiles, cotton machinery, electric meters, radios, sewing machines, spinning machinery, sulky plows, telegraphy, telephony, typewriters, and weaving machinery (Hart 1945: 338). He also noted that the same patterns are evident in the major inventions and discoveries of the Western world, and in patents sealed in Great Britain between 1751 and 1820, and between 1821 and 1938 (Hart 1945: 338).

Thus, it seems that military R&D cannot account for more than a small part of the decline in patents. Furthermore, the decline is widespread in so many fields, over such a long time, that declining propensity to patent can hardly account for it either. Recent research shows that there is in fact a strong positive relationship between R&D and patenting (Schmookler 1966: 44-6; Bound et al. 1984: 39; Pakes and Griliches 1984: 63). Thus the patent statistics appear to be a reliable indicator of inventive accomplishment.

It would appear that there has indeed been a genuine drop in the inventive productivity of research and development, and that as investments in R&D have increased (from 0.1 percent of gross national product in 1920 to 2.6 percent in 1960 [Rescher 1978: 67]), the marginal product of these investments has declined. Although there are some demurrals (e.g., Clark and Griliches 1984), many economists recognize this trend (e.g., Mansfield 1971: 32, 34-5; Nordhaus 1969: 20-4; Denison 1979: 126; Sato and Suzawa 1983: 65).

Medical research and application provide a good example of a declining marginal return for increased investment in a scientific field. While it is less easy to measure the benefits of medicine than its costs, one sure indicator is life expectancy. Unfortunately, ever larger investments in health care do not yield proportionate increases in longevity. In 1930 the United States expended 3.3 percent of its gross national product (GNP) to produce an average life expectancy of 59.7 years. By 1982, 10.5 percent of GNP was producing a life expectancy of 74.5 years. The pattern in the intervening years is shown in Fig. 11. It can be seen from this chart that from 1930 to 1982 the productivity of the U.S. national health care system (measured thus) declined by over 57 percent (after Worthington [1975: 5] and U.S. Bureau of the Census [1983: 73, 102]). (In fact, it is likely that the decline in the productivity of medicine has been even greater, for the effects of improved nutrition and sanitation on increasing life expectancy have not been included.)

As surprising as it may seem, investment in education also shows a trend of declining marginal productivity. To begin with, a complex society that must process large quantities of information will be faced with costs for education that will almost certainly rise. Between 1870 and 1960 the proportion of the population between the ages of 18 and 21 enrolled in institutions of higher education in the United States increased from 1.7 percent to 33.5 percent (Machlup 1962: 78). Moreover, the institutions of higher learning in which these students were enrolled consumed a portion of the gross national product that rose from 0.26 percent in 1900 to 1.23 percent in 1960 (Fig. 12) (Machlup 1962: 79). The number of students per faculty member declined from 12.8 in 1900 to 9.5 in 1958 (Machlup 1962: 81). At the same time, more and more students pursued educational courses that were longer and more specialized (Fig. 13), and more costly (Fig. 12) (Machlup 1962: 79, 91). The national cost of higher education, both actual and relative, has clearly increased.

But hasn't this increased investment in higher education brought at least equivalent, if not greater, returns? While the returns on investment in education are difficult to assess, most people would assume that the answer to that question must be yes. But there are ways of looking at the matter that suggest that this investment has

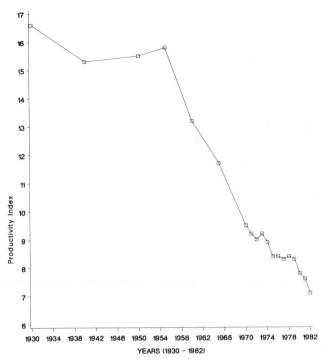

Fig. 11. Productivity of the U.S. health care system, 1930–82 (data from Worthington [1975: 5] and U.S. Bureau of the Census [1983: 73, 102]). Productivity index = (Life expectancy)/(National health expenditures as percent of GNP).

not brought greater *marginal* returns. With increasing time spent in education and greater specialization, the learning that occurs yields decreased *general* benefits for greater costs. The greatest *quantities* of learning are accomplished in infancy; learning that occurs earlier in life tends to be more generalized. Later, specialized learning is dependent upon this earlier, generalized knowledge, so that the benefits of generalized learning include all derivative specialized knowledge. Axiomatically, therefore, generalized learning is of overall greater value than specialized.

Moreover, this early, generalized learning is accomplished at substantially lower cost. Machlup (1962: 104-5) has compiled figures showing that, in 1957-8, education of pre-school children in the home cost the United States $4,432,000,000 (in income foregone by mothers), which yields $886,400,000 per year for ages 0 through 5. Elementary and secondary education cost $33,339,000,000, or $2,564,538,462 per year for ages 6 through 18. Higher education cost $12,757,000,000, or $2,514,000,000 per year for far fewer students, assuming an average of five years spent in higher education. In other words, the monetary cost to the nation of a year of education between pre-school, when the most generalized, highly useful education takes place, and college, when the most specialized learning is accomplished, increases by about 284 percent. And this increase would be even more dramatic if these figures took into account the fact that college enrollment is but a fraction of the available population.

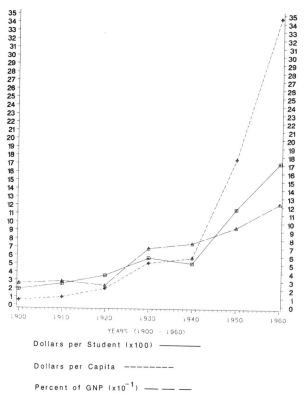

Fig. 12. American expenditures on higher education, 1900–60 (data from Machlup 1962: 79).

Similarly, Fig. 14 shows that the overall productivity of investment in higher education for the development of specialized expertise has declined substantially since 1900. D. Price has demonstrated, in regard to the education of scientists, that educating more scientists causes those of average ability to increase in number faster than those who are most productive (1963: 102-3). Thus, increasing investments in specialized education yield declines in both marginal and average returns.

In 1924, S.G. Strumilin collected in the Soviet Union a set of educational data that reveal a corroborative pattern. He showed that the marginal return on investment in education declines with increasing education. The first two years of education, according to Strumilin, raise a Soviet worker's production skills an average of 14.5 percent per year. Yet the third year of education yields an increase of only an additional 8 percent, while the fourth through sixth years raise skills only a further 4-5 percent per year (Tul'chinskii 1967: 51-2).

Such examples indicate the kinds of costs incurred by complex societies that must invest resources in preparing people for specialized tasks. While the performance of these tasks may be quite essential to the society's needs, it cannot be claimed that benefits for investment in education increase proportionate to costs. To the contrary, increasingly specialized training serves ever narrower segments of the system, at ever greater cost to the society as a whole. What is more, the benefits derived from

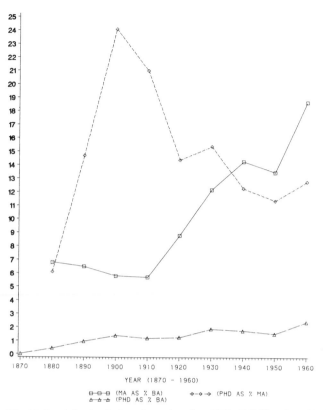

YEAR (1870 - 1960)

⊟─⊟─⊟ (MA AS % BA)   ◇─◇─◇ (PHD AS % MA)
△─△─△ (PHD AS % BA)

Fig. 13. Specialization in American education, 1870–1960 (data from Machlup 1962: 91).

specialized training are equally attributable to the generalized education which necessarily precedes it. Specialized training can be costly in other ways. Where flexibility is required in task performance, specialized personnel may not be capable of performing tasks for which they were not prepared. And where the need for certain kinds of specialized tasks arises and disappears, the investment in training may be largely wasted. Contemporary transformations in industry, and in its trained, specialized personnel, illustrate this point tragically.

A society able to meet its needs by generalized education will inevitably, then, obtain greater value for its investment than will a society dependent on specialized training. As complexity and specialization increase, the cost of education does also, while its marginal product declines.

A complex society must invest heavily in the development and maintenance of information channels. While it is not possible to show with available data that this yields a declining marginal product, it can be shown that it is an increasingly costly activity. Between 1940 and 1957, expenditures for radio and television services in the United States increased from 0.57 to 1.00 percent of GNP (Machlup 1962: 253). Telephone operating revenues, from 1880 to 1958, grew from 0.03 to 1.73 percent of GNP (Machlup 1962: 253). The important point to note from these figures is that when a sphere such as information processing acquires an increasing share of a

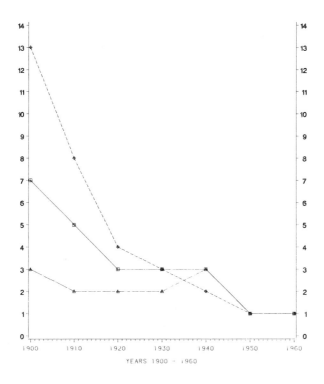

YEARS 1900 - 1960

(PHD/BA)/DOLLARS PER STUDENT X .001 —————
(PHD/MA)/DOLLARS PER STUDENT X .01 ————————
(MA/BA)/DOLLARS PER STUDENT X .01 — —— —

Fig. 14. Productivity of educational investment for the development of specialized expertise (data from Machlup 1962: 79, 91).

society's available resources (in this case, GNP), the share available for other spheres must automatically decline.

Sociopolitical control and specialization

There is in complex societies a recurrent and seemingly inexorable trend toward declining marginal productivity in hierarchical specialization. So widespread is this trend that, in democratic nations, entire political careers have been successfully based on rallying voters against it. C. Northcote Parkinson comes immediately to mind as the writer who has most effectively conjured the vision of bloated bureaucracies growing ever larger, devouring ever more of the produce of taxpayers, and producing ever less of real value (1957). And although much of his writing has a superficial tone, he has compiled some informative statistics to back up his view. Table 2 shows that, between 1914 and 1967, the number of capital ships in the British Navy declined by 78.9 percent, the number of officers and enlisted men by 32.9 percent, and the number of dockyard workers by 33.7 percent. Yet during this period the number of dockyard officials and clerks increased by 247 percent, and the number of Admiralty officials by 769 percent (Parkinson 1957: 8; 1971: 4). Table 3 shows that between 1935 and 1954 the number of officials in the British Colonial Office increased by 447

Table 2. *British Admiralty statistics, 1914-67*[1]

Year	Capital ships	Officers & men in Royal Navy	Dockyard workers	Dockyard officials and clerks	Admiralty officials and clerks
1914	542	125,000	57,000	3,249	4,366
1928	317	90,700	62,439	4,558	7,729
1938	308	89,500	39,022	4,423	11,270
1948	413	134,400	48,252	6,120	31,636
1958	238	94,900	40,164	6,219	32,237
1964	182	84,900	41,563	7,395	32,035
1967	114	83,900	37,798	8,013	33,574

[1]After Parkinson (1957: 8, 1971: 4).

Table 3. *British Colonial Office officials*[1]

Year	1935	1939	1943	1947	1954
Number of officials	372	450	817	1139	1661

[1]After Parkinson (1957: 11).

percent. During this same period, of course, the empire administered by these officials shrank considerably (Parkinson 1957: 11).

Parkinson has elsewhere suggested that, beyond a certain point, increasing taxation begins to yield declining marginal returns. Two of the reasons for this are increased avoidance on the part of taxpayers, requiring still further bureaucracy to enforce compliance, and inflation, which reduces the value of the money collected. Beyond a rate of 20 percent, Parkinson suggests, the marginal return on taxation declines (1960: 79). Such views, as is well known, figure prominently in current political and economic debates.

Parkinson (1957) indicted bureaucratic self-serving to account for declining marginal returns on investment in hierarchical specialists. However comforting to some, this is far too simplistic an explanation. Bendix (1956) has compiled for private industry, in several nations, data similar to those Parkinson has uncovered in government. He was able to show that a pattern of increasing hierarchical specialization characterizes the private sector as strongly as Parkinson has demonstrated for the public (Fig. 15). Clearly in the private sector, where economic success depends on efficiency, this pattern cannot be attributed to self-serving inefficiency. The reason why complex organizations must allocate ever larger portions of their personnel and other resources to administration is because (as discussed in Chapter 2) increased complexity requires greater quantities of information processing and greater integration of disparate parts.

Even popular government products are subject to the law of diminishing returns.

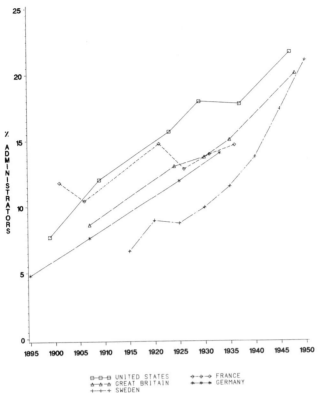

Fig. 15. Ratios of administrative and production employees in five countries for selected years (after Bendix 1956: 216).

Mohring (1965) has shown that as the ratio of high speed freeway capacity to street capacity increases, the marginal return on investment in freeway construction declines sharply.

Overall economic productivity

Complex societies with large, well-developed economies have historically been able to sustain only rather inferior rates of economic growth. Latecomers to economic growth tend to have higher growth rates than early starters (Rostow with Fordyce 1978: 48). This is evident in Table 4, which shows that rates of economic growth are highest in middle income countries, followed by high income and low income nations (Kristensen 1974: 27). Kristensen (1974: 28) infers from these data that, through time, rates of economic growth tend to slow down, as projected in Fig. 16. Such a trend suggests that societies with more developed economies face a situation in which the productivity of GNP for stimulating further growth tends to decline.

Although some authors (e.g. Schmookler 1962) believe that technical innovation responds to economic productivity, there are also data suggesting that technical innovation often occurs along a curve of declining marginal productivity. Fig. 17 shows reductions in fuel consumption of steam engines resulting from increases in

Table 4. *Variations in economic growth*[1]

GNP per capita (1967 dollars)	Percentage annual growth of GNP per capita, 1960-70
1801 or more	3.4
1101-1800	3.5
701-1100	6.5
401-700	4.4
201-400	2.9
101-200	2.6
100 or less	1.7

[1]After Kristensen (1974: 27).

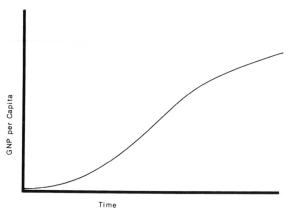

Fig. 16. Growth of GNP per capita. From *Development in Rich and Poor Countries* by Thorkil Kristensen, p. 28. Copyright © 1974 by Praeger Publishers, Inc. Reprinted by permission of Praeger Publishers.

thermal efficiency, from the early eighteenth to the middle twentieth centuries. In such a field, technical innovation slows down as returns for improvement diminish. For the steam engine, the remaining possibilities of fuel-saving were reduced as thermal efficiency was increased. A doubling of efficiency in this century would save much less fuel, per engine, than would a 10 percent increase in the eighteenth century, and the saving would be much harder to achieve (Wilkinson 1973: 144-5).

Zolotas has argued that the productivity of industrialism for producing social welfare is declining. In partial support of this assertion he points out that while U.S. per capita product increased 75 percent from 1950 to 1977, weekly work hours declined by only 9.5 percent (Zolotas 1981: 92-3).

Explaining declining marginal returns in complex societies

The discerning reader might reasonably question much that was presented in the preceding section. It might be said that examples of declining marginal productivity have deliberately been sought, and that the role of technological innovation in alleviating such problems was not considered. In fact, what was presented are simply

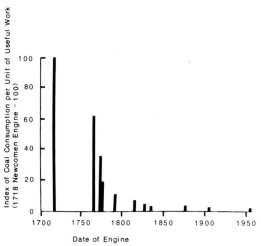

Fig. 17. Reductions in fuel consumption of steam engines resulting from increases in thermal efficiency (after Wilkinson 1973: 144). Reproduced by permission of Methuen & Co., London.

examples of what is proposed to be a problem common to many situations of increasing complexity, intensification in resource extraction, and economic growth. The fact that such examples can be compiled does not mean that all economic trends follow the same curve, nor that socioeconomic processes in complex societies follow only the law of diminishing returns. It also does not mean that such trends occurring in any specific sphere are irreversible. Where this law is operative, however, serious consequences can be expected, and those are the situations of interest here. The role of technological innovation is another matter; more will be said about it later. Suffice to say at this point that technical innovation in at least some cases (e.g., steam engines, as just described) can be shown to decline in its marginal product over time (e.g., Wilkinson 1973: 144-5).

The proposition that societies regularly face declining productivity for investment in complexity can be more securely demonstrated if it can be shown *why* this is so. This can indeed be done for the four spheres just discussed.

Agriculture and resource production

The reason why intensification in agriculture and resource production follows a pattern of declining marginal productivity is fairly easy to show, due to the work of Boserup (1965, 1981), Clark and Haswell (1966), and Wilkinson (1973). Simply put, rationally-acting human populations will first exploit those resources that yield the best return per unit of effort, and still meet the needs of the population. If this is so, then it follows that any change in resource extraction must be in the direction of using resources that are more costly to obtain, process, distribute, and/or market, so that the marginal product of labor and other inputs declines. Thus, hunters and gatherers first exploit foods that are higher in nutritional value, and easier to obtain and process, than resources that are less favorable for these characteristics (Asch, Ford, and Asch 1972). Populations employ labor-conserving, extensive patterns of land use, such as hunting and gathering, prior to labor-consuming, intensive patterns such as agriculture (Cohen 1977). Among those who practice agriculture, extensive systems, such as slash-and-burn, are preferred to intensive ones (Boserup 1965). Among intensive agriculturalists, lower labor quantities per unit of return are preferred to higher (Clark and Haswell 1966).

In other spheres of resource extraction, minerals and energy forms can be ranked in terms of their ease of discovery, extraction, processing, and use. Resources that rank higher in these dimensions will be used before resources that don't, and when these are no longer sufficient, secondary resources will be employed. The shift from wood to coal in England and the United States is a case in point (Wilkinson 1973). In the contemporary petroleum industry, the extraction of less readily available deposits by secondary and tertiary recovery techniques yields a product with a substantially higher monetary cost but no greater energy value.

There are of course ambiguities in these matters. It would be unwise to assume that human populations always behave with economic rationality, and even when they attempt to, information may not be available to ensure success. Further, people do some things for reasons that are not *directly* economic, but these activities nonetheless consume resources. Acquisition of distant, costly, and rare prestige goods is a ready example.

Such uncertainties are easily answered. Among *whatever* set of resources a population obtains, for *whatever* reasons, the law of diminishing returns is likely to apply. As demand for a commodity grows, increased production will at some point mean depletion or insufficiency of the least costly sources. At that point, more costly sources must be used, with declining marginal returns.

For the present purposes, it need not be argued that population growth is the sole driving force behind intensification in resource production. No doubt it often is, as in post-Medieval England (Wilkinson 1973), but other factors can also create rising commodity demands.

Information processing

Why does information processing often show a declining marginal return? Why do investment in education, and in research and development, result in decreasing productivity? The answers in both spheres are similar.

The case of education was touched on earlier. Reiterating in brief: general education, which occurs in the earliest years of life, is of the most lasting, widespread value. It is also attained at the lowest comparative cost. Later, more specialized training is considerably costlier. Its benefits may apply only to narrow segments of the society, while its costs are spread throughout the system. It may institutionalize rigidity where flexibility is called for. What is more, the benefits of specialized training are at least partly attributable to the generalized knowledge on which it depends. Axiomatically, then, general knowledge will always yield greater benefits than specialized. A society that can meet its needs through generalized education will obtain greater marginal returns on its investment than a society dependent on specialized training.

The situation in research and development is similar. As with education, specialized scientific knowledge depends upon prior, general principles. Within a scientific field, early work develops the general parameters of the discipline, the nature of the subject matter, the scope of inquiry, broad research questions, and like matters. And although much of this early work may come to be rejected by later scholars (Kuhn 1962), nevertheless there is also substantial derivation from it (Schwartz 1971: 43). Thus, the product of early, generalized work in a scientific field includes all knowledge derived from later, specialized research. And so – again axiomatically – specialized work can never yield the benefits achieved by earlier, generalized research. It is no coincidence that the most famous practitioners historically in each field tend to be persons who were instrumental in developing the field, and in establishing its basic outline. No Einsteinian physicist, no Darwinian biologist, and no Marxist social scientist will ever achieve the fame and influence of these masters who revolutionized their fields.

Yet science is not completely a cumulative, linear process. Rethinking, reformulation, and outright rejection of earlier work are commonplace (Kuhn 1962). When new schools of thought (what Kuhn [1962] calls 'paradigms') emerge through scientific revolutions, a new, generalized groundwork is laid upon which later, specialized work is built. The movement from general and most widely applicable, to specific and most narrowly focused (which characterizes the history of a scientific field), is duplicated repeatedly in the cycle of revolution, paradigm development, paradigm application, and revolution that Kuhn (1962) has noted. Again, the knowledge of greatest lasting benefit comes from the general formulations which initiate a paradigm, while the scientists who accomplish this tend to become more famous than their successors who produce derivative work.

Rostow (1980: 170-1) has graphed what he argues is the characteristic marginal product curve of individual branches of science. As shown in Fig. 18, Rostow projects that marginal productivity will first rise and then decline in each specific field (although he asserts that the marginal product for science as a whole continually rises). Sato and Suzawa argue analogously for technical progress: that its production function has the standard neoclassical properties of diminishing returns to R&D expenditures (1983: 65).

The decreasing benefits from specialized, derivative work, viewed from the perspective of the overall history of science, are acquired at substantially greater cost. The costs to societies of early support of science tended to be minimal (and as D. Price cogently noted, in many cases '...society almost dared [scientists] to exist' [1963: 107]). Generally, as in the ancient Mediterranean or Medieval Europe, it consisted of little more than the support of individual naturalists or mathematicians and their students, or the support of religious specialists who also performed scientific inquiry. Science today, in contrast, is a costly process involving complex institutions, sophisticated technology, and large, interdisciplinary research teams (cf. Schwartz 1971: 267-8). This costly science certainly produces astonishing results, but these cannot be claimed to be more valuable than the generalized knowledge of earlier, less expensive science. As impressive, for example, as modern travel technology is, it is

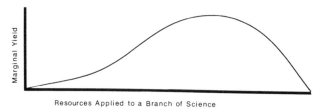

Fig. 18. Marginal yield in a branch of science (after Rostow 1980: 171). Reproduced by permission of Macmillan Publishers Ltd., London and Basingstoke.

hard to argue that it is of greater consequence than the development of the wheel, or of water craft, or of the steam engine. As astounding as it is to put human beings on the moon, this is not of greater import than the principles of geometry or the theory of gravity. However valuable may be genetic engineering, the benefits of this complex process must always be attributed in part to the nearly cost-free work of Gregor Mendel.

The contemporary field of archaeology provides a useful, if anecdotal, example. Archaeology in the United States during the nineteenth and early twentieth centuries was a low-cost, generalized affair, supported initially by individuals, local interest societies, and philanthropic institutions. Government spending in support of archaeology during the nineteenth century was comparatively small. By the mid-twentieth century Federal support, primarily through the National Science Foundation, had substantially increased. In the 1970s and 1980s Federal and private support grew exponentially, due to Federally-mandated conservation and recovery of archaeological data in the face of land development. Vastly larger sums have been expended on archaeology in the United States in the last fifteen years than ever before.

Has this produced knowledge exceeding, or even equivalent to, that derived from earlier, low-cost research? While the question is impossible to respond to in any quantitative sense, many professionals feel the answer is no. Early archaeology established the parameters of the field, defined regional and temporal variation, established rudimentary chronologies, and did a remarkably good job of setting out basic lines of inquiry. More recent, highly funded archaeology, asserts one critic, has not succeeded in answering a single, major research question (King 1981). (A related point worth recalling here is the fact, discussed in Chapter 2, that the major current explanations for the origin of the state were basically set out over 2000 years ago [Haas 1982]. Modern, costly research has still achieved no universally acceptable answer to these ancient questions.)

What has happened? Are archaeologists, as some assert, interested more in material rewards than in production of knowledge? Are we, as others believe, merely a profession of unimaginative muddlers? While these characterizations might describe some practitioners, they do not account for the current lack of scientific breakthroughs. The answer is that archaeology has followed the direction taken by other disciplines. It has become highly specialized and costly. Furthermore, the narrowly-focused, intensive research questions being asked today are harder to answer than those of the past. There are two reasons for this. One is that the profession now demands higher standards of fieldwork and analysis. But perhaps more importantly, in any field, as each research question among the stock waiting to be answered is resolved, the costliness of deciphering the remainder increases.

Admittedly such a view is oversimplified, for it is unlikely that there is any finite 'stock' of research questions waiting to be answered in a field (cf. Kuhn 1962). The point, however, has illustrative value. As more generalized knowledge is established early in the history of a discipline, only more specialized work remains to be done. This tends to be more costly and difficult to resolve, so that increasing investments yield declining marginal returns. Hence, contemporary archaeology appears to be unproductive, not because its practitioners are so, but because they are forced to grapple with increasingly complex questions. Where archaeology once asked primarily factual questions (what, where, and when?) that were inexpensive to answer, the focus today is more often on the difficult topic of *explaining* cultural processes.

This is probably a good part of the reason for the declining productivity of research and development. Modern science is becoming less productive *overall* (there are always countervailing trends in some fields) because it has become increasingly specialized and expensive, and has depleted much of the stock of less costly questions. The principles of gravity and of natural selection no longer wait to be discovered. They have been replaced as research foci by more complex matters such as space exploration and genetic engineering. As McCain and Segal have observed, it is not likely that science can still be advanced by flying a kite in a thunderstorm or peering through a homemade microscope (1973: 158).

The great physicist Max Planck, in a statement that Rescher calls 'Planck's Principle of Increasing Effort,' noted that '...with every advance [in science] the difficulty of the task is increased' (Rescher 1980: 80). As easier questions are resolved, science moves inevitably to more complex research areas and to larger, costlier organizations (Rescher 1980: 93-4). It is at least in part for this reason that U.S. defense expenditures (with their great emphasis on complex technologies and R&D) grew from 0.7 percent of GNP in 1913 to 10 percent in 1970 (Mishan 1977: 239). 'As science progresses within any of its specialized branches,' writes Rescher, 'there is a marked increase in the over-all resource-cost to realizing scientific findings of a given level [of] intrinsic significance...' (1978: 80). Thus from 1966 to 1971 constant dollar expenditures in the average National Institutes of Health project rose 13 percent, with no comparable increase in the apparent merit of the research (Rescher 1980: 85). *Exponential* growth in the size and costliness of science, in fact, is necessary simply to maintain a *constant* rate of progress (Rescher 1980: 92). So as D. Price noted in 1963, science is growing faster than either the population or the economy, and of all scientists who had ever lived, 80-90 percent were still alive at the time of his writing.

The declining productivity of the U.S. health care system becomes intelligible in this light. Rescher points out:

> Once all of the findings at a given state-of-the-art level of investigative technolo-
> gy have been realized, one must move to a more expensive level... In natural
> science we are involved in a technological arms race: with every 'victory over

nature' the difficulty of achieving the breakthroughs which lie ahead is increased (1980: 94, 97).

The declining productivity of medicine is due to the fact that the inexpensive diseases and ailments were conquered first (the basic research that led to penicillin costing no more than $20,000), so that those remaining are more difficult and costly to resolve (Rescher 1978: 85-6, 1980: 52). Moreover, as each increasingly expensive disease is conquered, the increment to average life expectancy becomes ever smaller. And in fighting a new malady such as Acquired Immune Deficiency Syndrome, large sums are spent simply trying to prevent a *drop* in life expectancy.

Sociopolitical control and specialization

Control and specialization are the very essence of a complex society. The reasons why investment in complexity yields a declining marginal return are: (a) increasing size of bureaucracies; (b) increasing specialization of bureaucracies; (c) the cumulative nature of organizational solutions; (d) increasing taxation; (e) increasing costs of legitimizing activities; and (f) increasing costs of internal control and external defense. These spheres are intertwined, and will be discussed together.

Human social evolution has proceeded from lower to higher cost. As discussed earlier in this chapter, more complex social forms require greater support costs per capita. In the process of increasing complexity, less costly social features have been added before more costly ones. Thus, part-time leadership has preceded full-time; generalized administration has preceded and given way to specialized. Where at one stage in the development of a political hierarchy multiple administrative functions tend to be carried out by a single individual, a common trend among human organizations is to respond to problems by developing specialized administrators, and by increasing the proportion of the population engaged in administrative tasks. In many cases this increased, more costly complexity will yield *no* increased benefits, at other times the benefits will not be proportionate to the added costs.

If increased complexity develops to deal with internal unrest or external threats, this solution may yield no tangible benefit for much of the population. Arms races present a classic example. Increasing costs of military hardware, and military and civilian personnel, when undertaken to meet a competitor's like increases, yield no increased security for the added cost. Such increased costs are often undertaken merely to maintain the balance-of-power status quo. As a military apparatus increases in complexity its administrative costs increase disproportionately, as Parkinson's (1957, 1971) figures indicate, usually to little or no competitive advantage.

Technological investments in military hardware, moreover, follow the marginal return curve of all technological developments. Improvement innovations (as in the steam engine) become harder to achieve and yield declining marginal benefits. Scherer concludes, for example, that the F-4 warplane was a greater technological leap relative to the subsonic F-85 or F-86 than the more recent F-15 was to the F-4 (1984: 266).

Similarly, if increased complexity is undertaken because of a need for hierarchical administration of, say, agricultural production, the results are likely to be the provision of no more than the base subsistence level for the population so served. This would probably average around 2000 calories per person per day. Now this same population, at a previous point in their history, were probably able to provide themselves with these same 2000 calories without the cost of an administrative hierarchy. For whatever reason – whether population growth, soil deterioration, or climatic fluctuation – the population later comes to require the development of a hierarchy to reverse a trend of declining agricultural output. When this occurs, the per capita subsistence yield may be returned to the base level, yet now this is accomplished at considerably greater cost. The marginal productivity of the interlinked administrative-agricultural system has declined.

Organizational solutions tend to be cumulative. Once developed, complex social features are rarely dropped. Tax rates go up more often than they go down. Information processing needs tend to move in only one direction. Numbers of specialists ordinarily don't decline. Standing armies rarely get smaller. Welfare and legitimizing costs are not likely to drop. An ever increasing stock of monumental architecture requires maintenance. Compensation of elites rarely goes down. What this means is that when there is growth in complexity it tends to be exponential, always increasing by some fraction of an already inflated size.

Complex societies, by their very nature, tend to experience cumulative organizational problems. As systems develop more parts, and more complex interactions among these parts, the potential for problems, conflicts, and incongruities develops disproportionately. Mancur Olson has produced a good example of how complexity itself breeds further costs. Among contemporary societies, as regulations are issued and taxes established, lobbyists seek loopholes and regulators strive to close these. There is increased need for specialists to deal with such matters. An unending spiral unfolds of loophole discovery and closure, with complexity and costs continuously increasing (Olson 1982: 69-73). Perrow (1984) has shown how in technological systems, the potential for catastrophic accidents increases solely by virtue of more complex linkages among parts. The cost of preventing accidents must therefore also rise.

Any complex hierarchy must allocate a portion of its resource base to solving the problems of the population it administers, but must also set aside resources to solve problems created by its own existence, and created by virtue of overall societal complexity. Prior to the development of modern welfare states it is likely that these increased administrative costs did little for the population as a whole other than to maintain some semblance of basic needs. And often even that was not accomplished.

To maintain growth in complexity, hierarchies levy heavier taxes on their populations. At some point even this yields declining marginal returns. This happens when rates are so high that avoidance increases, and taxation-induced inflation erodes the value of the money collected (Parkinson 1960: 79; Eisenstadt 1963: 152).

Rulers, as discussed in Chapter 2, must constantly legitimize their reigns. Legitimizing activities include such things as external defense and internal order, alleviating the effects of local productivity fluctuations, undertaking local development projects, and providing food and entertainment (as in Imperial Rome) for urban masses. In many cases the productivity of these legitimizing investments will decline. Whatever activities a hierarchy undertakes *initially* to bond a population to itself (providing defense, agricultural development, public works, bread and circuses, and the like) often thereafter become *de rigueur*, so that further bonding activities are at higher cost, with little or no additional benefit to the hierarchy.

This point may require clarification. Consider the situation of a hierarchy that must invest in legitimizing activities among a politically potent but minimally compliant segment of the population. Once this population segment has become accustomed to any pattern of increasing investment in legitimization, continuance of this trajectory is necessary to maintain the compliance status quo. Increased investment in legitimizing activities brings little or no increased compliance, and the marginal return on investment in legitimization correspondingly declines.

The appeasement of urban mobs presents the classic illustration of this principle. Any level of activities undertaken to appease such populations – the bread and circuses syndrome – eventually becomes the expected *minimum*. An increase in the cost of bread and circuses, which seems to have been required in Imperial Rome to legitimize such things as the accession of a new ruler or his continued reign, may bring no increased return beyond a state of non-revolt. Rewards to Roman military personnel would often follow the same pattern, particularly when bounties were granted upon a ruler's accession. Roman soldiers regarded such bounties as a right (Mattingly 1960: 184).

The alternative course is to reduce legitimizing activities and increase other means of behavioral control. Yet in such situations, as resources committed to benefits decline, resources committed to control must increase (Wittfogel 1957: 112; Lenski 1966: 51). Although quantitative cost/benefit data for such control systems are rare, it seems reasonable to infer that as the costs of coercion increase, the benefits (in the form of population compliance) probably do not grow proportionately (Haas 1982: 211). In the United States from 1960 to 1973, for example, an increase in total crime of 258 percent required a rise in law enforcement expenditures of 332 percent (Rescher 1980: 64). Thus the marginal cost of coercion increases, and the marginal return declines.

These remarks are not meant to suggest that social evolution carries *no* benefits, nor that the marginal product of social complexity *always* declines. The marginal product of any investment, as illustrated in Fig. 1, declines only after a certain point; prior to that point benefits increase faster than costs. *Very often*, though, societies do reach a level where continued investment in complexity yields a declining marginal return. At that point the society is investing heavily in an evolutionary course that is becoming less and less productive, where at increased cost it is able to do little more than maintain the status quo.

Overall economic productivity

Per capita rates of economic growth decline with increasing GNP, so that as the economy of a society expands, its rate of growth slows down. Various economists (e.g., Kristensen 1974; Rostow with Fordyce 1978) attribute this in large part to the cost of producing technical knowledge. It has been suggested that high growth rates use up the existing backlog of knowledge, so that growth thereafter must rely on the rate at which new knowledge is created. Growth, therefore, follows a logistic curve. Middle income nations develop a faster growth rate because they are able to simply absorb knowledge and technology developed elsewhere.

This is an interesting perspective, although it may not be readily applicable to the non-capitalist economies of early complex societies. There are, however, reasons to suspect that there is more behind declining economic growth than simply using up existing knowledge. It may well be that an overall trend of declining marginal productivity in a society simply leaves proportionately less capital for investment in future growth. Consider, for example, the plight of a society that must simultaneously face declining marginal productivity in any combination of the following: agriculture, minerals and energy extraction, science, education and information processing, size and costs of civil and military organizations, upkeep of capital stock (such as monumental architecture, or more practical things like aqueducts and bridges), etc. As each of these spheres requires an increased proportion of the society's budget, the portion available for investment in future growth must decline. Such a condition is more likely to characterize a country that has been growing for some time, than a newly emerging nation just entering a phase of growth.

Productivity growth is highly dependent on research and development (Mansfield 1968: 4-5; Sato and Suzawa 1983: 58), which like any scientific endeavor is susceptible to declining marginal returns. Cost records from seventeen research laboratories from 1950 to 1960, compiled by Ellis A. Johnson and Helen S. Milton, show that a doubling of R&D activity was gained only by an investment that grew 450 percent (Wolfle 1960: 517). Productivity growth requires technical innovation, but in the United States each one percent increase in the rate of cumulative R&D can yield an increase in the rate of technical change of only 0.1 to 0.7 percent (Mansfield 1971: 34-5). And once basic innovations have been achieved, derivative work and improvement innovations occur at high cost, with a declining marginal return (Mensch 1979; Scherer 1984).

Explaining collapse
At the beginning of this chapter it was proposed that four concepts would lead to an understanding of collapse. These are:

1. human societies are problem-solving organizations;
2. sociopolitical systems require energy for their maintenance;
3. increased complexity carries with it increased costs per capita; and
4. investment in sociopolitical complexity as a problem-solving response often reaches a point of declining marginal returns.

The first three points may be thought of as the conceptual underpinnings of the fourth, which is the crucial element in the explanation.

A society increasing in complexity does so as a system. That is to say, as some of its interlinked parts are forced in a direction of growth, others must adjust accordingly. For example, if complexity increases to regulate regional subsistence production, investments will be made in hierarchy, in bureaucracy, and in agricultural facilities (such as irrigation networks). The expanding hierarchy requires still further agricultural output for its own needs, as well as increased investment in energy and minerals extraction. An expanded military is needed to protect the assets thus created, requiring in turn its own increased sphere of agricultural and other resources. As more and more resources are drained from the support population to maintain this system, an increased share must be allocated to legitimization or coercion. This increased complexity requires specialized administrators, who consume further shares of subsistence resources and wealth. To maintain the productive capacity of the base population, further investment is made in agriculture, and so on.

The illustration could be expanded, tracing still further the interdependencies within such a growing system, but the point has been made: a society grows in complexity as a system. To be sure, there are instances where one sector of a society grows at the expense of others, but to be maintained as a cohesive whole, a social system can tolerate only certain limits to such conditions.

Thus, it is possible to speak of sociocultural evolution by the encompassing term 'complexity,' meaning by this the interlinked growth of the several subsystems that comprise a society. This growth carries an associated energy cost, which before the development of fossil-fuel economies was largely met by human labor. Growth also yields an array of benefits, including administration of resource storage and distribution, investment in agricultural, energy, and minerals production, internal order and external defense, information processing, and public works. Growth in benefits relative to costs will regularly follow the curve shown in Fig. 19, which is to say that *at*

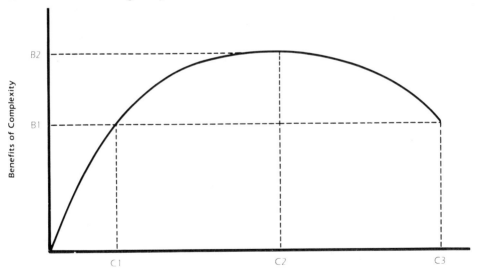

Fig. 19. The marginal product of increasing complexity.

some point in the evolution of a society, continued investment in complexity as a problem-solving strategy yields a declining marginal return. Let us examine this proposition in more detail.

The hypothetical society discussed a few paragraphs above responds to stress by increasing complexity. In so doing it increases investment in agricultural and other resource production, in hierarchy, in information processing, in education and specialized training, in defense, and so forth. The cost-benefit curve for these investments increases at first favorably, for the easiest, most general, most accessible, and least expensive solutions are attempted first. As these solutions are exhausted, however, continued stresses require further investments in complexity. The least costly solutions having been used, evolution now proceeds in a more expensive direction. The hierarchy expands in size, complexity, and specialization; resource production focuses increasingly on sources of supply that are more difficult to acquire and process; agricultural labor intensifies; information processing and training requirements become less generalized; and most likely, an increased military apparatus is seen as the solution to these problems.

What benefits derive from these adjustments? Barring the acquisition of new energy sources, most often through conquest, such increased costs are usually undertaken *merely to maintain the status quo.* Stress that is met by increased complexity might come from such sources as agricultural deterioration, population growth, external danger, internal unrest, and threats to foreign sources of important commodities. When complexity increases to counter such stress, it achieves success when the factors that threaten stability no longer do so. So if agricultural production drops below about 2000 calories per person per day, increased complexity, and attendant agricultural development, may restore it to that level. Where stability is threatened by internal or external sources, increased complexity will achieve success when the prior state of orderliness has been restored, or the frontiers defended. Where the supply of a commodity is threatened, increased complexity and military adventures may ultimately secure an even greater supply of the commodity, but just as often they may not.

Thus a growing sociocultural system ultimately reaches a point such as B1, C1 on the curve in Fig. 19, whereafter investment in further complexity yields increased returns, but at a declining marginal rate. When this point is reached, a complex society enters the phase where it becomes increasingly vulnerable to collapse.

There are two general factors that combine to make a society vulnerable to collapse when investment in complexity begins to yield a declining marginal return. First, stress and perturbation are a constant feature of any complex society, always occurring somewhere in its territory. Such a society will have a developed and operating regulatory apparatus that is designed to deal with such things as localized agricultural failures, border conflicts, and unrest. Since such continuous, localized stress can be expected to recur with regularity it can, to a degree, be anticipated and prepared for. Major, unexpected stress surges, however, will also occur given enough time, as such things as major climatic fluctuations and foreign incursions take place. To meet these major stresses the society must have some kind of net reserve. This can take the form of excess productive capacities in agriculture, energy, or minerals, or hoarded surpluses from past production. Stress surges of great magnitude cannot be accommodated without such a reserve.

Yet a society experiencing declining marginal returns is investing ever more heavily in a strategy that is yielding proportionately less. Excess productive capacity will at some point be used up, and accumulated surpluses allocated to current operating needs. There is, then, little or no surplus with which to counter major adversities. Unexpected stress surges must be dealt with out of the current operating budget, often ineffectually, and always to the detriment of the system as a whole. Even if the stress is successfully met, the society is weakened in the process, and made even more vulnerable to the next crisis. Once a complex society develops the vulnerabilities of declining marginal returns, collapse may merely require sufficient passage of time to render probable the occurrence of an insurmountable calamity.

Secondly, declining marginal returns make complexity a less attractive problem-solving strategy. Where marginal returns decline, the advantages to complexity become ultimately no greater (for the society as a whole) than for less costly social forms. The marginal cost of evolution to a higher level of complexity, or of remaining at the present level, is high compared with the alternative of disintegration.

Under such conditions, the option to decompose (that is, to sever the ties that link localized groups to a regional entity) becomes attractive to certain components of a complex society. As marginal returns deteriorate, tax rates rise with less and less return to the local level. Irrigation systems go untended, bridges and roads are not kept up, and the frontier is not adequately defended. The population, meanwhile, must contribute ever more of a shrinking productive base to support whatever projects the hierarchy is still able to accomplish. Many of the social units that comprise a complex society perceive increased advantage to a strategy of independence, and begin to pursue their own immediate goals rather than the long-term goals of the hierarchy. Behavioral interdependence gives way to behavioral independence, requiring the hierarchy to allocate still more of a shrinking resource base to legitimization and/or control.

Thus, when the marginal cost of participating in a complex society becomes too high, productive units across the economic spectrum increase resistance (passive or active) to the demands of the hierarchy, or overtly attempt to break away. Both the lower ranking strata (the peasant producers of agricultural commodities) and upper ranking strata of wealthy merchants and nobility (who are often called upon to subsidize the costs of complexity) are vulnerable to such temptations. Effective political action on the part of peasantry can generally take place only when they are allied with other strata. This strategy is rarely employed, the usual course being recurrent peasant upheavals. Even still, peasantry can effectively weaken a hierarchy by other means when their marginal return for participating in a complex system is too low. A common strategy is the development of apathy to the well-being of the polity (Eisenstadt 1963: 207-10). In both the later Roman and Byzantine Empires the overtaxed peasantry offered little resistance to the foreign incursions that ultimately toppled these regimes (A. Jones 1964, 1974; Charanis 1953: 420).

And so, societies faced with declining marginal returns for investment in complexity face a downward spiral from problems that seem insurmountable. Declining resources and rising marginal costs sap economic strength, so that services to the population cannot be sustained. As unrest grows among producers, increased resources from a dwindling supply must be allocated to legitimization and/or control. The economic sustaining base becomes weakened, and its members either actively or passively reduce their support for the polity. Reserve resources to meet unexpected stress surges are consumed for operating expenses. Ultimately, the society either disintegrates as localized entities break away, or is so weakened that it is toppled militarily, often with very little resistance. In either case, sociopolitical organization is reduced to the level that can be sustained by local resources.

At this point it would be profitable to discuss Fig. 19 in further detail. A society evolving in complexity undertakes a continuously escalating set of investments, as discussed throughout this chapter. At some point the investment/benefit ratio for this strategy reaches point B1, C1 in Fig. 19. Marginal productivity has reached the point where it can no longer rise, *given the basic technology and energy resources available.* Beyond this point, for at least a while, benefits still rise in response to increasing complexity, but at a declining *marginal* rate.

The region on the marginal product curve (Fig. 19) between B1, C1, and B2, C2 depicts a realm in which a complex society experiences increased adversity and dissatisfaction. Stress begins to be increasingly perceived, and if modern history is any guide, ideological strife (for example, between growth and no-growth factions) may become noticeable. The system as a whole engages in 'scanning' behavior, seeking alternatives that might provide a preferable adaptation. This scanning may result in the adoption by segments of the society of a variety of new ideologies and life-styles, many of them of foreign derivation (such as the proliferation of new religions in Imperial Rome). Some of these may be perceived by the hierarchy as hostile and subversive, others become briefly fashionable. At the same time, in an industrial society facing declining marginal returns, there may be increased investment in research and development (to the extent that declining resources permit), as solutions to declining productivity are sought, and in education, as individuals position themselves to reap a maximum share of a perceptibly faltering economy. Taxes rise, and inflation becomes noticeable. Prior to point B2, C2 investment and intensification can still produce positive benefits, but collapse becomes increasingly likely.

The region between B2, C2 and B1, C3 is critical. In this part of the curve increasing complexity may actually bring decreased overall benefits, as the economic system and the sustaining base are taxed to the point where productivity declines. All segments of the society compete for a shrinking economic product. This is a realm of extreme vulnerability, as a major perturbation or stress surge will impinge on a society that has inadequate reserves. Surplus production for investment in research and development has declined. The scanning behavior of the previous stage may be terminated, as the hierarchy imposes rigid behavioral controls (as in later Imperial Rome) in an attempt to increase efficiency.

As such a society evolves along the curve beyond B2, C2 it traverses a continuum of points, such as B1, C3, where costs for complexity are increasing but the benefits have actually declined to those previously available at some lower level of investment. Thus the benefits derived from investment at B1, C3 are no higher than those available at B1, C1, but the marginal productivity of this latter point is far preferable. A society at B1, C3 is in serious danger of collapse from decomposition (as well as from any external threat), as constituent social units recognize that a strategy of severing their ties to the regional entity might yield highly increased marginal productivity (or however it may be conceptualized). The resulting rebellions and peasant wars further weaken the polity. At a point such as B1, C3 rapid disintegration, of the type that Renfrew (1979) predicts from the topological mathematics of Catastrophe Theory, is likely and expectable.

One important question is why an equilibrium situation does not develop when marginal productivity can no longer rise. Why can't a society that has reached some optimum cost/benefit ratio for its investment in complexity simply rest on its accomplishments? While long-term equilibrium may be possible in comparatively simple foraging societies that are demographically flexible, it is less likely in more complex settings of greater density. Hunter-gatherers typically have the option of dispersing under resource shortages, so that population density is lowered in a distressed area. So long as new land is available, agriculturalists often have the same option (e.g., Renfrew 1982: 275; North and Thomas 1973; Rostow 1960: 34). Where demographic and/or sociopolitical factors limit the option of dispersal for a large segment of a population, though, the solution to stress must often be greater economic and/or sociopolitical investment. Since all human populations experience recurrent stresses, complex societies must constantly develop organizational features designed to alleviate new problems. To the extent that such problem-solving requires greater organizational investment, following the argument developed in this chapter, marginal returns on complexity will ultimately decline.

Alternatives to collapse

Much of the foregoing may read like the doom and gloom that issues from the Club of Rome (e.g., Meadows et al. 1972). Economists and others will rightly ask whether all this is really inevitable, or whether some salvation such as technical innovation can stave off collapse and permit continued growth. Tied up in all this is the question of the future of contemporary complex societies. Although contemporary societies will be discussed, that is deferred for a later chapter. For now the matter of innovation and growth, particularly in regard to ancient societies, will be briefly addressed.

Technical innovation, particularly the institutionalized variety we know today, is unusual in human history (Elster 1983: 105). It requires some level of investment in research and development. Such investment is difficult to capitalize in an agriculturally-based society that produces little surplus per capita. Technical innovation often responds to labor shortages, which in the ancient world were the exception (Walbank 1967: 79-80). As a result, technical development in societies not based on a fossil fuel economy tends to be minimal. Where technical innovation in ancient societies did occur, it often tended actually to depress the productivity of labor (Renfrew 1982: 272; see also Wilkinson [1973]).

In industrial societies, technical innovation responds to market factors, particularly physical needs and economic distress (Wilkinson 1973; Mensch 1979). It is not, though, always the panacea that is imagined. In an input-output analysis of the U.S. economy from 1947-58, corrected for inflation, Carter found that 'technological change (or progress!) had actually added about $14 billion to the task of satisfying the same final [national] demand' (1966: 29). Technological innovation, as discussed above, is subject to the law of diminishing returns, and this tends to reduce (but not eliminate) its long-term potential for resolving economic weakness. Using the data cited by Wolfle (1960), Scherer observes that if R&D expenditures must grow at 4-5 percent per year to boost productivity 2 percent, such a trend cannot be continued indefinitely or the day will come when we must all be scientists. He is accordingly pessimistic about the prospects for long-term productivity growth (Scherer 1984: 239, 268-9). Colin Renfrew correctly points out (in the context of discussing the development of civilization in the Aegean) that economic growth is itself susceptible to declining marginal productivity (1972: 36-7).

For human societies, the best key to continued socioeconomic growth, and to avoiding or circumventing (or at least financing) declines in marginal productivity, is to obtain a new energy subsidy when it becomes apparent that marginal productivity is beginning to drop. Among modern societies this has been accomplished by tapping fossil fuel reserves and the atom. Among societies without the technical springboard necessary for such development, the usual temptation is to acquire an energy subsidy through territorial expansion. The occurrence of this temptation runs the gamut from simple agriculturalists (Vayda 1961a) to great empires. Whenever the marginal cost of financing a social system's needs out of local yearly productivity becomes perceptibly too high, this solution must seem attractive.

The force of this attraction need hardly be argued, for the rise and expansion of empires provides one of the unequivocal touchstones of history. Such expansion, where successful, has at least the short-term advantage of providing the subsidy sought, as the accumulated reserves of the subject population, and a portion of their yearly productivity, are allocated to the dominant polity.

When some new input to an economic system is brought on line, whether a technical innovation or an energy subsidy, it will often have the potential at least temporarily to raise marginal productivity. In the long run, however, marginal returns will ultimately begin to decline again, for the reasons discussed throughout this chapter. This process is illustrated in Fig. 20. In the curve produced here, B1, C1 represents the point where, under the pressure of diminishing returns, a productive technical innovation or a new energy subsidy is adopted. Marginal productivity starts to rise for those aspects of complexity related to acquiring and initially developing the subsidy. (This may occur immediately or after some delay, as in Wilkinson's [1973] account of the development of a coal-based economy.) Ultimately, though, another point of declining marginal returns is reached, presaging further innovation and expansion, or collapse. The curve shown in Fig. 20 presents a more realistic expression of the economic history of some societies than does Fig. 19, but this only emphasizes the recurring problem of marginal decline.

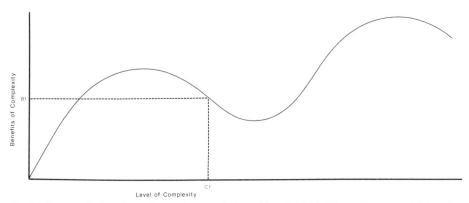

Fig. 20. The marginal product of increasing complexity, with technological innovation or acquisition of an energy subsidy.

A complex society pursuing the expansion option, if it is successful, ultimately reaches a point where further expansion requires too high a marginal cost. Linear miles of border to be defended, size of area to be administered, size of the required administration, internal pacification costs, travel distance between the capital and the frontier, and the presence of competitors combine to exert a depressing effect on further growth. Thus, as Taagepera (1968) has demonstrated, empire growth tends to follow a logistic curve (Fig. 21). Growth begins slowly, accelerates as the energy

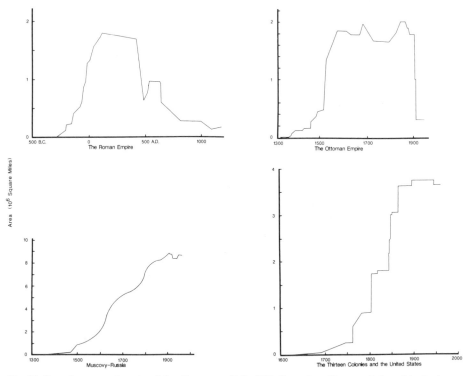

Fig. 21. Growth curves of empires (after Taagepera 1968: 172). Reproduced by permission of the Society for General Systems Research.

subsidy is partially invested in further expansion, and falls off when the marginal cost of further growth becomes too high.

Once conquered, subject lands and their populations must be controlled, administered, and defended. Given enough time, subject populations often achieve, at least partially, the status of citizens, which entitles them to certain benefits in return for their contributions to the hierarchy, and makes them less suitable for exploitation. The energy subsidy obtained from a conquest is highest initially, due to plunder of accumulated surpluses, and then begins to decline. It declines as administrative and occupation costs rise, and as the subject population gains political rights and benefits. Ultimately the marginal returns for the conquest start to fall, whereupon the society is back to its previous predicament. Now, however, the marginal cost of further expansion has risen even higher.

Thus, lacking dependence on such energy sources as fossil fuels, the limited technical development of which the ancient world was capable, and the extensive territorial expansion for which it is noted, could only provide a temporary respite from declining marginal productivity. The latter tendency in particular resulted in a situation where collapse, when it did occur, affected a wider territorial sphere in a more devastating manner than might have otherwise been the case.

5

Evaluation: complexity and marginal returns in collapsing societies

The people desire disorder.
    A Chinese poet on the Chou collapse (quoted in Creel [1970: 431])

The framework developed in the preceding chapter focused on changing cost/benefit ratios for investment in complexity. The shift to increasing complexity, undertaken initially to relieve stress or realize an opportunity, is at first a rational, productive strategy that yields a favorable marginal return. Typically, however, continued stresses, unanticipated challenges, and the costliness of sociopolitical integration combine to lower this marginal return. As the marginal return on complexity declines, complexity as a strategy yields comparatively lower benefits at higher and higher costs. A society that cannot counter this trend, such as through acquisition of an energy subsidy, becomes vulnerable to stress surges that it is too weak or impoverished to meet, and to waning support in its population. With continuation of this trend collapse becomes a matter of mathematical probability, as over time an insurmountable stress surge becomes increasingly likely. Until such a challenge occurs, there may be a period of economic stagnation, political decline, and territorial shrinkage.

The ideal way to evaluate this model would be to isolate and quantify the costs and benefits of various instances of social complexity, and to plot changes in these costs and benefits through time. Long-term periods of significantly declining marginal returns in complexity should be periods of vulnerability to collapse. None of the ancient societies that have collapsed, however, have kept the kinds of detailed records necessary for such a quantitative test, and indeed, many have kept no written records at all. (Such data are difficult to acquire even for contemporary societies [Mansfield 1971: 35-6].)

Strategy in this chapter will be instead to investigate in detail three complex societies that have collapsed. The objective is not to perform a quantitative test of the explanatory framework (for that is impossible) but to ascertain whether this framework helps us to *understand* collapse in actual cases.

The three test cases have been selected to represent a broad spectrum of sociopolitical complexity, to ensure that the explanation applies to different kinds of societies. Given this restriction, the cases chosen represent probably the best documented examples for their respective levels of complexity. The cases are:

1. *The Western Roman Empire.* The Roman Empire was certainly among the most complex, entrenched, and territorially extensive societies that have collapsed. It

127

is also one of the best documented through literary sources. This literature will be the main basis for the investigation.

2. *The Classic Maya of the Southern Lowlands.* Classic Maya Civilization evolved from small, independent hamlets, to polities that existed at a city-state level of organization, and to regional systems in which major political centers dominated territories of perhaps a few thousand square kilometers. Although the Maya were a literate civilization, their writing is at present not fully understood. Our knowledge of the Mayan collapse comes primarily from archaeological research.

3. *Chacoan Society of the American Southwest.* Organized as a hierarchical, regional confederation, the Chacoans represent the most complex prehistoric society that developed on the Colorado Plateaux of North America. They were also the least complex of the societies examined in this chapter, never organized as a true, coercive state. The Chacoans had no written records, and are solely known archaeologically.

These cases, besides representing very different levels of complexity, allow us to assess the usefulness of the framework for understanding both historically and archaeologically known cases of collapse.

The collapse of the Western Roman Empire

The Roman Empire is paradoxically one of the great successes and one of the great failures of history. The fact that it could be both is readily understandable by investigating its marginal return on investment in complexity during the periods of its rise and its decline.

The collapse of the Roman Empire in the West cannot be attributed solely to an upsurge in barbarian incursions, to economic stagnation, or to civil wars, nor to such vague processes as decline of civic responsibility, conversion to Christianity, or poor leadership. Several of these factors were indeed involved in the collapse process, but to understand that process it is necessary to go back in time to the formation of the entity that ultimately fell.

Whatever the factors that led to the Roman expansion in the last few centuries B.C., some of its economic consequences were striking. One of these was a tendency for Romans to migrate to the newly conquered provinces (Gibbon 1776-88: 32; Levy 1967: 56; Weber 1976: 394-5; Rostovtzeff 1926: 15). It is noteworthy that the Roman expansion followed the political strife between plebians and patricians of the fifth and fourth centuries B.C., and the land divisions among peasants of the Licinian Law of 367 B.C. While these facts entice speculation about the causes of the Roman expansion – whether it was induced by irresistible opportunities, by perceived threat, by abstract policy, by demographic pressure in Italy, or by some combination of these and other factors – such speculation is beyond the scope of the present work. What does seem fairly certain is that the willingness, even readiness, of the Romans to emigrate must indicate some lack of comparable opportunity in the homeland. To the extent that foreign acquisitions helped to meet this need, there was a valid social, political, and economic outcome to the policy of expansion – at least for the conquerors.

The policy of expansion was at first highly successful. Not only were the conquered provinces looted of their accumulated surpluses, even their working capital, but permanent tributes, taxes, and land rentals were imposed. The consequences for Rome were bountiful. In 167 B.C. the Romans seized the treasury of the King of Macedonia, a feat that allowed them to eliminate taxation of themselves. After the Kingdom of Pergamon was annexed in 130 B.C. the state budget doubled, from 100 million to 200 million sesterces. Pompey raised it further to 340 million sesterces after the conquest of Syria in 63 B.C. Julius Caesar's conquest of Gaul acquired so much gold that this metal dropped 36 percent in value (Levy 1967: 62-5).

With this kind of payoff, Rome's conquests under the Republic were economically self-perpetuating. The initial series of victories, undertaken as a matter of self-preservation, began increasingly to provide the economic base for further conquests. By the last two centuries B.C. Rome's victories may have become nearly costless, in an economic sense, as conquered nations footed the bill for further expansion (A. Jones 1974: 114-15).

This process culminated with Octavian's (later Augustus) conquest of Egypt. The booty of Egypt allowed Augustus to distribute money to the plebians of Rome – and even, when necessary, to relieve shortages in the state budget out of his personal fortune (Frank 1940: 7-9, 15). Yet the geometric Roman expansion of the Republic ended under the Principate (the emperors from Augustus up to the accession of Diocletian [284 A.D.]) (see Fig. 22). Augustus (27 B.C.-14 A.D.) terminated the policy of expansion, particularly after losses to the Germans, and concentrated instead on maintaining a stable army and restoring the prosperity that had been ruptured by the civil wars.

With the establishment of Imperial rule, historians usually refer to events by the chronology of the succession of emperors. To facilitate the discussion Table 5 has been prepared, giving the dates of rule for each emperor. These dates will also be occasionally incorporated into the text, whenever that might serve to clarify the discussion.

With the end of geographic expansion there was a corresponding drop in the windfalls of conquest (A. Jones 1974: 124). From Augustus to Diocletian, most emperors were faced with at least some insufficiencies of revenue (Heichelheim 1970: 270). Augustus frequently complained of fiscal shortage, and was often hard put to finance even the modest administration and foreign policy that he established (Gibbon 1776-88: 140; M. Hammond 1946: 75). He instituted for Roman citizens a five percent tax on legacies and inheritances (Gibbon 1776-88: 142). This tax, established to provide for military retirement (Frank 1940: 7), was highly unpopular, since the Roman population had been relieved of taxes in the late Republic.

The major Imperial costs, at various times, included pay, rations, and fodder for the army, the civil service, and other state employees (e.g., in later times workers in the Imperial arms factories), public works, the postal service, uniforms for the army and civil service, education, and the public dole (A. Jones 1974: 35). At all times the

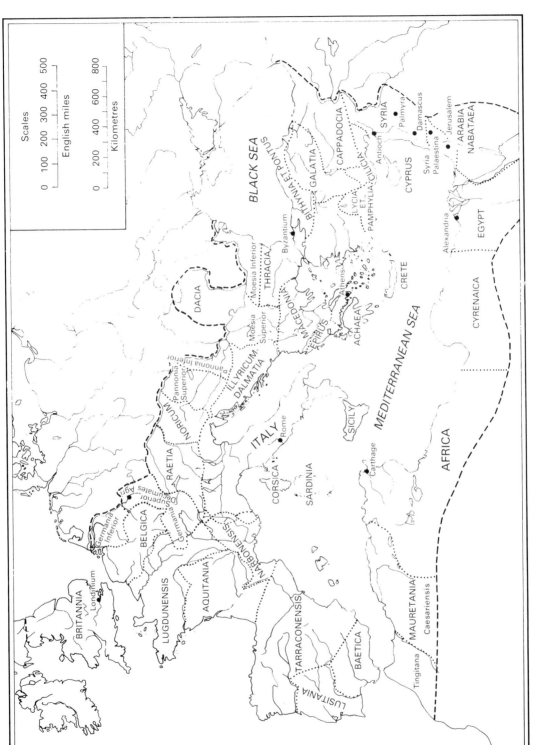

Fig. 22. The Roman Empire at the time of Hadrian.

Table 5. *Roman emperors*[1]

Emperor	Reign
Augustus	27 B.C.-14 A.D.
Tiberius	14-37 A.D.
Caligula	37-41
Claudius	41-54
Nero	54-68
Galba	68-9
Otho	69
Vitellius	69
Vespasian	69-79
Titus	79-81
Domitian	81-96
Nerva	96-8
Trajan	98-117
Hadrian	117-38
Antoninus Pius	138-61
Marcus Aurelius	161-80
Lucius Verus	161-9
Commodus	180-92
Pertinax	193
Didius Julianus	193
Septimius Severus	193-211
Clodius Albinus	193-7
Pescennius Niger	193-4
Caracalla	211-17
Geta	209-12
Macrinus	217-18
Diadumenianus	218
Elagabalus	218-22
Severus Alexander	222-35
Maximinus	235-8
Gordian I	238
Gordian II	238
Balbinus	238
Pupienus	238
Gordian III	238-44
Philip	244-9
Decius	249-51
Trebonianius Gallus	251-3
Volusianus	251-3
Aemilianus	253
Valerian	253-60
Gallienus	260-8
Claudius II	268-70
Quintillus	270
Aurelian	270-5
Tacitus	275-6
Florianus	276
Probus	276-82

Table 5 *continued*

Emperor	Reign
Carus	282-3
Carinus	283-5
Numerianus	283-4
Diocletian	284-305
Maximianus	286-305
Constantius I	305-6
Galerius	305-11
Constantine I	306-37
Constantine II	337-40
Constans	337-50
Constantius II	337-61
Julian	360-3
Jovian	363-4
Valentinian I	364-75
Valens	364-78
Gratian	367-83
Valentinian II	375-92
Theodosius I	379-95
Arcadius (E)[2]	395-408
Honorius (W)	395-423
Theodosius II (E)	408-50
Valentinian III (W)	423-55
Marcian (E)	450-7
Maximus (W)	455
Avitus (W)	455-6
Leo I (E)	457-74
Majorian (W)	457-61
Severus (W)	461-5
Anthemius (W)	467-72
Olybrius (W)	472
Glycerius (W)	473-4
Leo II (E)	473-4
Nepos (W)	474-5
Zeno (E)	474-91
Romulus Augustulus (W)	475-6

[1]After Rostovtzeff (1926: 632-3), Boak and Sinnigen (1965: 533-5), and Gibbon (1776-88).
[2]Designates rulers of the Eastern (E) or Western (W) empires after the death of Theodosius I (395).

major expense was the military, although the Roman dole was not inconsequential. Julius Caesar found 320,000 beneficiaries, nearly one citizen in three. He reduced this to 150,000, but the figure rose again. From Augustus to Claudius (41-54 A.D.) approximately 200,000 heads of families received free wheat. A special fleet was needed to transport this, as were wharves on the Tiber River and at the port of Ostia, and numerous shipowners and bakers (Levy 1967: 69, 77). In the middle of Augustus' reign Rome's annual income was about 500 million sesterces (Frank 1940: 53) (the sestertius was a coin valued initially at four to the silver denarius [Mattingly 1960: 122]). With this income, Augustus established an army of 25 legions. The pay of individual legionaries was set at 225 denarii per year.

Despite the stagnation of revenue when expansion fell off, and the often heavy rule in the provinces, there were definite benefits to the early Empire. There were foreign and internal peace and security, the borders were maintained, commerce was protected, and public works projects were undertaken (Toutain 1968: 253-9). The early Empire was relatively prosperous (M. Hammond 1946: 34) even if the State was not able to command the wealth temporarily made available by earlier conquests.

The Roman economy was overwhelmingly an agricultural one. It has been estimated that in the later Empire agriculture provided fully 90 percent of the government's revenue. Trade and industry, by contrast, were relatively insignificant. One of the main reasons for this was the high cost of land transport. A wagon load of wheat, for example, would double in value with a land journey of only 480 kilometers, a camel load in 600 kilometers. Land transport was so costly and inefficient that it was often impossible to relieve inland famines; local surpluses could not be economically carted to areas of shortage. Ship transport, while risky and seasonally restricted, was much more economical. It was, for example, less costly to ship grain from one end of the Mediterranean to the other than to cart it 120 kilometers. Under the Edict on Prices, issued by Diocletian in 301 A.D., transport by road was 28 to 56 times more costly than by sea. The importance of Egypt to feeding the Empire was not just its agricultural productivity, but also its proximity to water transport.

Thus, the only goods that could profitably be transported long distances were those of high relative value – i.e., luxury goods. The bulk of the population, existing on their own agricultural production, could not afford such goods. Large-scale industry thus existed in only a few towns, while most local needs were supplied by village craftsmen (A. Jones 1964: 841-4, 1974: 30, 37-9, 83, 138; Duncan-Jones 1974: 1, 368; M. Hammond 1946: 70-1).

The Imperial superstructure built on this agricultural base could usually support ongoing expenses, but had difficulty dealing financially with crises. Taxes were initially levied at fixed rates, and were typically not flexible enough to be increased in crises. The government operated strictly on a cash basis and rarely borrowed; its budget was at best minimally planned. Costs tended to rise, although so for a time did State income. Rome's revenues grew from about 500,000 sesterces in the middle of Augustus' reign to about 1,200,000 to 1,500,000 under Vespasian (69-79 A.D.). Some reigns were excessively expensive, such as that of Claudius (41-54 A.D.), who engaged in major public works and conquered Britain. Reserves built up by prudent emperors were quickly spent by their successors (Frank 1940: 42, 53; Heichelheim 1970: 249, 270; A. Jones 1974: 189).

Emperors upon accession were often faced with an insolvent government, and rarely were able to accumulate reserves for emergencies. When extraordinary expenses arose the supply of coinage was frequently insufficient. To counter this problem, Nero began in 64 A.D. a policy that subsequent emperors found increasingly irresistible (see Table 6 and Fig. 23). He debased the silver denarius, raising the content of base metal to ten percent. He also reduced somewhat the size of both the denarius and the gold aureus (a coin initially worth 25 denarii) (A. Jones 1974: 191; Heichelheim 1970: 213-14; Mattingly 1960: 121).

This proved no solution, for Vespasian, who increased the number of legions to 30 (M. Hammond 1946: 76), encountered a pressing need for money, and so both raised taxes and debased the currency further (Frank 1940: 44-7; Finley 1973: 90). Adding to the problem, Domitian (81-96 A.D.) increased the pay of legionaries to 300 denarii per year, while Nerva (96-8) established a public system for the care of Italian orphans (M. Hammond 1946: 82; Duncan-Jones 1974: 288).

The emperor Trajan (98-117 A.D.) embarked on an ambitious – and expensive – program of military expansion. While successful in the field, the booty taken from the conquered lands apparently did not even cover the costs of his campaigns. And of that booty, more than 1/3 was distributed among the urban poor (at some 650 denarii per head). Consequently, the denarius, which had been restored under Domitian and Nerva to its Neronian standard, was devalued by 15 percent, to a level of 79-88 percent purity (Rostovtzeff 1926: 309; M. Hammond 1946: 75-6, 78; Frank 1940: 68, 91; Mattingly 1960: 184).

Trajan's successor, Hadrian (117-38), dropped the financially untenable policy of expansion, and abandoned the new acquisitions in Mesopotamia and Assyria. At the same time, however, he instituted a public dole at Athens, gave largess to the poor at 1000 denarii per head, and incurred heavy costs in his travels and building programs. To economize in military costs, from Hadrian's time on army units were raised as often as possible from the locality where they would be stationed. Hadrian occasionally granted tax waivers, perhaps indicating that by this time higher taxation would have created difficulties (Bernardi 1970: 38).

The next Emperor, Antoninus Pius (138-61), attempted to shrink the level of Hadrian's administration. He tried to reduce the number of government officials, and even sold some of the Imperial property and estates. Although he repeatedly gave largess to the people of Rome (at 800 denarii per head), Antoninus Pius left in the treasury at his death a substantial surplus, totaling 675 million denarii (A. Jones 1974: 189; Weber 1976: 406; Frank 1940: 71, 72, 76; Rostovtzeff 1926: 315; Mattingly 1960: 184).

This surplus proved short-lived. During the reign of Marcus Aurelius (161-80) the edifice of the Empire began to crack. Two major crises confronted the Empire while he held the throne. First, a devastating plague began in 165 or 166 A.D.; it lasted about 15 years and caused significant loss of life (as much as 1/4 to 1/3 of the populace in some areas [McNeill 1976: 116]). Secondly, wars with Germanic tribes kept the Emperor in the field for much of his reign. The Roman Empire that had thrived on the plunder of expansion, and that had at least maintained stability when expansion ceased and revenues leveled off, found itself hard pressed to deal with stress surges of this magnitude.

The cost of Marcus Aurelius' barbarian wars exceeded the level that could be supported by the Empire's normal income. One consequence, as might be expected,

Table 6. *Debasement of the denarius from Nero to Septimius Severus*[1]

Emperor	Average Silver Percent
Nero (54-68 A.D.)	91.8
Galba (68-9)	92.6
Otho (69)	98.2
Vitellius (69)	86.1
Vespasian (69-79)	84.9
Titus (79-81)	80.3
Domitian (81-96)	90.8
Nerva (96-8)	90.7
Trajan (98-117)	85.4
Hadrian (117-38)	84.1
Antoninus Pius (138-61)	80.0
Marcus Aurelius (161-80)	76.2
Commodus (180-92)	72.2
Pertinax (193)	76.0
Didius Julianus (193)	81.0
Septimius Severus (193-211)	58.3

[1] After Bolin (1958: 211).

was the depletion of Antoninus Pius' surplus. Yet even with this surplus, Marcus Aurelius found his wars too expensive for revenues, and was forced to finance the Empire's efforts by conducting public auctions of Imperial valuables. He also had to raise new taxes, and debased the denarius to between 70 and 78 percent silver. Despite these difficulties, he still made donations to his soldiers and the poor.

In addition to the problems of financing the barbarian wars, Marcus Aurelius faced a shortage of recruits for his army. Because of this he was forced to settle the defeated Marcomanni within the borders of the Empire, on the condition that they furnish recruits. This is in some ways not surprising, for although population may have risen under the early Principate, by the second century A.D. there was a shortage of free agricultural labor. Not only did this have consequences for agriculture, but also for the military, which depended on the peasant population for recruits (Boak 1955: 15, 17-19; Frank 1940: 77, 92; A. Jones 1974: 194; Rostovtzeff 1926: 326).

There are indications that these financial exigencies extended to more than foreign and military affairs. The cities of the Empire had few sources of revenue, so elected officials were usually drawn from the local wealthy classes, and were expected personally to finance all or part of the duties of their offices. As these expenditures increased through time, the amounts paid by these magistrates rose. By the second century A.D. these duties grew to be so burdensome that candidates for office began to fall off (A. Jones 1974: 13, 28; Rostovtzeff 1926: 342).

Commodus (180-92), who succeeded Marcus Aurelius, is of interest to this study

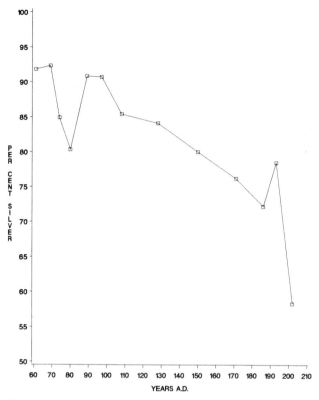

Fig. 23. Debasement of the denarius from Nero to Septimius Severus (data from Bolin 1958: 211). Silver percentages plotted at midpoint of an Emperor's reign. For A.D. 69 and 193 (which were years of successional struggles), values plotted are an average of all unsuccessful Emperors.

primarily for further debasement of the denarius. Under his rule it dropped to as low as 67 percent silver (Frank 1940: 92).

The death of Commodus marked the end of the Antonine dynasty. In the successional struggles that followed, Septimius Severus (193-211) ultimately emerged, but with an uncertain hold on the throne. To secure his position, he and his successors of the Severan dynasty courted the army. The resultant military costs strained finances. Septimius Severus increased the pay of troops to 400 denarii per year. His successor, Caracalla (211-17), raised it to 600, while by the end of the Severan dynasty (235) it stood at 750. The size of the military was also increased to 33 legions. Nor were military costs the sole problem. Septimius Severus supplemented the Roman dole with the addition of oil to the list of free commodities. Mattingly has noted of this time, 'The expenses of government were steadily increasing out of proportion to any increase in receipts and the State was moving steadily in the direction of bankruptcy' (1960: 124).

To pay for all this, Septimius Severus debased the denarius to between 43 and 56 percent silver. The denarius by the early third century was so reduced in value that Caracalla introduced a new coin, the Antoninianus, which was supposedly equal to two denarii, but of lower real value (Mattingly 1960: 215). His successors did not hesitate to debase it further. Caracalla also reduced the gold content of the aureus. The denarius, however, was the coin most worth debasing, since it was used to pay the troops, and this was the major item in the Imperial budget. Caracalla is perhaps best known for his act of 212 extending Roman citizenship to all free inhabitants of the Empire. This had the consequence of vastly extending the pool of those liable to the Roman inheritance tax, which he incidentally doubled.

Although good data are lacking for the early Empire, these continued debasements were clearly inflationary. A slave that in Commodus' reign cost 500 denarii, for example, sold for 2500 under the Severi (Mazzarino 1966: 153). The older, more valuable coins would have been withdrawn, since people would naturally prefer to pay obligations in the newer, debased currency.

Bands of military deserters plagued parts of the Empire under Commodus, Septimius Severus, and Severus Alexander (222-35). Order was beginning to break down. Yet the disturbances of the early third century were nothing compared with what would follow the end of the Severan dynasty in 235 A.D. (Rostovtzeff 1926: 344-80; A. Jones 1974: 194-5; Frank 1940: 86-7, 92-3; Boak 1955: 66; M. Hammond 1946: 76).

The half century from 235 to 284 A.D. was a period of unparalleled crisis, during which the Roman Empire nearly came to an end. The chief features of this time were foreign and civil wars, barbarian incursions, devastation of many provinces, increases in the size of the army and the bureaucracy, financial exigency and increased taxes, debasement of the currency, and unparalleled inflation. MacMullen has aptly characterized the time: 'So extensive and complex was the unraveling of the empire's power to defend itself, it strained every power of comprehension' (1976: 69). The Empire survived this period of crisis, but at great cost, and emerged at the turn of the fourth century A.D. as a very different entity.

This is a period for which comparatively little documentation exists, but that in itself may be symptomatic. Literacy and mathematical training apparently declined during the third century. This resulted not only in the unsatisfactory documentation of the period with which historians must deal, but must also have affected the Imperial government. As fewer people could read or count, the quality and quantity of information reaching the government during this critical time would have declined. In Egypt after 250 A.D. census registration came to a halt, and Egypt was a province that was relatively untouched by the troubles. The major emphasis of what education remained was rhetoric, and that was not really relevant to the needs of the government. There was at the same time an increase in mysticism, and knowledge by revelation. The external threats brought increased propaganda about patriotism, ancient Roman virtues, and superiority over the barbarians (MacMullen 1976: 13, 38-44, 50-1, 58-60, 65-6; Clough 1951: 159; Burckhardt 1949: 129).

The average reign during this period of violent political instability was only a few months, and there were many usurpers (A. Jones 1964: 23). There were in this 50 year period at least 27 recognized Emperors, at least twice that many usurpers who were killed, and at one time thirty claimants to the throne. A partial list of these is given in Table 7. By the time of Diocletian (284-305), the number of Emperors and pretenders

Table 7. *Emperors and pretenders from 235 to 285 A.D.*[1]

Emperors	Pretenders	
Maximinus, 235-8	Quartinus, 235	
Pupienus Balbinus, 238		
Gordian III, 238-44		
Philip, 244-9	Iotapianus, 248-9	Pacatianus, 248-9
Decius, 249-51	Licinianus, 250-1	
Gallus, 251-3		
Aemilianus, 253	Uranius, (248?) 253-4	
Valerian, 253-60	Ingenuus, 258 (259?)	
Gallienus, 260-8	Regalianus, 260	Postumus, 260(?)-8
Claudius II, 268-70	Aureolus, 268	Odenathus, 262-7
Aurelian, 270-5	(?)Domitianus, 271(?)	Zenobia, 267-73
Tacitus, 275-6	Florianus, 276	Laelianus, 268
Probus, 276-82		Marius 268
Carus, 282-3		Victorinus, 268-70
Carinus, 283-5		Tetricus 270-3 (274?)

[1]After MacMullen (1976: 93).

averaged out to at least one per year for half a century. Many commoners did not know who the Emperor at any time was – only that there was one (MacMullen 1976: 93-4; Boak 1955: 23; Clough 1951: 155).

An Emperor's rule during this time was tenuous, and highly dependent on the favor of the military. Rulers were forced to take extraordinary actions to convince the populace of their legitimacy, and to maintain military support. These legitimizing activities carried associated costs; they were politically essential but came at a time of unprecedented financial crisis. Portrait busts were churned out upon the ascendancy of a ruler. False exploits and titles were manufactured. Coinage addressed to key army units was issued. Increased subsidies were given to those who manufactured luxuries for wear or use in palaces. During some of the darkest times, Aurelian (270-5) felt compelled to increase the expense of the Roman dole, issuing loaves of bread rather than wheat flour, and offering pork, salt, and wine at reduced prices. In the decade before Aurelian, Alexandria and other Egyptian cities had been added to the dole (MacMullen 1976: 45-6, 93-4, 98; Boak 1955: 66).

Central control over many provinces waned, and successful independent empires were temporarily established in several areas. Gaul, Britain, and Spain, for example, were independent from 260-74. Semi-successful revolts included those of Carausius and Allectus in the northwest (287-96), Domitianus and Achilleus in Egypt (297), and Zenobia in the east (267-73). Provinces such as Gaul and Palmyra found Imperial assistance during the crisis so ineffectual that for local pretenders usurpation was comparatively successful. Each new center of power, whether legitimate or not, needed a court and full bureaucracy, a complement of servants, and of course an army (MacMullen 1976: 93, 100; Boak 1955: 23; Rostovtzeff 1926: 391).

This was a time of local disintegration. Lawlessness and banditry increased in places such as Sicily. Tenant farmers left the land, and there were numerous bands of brigands. Farmers in Egypt fled to the swamps of the Delta. In Gaul, rebellious bands formed called the Bagaudae. Suppressed by Maximinian in 286, but reappearing in the mid fourth century, they remained to the end of Roman rule (Gibbon 1776-88: 242-43; Rostovtzeff 1926: 424, 437; Boak 1955: 27, 38-40).

Government costs rose in the areas still under Imperial control. There were increased costs for the expansion and care of cities, for the dole, and for the construction of roads, palaces, and storage buildings. The size and payroll of the army grew, as did campaigning costs. The government's fiscal obligations may well have doubled, and yet this was a government that even before the crisis had been strapped for funds (MacMullen 1976: 102-4, 107-8). Despite the increased expenditures, civil services declined, and buildings fell into disrepair (A. Jones 1974: 29).

The only solution for the government was to raise taxes and debase the currency further. Caracalla had increased army pay at a cost of 70,000,000 denarii per year. To pay for this, as noted, he introduced the Antoninianus, a new coin. It was half the weight of the denarius but tariffed at two denarii. More than 50 years later, after devastating inflation, Aurelian tried the same trick: in the context of reforming the currency he placed a nominal value on coins that was far higher than their actual worth. Prices skyrocketed. Money changers in the east refused to give small change for Imperial coinage. Under Gallienus (260-8) the Antoninianus had less than five percent silver. 'The Empire,' wrote Mattingly of this period, 'had, in all but words, declared itself bankrupt and thrown the burden of its insolvency on its citizens' (1960: 186). By Aurelian's time further debasement was essentially impossible (A. Jones 1964: 16, 26, 1974: 196; Levy 1967: 87; Heichelheim 1970: 214; MacMullen 1976: 108-9, 112; Mattingly 1960: 186).

Due to the decline in literary and mathematical training during the period of crisis, few data are available on actual inflationary rates between 235 and 284. Good quantitative data again become available with the reign of Diocletian. These data will be discussed when the narrative reaches that point. Some of the effects of the inflation can be perceived, however, even before Diocletian. The main victims, as always, were those on fixed incomes. Unlike current times, though, this included the government and its employees. The Roman government before Diocletian had no real budget, nor any economic policy, as we would know these today. It depended on tax rates that rarely changed. As a result, when crises arose, revenue could not be increased. By the latter part of the third century the currency was so worthless that the State resorted to forced labor and an economy in kind. The earliest example of the former may be Aurelian's conscription of craft associations to build the walls around Rome. By the time of Diocletian the State was so unable to rely on money to meet its needs that it collected its taxes in the form of supplies directly usable by the military and other branches of government, or in bullion to avoid having to accept its own worthless coins (A. Jones 1964: 29-30 1974: 137, 197; MacMullen 1976: 125, 158, 205; Mattingly 1960: 186).

Barbarian incursions were frequent and ruinous between 248 and 268. The usurpations and regular murder of sitting Emperors meant that civil war was common. Many local populations were devastated by these events. The barbarians were unskilled at siege warfare, so they tended to concentrate in the countryside. Even so, some cities were sacked and burned. In rural areas crops were destroyed, cattle seized, and the population carried off into slavery. Roman armies were almost as destructive. Despite pay increases, inflation sapped the value of military compensation so thoroughly that army units were often forced to seize what they needed from local populations. Under the expense of defending the Empire against incursions, some frontier provinces were abandoned, including the area between the Rhine and the Danube in the 230s and 260s, Dacia in the 260s and 270s, the larger parts of Moesia in the 270s and Mauretania Tingitana in the 280s, and the Low Countries in the late third century. There was increased investment in fortifications, and troops withdrew from border installations to walled cities. In Britain, large coastal forts were constructed, and massive stone walls built around even rather small population centers (A. Jones 1964: 25, 31-2; MacMullen 1976: 1, 189-90; Gibbon 1776-88: 206-7; Rostovtzeff 1926: 444-5; Boak 1955: 232; Frank 1940: 302; Frere and St Joseph 1983).

The population of the Empire, under the effects of ravaging of the countryside by both foreign and friendly forces, rampant inflation, and changing leadership, cannot have recovered from the plague outbreak of 165/166 to 180. The catastrophes of 235-84 fell on a declining population, which suffered further when the plague returned from 250 to 270 A.D. The agricultural population of a province so essential as Gaul declined, either killed or captured by barbarians, or having deserted fields to join the bands of brigands. Town populations fell before and during the crisis, due to plague, pillage by armies engaged in civil wars or by barbarians, and the declining rural population (Rostovtzeff 1926: 424; Boak 1955: 19, 26, 38-9, 55-6, 113; MacMullen 1976: 18, 183).

The wealthy, as long as they avoided injudicious political entanglements, generally continued to fare well. Large landowners emerged during the third century in increased numbers in all parts of the Empire. The middle class in towns, however, was burdened by the cost of civil obligations. After the second century, while portrait busts of Emperors were being turned out in increasing numbers, there were fewer and fewer local inscriptions. Townspeople could no longer afford them. Small peasant proprietors lost their holdings, attaching themselves as tenants to large estates. Commerce declined, due to the unsafe nature of the countryside and the seas (M. Hammond 1946: 75; Boak 1955: 57; Heichelheim 1970: 297).

The Roman Empire was in a crisis in which its survival was imperiled. The situation was rescued for a time by Aurelian, who in a brief reign (270-5) pushed back the barbarians, 'reformed' the coinage, and reattached the rebellious provinces. Yet he failed, or did not have sufficient time, to enact the sweeping administrative and economic changes needed to ensure the Empire's survival. He did, however, begin these, by conscripting labor when needed for the walls of Rome, and by ordering that deserted lands be obligatorily farmed under the direction of local city Senates. The effect of the latter directive was to draft peasants and whole villages into enlarged agricultural labor forces (MacMullen 1976: 205-6). Yet the situation began to unravel again after his death. It was Diocletian who, in a reign from 284 to his voluntary abdication in 305, quelled the barbarians, defeated usurpers, and at the same time initiated sweeping political and economic changes that transformed the nature of the Empire, and ensured its survival for a while longer.

It is difficult always to determine the starting date of the changes that transformed the later Empire. Some can be traced to Diocletian, to Constantine, or to their successors. Others probably originated in the dark times of the crisis, from which so little documentation has emerged. For this reason the discussion that follows will be temporally eclectic, chronologically consistent insofar as possible, but concerned more with the processes of change than with the dates of administrative actions.

The Empire that emerged under Diocletian and Constantine was administered by a government that was larger, more complex, more highly organized, and that commanded larger and more powerful military forces. It taxed its citizens more heavily, conscripted their labor, and regulated their lives and their occupations. It was a coercive, omnipresent, all-powerful organization that subdued individual interests and levied all resources toward one overarching goal: the survival of the State.

The most pressing need was increased military manpower. It has been estimated that the Severan army (prior to 235 A.D.) was just over 300,000. During the next half-century it was increased, standing at 400,000 when Diocletian took office. The level was raised again by Diocletian and Constantine, to between 500,000 and 600,000. By Diocletian's time, in other words, the size of the army may have doubled in 70 years. It was increased again by Constantine, and stood at 650,000 by the end of the fourth century. The recruitment rate for a force of this size has been estimated at around 96,000 per year. Diocletian built networks of strategic roads and fortresses along the frontiers. Constantine drew back slightly from this strategy, reducing frontier garrisons, and creating instead a central, mobile striking force, with a greatly increased proportion of cavalry. The army of the later Empire was probably better officered, since most were professional soldiers rather than civilians with temporary commissions (Boak 1955: 87, 91, 94; A. Jones 1964: 55, 57, 60, 97-8, 1037, 1046, 1974: 129; MacMullen 1976: 185-7, 204; Brown 1971: 24).

A second major transformation was in the administration of the Empire. A serious revolt in Egypt in 297 convinced Diocletian that more than one ruler was needed to deal with the multiple crises besetting the Empire on so many fronts at once. His solution was the establishment of the Tetrarchy, the system whereby the eastern and western halves of the Roman world were ruled by separate Emperors, each assisted by a subordinate with the title 'Caesar.' Diocletian also greatly increased the number of provinces, by subdividing existing provinces into many smaller ones (and thereby depriving provincial governors of the opportunity to rebel). He increased the size of the Imperial administration, which now had to move with him as he traversed his domains. The size of the bureaucracy was greatly expanded, perhaps doubling by Diocletian's abdication. Moreover, this increased, peripatetic administration was largely duplicated four times, in each of the Imperial courts (two Emperors, two Caesars). The number of capital cities correspondingly increased, making permanent the temporary proliferation of capitals under the pretenders.

Diocletian built state factories to make arms for the military, and also to provide for the material needs of the Imperial court. A vast state transport system was maintained. Under Diocletian and Constantine not only was the size of the administration expanded, but it was increasingly segmented and specialized. Indeed, this process can be traced back to the years of crisis. From Gallienus (260-8) on the civil and military functions of government were split. Within the military, the tactical was split from the stationary. Within the civil area, Constantine subdivided financial functions.

Although the number of usurpers, and consequent civil wars, declined between the third and fourth centuries, Emperors nevertheless felt a continuing need to spend on public display in order to legitimize their reigns and deter rivals. There was increased new construction in the fourth century, as the Tetrarchy returned to the task of embellishing cities. But much of the rebuilding (and the building of Constantinople) was done by stealing accumulated treasures from other places. Despite this, the building of Constantinople was a major drain, as was the support of its 80,000 citizens placed on the dole. Meanwhile, the city of Rome was a continuing burden: in the fourth century it had some 300,000 inhabitants receiving public distributions.

Whatever the personal motivation behind Constantine's backing of Christianity, it had an important political consequence: by providing a universal religious focus it legitimized the sitting Emperor as sanctioned by divinity. Coins from this time on placed emphasis on symbols of the Emperor's power (showing, for example, the diadem, mantle, scepter, and orb) rather than on personal attributes. Both were important strategies for maintaining the increased authoritarianism of the Imperium from Diocletian on, which historians label the Dominate (Gibbon 1776-88: 332, 537; Rostovtzeff 1926: 456; M. Hammond 1946: 77; Boak 1955: 126; A. Jones 1964: 39, 49, 1033, 1045-6; Mazzarino 1966: 169; Heichelheim 1970: 336; MacMullen 1976: 96-7, 100-1, 159, 204; Mattingly 1960: 226).

The changes instituted by Diocletian and Constantine made the Empire more efficient and better defended, but at considerable cost. When evaluating these costs it must be kept in mind that each new governmental office cost little in the degraded currency. The old maximum salary for equestrian-class officials of 300,000 sesterces was by now worth only about 400 second-century denarii. But salaries in kind were considerable. Even though compensation per individual remained below second century levels, the total cost of the new civil administration was the equivalent of adding perhaps two or three new legions to the army. By the fifth century the civil service was over 30,000 strong. This was a heavy burden on the exhausted Empire, and yet it was the lesser part of the increase. The expanded military costs were substantially greater. Not only was the increase in military personnel greater than the civilian, but the increased emphasis on cavalry was particularly expensive. Fodder for a horse cost as much as the rations of a soldier.

After the political disintegration of the third century, the Tetrarchy had to reestablish links with local-level organizations, and to obtain tax-related information. In Egypt, for example (and probably elsewhere), lands had to be resurveyed. Taxes were inevitably increased, and continued to rise thereafter. Overall, the role of government in the economic life of the Empire increased (Gibbon 1776-88: 333; M. Hammond

1946: 77; A. Jones 1964: 51-2, 130-1, 1035, 1974: 129, 131-2; MacMullen 1976: 126, 186-7).

Inflation continued unabated under Diocletian, forcing the government to continue the economy in kind. One of Diocletian's major accomplishments was to establish the first mechanism whereby the rate of tax in any given year could be geared to estimated expenditures.

Diocletian attempted to restore a sound currency, but may not have had enough metal, for earlier coins continued in circulation. He introduced a new coin worth 25 denarii, which by the 320s had shrunk to 1/3 of its original weight. There were two currencies during the fourth century: gold and copper. The gold solidus was introduced by Constantine, and retained its value for seven centuries. Copper currency, however, was inflated by assigning face values to the coins that were artificially high. The inflated copper coins went to cover military pay, and to buy gold solidi on the open market. Only by the end of the fourth century were payments in kind fully commuted to gold (A. Jones 1964: 60-6, 107, 109, 442, 1974: 169-70, 197-200, 202-3, 215, 224; Levy 1967: 88).

In the second century a modius of wheat (approximately nine liters), during normal times, had sold for 1/2 denarius. In Diocletian's Edict on Prices (301 A.D.), the price was fixed at 100 denarii, which was itself probably too low. Thus the real value of the denarius had sunk to no more than 0.5 percent of its former value, while wheat, conversely, had gone up 200 times. And that was not the end. In Egypt, the grain basket of the Empire, the same modius of wheat sold in 335 A.D. for over 6000 denarii, and in 338 for over 10,000. In 324 the gold solidus was worth 4250 denarii, yet by 337 it was worth 250,000. By 363 the value stood at 30,000,000 denarii to the solidus. Inflation by this time abated somewhat, for in the next 30 years the value of the denarius with respect to gold fell only another 50 percent. In Egypt in the fourth century the value of the solidus went from 4000 to 180,000,000 Egyptian drachmae. (The Egyptian tetradrachm was considered equal in value to one denarius, and was debased to match the latter. Part of the reason for the Egyptian hyperinflation was apparently a political decision not to back Egyptian coinage with gold or silver [Mattingly 1960: 194, 224, 248].)

It was the coinage of everyday commerce that was debased, for this was the currency that the government used to meet its military obligations. In the 150 years prior to Diocletian's Edict of 301, the value of gold rose 45 times, the value of silver 86 times. The silver that once went into one denarius could now produce 150. The result was hyperinflation that must have disrupted local-level commerce. In Diocletian's Edict a pound of pork was fixed at 12 denarii. By 412 it cost 90 denarii. In Egypt, from which the best documentation has survived, a measure of wheat that in the first century A.D. sold for six drachmae, had increased to 200 drachmae in 276 A.D., 9000 in 314, 78,000 in 324, and to more than 2,000,000 drachmae in 334 A.D. Not surprisingly, Egyptian loans of money were made for increasingly shorter periods in the third and fourth centuries. Gradually, though, more and more gold solidi came into circulation, and the copper output was reduced. By the fifth century the inflation was largely spent (A. Jones 1964: 27, 109, 443, 1974: 200-1, 213, 215, 224; Levy 1967: 88-9; MacMullen 1976: 118; Mattingly 1960: 222-3).

Other approaches failing, Diocletian attempted to control inflation by his famous (and famously unsuccessful) Edict on Prices, issued in 301 A.D. It was no novelty, having been tried before. In general, it set prices too low, was rigged in favor of creditors, and – much to the government's advantage – depressed the cost of transport (Rostovtzeff 1926: 463; A. Jones 1964: 27, 61; Levy 1967: 94; MacMullen 1976: 122).

The increases in military strength and civil administration had to be supported by a depleted population. After the plagues of the second and third centuries, and consequent depopulation, conditions favorable to population reestablishment never did emerge in the fourth and fifth centuries (Russell 1958: 140; McNeill 1976: 116). After Diocletian there was relative peace in the West for over a century, and in the Asiatic provinces until the beginning of the seventh century. Nevertheless, economic factors created by the establishment of the Dominate did not favor population recovery. This point will be discussed further below.

The consequence for the Empire was a decline in personnel for agriculture, industry, the military, and the civil service. Agriculture and industry accordingly declined. Agricultural labor became so scarce that landowners, to avoid conscription of their own laborers, bribed vagabonds to enlist instead. In Gaul, shortages of agricultural labor continued until the collapse, so that the victorious barbarians were able to appropriate land with minimal impact on the local population. Many barbarians were enlisted in the military, indeed in the later Empire barbarian colonies were planted within the depopulated lands under Roman rule. Height requirements for military recruits were lowered. By the late fourth century in the West even slaves were sometimes enlisted. In 315 Constantine ordered assistance for poor and orphaned children in an attempt to reverse the demographic trend (Boak 1955: 42, 97-8, 113-14; A. Jones 1964: 149, 158-9, 1041-3, 1974: 87; MacMullen 1976: 182-3).

This decline in population and in the supply of essential labor does much to explain the social and economic policies of Diocletian and Constantine. Conscription, which had been practiced before, was instituted as a regular practice by Diocletian. He levied guilds to supply the armies and the Imperium. Gradually families came to be frozen into essential occupations. In 313 Constantine required that soldiers' sons be likewise. A hereditary soldiery emerged, with predictable problems. From 319 to 398 at least 22 laws were issued dealing with the sons of soldiers who sought to evade military service.

From the early fourth century on sons of civil servants were made to enter their fathers' offices. The same was required of workers in government factories, as well as many private sector occupations. Indeed, the distinction between the public and private sectors blurred, as the State directed persons into occupations and levied their output. By the time of Diocletian city offices, which were such a financial burden on their holders, had become hereditary. Since the very wealthy had by this time largely fled the towns to establish country villas, or obtained exemptions, this burden fell on the middle income segment.

Perhaps most important to the economy of the Empire was the tying of agricultural labor to the soil. First mentioned in an announcement of Constantine's in 332, this had the effect of establishing a system of serfdom in which tenants were bound to large estates. The colonate, as it is known, was a boon to large landowners during a time of agricultural labor shortages. Colonates continuously tried to escape unsatisfactory conditions, to the army, the church, the civil service, the professions, and other proprietors (Boak 1955: 49, 95, 97, 102-3; A. Jones 1964: 615, 1042, 1974: 16, 18, 87-8, 299; Levy 1967: 98; MacMullen 1976: 159, 172, 180, 185).

Concomitant with the decline in population and in agricultural labor there was a significant abandonment of arable, and formerly cultivated, land. In some provinces under Valens (364-78) from 1/3 to 1/2 of arable lands were abandoned. This problem first appeared in the late second century, perhaps due to the plague, and was a subject of Imperial legislation from before Diocletian's time to that of Justinian (527-65). In the late third century Aurelian had held city councils responsible for the taxes due on deserted lands.

The shrinkage in areas cultivated was considerable in many localities. Of Imperial lands in Africa Proconsularis in 422 A.D., over 1/3 were deserted. In adjacent Byzacene more than 1/2 of the lands were untilled. Around the city of Cyrhhus, in 451, over 1/6 of the lands were deserted. Abandoned lands by the fifth century in Africa were between 10 and 15 percent in some provinces, but ranged up to 50 percent in others. Responding to this situation, Constantine made the following discharge offer to his veterans: if they became farmers they would be given free, vacant land, 100 measures of seed, and 25,000 folles (the follis being worth three-fourths of a denarius). If they became anything else the offer was 100 folles (Boak 1955: 45-6; A. Jones 1964: 812, 816, 1039, 1974: 84; MacMullen 1976: 193; Mattingly 1960: 223).

Three explanations are commonly offered for the abandonment: soil exhaustion, labor deficiencies, and barbarian raids. None of these is really satisfactory. The same agricultural techniques had been employed for centuries before Diocletian, and continued for centuries after. The bulk of deforestation and erosion apparently came later, in the Middle Ages, and resulted from disregard of water and soil conservation measures in late Roman times (Vita-Finzi 1969: 101-2). In Egypt, where the fertility of the soil was annually renewed by the Nile, abandonments were just as severe as elsewhere (Baynes 1943: 30).

Shortages of labor are more plausible, for landlords were always short of tenants, and welcomed allocations of barbarian prisoners. But some landowners abandoned estates with agricultural slaves and tenants in place. Clearly, then, labor shortages were not the sole responsible factor.

Barbarians ravaged only some parts of the Empire, and not necessarily those with the greatest percentages of abandoned lands (A. Jones 1964: 816-18, 1974: 85). They alone were not responsible for agricultural abandonment.

Contemporaries of the event attributed it to overtaxation, and there is much to recommend this interpretation. The expensive government and military of the Dominate are clearly implicated. One writer of the period went so far as to suggest that those who lived off the treasury were more numerous than those paying into it. Another complained that taxes, which were high even before the Dominate, doubled from 324 to 364. In the sixth century A.D. (which post-dates the fall of the West, but illustrates the trend), even privileged landowners paid twice as much tax as provincials had in the first century B.C., and ordinary landowners paid well over three times as much. Even Italians now found themselves taxed again.

A major problem, in addition to the rate of the levy, was the rigidity of Diocletian's tax system. It was not designed to accommodate variations in the quality of land or fluctuations in yield. This was a flat tax levied on the land and on the number of residents. The government required that the land tax be paid whether a parcel was cultivated or not. Where possible, abandoned lands were sold or granted to new owners with a tax rebate, but if this failed, they were assigned compulsorily to other landowners, to all local landowners, or to municipalities for payment of taxes. Population figures for the poll tax remained as originally calculated, regardless of how population actually changed. Villages were held corporately liable for these taxes on their members, and one village could even be held liable for another. The rate of taxation was generally not progressive, so it rested more heavily on the poor and on those with large families. When wealthy influentials got their land under-assessed, the extra share was distributed among the remainder. And the State always had a back-up on taxes due, extending obligations to widows or children, even to dowries.

The tax burden was such that peasant proprietors could accumulate no reserves, so if barbarians raided, or drought or locusts diminished the crop, they either borrowed or starved. Eventually their lands passed to creditors, to whom they became tenants. As tenants they paid 1/2 of their crops in rent, while proprietors owed 1/3 in taxes. Whatever crops were brought in had to be sold for taxes, even if it meant starvation for the farmer. Under conditions of famine it was the farmers, amazingly enough, who were the first to suffer, often flocking to cities that held stores of grain.

It is little wonder that the peasant population failed to recover. The collection of taxes and rents was so unvarying that, however poor the crop, the amount due was seized even if the cultivators were left without enough. People couldn't meet taxes and so were jailed, sold their children into slavery, or abandoned their homes and fields. Circumstances were highly unfavorable for the formation of large families.

Under these conditions the cultivation of marginal land became unprofitable, as too frequently it would not yield enough for taxes and a surplus. Hence, lands came to be progressively deserted. Faced with taxes, a small holder might abandon his land to work for a neighbor, who in turn would be glad of the extra agricultural labor. A patronage system developed wherein powerful local land-holders extended protection over peasants against the government's demands. The government legislated unsuccessfully against this source of lost revenue.

It was not only the countryside that suffered. Toward the end of his reign Constantius II (337-61) appropriated the landed endowments of cities. All local services now had to be financed by city magistrates, upon whom the burden was hereditary. Julian (360-3) restored land rents and taxes to cities, but these were reconfiscated under Valentinian I (364-75) and Valens (364-78). A few years later a portion was refunded for public building repair. In Gaul of the later Empire cities contracted, sometimes to the size of the Celtic villages from which they had earlier sprung (Rostovtzeff 1926:

465, 470-1; Boak 1955: 33, 58, 112, 125; A. Jones 1964: 68, 131, 146, 455, 465, 755-6, 773-6, 810-12, 819, 822, 1043-4, 1974: 18, 82-8, 130, 135-6; Heichelheim 1970: 332; MacMullen 1976: 100-1, 170, 173, 209).

The system established by Diocletian involved rigid control of individuals and their output. Each citizen, each guild, and each locality was expected to produce needed essentials for the survival of the Empire. For a time the Empire did indeed survive, but at a cost of the progressive abandonment of land, declining agricultural yields, depopulation of the countryside, and impoverishment of the cities. As different occupations competed for personnel, military strength declined until finally barbarians were relied on to staff the army. When Attila was defeated in Gaul in 451 it was by a federation of local Germanic kingdoms, not by Roman arms.

Taxes in the later Empire continued to be crushing. Although Valens stopped their rise in the East, and later reduced them somewhat, in the West under co-Emperor Valentinian II taxes were still too heavy. His successor, Valentinian III, publicly admitted in 444-5 that additional taxes on landowners or merchants would be devastating. Even still, he was forced in 444 to impose a 1/24 sales tax, which required that all sales be conducted in the presence of a tax collector. In the early fifth century in the West there were widespread revolts (in 417, 435-7, and 442), which had to be suppressed by the military. Delinquent taxes were remitted occasionally in the early and middle fourth century, but so frequently after 395 that a general agricultural breakdown in the West seems indicated.

Contemporary records indicate that, more than once, both rich and poor wished that the barbarians would deliver them from the burdens of the Empire. While some of the civilian population resisted the barbarians (with varying degrees of earnestness), and many more were simply inert in the presence of the invaders, some actively fought for the barbarians. In 378, for example, Balkan miners went over en masse to the Visigoths. In Gaul the invaders were sometimes welcomed as liberators from the Imperial burden, and were even invited to occupy territory. To ensure the doubtful loyalty of frontier areas, the government was on occasion forced to make up local deficits of grain.

Zosimus, a writer of the second half of the fifth century A.D., wrote of Thessaly and Macedonia that '...as a result of this exaction of taxes city and countryside were full of laments and complaints and all invoked the barbarians and sought the help of the barbarians' (quoted in Mazzarino [1966: 65]). '[B]y the fifth century,' concludes R. M. Adams, 'men were ready to abandon civilization itself in order to escape the fearful load of taxes' (1983: 47).

The decreased manpower and wealth of the Western Empire helped contribute to the military successes of the invaders. In turn, the military disasters of the West further weakened its finances. In the mid fifth century the West was gradually lost. Areas like Spain and Africa were temporarily or permanently lost to the barbarians. Substantial tax remissions had to be given to the areas devastated by the invasions. In 439 the Vandals took Carthage, which had supplied grain to the city of Rome. There were widespread breakdowns in civil services.

In the 20 years following the death of Valentinian III (455 A.D.), the Roman Army proper dwindled to nothing. The recruiting ground shrank to Italy itself. The government came to rely almost exclusively on barbarian troops. When finally these could not be paid they demanded land in Italy instead. This being refused, they mutinied, elected Odoacer their king, and deposed the last Emperor of the West, Romulus Augustulus, in 476.

Although this is the official date for the end of the Western Empire, in fact most of the provinces had been lost years before. One small section of Gaul remained under Roman administration until annexed by the Franks in 486. The Germanic kings initially maintained approximately the same civil administration they found in the conquered lands, for this was the only administration they knew. In Italy the Senate continued to meet under Odoacer and Theoderic. But even these vestiges of the Empire disappeared within a few years (Gibbon 1776-88: 1238, 1254-5, 1301; Dill 1899: 237-40; Frank 1940: 303-4; Boak 1955: 52; A. Jones 1964: 147-8, 190, 201, 204-6, 243-4, 247-8, 253, 812, 826, 1059-61, 1974: 82, 84, 88; Levy 1967: 99; Heichelheim 1970: 300; Isaac 1971: 127; Weber 1976: 407; MacMullen 1976: 207).

Assessment of the Roman collapse

Whatever the stimulus for the Roman expansion – and this no doubt varied over time – it was for the conquerors a highly successful policy. From the middle of the third century B.C. ever increasing quantities of gold and silver flowed into the Roman treasury. The result was that the Roman people paid little or nothing for continuing conquests and for garrison costs. The captive populations underwrote the cost of further expansion (A. Jones 1974: 114-15). At this point in their history the Roman people were investing in a policy of territorial expansion (with associated rise in administrative costs), and reaped the return on that investment. After the initial series of successes, the benefit/cost ratio for this policy was for a time spectacularly high. It was an enterprise with a marginal return that was most favorable.

Inevitably, though, this high rate of return could not be maintained. Three factors combine ultimately to lower the marginal return for any such policy. First, the number of profitable conquests declines. A geographically expanding state ultimately encounters a competitor with equivalent capabilities, whose conquest would be too expensive, if not impossible. Rome met such a competitor in the Persian (Parthian, later Sassanian) Empire to the east. Although in the many contests between these powers Rome generally came out best, Parthia was a long overland trek from the Mediterranean. It had lengthy borders, external enemies of its own, and a potentially subversive population. Trajan's conquest of parts of this empire was abandoned by Hadrian as too expensive to administer (Rostovtzeff 1926: 315). On other fronts, if powers demanding respect are not found, an expanding polity is likely to meet populations whose conquest would not bear the cost. The Romans found such peoples on many fronts, such as the northern frontier with Germany. Thus, the economics of territorial expansion dictate, as a simple matter of mathematical probability, that an expanding power will ultimately encounter a frontier beyond which conquest and garrisoning are unprofitable.

Secondly, the logistics of transport and communication dictate that, beyond a certain distance from the capital, lands will be difficult to govern. For the Roman Empire this was especially the case the farther one traveled inland from the Mediterranean sea lanes.

The combined factors of increased costliness of conquest, and increased difficulty of administration with distance from the capital, effectively require that at some point a policy of expansion must end. This was the state reached by the Roman Empire by the beginning of the current era. Under Augustus the size of the Roman Empire was essentially capped. Later additions were comparatively insignificant, and costly. The conquests of Britain by Claudius, and of Dacia by Trajan, probably never paid for themselves, for these were poor, distant, frontier provinces (M. Hammond 1946: 75-6).

Thirdly, once the accumulated surpluses of conquered nations have been appropriated, a conqueror must thereafter incur costs to administer, garrison, and defend the province. And when the accumulated surpluses have been spent, this must be paid for out of yearly income. Costs rise and benefits decline. For a one-time infusion of wealth from each conquered province, Rome had to undertake administrative and military responsibilities that lasted centuries. For Rome, the costs of administering some provinces (such as Spain and Macedonia) exceeded their revenues. And although he was probably exaggerating, Cicero complained in 66 B.C. that, of all Roman conquests, only Asia yielded a surplus. In general, most revenues were raised in the richer lands of the Mediterranean, and spent on the army in the poorer frontier areas such as Britain, the Rhineland, and the Danube (A. Jones 1974: 116, 127).

So the process of geographical expansion, if successful, yields a marginal return that initially is very high, but which inevitably begins to decline. By the time the conquest of the rich Mediterranean lands was completed, this was the situation in the Roman Empire. An imperial administration that had been developed following the major influxes of wealth that were the benefits of conquest thereafter had to be supported by the Empire's yearly agricultural output. The result was that under the Principate the Empire had to maintain a far-flung, inflexible administrative and military structure on the basis of variable agricultural output, and in the face of an increasingly hostile political environment. The Roman Empire was the first state, and the only one until recent times, to maintain a standing military force sufficient for all its needs (A. Jones 1974: 135).

As a result, from Augustus on, the Empire regularly faced fiscal insufficiencies. The Imperial budget was generally sufficient for the normal needs of the government, but stress surges required extraordinary fiscal measures. Augustus' successors dealt with financial crises occasionally by selling their capital – Imperial lands and treasures. This was obviously a limited solution. The more common stratagem was to defer the true costs of government by debasing the currency. This had the politically expedient advantage of shifting to some indefinite point in the future the cost of current crises. The inflation that would inevitably follow would tax the future to pay for the present, but the future could not protest. Viewed from the perspective of history, it is clear that by the time of the Principate the marginal return on investment in empire had declined considerably from the level of the later Republic. When the stresses impinging on the Empire grew, it would decline further still. What had once been a windfall was becoming a burden.

The weaknesses of the Empire that were exposed when Marcus Aurelius confronted the Marcomanni proved nearly fatal during the succeeding crises. The reduced marginal return on organizational investment left the Roman Empire without sufficient reserves to meet such emergencies. The only alternatives were to raise taxes directly, or to raise them indirectly by debasement and inflation. Both courses were adopted. And yet the crises of civil war and barbarian incursions required increased expenditures that yielded no increased return. The Empire was not expanded, no major booty was acquired, and there was no increase in agricultural output. The increased costs of the third century were incurred merely to maintain the status quo. Costs rose precipitously while benefits, at best, remained level. Axiomatically, the marginal return on investment in empire declined.

This process intensified with the establishment of the Dominate during the reign of Diocletian. In the third century taxation had become so heavy as to consume the capital resources of taxpayers (Boak 1955: 111). In the fourth and fifth centuries it became even worse. As the sizes of both the military and the civil administrations doubled, taxes had to be raised from a weakened Empire to foot the bill. The effect on the support population, as described, was devastating.

The cost of saving the Empire was extremely high for a non-industrial population. And as in the third century, payment of this cost yielded no increase in benefits. Yet what happened during the fourth and fifth centuries was more than simply a further decline in the marginal return. The Empire was by this time sustaining itself by the consumption of its capital resources: producing lands and peasant population. Continued investment in empire was creating not only a drop in marginal output, but also a drop in *actual* output. Where under the Principate the strategy had been to tax the future to pay for the present, the Dominate paid for the present by undermining the future's ability to pay taxes. The Empire emerged from the third century crisis, but at a cost that weakened its ability to meet future crises. At least in the West, a downward spiral ensued: reduced finances weakened military defense, while military disasters in turn meant further loss of producing lands and population. Collapse was in the end inevitable, as indeed it had always been.

In Chapter 4 it was suggested that, when a complex society enters a situation of declining marginal returns, collapse can occur from one or both of two reasons: lack of sufficient reserves with which to meet stress surges, and alienation of the over-taxed support population. The former was a clear problem faced by the Empire since at least the days of Marcus Aurelius, if not before. The latter evidently became part of the Empire's problems under the Dominate, or possibly even during the third century crisis. If accounts are to be believed, at least a portion of the overtaxed peasantry openly welcomed the relief they thought the barbarians would bring from the burdens of Roman rule. And a much larger portion were evidently apathetic to the impending collapse. It seems clear that the Empire had at least partially lost its legitimacy. The costs of empire had risen dramatically, while in the face of barbarian successes the protection that the State could offer to many of its citizens proved increasingly ineffectual. To many, there were simply no remaining benefits to the Empire, as both barbarians and tax collectors crossed and ravaged their lands. As Gunderson notes, '...the net value of local autonomy exceeded that of membership in the Empire' (1976: 61). Complexity was no longer yielding benefits superior to disintegration, and yet it cost so much more.

The collapse yielded at the same time both a reduction in the costs of complexity and an increase in the marginal return on its investment. The smaller, Germanic kingdoms that succeeded Roman rule in the West were more successful at resisting foreign incursions (e.g., Huns and Arabs) than had been the later Empire (Weber 1976: 389). They did so, moreover, at lower administrative and military costs. The economic prosperity of North Africa actually rose under the Vandals, but declined again under Justinian's reconquest when Imperial taxes were reimposed (Hodges and Whitehouse 1983: 28). Thus the paradox of collapse: a drop in complexity brings with it a corresponding rise in the marginal return on social investment (see Fig. 19).

Two matters remain to be addressed: why the East survived when the West failed, and why the Empire did not develop the economic strength necessary to avoid collapse.

Three factors account for the continued survival of the East. Two of these are that it was economically stronger than the West and strategically less vulnerable. The provinces of the Eastern Empire included the older, more economically developed and populous parts of the Mediterranean world. Such provinces were better able to bear the costs of defense and administration than those of the West. It has been estimated that in the later Empire the budget of the West was only 1/3 that of the East. And yet the West had over twice as long a northern frontier to defend. While in the fourth and fifth centuries the West was overrun by invaders, the East had major problems along only the Danubian frontier. To the east, wars with Persia were infrequent, with long periods of peace (Baynes 1943: 34-5; A. Jones 1964: 1027, 1030-1; Levy 1967: 92, 99).

Within the framework developed here it may be observed that the East survived because, with its greater wealth and its smaller border problems, its investment in complexity was more easily financed, and its marginal return higher. The support population was wealthier and more numerous, and thus less easily overtaxed. And its government was, if not more successful militarily than the West, at least less unsuccessful. The government of the East continued to rule not just because of wealth and geography, but also because these happy circumstances combined to give it greater legitimacy.

The third factor accounting for the survival of the empire in the eastern Mediterranean is that it *could not* collapse. To discuss this point requires concepts that will be introduced in the final chapter. The survival of the Eastern Roman Empire will be raised again at that point.

The matter of economic development is more subtle. Many authors concentrate on the expense of transport, and the poverty of the rural population, as reasons why industry did not develop, nor agriculture intensify (e.g., A. Jones 1964: 1048). Yet there is more to the matter. As Elster has pointed out, 'Innovation and technical change are not universal phenomena, but are restricted in time and space to a very small subset of historical societies' (1983: 105). In this light the question 'Why didn't Rome develop economically?' can be rephrased 'Why wasn't Rome economically abnormal?' Viewed thus, the question of Rome's lack of economic development becomes substantially less problematical.

It might be worthwhile to consider the matter by comparison to the later development of industrialism in northwestern Europe. As described in previous chapters, Wilkinson (1973) has argued that, at least in its initial phases, industrialism in England was stress-induced. Overpopulation in the later Medieval period led to clearing of forests for agricultural land. The resulting drop in fuelwood regeneration required the populace to shift to increased dependence on coal. Reliance on coal in turn necessitated a host of concomitant changes, many associated with the industrial 'revolution.' These included the steam engine, high capacity water pumps (for mining below the water table), and both canal and rail transportation.

While I don't wish to draw any *direct* contrasts between industrialism in England and its absence in the Roman Empire, one difference is glaring: the later Empire was substantially underpopulated. Lands that had once been cultivated were in late Classical times deserted, while agricultural labor was in short supply. Government attempts to reclaim the abandoned lands and to foster population growth were notably unsuccessful. It has been argued that such attempts at intensifying the use of land will typically be unsuccessful, if imposed from the top in a situation in which they are inappropriate (cf. Boserup 1965; Rostow 1960: 34). Intensification, whether in the use of land or in any economic sphere, would have had to emerge from demographic and/or economic pressures operating on the bulk of the Roman population (Wilkinson 1973; North and Thomas 1973). With low population and free available land, such pressures were simply absent. Other pressures, to be sure, were affecting the population of the Empire, but not a lack of economic opportunity. There were simply too much unused land and too many unfilled occupations. In Britain, for example, the heavy plow needed to take in the clay lands was probably known from before Roman times, and yet population was so low that the clay lands were largely avoided until later (Boak 1955: 36; Wailes 1972). If the later Roman government had attempted a policy of economic development, it would have experienced a frustration often found by contemporary governments attempting the same thing: development cannot be forced in the absence of demand. Colloquially, it is called pushing on a string.

The Classic Maya collapse

The setting

Lowland Classic Maya Civilization is often regarded as a puzzle of human history. One of the few early civilizations that did not develop in a semi-arid setting (Sanders 1962: 79), the Maya are, as Netting has observed, '...a people whose greatest mystery is their abrupt departure from the stage of world history...' (1977: 299).

This discussion will concentrate on the Maya of the Southern Lowlands, whose society underwent a rapid, dramatic, and justly famous collapse between about 790 and 890 A.D. (Pertinent material from surrounding Mayan areas will also be discussed where appropriate.) The Southern Lowlands region encompasses roughly the Peten of northern Guatemala and surrounding lands. The Mayan political centers of this region (Fig. 24) are numerous and varied. The record of their rise and fall can be most clearly discussed in the context of Mayan archaeological chronology. In actuality, a number of chronologies exist for the Southern Lowlands, most of which are sufficiently similar that their differences need not concern us. Gordon Willey's (1982), given below, will satisfy our present needs:

Middle Preclassic	1000-400 B.C.
Late Preclassic	400-50 B.C.
Protoclassic	50 B.C.-250 A.D.
Early Classic	250-550 A.D.
Hiatus	550-600 A.D.
Late Classic	600-800 A.D.
Terminal Classic	800-1000 A.D.
Postclassic	post-1000 A.D.

As with most archaeological chronologies, this one is highly generalized, and the dates are of course rounded averages. Not all authors make the distinction between Late Preclassic and Protoclassic, and between Terminal Classic and Postclassic, so in the discussion that follows there may be some blurring of these phases.

The Maya produced a form of hieroglyphic script that cannot at present be fully read, although considerable progress has been made toward its decipherment. Mayan civilization, as noted above, is mainly known archaeologically.

The vegetation of the Southern Lowlands is today a tropical rainforest, as it was when the Maya first began to clear the land for planting. The central Peten zone is characterized by flat-topped limestone ridges, on which the Maya settled, interspersed with seasonal swamps called *bajos*. Rainfall concentrates between May and November, which is also the main agricultural season. Single cropping is today the norm, but limited replanting and double cropping are possible in an emergency (Culbert 1973a: 6, 11, 1974: 6). Rainfall, which varies across the Central Lowlands from 1000 to 2000 millimeters per year, displays some variation. Droughts occur, but tend to be minor. Long-term rainfall fluctuations in the Northern Lowlands range only about 9 percent from maximum to minimum, compared with 17-22 percent in the Mesoamerican Highlands. Annual rainfall fluctuations in the area of concern are less than 15-20 percent, and generally do not adversely affect agriculture today (Culbert 1974: 6; Hammond and Ashmore 1981: 24; Vivo Escoto 1964: 203-4; Wallen 1956: 147, 149).

A major debate among students of the Maya is the degree of ecological diversity across the Lowlands. This debate has important implications for Mayan sociopolitical evolution, and is a topic that will be raised again in a few pages. In essence, the difference is between scholars who emphasize the comparative topographical redundancy and ecological homogeneity of the central Peten (e.g., Culbert 1973a: 3;

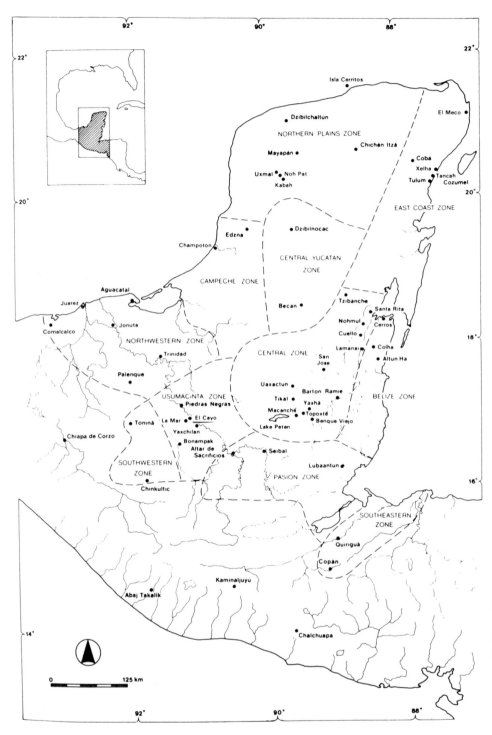

Fig. 24. The Mayan area, showing major subdivisions and selected sites (after Hammond and Ashmore 1981: 21). Reproduced by permission of Wendy Ashmore and the University of New Mexico Press.

Sanders 1973: 335, 1977: 288; Tourtellot and Sabloff 1972: 128; Rathje 1973: 408), and those who see the Southern Lowlands as nevertheless significantly diverse (e.g., Harris 1978: 302; Wiseman 1978: 72). Sanders notes that 26 varieties of soil, with differing potentials for agriculture, have been mapped in the Peten (1973: 375), although greater soil variation is to be found in the Guatemalan Highlands (Sanders and Webster 1978: 262, 264). Others note that at some of the peripheries of the Peten, ecological diversity is higher. This is especially so in Belize, which is characterized by riverine environments, the coastal strip, the Maya Mountains (which rise to about 1000 meters), as well as lowland rain forest (Culbert 1973a: 8, 1974: 3-4; N. Hammond 1981: 159). Viewed on a broad level, the central Peten, which witnessed the earliest and most complex Mayan developments, is characterized by somewhat better soils than surrounding areas. Yet this has drawbacks, for the best soils in the area are susceptible to erosion (Adams and Jones 1981: 302; Sanders 1973: 337, 339).

Several factors are pertinent to the diversity argument. Although tropical rainforests are as a rule notably diverse in *species* (MacArthur 1972: 210-11), the important factor here may be *topographic* diversity. Since climate and vegetation change with altitude, the topographic redundancy of the Peten creates a situation where diversity of ecological *zones* (not necessarily diversity of species) per unit of horizontal space must be lower than in the Mesoamerican Highlands. Zonal diversity is important for developing different resource production systems within an area. Where zonal diversity is high, there is a greater likelihood that different production systems will exist that will fluctuate non-synchronously in their ability to support human populations. Such a condition is important in the evolution of complex, regional exchange systems. This is not to suggest that diverse production systems did not exist in the Lowlands, only that the potential for such systems was greater in the Highlands. It is noteworthy that the Maya Mountains may not contribute significantly to Lowlands diversity, for tropical mountaintops tend to have fewer species than tropical lowlands (MacArthur 1972: 211, 214).

Views of the Maya
Only recently have archaeologists begun to understand the true complexity of Maya Civilization. Our previous ignorance is part of the reason why the Maya, and their collapse, have seemed so mysterious. The Classic Maya were at one time thought to have been a low density people scattered, as today, across the Lowlands, practicing slash-and-burn (swidden, milpa, or forest-fallow) agriculture, and residentially mobile to the extent that milpa requires. The Maya centers were thought to be ceremonial in nature, with little permanent occupation. The rural populace visited these centers on ceremonial occasions, but did not reside at them. The ceremonial centers were staffed by a small caste of priests and nobles who concerned themselves largely with ceremonialism and its calendrical details. The Maya, depicted thus, were thought to be a peaceful people, whose centers were open and without fortifications. Elite demands were as a rule low, but did eventually reach the point where the peasants were no longer willing to satisfy continual or increased demands for services, labor, and food. At this point a peasant revolt or withdrawal of support brought about

the collapse (e.g., Altschuler 1958: 194-6; Cowgill 1964: 154; J. E. S. Thompson 1966 [not all of whom would necessarily agree with each of the above points]; for discussions see Mathewson [1977: 204-5] and Turner [1974: 118]).

Maya Civilization, as thus reconstructed, seems anomalous. The low, dispersed population of swidden farmers would be unusual among early civilizations, which were generally characterized by high population densities and labor-intensive farming often involving hydro-agricultural engineering. The vacant ceremonial center notion is out of place considering the relationship in many early civilizations between urbanism and sociopolitical complexity. The notion of the Maya elite as relatively powerless priests and nobles, concerned only with ceremonialism and ritual calendars, presents a startling departure from the normal condition of hierarchical organization in complex societies. And the view of the Maya as a peaceful civilization is, to say the least, unusual.

Within the last 20 to 30 years archaeological fieldwork has produced finds that require a major reassessment of the Maya. The University of Pennsylvania project at Tikal, the largest Mayan site, has produced evidence of a center that was urban in its proportions, with population numbering in the tens of thousands (Haviland 1969, 1970). Such population densities seem to exceed the support capabilities of swidden agriculture (e.g., Harrison 1977: 479, 484; Rice and Puleston 1981: 144-5), leading to the suggestion that past Mayan agriculture may have been more intensive than that of today. Not surprisingly, both aerial and ground surveys in recent years have found substantial evidence for intensive agriculture in the form of terraces, canals, and raised fields (Adams and Hammond 1982: 502). The Maya elite appear to have been interested in more than calendrics, as their inscriptions are showing evidence of concern with dynastic succession, political struggles, alliances, royal marriages, and the like (e.g., Proskouriakoff 1960, 1963, 1964). Evidence of warfare is found in both art and fortifications (Webster 1976a, 1977), evidence which Webster suggests has '...further reduced the "peaceful Maya" to the same level as the rest of contentious humanity...' (1976a: 113).

The new findings suggest that the Maya may not have been unusual among early civilizations, and require a revised synthesis of the Lowland Classic. Mayan archaeologists have responded with such a synthesis.

The evolution of Maya Civilization

The emergence of Maya Civilization apparently lies in the Preclassic, when many Classic period characteristics began to develop. Early Preclassic villages existed as early as 2000 B.C. (Culbert n.d.). Maize (*Zea*) pollen has been found in the central Peten Lakes dating to the same period (Rice 1976: 425). By the Middle Preclassic there were settlements containing at least 200 to 300 persons each (Willey 1982: 261).

The Middle and Late Preclassic farmers of the Southern Lowlands were undeniably successful, for their archaeological record reveals a continuously rising population (R. E. W. Adams 1977b: 320; Deevey et al. 1979: 301; Rice 1976: 439, 444-5; 1978: 44; Webster 1977: 343; Willey 1977a: 138-9, 1982: 262; Willey et al. 1965: 569). Webster suggests that there was population pressure in the Becan region by about 500

B.C. (1977: 343), while N. Hammond concludes that by the Late Preclassic, population density and site spacing were such that any further growth would have led to competition (1977: 65; see also Rice [1976: 444-5]). Based on their research in the central Peten Lakes region, Deevey et al. calculate a constant population growth rate through the Preclassic and Classic periods of about 0.17 percent per year, which yields a doubling interval of about 408 years (1979: 301).

At some point in the Preclassic, probably varying across the region, this continued population growth led inevitably to strains on existing food production systems. A variety of responses followed. Agricultural strategies had to change, and did so through the formation of systems that were increasingly labor intensive. R. E. W. Adams suggests that there may have been a conversion from swidden to more intensive agricultural systems in the central and northern Peten by the Late Preclassic or Early Classic (1981: 249; see also Freidel [1981: 373-4] and Sanders [1977: 296]). There is good evidence for this. A major system of hydraulic engineering, involving reservoirs and canals, was constructed at the Belizean site of Cerros in the Late Preclassic, with some parts of the system dated to between 200 and 50 B.C. (Freidel and Scarborough 1982; Scarborough 1983). (Freidel and Scarborough suggest that this development represents commercial rather than subsistence production [1982: 152-3].) A similar system was started at the site of Edzna, in northern Yucatan, in the Late Preclassic (Matheny 1978: 199).

Calculations of population levels and subsistence production indicate that by the Late Preclassic subsistence stress in the central Peten may have required shorter fallow periods and the addition of less productive lands (Rice 1978: 50). In this region, an early lacustrine settlement pattern, associated with reliable water sources and aquatic protein, gave way to increased Middle Preclassic settlement in the water-deficient interior (Rice 1976: 440-1; Rice and Puleston 1981: 151-2).

This early shift to more intensive agriculture may have been widespread, for by the Late Preclassic much of the central area had been deforested (Deevey et al. 1979: 298). Such a condition would make long-fallow swidden impossible. Pollen samples indicate that the Preclassic landscape was a mosaic of cornfields and scrubland, with occasional hamlets. Human population density may have been around 25-60 per square kilometer (Wiseman 1978: 112).

Major fortifications at the site of Becan (a ditch and parapet surrounding the site) have been dated to between 150 and 300 A.D. (Thomas 1981: 96; see also Webster 1976a, 1977). It seems likely, therefore, that the competition and conflict which characterized later Maya Civilization began in the Pre- or Protoclassic. Its origin can be probably attributed to the pressure of population on resources (R. E. W. Adams 1977b: 320; Freidel 1979: 38; N. Hammond 1977: 65).

The Late Preclassic Maya were faced then with population pressure, a strained resource base, and an increasingly competitive environment. At least two solutions were sought: agricultural intensification (as noted) and increased sociopolitical complexity (Rice 1976: 444-5). The evidence for the latter is striking by the Middle and Late Preclassic. Formal, public architecture and social differentiation become evident by early in the Middle Preclassic, and increasingly thereafter. Public buildings on platforms, and status differentiation in burials, occur by about 400 B.C. (Culbert 1977b: 42; N. Hammond 1982: 123; Marcus 1983: 461; Rice 1976: 438-9; Willey 1977a: 145, 1977b: 388, 1980: 258, 1982: 262).

The site of Altar de Sacrificios has yielded an interesting record of the emergence of local hierarchies. At the end of the Middle Preclassic one of several residential clusters was rebuilt so that it was noticeably larger than the rest, with the largest monument some four meters high. Successive rebuildings transformed this into a Classic temple-palace complex, with a 13-meter-high pyramid mound, and a stone-faced stairway. This transformation seems to record the emergence of a ruling descent group from an earlier dominant residential unit (Willey 1980: 258, 1982: 262).

In the Late Preclassic a two or three level administrative hierarchy was present in the Southern Lowlands. Public architecture became truly monumental at some Lowlands sites (Marcus 1983: 461; Willey 1982: 262). By 100 B.C.– 150 A.D. Tikal was emerging as a center of considerable magnitude (Culbert 1977b: 39).

These patterns intensified throughout the Classic. Population, agricultural investment, sociopolitical complexity, architectural elaboration, and conflict continued to grow. In the Early Classic regional political organization developed into increasingly formal and hierarchical patterns. Prior to 434 A.D. centers were spaced about equidistantly, and seem to have been roughly equivalent in rank. Tikal and Uaxactun, however, may have been early dominant centers, for they have the earliest dated monuments and together account for 50 percent of all monuments between 292 and 434 A.D. (Marcus 1976: 191). One prominent Mayanist, Gordon Willey, suggests that Tikal actually attained a measure of dominance over the entire Southern Lowlands during the Early Classic, possibly constituting the capital of a Southern Lowland state (1980: 259, 1982: 265).

The maximum areal extent for Classic monuments and art styles was reached in the early sixth century A.D. Major centers emerged that may have been regional capitals. There was a hierarchy of at least four levels of sites, with hexagonal lattices of secondary centers around regional capitals (Marcus 1976: 191). The earliest Mayan writing can be dated to the third century A.D. Early texts deal with the birth, death, accession, and conquests of rulers (Marcus 1983: 461). At Tikal, a defensive earthwork and moat were constructed at the site's north end, spanning the 9.5 kilometers between the two swamps that bounded Tikal to the east and west. A similar feature lies south of the site (R. E. W. Adams 1977b: 148-9).

An intriguing development at the end of the Early Classic is a sharp decline in the number of monuments newly dedicated, and in the number of sites at which these occur. There are indications of a decline in other construction, as well as changes in ceramic and architectural styles. Dating between 534 and 593 A.D., the event has been termed the Hiatus (Willey 1974). One of the interesting aspects of the episode is an apparent degree of political decentralization, as stelae (stone monuments that marked political events) were erected for the first time on the peripheries of the Southern Lowlands. (The core area, in other words, no longer held a political monopoly.) Although there is no evidence to indicate a marked reduction in sociopolitical complexity across the region, the Hiatus seems in some ways similar to the political decentralization that, as will be seen, marked the collapse (Willey 1974).

The Late Classic witnessed the resurgence and culmination of the trends begun in the Preclassic. Between 652 and 751 A.D. there was a high degree of homogeneity across the Southern Lowlands in the style and iconography of monuments. A standardized (and highly sophisticated) lunar calendar was adopted throughout the region within a ten year period. Major sites may have served as regional capitals, engaging in alliances with each other. Integration within a region was accomplished by marriage alliances between regional capitals and their dependencies. Major centers were surrounded by secondary centers that were spaced almost equidistantly from each other (Marcus 1976: 191, 1983: 461). The stature of Tikal seems to have comparatively declined. Although it remained the largest state it was forced to compete politically with many new centers (Willey 1982: 266). Investment in monumental architecture increased substantially over earlier times (Willey and Shimkin 1973: 459-61).

Several aspects of the Classic period merit detailed discussion in order to understand the collapse. These include population, subsistence, sociopolitical complexity and related phenomena, and warfare.

Population

There is evidence across the Southern Lowlands for continued population growth during the Classic, reaching a peak at different times in the Late Classic in various localities (e.g., R. E. W. Adams 1977a: 93; Culbert n.d.; Deevey et al. 1979: 301; Rice and Puleston 1981: 153; Willey 1973: 96; Willey et al. 1965: Willey and Shimkin 1973: 490). Late Classic population levels, despite agricultural intensification, were apparently approaching an upper limitation, for the earlier pattern of exponential growth was beginning to level off. G. Cowgill suggests that there was little growth in the Lowlands after 550 A.D. (1979: 57-8), while R. E. W. Adams, agreeing with the pattern, would push the date of growth cessation forward to about 650 (1977b: 221). Focusing on patterns in individual localities, Culbert (n.d.) observes that in some parts of the Southern Lowlands population peaked between 600 and 700 A.D. (the Tepeu 1 ceramic period), while elsewhere it peaked between 700 and 830 (Tepeu 2). Tikal and Yaxha reached maximum population in the Late Classic, Seibal and Altar de Sacrificios in the Terminal Classic (Lowe 1985: 34). Away from the major political centers, there was also a late peak among the rural population of the Belize Valley (Willey 1973; Willey et al. 1965).

Tikal is the most intensively studied of the Mayan centers. The most densely occupied, central 16 square kilometers of the site may have had a peak, Late Classic population of 10,000 to 11,000 (Haviland 1969, 1970). The periphery of Tikal, bounded by swamps on east and west and earthworks on north and south, was home to another 39,000, for a total population of 49,000. Haviland notes that this figure compares closely to the estimate of about 50,000 for ancient Sumerian cities (1970: 193).

For the entire Southern Lowlands, Culbert (n.d.) projects an average of about 200 persons per square kilometer, and notes that this would make the Lowlands one of the most densely populated areas of the preindustrial world. The population density of Tikal was about 350 to 400 per square kilometer, while swidden agriculture would have been able to support only 30-60 per square kilometer (Culbert 1973b: 72). Several investigators have concluded from such figures that slash-and-burn farming was incapable of sustaining much of the population (e.g., R. E. W. Adams 1977a: 91; Deevey et al. 1979: 299; Harrison 1977: 479, 484; Rice 1978: 50; Sanders 1973: 330-1). Harrison, for example, estimates that from 61-74 percent of the Tikal population must have been supported by other means (1977: 479, 484). The question of how Lowland populations were supported is thus of considerable importance.

Subsistence

Research in the Lowlands over the past few years has revealed a widespread complex of features reflecting intensive agriculture. Intensive agricultural methods were relatively permanent and organized, and included at least the following techniques: (a) canalization and draining of river margins and *bajo* swamps to create raised and channeled fields; (b) water channeling and storage; (c) terracing of both steep and shallow hillslopes to direct drainage, trap silt, and create fertile areas; and (d) a variety of miscellaneous features (R. E. W. Adams 1977a: 93; Adams and Hammond 1982: 502). These techniques have been found in various areas across the Lowlands.

Canalization/raised fields. Raised field systems and associated canals provided dry, cultivable land in areas otherwise subject to inundation. This includes lakes and lagoons, river margins, and, primarily, *bajos*. Other benefits of raised fields/canals would be fish propagation in the canals between fields, maintenance of a moist root-level soil environment, fertilization of fields with organically-rich soil derived from canal bottoms, and use of canals for transporting crops (R. E. W. Adams 1980: 209; Puleston 1977: 455-7; Siemens 1982; Turner 1974, 1978). With fertilization from canal bottoms, these fields could have supported continuous cropping (Siemens 1982: 221), although it is uncertain whether this was done (Antoine et al. 1982: 234; Siemens 1982: 219).

Most raised field systems have been discerned through aerial photography. Ground checking has regularly confirmed the observations made on the aerial imagery; and with the passage of time, more and more areas of the Lowlands have been shown to have such remains (e.g., R. E. W. Adams 1983; N. Hammond 1981: 170; Harrison 1977: 477, 1978: 247, 249, 1982: 123-6; Puleston 1977; Siemens 1978, 1982; Turner 1978; Willey 1980: 253). Recent work by R. E. W. Adams involved radar mapping of about one-half of the Southern Lowlands (1980). Adams' results lead him to estimate that between 1250 and 2500 square kilometers of the Lowlands were modified by canals. Such figures compare impressively with the 120 square kilometers of the famous Aztec *chinampas* of the Valley of Mexico, which were similar in nature and function. Drained, modified, and intensively cultivated swamps, suggests Adams, may have been the most valuable land by the Late Classic (1980: 210). There is a noticeable association between swamps and the larger sites. Tikal, significantly, had the largest quantity of readily available swamp of any major center (R. E. W. Adams 1980: 210-11).

Raised field complexes date as early as ca. 1100 B.C., as well as to the Late Preclassic. With the population maximum that was reached in the Late Classic, raised field cultivation was at its height in this period (Puleston 1977: 452; Siemens and Puleston 1972: 234; Willey 1982: 264).

Water channeling and storage. Water channeling and storage involved a variety of techniques, some of which were only partially related to agriculture, but which were all characteristically labor-intensive. The Lowlands as a whole are deficient in surface water, particularly during the dry season. The Maya dealt with this was by constructing canals, dams, reservoirs, and small wells, and by altering *cenotes* (large limestone sinkholes) (Healy 1983; Matheny 1982). In some areas hydraulic engineering reached major levels. Reservoirs are common in the Rio Bec area (R. E. W. Adams 1981: 227). At the west Yucatan site of Edzna, a water-control system consisting of a moat, canal, and reservoir complex was designed to collect and store rainwater for agriculture, human consumption, and defense. The volume of earth moved for this complex, begun in the Late Preclassic, made its construction as large an undertaking as the Pyramids of the Sun and the Moon at Teotihuacan (Matheny 1976, 1978). A major Late Preclassic canal system was also built, as noted above, at the site of Cerros in northern Belize (Freidel and Scarborough 1982; Scarborough 1983).

Canal systems that were probably used for water transportation have been documented along the Rio Candelaria (Siemens and Puleston 1972). Hundreds of narrow (3-10 meters wide), short (1-2 kilometers) canals have been recorded. Matheny's calculations on the volume of earth moved to create the 180 kilometers of documented canals suggest that 500,000 labor-days are represented. The 10,000,000 cubic meters of material excavated is ten times the volume of the Pyramid of the Sun (Matheny 1978: 193, 195).

Terraces. Terraces are found across a wide area of the Lowlands, including southern Campeche and Quintana Roo (and the Rio Bec region), portions of the Peten, and the Maya Mountains of Belize (R. E. W. Adams 1981; Turner 1974, 1978, 1979; Wilken 1971; Willey 1980: 252-3). Hundreds of thousands of terraces and related stone works were spread across 10,000 square kilometers of southern Campeche and Quintana Roo hillsides. An additional 1400 square kilometers of terraces have been noted in Belize (Turner 1974, 1978, 1979). Available dates on terrace systems seem to consistently point to the late Early Classic and the Late Classic (R. E. W. Adams 1981: 246; Thomas 1981: 100-1, 106; Turner 1974: 121; Turner and Harrison 1978: 343).

Miscellaneous features. Other agricultural features found in the Lowlands include check dams and walled fields (R. E. W. Adams 1981: 243, 246-7; Turner 1978: 170; Wiseman 1983: 156). The walled field complexes may occur over much of the Peten (Turner 1974: 170; Wiseman 1983: 156), and are sometimes found as parts of terrace systems (R. E. W. Adams 1981: 246). Such field demarcation is absolutely incongruent with anything but permanent or short-fallow cultivation (cf. Turner 1978: 170).

Mayan crops. Although a great deal is known about Mayan agricultural production systems, little is known about crops actually grown. It has always been assumed that maize was the major crop, and indeed most archaeobotanical remains are of this plant (Marcus 1983: 476). Bronson has suggested that the Maya grew root crops of various kinds (1966), while Puleston (e.g., 1978) has argued for reliance on the nut yields of the Ramon tree. Archaeobotanical and palynological evidence definitely establishes the cultivation of maize, squash, avocado, cacao, cotton, and *Xanthosoma* root. Classic Maya art suggests the cultivation of *Achras*, *Byrsonima*, and *Psidium*, which are fruit-bearing trees (Wiseman 1983: 161, 163). Ramon is currently a famine food among the Maya (Sanders 1973: 339-41).

Palynological studies in the Peten suggest that in the Classic period agricultural practice involved a suite of techniques, each fitted to peculiar circumstances, with differing levels of intensification and productivity (Wiseman 1978: 113, 1983: 158). Wiseman suggests that, with Classic period population densities and forest clearing, the Maya would have had to maintain woodlots for firewood, and production lots for the palm fronds needed for thatched roofs (1983: 151-3).

Sociopolitical complexity

Aspects of Mayan sociopolitical organization have been discussed previously. This is a topic that crosscuts all other facets of the Maya, but can be briefly isolated to characterize its nature.

Mayan society was complex and highly stratified. The social order consisted minimally of a ruling class, a mid-level hierarchy of artisans and bureaucrats, and the peasants. In actuality, each of these classes was itself subdivided into appropriate gradations (R. E. W. Adams 1973b: 138; Adams and Smith 1981; Becker 1973). Leadership was hereditary within descent groups (C. Jones 1977) from at least the first century B.C. (Haviland 1977: 66), or possibly even as early as the Middle Preclassic (Willey 1980: 258). Rulers legitimized their reigns by erecting sculptural art that proclaimed ties to ancestors and deeds of conquest (Adams and Jones 1981: 301; Marcus 1983: 461; Proskouriakoff 1960, 1963, 1964; Willey 1980: 259-62).

The sculptures of Tikal offer an interesting glimpse into Mayan sociopolitical succession. In A.D. 378 Tikal was ruled by a man whose identifying glyph is today given the descriptive designation 'Curl Snout.' Curl Snout is shown in the ornament and dress of Teotihuacan, symbolizing linkages with that dominant Highland power. The accession of 'Stormy Sky,' son of Curl Snout, is associated with a burst of major, new construction. Some time later (in the period now known as the Late Classic) after a phase of leadership struggles, 'Ruler A' acceded to the throne. His possibly precarious position was buttressed in sculptural art by a conspicuous display of Curl Snout and Stormy Sky symbols (Willey 1980: 259-60). Such legitimization of rule by display of ancestral ties occurs elsewhere in Mayan art at stressful times, such as when a ruler's accomplishments were less than those of his ancestors (Proskouriakoff 1963: 166, 1964: 178), and at the collapse (Marcus 1976: 193).

Sculptural and ceramic art portray a Maya elite concerned with alliances, royal marriages, conflict, hierarchical relationships, and political intrigue (Adams and Jones 1981: 301). Important persons visited distant centers to participate in the burial ceremonies of other elites (R. E. W. Adams 1969: 25, 1973b: 138), arranged marriages as vehicles of political aspiration (Molloy and Rathje 1974), celebrated conquests, and generally engaged in the kinds of political maneuvering expectable in a complex society.

The distribution of population and settlements across space reflects the political climate of the Lowlands. The view of Mayan socio-spatial organization that has gained widest acceptance was developed by Bullard, based on surveys in the Peten (1960). The organization of settlement mirrored the organization of the society. At the apex of each polity was a Major Center such as Tikal. Each Major Center established dominance over a set of smaller Minor Centers that were characterized by lesser amounts of sculptural art and monumental architecture. Each Minor Center in turn administered, and served as the political focus of, a localized peasant population (see also Willey et al. 1965; Willey 1981; Sanders 1973: 326-7).

There were regional and temporal variations in this idealized pattern, and since Bullard's work finer details have emerged. Within centers, residential areas were segregated by status (Folan et al. 1979; Kurjack 1974). Between centers, in some areas, the density of settlement declined (Puleston 1974: 303-8; Sanders 1981a). In other regions the distribution of settlements is continuous (Sanders 1981a: 360; Thomas 1981: 26; Willey et al. 1965). In southern Quintana Roo, for example, there are stretches of terrain 40 to 50 kilometers in length in which there is no gap of more than 100 meters between structures (Willey 1981: 397).

Settlement nucleation increased through time, as population aggregated into centers. This is particularly a characteristic of the Late Classic (Puleston 1974: 309; Rice and Puleston 1981: 153; Sanders 1981a: 361). Significant numbers of people nevertheless still lived in rural areas between centers (Puleston 1974; Sanders 1981a: 360-1; Willey 1980: 257). Some rural areas, such as Barton Ramie in Belize (Willey et al. 1965) and the central Peten Lakes (Rice and Puleston 1981: 153), experienced continued dense settlement throughout the Classic.

It is possible that dominance hierarchies existed among major centers. Gordon Willey, as noted, has argued for the existence of a pan-Southern Lowland state, headed by Tikal, in the Early Classic (1977a, 1980, 1981, 1982). He notes that Tikal in this period founded dynasties at Quirigua and Copan, and married its royal daughters to the rulers of other centers (Willey 1982: 265). In the Late Classic this regional state broke down into a number of local polities (Willey 1977, 1980, 1981, 1982), each headed by a dominant center such as Tikal, Calakmul, Copan, Naranjo, Palenque, or Yaxchilan (Adams and Jones 1981; Culbert 1974, 1977a; Marcus 1976, 1983). (It should be pointed out that this model differs from the Major Center/Minor Center hierarchy formulated by Bullard [1960], for here the model is of hierarchies among Major Centers.) Culbert interprets the glyphic evidence as indicating a domain for Tikal that extended more than 100 kilometers in each direction (n.d.; see also Adams and Jones [1981: 318]). The hierarchy headed by Naranjo (or Tikal and Naranjo) included six subordinate centers, each with the same number of courtyards. With one exception, these are distributed in a manner suggesting that they were administrative centers (Adams and Jones 1981: 318-19).

As might be expected, these hierarchies were not fixed. Political fortunes rose and fell, centers achieved dominance and declined, allegiances and competitive relations changed (Freidel 1983; Graham 1973: 217). Marcus, who proposes that there were four regional capitals, notes that their membership changed through time (1976).

A number of scholars, it should be noted, dissent from this reconstruction. Cowgill suggests that there is no evidence that any Southern Maya center gained firm, long-term political or economic control over any large region, but that there is plenty of evidence of brief dominations, alliances, and royal marriages (1979: 56). Sanders makes the important observation that, with relatively uniform productivity over large areas of the Lowlands, there was no economic basis for any one center to achieve dominance over another (1977: 296-7); to this it might be added that there was also no advantage to doing so (Sabloff 1986; Webster 1977: 366).

Complexity, and its costly manifestations, increased through time, reaching a peak in the Late Classic. At Altar de Sacrificios the size and extent of formal architecture, number of stelae, and amounts of elaborate pottery reached a peak between 613 and 771 A.D. (R. E. W. Adams 1973b: 137). At the sites of Yaxchilan and Bonampak, the greatest quantities of sculptural art preceded the end of monumental construction by a relatively brief time (Rands 1973: 172). The greatest building period at Tikal was between 692 and 751 A.D. (Culbert 1973b: 72). Across the Southern Lowlands as a whole, 60 percent of all dated monuments were built in a period of 69 years, between 687 and 756 A.D. (Marcus 1976: 17, 19). At the same time, Late Classic architecture shifted increasingly to secular functions, with proportionately more investment in those buildings that Mayan archaeologists have called 'palaces' (Culbert 1974: 96; Rathje 1970: 368; Sanders 1973: 346; Willey and Shimkin 1973: 459). Culbert suggests, based on this development, that there was increased importance of administrators and nobles (1974: 101).

The increasing costliness of Late Classic sociopolitical complexity is well illustrated in Figs. 25 and 26, which depict monument construction and occupation of centers through time.

Warfare
There was military competition among the Lowland Maya from at least the Protoclassic, which is the date of the major fortifications at Becan (Thomas 1981: 96; Webster 1977: 360). The ditch and parapet at Becan are so massive (Webster 1976a, 1977) that they are not likely to represent the earliest instance of Mayan warfare. The Tikal defenses most likely date to the Early Classic (Webster 1976a: 3). Leadership was associated with militarism by at least the latter period (R. E. W. Adams 1977a: 3).

Warfare and militarism intensified in the Late Classic, and the art of this period shows greater emphasis on captives and conquest (R. E. W. Adams 1969: 29; Cowgill

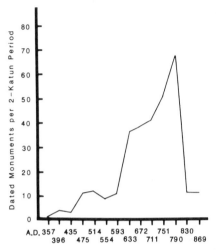

Fig. 25. Construction of dated monuments at Classic Maya sites (after Erickson 1973: 151). Reproduced by permission of Human Relations Area Files, Inc., New Haven. One katun is approximately 20 years.

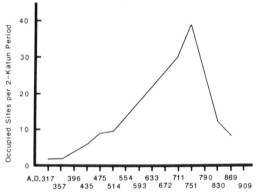

Fig. 26. Occupation of Classic Maya centers (after Erickson 1975: 40). Reproduced by permission of Human Relations Area Files, Inc., New Haven. One katun is approximately 20 years.

1979: 51; Culbert 1974: 101; Marcus 1976: 22, 190; Rands 1973: 174; Willey 1974: 422; Willey and Shimkin 1973: 461). Major fortifications in the Rio Bec area at the sites of Calakmul and Oxpemul (R. E. W. Adams 1981: 234) may date to this time (Demarest 1979: 108).

Many Mayan archaeologists have argued that the population growth evident in the Lowlands ultimately stimulated competition and conflict (R. E. W. Adams 1969: 30, 1973b: 152, 1977a: 96, 1983: 334; Ball 1977: 123-5; Freidel 1979: 37; Rice 1976: 444-5; Webster 1976a: 110, 1977: 343). Cowgill disagrees, suggesting that population growth was a concomitant of militarism (1979: 61). The two processes are not incompatible: a competitive situation, perhaps stimulated by pressure on resources, would yield advantages to a center with a policy of further population growth (Webster 1977: 359). Warfare had as one result the concentration of population in centers, which offered greater safety from attack (Sanders 1973: 358-9, 1981: 361).

There were major logistical limitations to prehistoric Lowland warfare, including the agricultural cycle and the lack of beasts of burden. Prolonged sieges were virtually impossible (Webster 1976a: 94). For the most part Classic warfare was sporadic and small in scale (Demarest 1979: 101-2). In the Rio Bec region, though, the presence of fortified sites suggests a different pattern – perhaps conflict at a major regional boundary (Demarest 1979: 107-8; Webster 1976a: 106). The intensity of conflict most likely varied with economic and sociopolitical conditions.

The most thorough treatment of the role of warfare in the evolution of Mayan society is that of Webster (1976a, 1977). Suggesting that by the Late Preclassic population growth had left little room for expansion, Webster argues that security requirements and management of conflicts selected for leadership, hierarchical organization, and economic stratification.

The collapse

The Maya collapse, as noted, was preceded in many centers by a burst of monumental construction (R. E. W. Adams 1973b: 137, 1977b: 224; Culbert 1973b: 72-3; Marcus 1976: 17, 19; Rands 1973: 172; Willey and Shimkin 1973: 460-1). There is evidence for political decentralization before the collapse was completed. New centers proliferated along the western, southern, and eastern peripheries of the Peten (Willey and Shimkin 1973: 460). Even as construction ceased at the major centers, many small sites began to erect monuments for the first time. Between 830 and 909 A.D. 65 percent of monuments were erected at minor centers. More than 40 percent of the centers that erected monuments at this time did so for the first time (Marcus 1976: 192-3). Often, this was the only monument such sites dedicated before they, too, were swept up in the collapse (Culbert n.d.). This decentralization seems to duplicate events of the sixth century Hiatus (Willey 1974).

The collapse was swift. (Actually, there were many individual instances of collapse repeated, in varying form, at individual sites across the Southern Lowlands.) In A.D. 790, 19 centers erected dated monuments. In 810, 12 did so. In 830, there were only three. And A.D. 889 is the date of the last stela with full calendrical inscriptions (Culbert 1974: 105) (although J. E. S. Thompson suggests that there may be late monuments dating to 909 and 928 [1966: 102]). The collapses at Bonampak, Palenque, and Piedras Negras occurred about 800 (Rands 1973: 171; Willey and Shimkin 1973: 463), as did that of Copan. Quirigua and Piedras Negras display terminal dates of 810. Other centers fell in the mid ninth century (J. E. S. Thompson 1966: 100). There is no evidence for any major construction at Tikal after 830 (Culbert 1973b: 73).

A number of archaeologists find evidence for foreign incursions on the western Mayan periphery at the time of the collapse. It was once thought that such an invasion actually triggered the collapse, if only indirectly (R. E. W. Adams 1973b: 152; Cowgill 1964: 155; Sabloff and Willey 1967). Others think such incursions were the result, rather than the cause, of collapse, as peripheral populations moved to exploit a power vacuum (Culbert 1973b: 92). The evidence for foreign invasions is found primarily at Altar de Sacrificios and Seibal, where sculptural and ceramic art in the ninth and tenth centuries are reminiscent of Yucatan, Gulf Coast, and central Mexican art. A florescence of architectural construction at Seibal coincides with the change in artistic styles, leading to the inference of a military take-over (R. E. W. Adams 1973b; Sabloff 1973b; Sabloff and Willey 1967; Willey and Shimkin 1973: 464-5). Not all Mayanists, though, are convinced by this evidence. Graham adds the important caveat that some of these artistic similarities may reflect imitation of foreign styles by local elites (1973: 213). Saul's analysis of the skeletal remains of the occupants of Altar de Sacrificios discloses no evidence for the intrusion of a genetically different population (1972: 30).

With collapse, the following elements of complexity were lost: administrative and residential structures, the erection and refurbishment of temples, stela construction, manufacture of luxury items, and Classic calendrical and writing systems. The elite class associated with these elements correspondingly ceased to exist (R. E. W. Adams 1973a: 22).

The Mayan collapse involved not only a decline in sociopolitical complexity, but also a major loss of population. R. E. W. Adams estimates that population was reduced over a 75 year period from 3,000,000 to 450,000. He suggests that this could have come about by an increase in the mortality rate of 10 to 15 percent (R. E. W. Adams 1973b: 225). Culbert is more conservative on this topic, suggesting that the Lowlands lost 1,000,000 people in 100 years (1974: 109). Either scenario represents a significant demographic disaster. Various authors (e.g., Culbert n.d.; Sanders 1973: 364) suggest that emigration might have contributed to the population decline.

In actuality, the exact relationship between collapse and the population loss is not clear. It may be reiterated that in many areas population leveled off some time before the collapse. The timing of the depopulation varied across the region, from the last 100 years of the Classic to well within the Terminal Classic or Postclassic (Sanders 1973: 361-2). Reduced populations remained in and near some centers, including Tikal (Culbert 1973b, 1974), Benque Viejo (Barton Ramie area) (Mackie 1961), and Uaxactun (J. E. S. Thompson 1966: 106) for several decades following the political demise. At Barton Ramie (Willey 1973; Willey et al. 1965), and elsewhere in Belize (Culbert n.d.), sizeable populations remained past 1000 A.D. Barton Ramie is a particularly informative area. Here, despite collapse of the Benque Viejo center around 830, the total of 65 rural mounds displaying occupation between 700 and 950 drops only to 62 mounds thereafter (Willey 1973; Willey et al. 1965). There was substantial post-collapse occupation in the central Peten Lakes region, where a new political center was established. Even here, though, there is an 81 percent drop in the number of occupied structures between Late and Terminal Classic times (Bullard 1973; Culbert n.d.; N. Hammond 1982: 143; Rice and Rice 1985; D. Rice 1986; P. Rice 1986).

The radiocarbon dates associated with elite and commoner archaeological contexts confound an interpretation of a simple relationship between collapse and depopulation. As compiled by Sidrys and Berger (1979), radiocarbon dates from elite contexts rise to a peak in the mid eighth century and, as expected, thereafter decline sharply (Fig. 27). In contrast, dates from commoner contexts follow no such pattern,

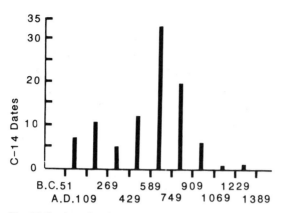

Fig. 27. Southern Lowland Maya radiocarbon dates from elite contexts (after Sidrys and Berger 1979: 271). Reproduced by permission of Macmillan Journals Ltd. and Raymond Sidrys from *Nature*, Vol. 277, p. 271. Copyright © 1979 Macmillan Journals Ltd.

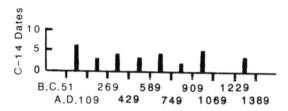

Fig. 28. Southern Lowland Maya radiocarbon dates from commoner contexts (after Sidrys and Berger 1979: 271). Reproduced by permission of Macmillan Journals Ltd. and Raymond Sidrys from *Nature*, Vol. 277, p. 271. Copyright © 1979 Macmillan Journals Ltd.

and give no evidence of a concurrent peasant population crash (Fig. 28). Some points need to be mentioned about this pattern: the sample size of commoner-associated dates is small; and there is a real possibility of significant sampling error, or even bias (cf. Culbert n.d.). Keeping these points in mind, the patterns graphed by Sidrys and Berger are provocative.

There is no reason at this point to suggest that the collapse and the depopulation were unrelated. There is, however, ample basis for suggesting that the relationship between them was complex, and varied across space and time. Further research into the Terminal Classic and Postclassic population decline is certainly needed.

The collapse affected each site according to the peculiarities of its circumstances. It was transmitted between centers, though, as distressed cities raided and caused devastation among their neighbors, and as support populations moved to less affected areas (Lowe 1985: 190).

The behavior of post-collapse populations is best illustrated at Tikal. Population at the center may have declined by 90 percent or more, leaving a remnant band of 1000 to 2000 persons. Tikal's sustaining area shows a corresponding drop. The Eznab occupation, from ca. 830 to 900 A.D., was by an impoverished population that attempted to carry on a semblance of Classic ceremonialism. The Eznab people lived in the great vaulted structures, and deposited their refuse in courtyards, down stairways, even within rooms. When these structures deteriorated, there was no rebuilding. Eznab constructions were small and rudimentary, and their pottery compares unfavorably with the technical perfection of Classic ceramics. Eznab burials are in the same places as Classic elites, but contain minimal accompaniments. Classic tombs and caches were looted. The attempts at imitating Classic ceremonialism betray the loss of Classic elite knowledge. As many as 40 percent of Tikal stelae were reset by the Eznab occupants, but this was done improperly by Classic standards (i.e., in the wrong places, or upside down). With the departure or demise of this remnant population the political and demographic collapses at Tikal were complete (Culbert 1973b, 1974).

Similar patterns are seen at such sites as Uaxactun, San José, Palenque, and Piedras Negras (Culbert 1974: 107-8). The rural population of Barton Ramie shows analogous behavior, because although the post-collapse occupation was extensive, new construction was comparatively minimal (Willey 1973: 102-3).

Yet the collapse was not uniform across the Lowlands. The Puuc sites of the Northern Lowlands show a Terminal Classic occupation that is in no way diminished from former times (and which may have even been assisted by populations fleeing the southern disaster) (Lowe 1985: 40-1; Freidel 1985; Andrews and Sabloff 1986). Nor is any collapse evident at the Belizean site of Lamanai (Pendergast 1985, 1986). Yet as a whole the Southern Lowlands were struck by what one authority describes as '...the most devastating demographic and cultural disjuncture prehistoric Mesoamerica ever experienced' (Freidel 1985: 293).

Assessment of the Maya collapse

The research synthesized in the preceding pages contradicts the traditional view of the Maya: a peaceful population of dispersed swidden farmers who cheerfully built, and occasionally visited, ceremonial centers that were staffed by an elite concerned only with calendrics and ritual. The Maya in fact were a high-density, stressed population, practicing intensive agriculture, living largely in political centers, supporting both an elite class and major public works programs, and competing for scarce resources. This more realistic view both makes the Maya less anomalous among early civilizations, and their collapse less mysterious.

The reasons for the collapse lie in the Preclassic and in earlier times. There was good reason for the development of military competition in association with the population/resource stress of the Middle and Late Preclassic. The topographic redundancy of the Southern Lowlands is pertinent to understanding this development.

As a population impinges on the capacity of its food production system, fluctuations in productivity become increasingly consequential. In environments characterized by high topographic diversity, where food procurement systems with different productivity cycles exist in close proximity, it is common to alleviate resource fluctuations by developing regional systems of economic symbiosis. By forming trading or reciprocal feasting relationships, or by contributing to a hierarchically-administered regional resource pool, a local group can insure itself against lean times by converting temporary surpluses into reciprocal obligations that are called in during times of scarcity. In essence, the scale of the production and consumption unit is raised from the local group, occupying a limited territory, to the regional population occupying diverse territories. Isbell has called such strategies 'energy averaging' systems, which is an apt term (1978). Energy averaging systems have been observed among hunter/gatherers and subsistence agriculturalists in many regions (Bean 1972; Bettinger and King 1971; Chagnon 1970; Ford 1972; Isbell 1978; Suttles 1960; Vayda 1961b, 1967), and were a crucial development in the evolution of densely populated, complex sociopolitical systems (Bettinger and King 1971; Isbell 1978; Tainter and Gillio 1980: 101-13). One energy averaging system, in the San Juan Basin of New Mexico, will be examined in detail later in this chapter.

Regional economic symbiosis and spatial energy averaging are a method of countering productivity fluctuations that can be efficient and successful, and that has important evolutionary consequences. Such a strategy can lead to the formation of regional sociopolitical aggregates that are based on economic cooperation directed by self-interest. Regional economic symbiosis can achieve long-term success, however, only in the right kinds of environmental settings. What are needed most fundamentally are diverse production systems that fluctuate non-synchronously, and that exist in sufficiently close proximity that resource transport is economical. Where these conditions are not met, and where groups in close proximity experience production cycles with synchronized periodicities, there is little basis for economic cooperation. When a number of local groups each experience lean times *concurrently*, their behavior is largely without option, and is entirely predictable: competition, raiding, and warfare. C. White has documented an interesting example of this pattern in the Colorado River region of the California/Arizona border. Environmental zones in this region trend north-south, so that if one travels east-west resource diversity is encountered, but travel north-south is likely to be within a single environmental zone. Not surprisingly, cooperative alliances among native groups in this region developed on an east-west basis, while competitive relationships tended to pattern north-south, between groups experiencing synchronized productivity fluctuations (C. White 1974).

Productivity fluctuations in the Lowlands, while not as severe as in more arid lands, were nevertheless of concern to a Mayan population that approached the densities of such areas as Java and parts of China (Culbert n.d.). Any productivity decline will adversely affect such a people. Historic swidden farmers in the central Peten experienced repeated food crises, and this among a comparatively small population that was nowhere near the support capacity of the region (Reina 1967: 15-18). The intensive systems of the high density Preclassic and Classic populations would have been particularly susceptible to climate, plant diseases, pests, and nutrient loss (Turner 1974: 123; Wiseman 1978: 113; Lowe 1985: 188).

Along the continuum from high regional diversity/unsynchronized productivity fluctuations/economic symbiosis to low regional diversity/synchronized productivity fluctuations/subsistence competition, the Lowland Maya fell somewhere toward the latter end of the scale. The topographical redundancy of the Lowlands environment (over relatively short distances) created a situation where highly diversified production systems were not likely to exist in any local setting, and where neighboring populations would be experiencing nearly the same productivity cycles. (And as a colleague has pointed out, the clearing of large areas of rainforest would have further reduced what diversity there was in the area [Gordon Dean, personal communication].) This is not to suggest that there was *no* regional diversity in Mayan agricultural practice (for clearly there was), nor that each local group was nothing more than a mechanical duplicate of its neighbors. The argument is simply that, compared with settings of high topographic diversity, the Lowlands environment presented the Maya with a situation where resource fluctuations were more likely to be resolved by raiding and competitive relations than by spatial energy averaging. To put it another way, in lean times the Maya could not profitably average that which was *uniformly* low.

When population in the Preclassic became sufficiently dense that productivity fluctuations were a matter of serious concern, the solution to each local group so affected must have been obvious: raid neighboring groups to make up a deficit. Since the only alternative over the short-term was famine, the development of warfare among the Maya was entirely expectable. Long-term solutions included agricultural intensification and the establishment of a hierarchically managed economy. These were not permanent solutions, however, for the archaeologically-evident pattern of population growth indicates that, with each establishment of a higher-capacity production system, population simply rose further. The military option must have been perpetually tempting.

The establishment of competitive relations among local Mayan groups had important implications for the further evolution of Mayan society. It is no accident that population pressure, warfare, and sociopolitical complexity emerged together in the Middle and Late Preclassic and the Protoclassic, for as Webster has argued, they were systemically related (1976a, 1977). Organization for the initiation, conduct, and resolution of war provided a significant managerial/leadership role that contributed to the emergence of a social hierarchy. Economic stratification resulted from success at war, as the bounty of a successful campaign was subject to expropriation and distribution by the leadership (Webster 1976a, 1977: 349-51).

Although major fortifications did exist, the majority of conflicts (if they were indeed related to subsistence stress) would have involved raids on fields, as crops neared maturity, and on peasant villages and storage complexes, after the harvest. The insecurity that this created among the rural population selected for nucleation around secure, regional centers (Sanders 1981a: 361; Webster 1977: 348). This in turn further intensified subsistence stress, as populations aggregated into smaller areas, leaving large hinterlands with comparatively fewer people and less agricultural production (Webster 1977: 348). R. McC. Adams has noted a similar response to warfare among early Sumerian city-states (1974: 3).

Complex feedback relations emerged among agricultural production, conflict, and complexity. Productivity fluctuations made military adventures tempting, even essential, while in turn military strategy came to influence agriculture. Dispersed, shifting swidden plots were essentially indefensible (at least at any reasonable cost), and yet were highly vulnerable and essential to subsistence. Concentrated, intensive systems, such as raised fields and terraces, were at the same time more easily defended (being compact, concentrated, and stationary) and productive enough to be *worthwhile* defending. The same consideration applies to centralized storage facilities. While it would be simplistic to suggest that warfare was the sole reason for agricultural intensification, it certainly made intensification that much more attractive. (And of course once present, such capital assets make tempting targets [Webster 1976a: 111, 1977: 367-8].) Similarly, management of conflict was probably not the only reason for the emergence of sociopolitical hierarchies, but both directly (through the need for military leadership) and indirectly (through the need for labor mobilization and agricultural management), it certainly influenced their development.

Mayan strategies for dealing with subsistence stress no doubt varied across time and space. In some instances raiding may have been a group's best option to relieve a deficit. At other times, as one's neighbors developed effective strategies of defense, agricultural intensification or increased economic management would have been more effective. Warfare was most likely not the only factor involved in Mayan sociopolitical evolution. It developed as a crucial part of a complex, adaptive system.

As Webster has pointed out (1977: 359), a genuine edge in both offense and defense accrues to larger populations, where other factors are equal. It was perhaps this point that led Cowgill to suggest that competition itself selected for Mayan population growth (1979: 61). If so, a positive feedback loop was in operation in which the factor causing stress (population) was further increased by the solution to that stress. In the absence of massive, regional diplomatic agreements, no single polity would dare withdraw from this competitive spiral.

The best strategy for any Mayan polity, once the competitive system was established, was deterrence. Without large standing armies (Adams and Hammond 1982: 508), some signaling system was needed to communicate relative strengths, to deter aggressors, and to facilitate conflict resolution without violence. While (again) not suggesting that this was the sole reason for their development, monumental architecture, painting, and sculptural art would have served as such a system. Massive, labor-consuming investments in public display would communicate quite effectively the relative strength of political centers. By engaging in architectural display a center could signal to potential competitors the relative population numbers that it could mobilize. It could also, in effect, convey the message that a polity which could squander so much wealth and labor on something as inconsequential as architecture, could certainly mobilize vast resources to cope with an external threat. Indeed, Mayan architecture conveys these subtle messages even to this day, centuries after the builders departed the scene, for architectural investment is a major criterion used by archaeologists to assess the relative political strengths of Mayan centers.

Sculptural and painted art fit squarely into such a signaling system. Mayan sculpture regularly depicts military themes, and rulers are often shown judging, even standing on, captives. At a center displaying such art, emissaries and visiting elites from potentially competitive centers would constantly encounter sculpture and painted surfaces showing the military prowess of their hosts, and the harsh manner in which they treated prisoners. Such visitors could not help but receive the correct message from art, such as the Bonampak murals, showing the torture and execution of prisoners. Although no expert on the subject, my impression is that Mayan art more frequently displays mistreatment of prisoners than, say, Roman Imperial art (e.g., Becatti 1968). Roman prisoners of war (especially notable ones) are often shown in, for example, the victory processions of emperors, but mistreatment of prisoners is not depicted so conspicuously as in Mayan art. The Romans maintained a powerful standing army, and their art does not concentrate on the mistreatment of prisoners. Classic Mayan states did not have standing armies. Their art depicts terrifying treatment of enemies. Without real strength, propaganda was the next best thing.

Signaling of strength did more than deter neighbors. It could also serve to attract unattached rural populations, and minor centers, into affiliating themselves with the major center that could promise the greatest protection and advantage. Although aggregation increased through time, much of the Mayan population continued to live in rural hamlets (Bullard 1960; Willey et al. 1965), and was probably a constant focus of recruitment by centers. Willey and Shimkin have suggested that in some areas by the Late Classic, commoners were actively recruited, and even captured from other centers (1973: 485).

The Maya of the Classic period were engaged, then, in a system of competitive relations in which advantage would accrue to those centers that were larger, that invested more in competitive display, and that could mobilize greater populations. By the Classic, certainly by the Late Classic, warfare had evolved far beyond its original stimulus of subsistence insecurity, and was an element of political relations and regional dominance hierarchies. Polities were differentially successful at such competition, for powerful centers began to emerge that dominated minor centers and large territories. Tikal occupied such a position in the Early Classic, while several regional powers did so in the Late Classic. Glyphic evidence suggests that the region dominated by Tikal spread 100 kilometers in each direction. Yet this domain was maintained with difficulty. Culbert (n.d.) believes that most depictions of military exploits refer to intraregional struggles, for captives shown in art can rarely be associated with known, major centers. A domain the size of Tikal's, though, raises the possibility that in later periods food stress in the central Peten could have been relieved by importation of food from such distant sources as the terraces of the Maya Mountains or the raised fields of Belize (Culbert n.d.). Long-distance transport of food (as in the Roman Empire) would have been costly. Culbert's calculations indicate that food transported 100 kilometers would have cost 33 percent of its own value in consumption by bearers (n.d.).

Although it is not possible, with available data, to fill in all details, it is clear that among the Classic Maya high population density occurred in association with vast hydraulic and agricultural engineering, sociopolitical complexity, massive public works, and military competition. More importantly, each of these variables was increasing (except for population, which eventually leveled off). Complexity and architectural investment grew significantly just prior to the collapse.

This was a system that was costly in human labor (e.g., Boserup 1981: 61). Although we have no written records of the status of the support population, as we do for the later Roman Empire, archaeologists have recovered the physical remains of the people themselves. In many ways these mute remains speak clearly about the conditions of the times.

In 1965, Gordon Willey and his colleagues noted that the human skeletal remains from Barton Ramie became, over time, increasingly fragile and lacking in robustness. Suggesting that the dense populations of the area may have been at or above their subsistence capacity, they propose that there was a growing crisis in food supply that climaxed in the Late Classic (Willey et al. 1965: 570).

Once again, the massive data base provided by the Tikal project has proven informative. By about A.D. 1 marked stature differences had developed at Tikal between tomb (higher status) and non-tomb (lower status) segments of the population. By the Early Classic tomb populations averaged seven centimeters taller, suggesting preferential access by the elites to nutritional resources during the childhood growth years. Yet during the Late Classic both groups were affected by the stresses of the time. Stature among males declined markedly, in both the tomb and non-tomb segments. Nutritional deterioration seems to be implicated. It is noteworthy that females were not so affected, for their stature showed no reduction (Haviland 1967).

A large burial population has also been analyzed from Altar de Sacrificios. At this site, from Preclassic times on, there was a high and continuing incidence of malnutrition and/or parasitic disorders, and perhaps childhood infection. There was a very high frequency of several varieties of anemia, indicated by a degenerative bone condition called porotic hyperostosis. Childhood growth interruption is reflected in enamel hypoplasia of teeth. Pathologic lesions occurred in moderate numbers. Male stature decreased between the Preclassic and Classic periods (females again show no such pattern), while life expectancy declined abruptly in the Late Classic. There is evidence for a high frequency of Vitamin C deficiency, and resulting scurvy. The pathologies evident in the population were debilitating, often on a long-term basis, and would have impaired normal functions (Saul 1972, 1973), and work capacity (Shimkin 1973).

More recent research, directed by William Sanders at the site of Copan, corroborates these findings. Both infectious and nutritional diseases were more prevalent in Copan's rural areas, but may have been more severe in the city. Urban residents died significantly earlier than did their rural counterparts, and the average age at death of city-dwellers declined in the Late Classic. The lower class population was unhealthy, and even experienced an unusually high number of deaths among older children and adolescents. In most populations such young persons die infrequently (Whittington 1986).

Late Preclassic and Classic Maya populations were clearly under stress, and this condition apparently worsened through time. It is tempting to draw parallels to the impoverished, overtaxed peasants of the later Roman Empire, except that the Roman records pertain to only the last 300 years or so before the fall of the Western Empire, while the Mayan data cover nearly a millennium.

The factors that led to the Mayan collapse can now be assembled in a systematic framework. The stresses and pressures of the Preclassic and Classic periods set in motion a dynamic, interlinked system of competition and warfare, support of an elite hierarchy, investment in monumental construction, hydraulic and agricultural engineering, and administration of growing regional domains. The costs of supporting this system fell entirely on the agricultural support population. To be sure, this growing investment in complexity must have had benefits, for a strategy pursued for 1200 years or more, and intensified through time, cannot have been entirely unsuccessful. Yet it is also clear that the marginal return on this investment deteriorated over time. Ever increasing investments in warfare, complexity, monumental construction, and agricultural intensification yielded no proportionately increasing returns in the health and nutritional status of the populace. To the contrary, as the demands on the support population increased the benefits accruing to that population actually declined. All of the monumental construction, and all of the agricultural engineering, apparently yielded little or no increase in nutrition per capita. (I must emphasize the *per capita* part of the previous sentence, since it is obvious that overall food production did increase.) This was especially so just prior to the collapse, when a dramatic increase in monumental construction fell on a stressed and weakened support population that was no longer growing.

The fact that females were apparently not as stressed as males (at least at some sites) leads one to speculate that the hierarchy, faced with increased needs for labor and military personnel, pursued a policy of deliberately favoring female nutrition to increase population. The later Roman Empire, as already seen, also encouraged population growth, but through taxation incentives and care of orphans. Closer at hand, both the Aztecs and the Incas had policies favoring population growth, in some instances honoring reproducing females (Conrad and Demarest 1984: 171-2). As in the Roman case, it is further tempting to ask whether the Late Classic leveling of Mayan population was partly due to excessive demands on the peasantry.

Mayan society of the Preclassic and Classic periods, then, evolved along a direction of increasing investment in complexity, and declining marginal returns for that investment. By the latter part of the eighth century A.D. the populace supporting Mayan Civilization was so weakened that the society was ripe for a stress surge. Although conflict was an intrinsic aspect of Mayan life, by the time of the collapse military conquest would not have provided even a temporary respite from their problems. The acquisition of larger territories would by this time have only meant greater impoverished populations to support, so that the marginal return on evolution to larger states would have been small. Whether the final push was from invaders, environmental deterioration, withdrawal of peasant support, internal conflict, or some combination of these, the fact of the collapse is no surprise. It was a predictable adjustment to an otherwise insolvable dilemma.

Over the short-term the collapse probably resulted in an improved standard of living for a peasant population suddenly relieved of the burden of supporting a

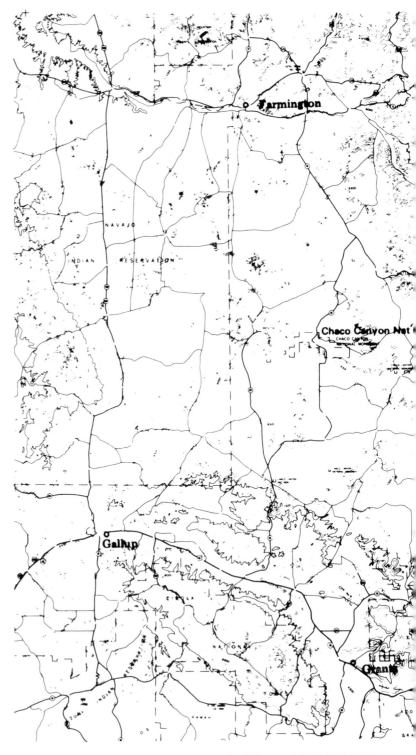

Fig. 29. San Juan Basin and surrounding terrain (after Tainter and Gillio 1980: 111).

hierarchy (cf. Sanders 1973). In the long run, though, the agricultural population was itself decimated. The fact that there was no population recovery seems to indicate that the Lowlands environment had deteriorated under intensification, and/or that the intensive agricultural systems could be maintained only with the hierarchical management that was by now proven infeasible.

As archaeologists are beginning to realize, while this was a political and demographic disaster of the greatest magnitude, it was not the end of Mayan Civilization. The Northern Maya Lowlands were not affected by the southern collapse, and indeed grew in strength. It now appears that there was much cultural continuity between the Southern Lowlands and the Puuc sites and even Chichen Itza to the north. The major transformation in Mayan Civilization came with the demise of Chichen Itza, and the rise of Mayapan, in the thirteenth century (Freidel 1985; Andrews and Sabloff 1986).

The Chacoan collapse

Chacoan society of the San Juan Basin of northwestern New Mexico is known only from its archaeological remains. In contrast to the tropical setting of the Mayan area, the San Juan Basin is an arid region. Social complexity in this area evolved in response to a very different set of challenges, but collapsed for reasons that parallel those of the cases already investigated.

The San Juan Basin is a structural subunit of the vast Colorado Plateaux. Its 85,000 square kilometers consist of broad plains, sharply and frequently dissected by mesas and buttes of relatively low relief. It is surrounded by mountains and plateaux of high relief (Fig. 29). Topographic elevation over short distances, in the central Basin, rarely exceeds 150 meters, while relief of 900 meters at the periphery is not uncommon (Judge 1982: 8; Powers 1984: 23).

In the center of the San Juan Basin lies its major topographic feature, Chaco Canyon. An east-west trending feature bounded on north and south by sharply rising cliffs, Chaco Canyon is an island of topographic relief and environmental variety in a sea of topographic homogeneity and environmental redundancy (cf. Judge et al. 1981: 68). The Canyon has several major tributary drainages, and so receives moisture from an extensive drainage basin. This is crucial for agriculture in an arid setting, for with characteristic spatial variability in localized summer rains, it is common to see some Canyon drainages running while others are dry. Chaco Canyon thus maximizes the potential for capturing runoff from variable (and often insufficient) precipitation, and is unusual in the Basin in this regard (Judge et al. 1981: 68).

In other ways, though, Chaco Canyon is not a good location for subsistence agriculture. It has, for example, some of the poorest soils in the region (Powers et al. 1983: 289; Schelberg 1982: 105). The maize of the Hopi of northeastern Arizona takes about 115 to 120 days to mature (Schelberg 1982: 16). Southwestern archaeologists often use these figures to estimate whether any given area can support maize agriculture. The average growing season for the San Juan Basin is between 140 and 160 days (Judge 1982: 8). Yet at the elevation of Chaco Canyon, 1866 meters, 60 percent of growing seasons are less than 120 days, and 30 percent are less than 100 days.

The only permanent water in the Canyon consists of about a dozen small seeps in the sandstone cliffs, the largest of which holds less than 380 liters. Recorded rainfall in Chaco averages 213 millimeters, but varies from 89 to 457 millimeters (Schelberg 1982: 16, 79, 81, 87).

Climatic conditions at the height of the Canyon's occupation were similar to those of today (Powers et al. 1983: 277-9). Dendrological (tree-ring) evidence suggests that between 900 and 1300 A.D. rainfall averaged 221 millimeters. Temporal and spatial variations were critical in such a moisture-deficient area, and droughts adversely affected the Chacoans. Between 920 and 1040 A.D., in 45 percent of years precipitation was greater than the 100 year mean. Between 1040 and 1120, this figure increased to 55 percent of years. Yet between 1120 and 1180 only 10 percent of all years experienced precipitation above the 100 year mean. From 1123 to 1178 A.D. only eleven years saw above-average precipitation (Schelberg 1982: 16, 95).

A regional system of social complexity, political stratification, and economic symbiosis developed in this marginal environment on a scale unparalleled in the prehistoric northern Southwest. Although research is beginning to disclose the existence of regional systems that existed at other times and other places in the Puebloan area (e.g., Upham 1982; Plog 1983), the Chacoan system reached a level of hierarchy, complexity, and costliness that exceeded all others.

The demarcating attribute of the Chacoan system is its architecture. Two generalized kinds of Chacoan structures have been characterized by archaeologists. The first, called 'Great Houses,' 'Chacoan Structures,' or 'Towns,' are distinctive among Southwestern pueblos. They are: (a) characteristically large compared with surrounding buildings (sometimes reaching several hundred rooms, and including multiple stories); (b) the result of large-scale planning, exhibiting large construction units, an ordered, compact, symmetrical layout, and a high level of labor organization; (c) characterized by a distinctive, elaborate form of masonry that was costly to construct; (d) filled with large, high-ceilinged rooms that were roofed with large timbers; and (e) associated with a distinctive form of religious architecture called the Great Kiva. Contrasting with these comparatively few Chacoan buildings are hundreds of small pueblos or villages that held the bulk of the Basin population. These pueblos are small and amorphous; they exhibit unplanned layouts, simpler masonry, smaller rooms with lower ceilings, and smaller, less elaborate kivas (Powers et al. 1983: 15-17; see also Vivian 1970; Marshall et al. 1979). The overall costliness of their construction, as Neller has demonstrated, was substantially lower than that of Great Houses (Lester and Neller 1978).

Chacoan structures (Great Houses) typically contain a large number of what appear to have been storage rooms, and would accordingly have had populations that were proportionately low compared to structure size (Judge 1979: 903; Marshall et al. 1979: 337-9; Schelberg 1982: 223). The burials in Chacoan Structures in the Canyon are often associated with exotic, imported goods, including turquoise beads and pendants, shell ornaments, decorated ceramic vessels, jet inlays, quartz crystals, and other valuable items. Sometimes such grave associations number in the hundreds or thousands of items. Village burials, in contrast, are far less frequently associated with valuable materials. Between 1030 and 1150 A.D., for example, 21 percent of Canyon Great House burials had turquoise beads, but less than one percent of village interments did (Schelberg 1982: 158-86; Akins and Schelberg 1984).

The evidence for labor mobilization and high energy expenditure in Great House architecture, and for social and economic differentiation in mortuary practices, identifies Chacoan society as socially stratified, with the higher status members of the population resident in the Great Houses (Schelberg 1982, 1984; Tainter and Gillio 1980; Powers 1984; cf. Cordy 1981; Tainter 1978). The distribution of Chacoan towns, both in the Canyon and throughout the San Juan Basin, demarcates the geographical extent of this system of hierarchical organization (Fig. 30).

Great Houses range in size from 1 to nearly 700 rooms (Powers et al. 1983: 313-15). The largest sites concentrate in and near Chaco Canyon, with a few along or near the San Juan River at the north edge of the Basin. The other Great Houses, scattered primarily about the periphery of the Basin and along the lower Chaco River (Fig. 30), are generally referred to as 'Chacoan Outliers' (Marshall et al. 1979; Powers et al. 1983). More than 70 of these have been identified (Schelberg 1982: 7).

A road network spread outward from Chaco Canyon to the Outliers. These roads are wide (up to 9-10 meters) and straight. They do not adhere to topographic contours, but were imposed on the landscape. The roads often contain masonry curbs, causeways over drainages, and, at cliff faces, carved stairways (Lyons and Hitchcock 1977). Recent research indicates that they were not merely the result of habitual use, but were systematically planned, engineered, constructed, and maintained (Nials 1983). More than 300 kilometers of such roads have been identified so far (Schelberg 1982: 209). A few Outliers seem to have served as way-stations associated with this road network (Marshall et al. 1979; Powers et al. 1983: 325), although the majority of Great Houses served as residences of high status individuals and descent groups in local agricultural communities (Tainter and Gillio 1980: 105; Schelberg 1984; Powers 1984).

The archaeological chronology of the San Juan Basin is as follows (after Schelberg 1982):

Basketmaker III	400/500-725/750 A.D.
Pueblo I	725/750-900 A.D.
Early Pueblo II	900-1100 A.D.
Late Pueblo II	1000-1050 A.D.
Early Pueblo III	1050-1150 A.D.
Late Pueblo III	1150-1225 A.D.

Developing social complexity is evident in the San Juan Basin as early as the Basketmaker III and Pueblo I periods. Great Kivas make their first appearance at this time in and around the region (Schelberg 1982: 11, 126-7, 144). (Great Kivas are large religious structures that probably served several groups.) From this early period Chaco maintained extensive trading relations with surrounding areas. Between 20 and 80 percent of the earliest ceramics were traded into Chaco from the Cibola area 80 kilometers to the southwest. Later, during Pueblo II, major quantities of decorated

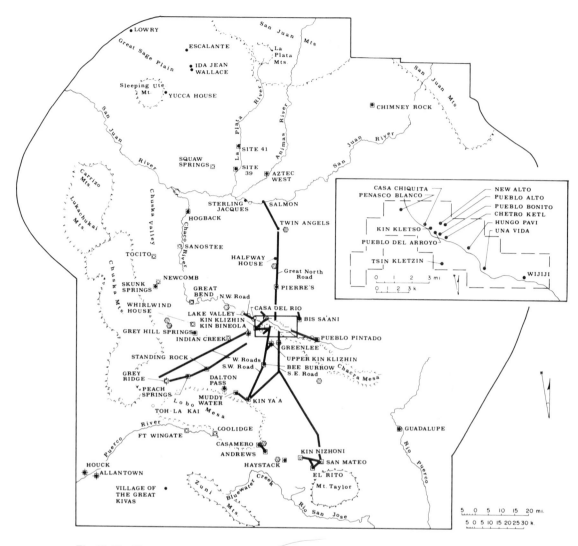

Fig. 30. The Chacoan regional system, A.D. 1050–1175 (after Powers et al. 1983: 2). Courtesy of the U.S. National Park Service.

pottery came from the Red Mesa Valley, 50 kilometers to the south, and much utility ware from the Chuska Mountains, 80 kilometers to the west. By the ninth century A.D. Chaco Canyon supported a sizeable population of small, independent pueblos, characterized by irregular masonry and unstructured ground plans (Judge 1979: 901-2; H. Toll 1984, and personal communication).

Around 900 A.D. major changes began. Three Canyon sites – Una Vida, Pueblo Bonito, and Peñasco Blanco – began to develop the large rooms and multi-storied, distinctive masonry that characterizes later Great Houses (Judge et al. 1981: 81, 84). By early Pueblo III at least 13 Great Houses were occupied in or near the Canyon. Several Great Kivas were concurrently built, and a water control system established (Vivian 1970). Luxury items were imported for use by the Great House elites, including turquoise, ocean shell, copper bells, macaws, and parrots (Mathien 1984).

Elsewhere in the San Juan Basin the period between 500 and 900 A.D. witnessed the establishment of agricultural villages in many areas that came later to support Outliers. Between 900 and 975 seven Chacoan structures were built along the southern and western edges of the Basin (Powers et al. 1983: 247), as sociopolitical hierarchies evolved in response to localized challenges, stresses, and opportunities (Tainter and Gillio 1980: 108-9). The South Road leading out of the Canyon dates to the same time as these early Outliers (Kincaid et al. 1983), indicating integration between Chaco and its southern periphery. Between 975 and 1050 initial construction began at another nine Chacoan structures. There was a florescence of construction during the next century, when 19 Great Houses were built. Yet after this final flurry construction dramatically declined. The last building date from a Great House is 1132 A.D., from Pueblo Alto overlooking Chaco Canyon (Powers et al. 1983: 247-53).

By the later periods of the Chacoan system there is pronounced evidence for regional economic integration. Some 150,000 to 200,000 trees were imported to roof the Canyon Great Houses. For the Canyon site of Chetro Ketl an estimated 5122 roofing timbers were cut between 1037 and 1039 A.D. An additional 4108 were felled in 1051 and 1052. Of 26,000 trees needed to build Chetro Ketl, 6,000 were fir obtained from high elevations at least 50 kilometers away. The remainder were pine from mountains at least 25 kilometers distant. Between 1020 and 1120 A.D., an estimated 40,500 pottery vessels were imported from the Chuska Mountains to one Canyon site alone (Pueblo Alto) (Schelberg 1982: 8, 206, 219). What may have been even more important was the contents of these vessels.

Research suggests that the population of the Canyon, at its peak, was between 4400 and 10,000 persons. Estimates of local environmental productivity indicate that at least some of these could not have been supported by adjacent agricultural lands or local faunal resources. The maize cobs from Pueblo Bonito, one of the major Canyon Great Houses, average 25 percent larger than those of other Canyon sites, suggesting that the elite residents of this site relied on imported maize. At another Great House, Pueblo Alto, archaeologists have found a greater variety of plant species than at the villages, suggesting greater access to outside resources. Many stone tools, and raw materials for these, were imported (Schelberg 1982: 109-21; Cameron 1984; Akins 1984; M. Toll 1984).

By the mid-to-late twelfth, or early thirteenth, century the Chacoan system had essentially collapsed. Population remnants hung on in the Canyon and other Basin areas, but Great House building was a thing of the past. Construction was either at village sites, or small, village-sized rooms were abutted against existing Great Houses. Masonry walls were often built with food-grinding implements scrounged from Great House trash. The days were gone when hierarchically mobilized labor forces shaped elaborate masonry into planned, symmetrical towns. Chaco was no longer the center of the economic universe. A late population in the region from 1225 to 1275 or 1300 may have had ties to the Mesa Verde region to the north. After 1300 A.D. the region was essentially abandoned by agricultural peoples (Powers et al. 1983: 345; Schelberg 1982: 129-30, 274; Lekson 1984: 66, 69).

Assessment of the Chacoan collapse

By the tenth century A.D. population growth in the San Juan Basin region had reached the point where local groups no longer had the option to move into alternative territories when faced with subsistence stress. Cultivation was thus forced into increasingly marginal lands (Judge et al. 1981: 75-8). Where population density is high, and where population units are territorially constrained, it becomes necessary to ensure access to the produce of larger territories to guard against the effects of such things as localized droughts, frosts, and raids. This is especially so in an environment where conditions of moisture, soil quality, and growing season are so marginal for agriculture. In discussing the Maya it was suggested that regional economic symbiosis (spatial energy averaging) is advantageous under such circumstances, and often develops where there is sufficient environmental diversity. San Juan Basin populations had greater opportunity to develop such a system than did the Lowland Maya. As a consequence, although both the Mayan and Chacoan societies developed along somewhat similar paths of increasing complexity followed by collapse, they did so under very different driving forces.

The San Juan Basin, as noted, is a topographically homogeneous, dry, featureless plain (Cordell 1982; Judge et al. 1981; Powers et al. 1983; Tainter and Gillio 1980). There is lower diversity and abundance of flora and fauna in the central Basin than at its margins (Cordell 1982: 61; Powers et al. 1983: 293; Powers 1984). For a territorially constrained population in Chaco Canyon, surrounded by the dry, redundant Basin floor, the most advantageous exchange relationships would have been with groups at the well-watered, high diversity lands at the Basin edge (Tainter and Gillio 1980: 110).

In the northern Southwest, as Kent Lightfoot has noted (as cited by Plog [1983: 300; and personal communication]), there is a tendency toward an inverse relationship between the agricultural productivity of high and low elevation terrain. In warm, dry years there is little precipitation in lower elevations, but sufficient moisture, with a long growing season, in high elevations. In cool, wet years the pattern is reversed: better moisture conditions for lowland planting, but a shorter growing season at highland agricultural areas. Such a pattern would have encouraged exchange relationships between Basin interior and Basin margin populations. Not surprisingly, from at least Basketmaker III times Chaco Canyon populations did trade extensively with such outlying areas (Judge 1979: 901-3).

For populations throughout the Basin, maximum insurance against productivity fluctuations would be gained by establishing economic access to territories as diverse as possible. Herein, though, lies a problem. If each local group had to allocate resources toward the tasks of identifying potential trading partners, identifying these partners' yearly production levels, and establishing reciprocal economic relations with each, the duplication of administrative costs by hundreds of local groups would have been enormous. These costs were substantially reduced when the regional population jointly supported a single administration that served the economic needs of all groups. Additional advantages to hierarchical management of regional economic symbiosis were:

> providing for equitable distribution of resources, thereby reducing competition and conflict;
> providing authority to requisition surpluses from those groups that had one, necessary when economic exchanges were imbalanced, or balance might be delayed;
> centralized pooling to serve a large, diverse territory;
> support of specialists whose role was to monitor surpluses and deficits throughout the region (i.e., to process information).

Situated as it was at the center of the San Juan Basin, Chaco Canyon was the most efficient, least-cost location from which to administer a Basin-wide energy averaging system. The presence of the largest Chacoan towns, with rich luxury goods, high status burials, and a variety of imports, coupled with the convergence of the regional road system, suggest that Chaco did indeed emerge as the administrative center of a Basin-wide system of hierarchical social and economic integration.

A three-level economic hierarchy appears to have operated in the Basin. Elites resident in Outliers mediated the participation of local agricultural villages in the system, and interacted directly with the regional elites resident in Canyon Great Houses. Resources exchanged up and down through this hierarchy would have included: agricultural crops, firewood, building materials, animal products, wild plant products, stone and pottery, and such extra-Basin resources as cotton, salt, and turquoise (Powers et al. 1983: 301-2; Powers 1984; Schelberg 1982: 9-10, 198-200, 1984; Tainter and Gillio 1980: 104-9).

If our present understanding of the Chacoan system is correct, it would seem that the population of the San Juan Basin obtained a valuable return on its investment in complexity by lowering the administrative cost, and increasing the effectiveness, of an energy averaging system. Beyond its initial establishment, however, further expansion of this system may not have been so advantageous.

In the Early Pueblo II period, as described, Outliers were located primarily at the productive, high diversity terrain of the Basin margins. These early Great Houses were situated an average of 54 kilometers apart. In Late Pueblo II Outliers continued to be established at the Basin periphery, but a few also began to be built elsewhere.

With the increase in number of Outliers, the mean distance between them dropped to 31 kilometers, with an average of 10 kilometers between five Outliers at the southwestern perimeter of the Basin. In Early Pueblo III the geographical pattern of Outlier development shifted. A few new ones were established on the periphery, but most appeared north of the San Juan River and in the San Juan Basin interior. Mean distance between Outliers declined to 17 kilometers. This distance was only 12 kilometers between Outliers that were road-connected.

The Chacoan system ca. 1100 A.D. was at its height, but on the eve of collapse. In Late Pueblo III the number of occupied Outliers declined substantially (to 17), while the mean distance between these increased to 26 kilometers Many of those that survived to this period were located north of the San Juan River, suggesting that the economic center of gravity had shifted at least partially from Chaco Canyon to points north (Powers et al. 1983: 263, 268).

The later development of the Chacoan system illuminates the process of collapse. Late trends, particularly in the Early Pueblo III period, include:

> increasing numbers of Outliers, each requiring the construction of a Great
> House;
> a spurt of building activity in the Chacoan towns of the Canyon itself, which
> doubled labor requirements (Lekson 1984: 60, 62);
> increasing functional specialization of architecture (Powers et al. 1983: 326);
> decreasing mean distance between Outliers;
> increasing establishment of Outliers in the low productivity, low diversity
> interior of the Basin.

This combination of trends increased the overall cost of the Chacoan system at the same time that it reduced its effectiveness.

With declining distance between Outliers, more and more Chacoan Towns were established that experienced productivity cycles similar to their ever-closer neighbors. As participants in the energy averaging system became spatially closer, their productivity fluctuations grew increasingly synchronized. After enough Outliers had been established in the region to maximally exploit its environmental diversity, the addition of each new one reduced the overall effectiveness of the system. This problem became particularly acute in the Early Pueblo III period.

The establishment of increasing numbers of Outliers in the low diversity Basin interior (Powers et al. 1983: 293; Doyel et al. 1984) exacerbated the problem. This marginal, low productivity environment offered *diversity* as its best characteristic. The Chacoans initially made wise use of this feature, but came ultimately to dilute its effectiveness. An energy averaging system is most effective when adding a new participating community means increasing the diversity and/or productivity of the regional exchange pool. The Chacoans initially pursued such a strategy. Increasingly, though, communities were added that did not augment the system's diversity, and that actually caused deterioration in the ratio of communities/diversity. Such communities created a drag on the efficient operation of the network. Incorporating communities from the Basin interior made this problem considerably worse than it might otherwise have been, for such areas intrinsically had less to contribute to regional well-being.

The florescence of Great House architectural construction in the Early Pueblo III period in Chaco Canyon may have been stimulated by the availability of enlarged labor pools from the addition of so many new participants in the system, and by increased storage requirements to serve these participants. Indeed, much of the late building was devoted to storage space (Lekson 1984: 66). This building boom, however, came at a very inopportune time, when the overall efficiency of the regional system was declining.

It is possible to see, then, that the Chacoan system, established initially to provide subsistence security for a regional population, came eventually to experience a declining marginal return on investment in complexity. With the establishment of ever more Outliers, in closer and closer proximity, and in increasingly unfavorable settings, the major resource of the system – diversity – was diluted. The overall effectiveness of the network deteriorated. The result was that later Chacoan communities realized a proportionately lower advantage when some region experienced a surplus, and proportionately less could be distributed to each community experiencing a deficit.

This deterioration coincided with a period of significantly increased investment in architectural construction. The net result was that Chacoan communities of the San Juan Basin, around 1100 A.D., derived less subsistence security at higher cost than had their ancestors of 100 to 150 years previously. Faced with such a declining marginal return they began to withdraw from the regional network, leading to the weakening of the system and its ultimate collapse. It was no coincidence that the most densely packed Outlier communities, those at the southern edge of the Basin, may have been the first to withdraw from the network (perhaps in the later eleventh century) (Gauthier, Acklen, and Stein 1977: 24). Their loss would have been detrimental to the system as a whole, for this area contained some of the most productive agricultural land in the Basin (Powers et al. 1983: 289). Lacking true coercive force, the Canyon administrators could not enforce participation, and as the number of participating Outliers dwindled those that were left were probably the weaker ones, less able to survive on their own, with less to contribute to the regional pool.

It is possible that the collapse of Chacoan society was partially a consequence of its success. By increasing subsistence security and reducing natural checks on population, the Chacoan system allowed regional population to rise to a level that would otherwise have never been attained. As a result, increasingly marginal lands had to be taken in for agriculture, and for incorporation into the exchange network. Outliers were established in precarious areas that could produce little surplus for export (Doyel et al. 1984: 44, 48, 49), but even these small surpluses may have been necessary. The great investment, during the later Chacoan era, in building storage rooms at Great Houses (Lekson 1984: 66) indicates increased concern with subsistence insecurity and the possibility of temporary food shortages. This costly investment in a low-return payoff is a classic example of a declining marginal return.

A final blow may have been administered by a severe, prolonged drought from 1134-81 A.D. (Powers et al. 1983: 345; Schelberg 1982: 273). Some archaeologists believe this drought caused the Chacoan collapse. The Chacoans had, however, previously survived droughts in the mid tenth, the early eleventh, and the late eleventh centuries without collapsing (Schelberg 1982: 273; Powers et al. 1983: 280). This final drought does not seem, then, to be a sufficient reason for the system's demise.

The Canyon inhabitants did have alternatives for dealing with the 1134-81 drought. Among the strategies they could have pursued are:

> military mobilization of the labor forces at their disposal, leading to forced participation of target communities in the Basin network, or even to conquest of other populations and imposition of tribute (the energy subsidy strategy);
> digging walk-in wells and practicing pot irrigation; or
> importing water for crops, pot by pot or (watertight) basket by basket, from the Basin margins.

Specialists in Southwestern prehistory will find these alternatives farfetched. I agree; they are indeed. I raise them because it is interesting to discuss *why* they seem farfetched. None of these was technically impossible; the Chacoans could have attempted any of these strategies. *They did not do so because of the extreme cost.* The marginal return for any of these practices was simply too low. It was not that the Canyon inhabitants had no alternatives; they simply had no *economical* ones. Sociopolitical collapse was preferable from an economic viewpoint. In this case, what the Chacoans did *not* do illustrates the thesis of this work as clearly as what they did.

What the final drought may have accomplished was to change the curve of marginal return on investment in complexity from a smoothly to a sharply declining one, and so to hasten the end. The drought did not cause the collapse. Given the trends in marginal productivity that the Chacoans faced, this complex society would have ultimately collapsed with or without the final drought.

Evaluation

The three cases examined in this chapter were significantly different in sociopolitical structure, level of complexity, economy, territorial extent, and evolutionary trend, and in details of their respective collapses. They were located in contrasting environments, and are known to us from very different data sources. And yet the collapse of each may be understood by the same general principles.

The collapses of these societies cannot be understood solely by reference to their environments and subsistence practices (or to changes in these), to the pressure of outside peoples, to internal conflict, to population growth, to catastrophes, or to sociopolitical dysfunction. What affected the Romans, Maya, and Chacoans so adversely was how one or more of these factors was related to the cost/benefit ratio of investment in complexity. When challenges and stresses caused this ratio to deteriorate excessively, or coincided with a declining marginal return, collapse became increasingly likely.

The Roman collapse

The Romans established an empire that was paid for largely by the monetary subsidy of successive conquests. Captive peoples financed further subjugations, until the Empire grew to the point where further expansion was exceedingly costly and decreasingly profitable. As windfalls from new conquests ceased to pour into the treasury, the administration and defense of the Empire had to be covered primarily out of yearly agricultural production. This proved to be both insufficient for the maintenance of the Empire, and costly to the support population. A strategy that at first yielded a high marginal return became, by the time of Augustus, an increasing burden, so that most emperors faced problems of fiscal insufficiency. The Empire, nevertheless, provided conditions of relative peace and prosperity through the first two centuries A.D. It might be argued, then, that although by this time the marginal return on investment in empire had declined, it had not yet declined to the point where continuation of that investment was not worthwhile.

Serious stress surges, in the form of barbarian incursions, began to affect the Empire in the mid second century A.D., and increasingly thereafter. Unable to bear the cost of meeting these challenges out of yearly productivity, the emperors adopted a strategy of artificially inflating the value of their yearly budgets by debasing the currency. This shifted the cost of current crises to future taxpayers. Such a strategy assumes that the future will experience no equivalent crisis. When this assumption proved grossly in error, the existence of the Empire was imperiled.

A series of escalating crises from the third through the fifth centuries, both internal and external, proved increasingly detrimental to the welfare of the State. The costs of meeting these crises fell on a decimated support population. By debasing the currency, increasing taxes, and imposing stringent regulations on the lives of individuals, the Empire was, for a time, able to survive. It did so, however, by vastly increasing its own costliness, and in so doing decreased the marginal return it could offer its population. These costs drained the Empire's peasantry so thoroughly that population could not recover from outbreaks of plague, producing lands were abandoned, and the ability of the State to support itself deteriorated. As a result, the barbarian incursions of the late fourth and fifth centuries were increasingly successful and devastating.

The burden and costliness of the Empire not only increased over time, but the benefits it afforded its members declined. As crops were confiscated for taxation and peasant's children sold into slavery, lands were increasingly ravaged by barbarians who could not be halted with the Empire's resources. The advantage of empire declined so precipitously that many peasants were apathetic about the dissolution of Roman rule, while some actively joined the invaders. In being unable to maintain an acceptable return on investment in complexity, the Roman Empire lost both its legitimacy and its survivability.

The Germanic kingdoms that succeeded Roman rule in the West were more successful at resisting invasions, and did so at lower levels of size, complexity, permanent military apparatus, and costliness. This indicates a significant development: with the fall of the Roman Empire, the marginal return on investment in complexity increased significantly in Western Europe.

The Mayan collapse

The Preclassic and Classic Maya of the Southern Lowlands were a densely packed, territorially constrained people, bounded by ocean, by highlands, and by other populations. Colloquially, it is tempting to describe the prehistoric Lowlands as like a sealed cauldron, where population growth, and the lack of an external outlet, produced a tense, pressurized atmosphere in which Mayan communities could do little but turn on each other.

By the last few centuries B.C. population pressure in some parts of the Lowlands had reached the point where a variety of stress responses developed. These included cultivation of marginal lands, agricultural intensification, the development of sociopolitical hierarchies and public architecture, and predation on neighbors to counter resource fluctuations. While many factors were involved in the development of Mayan Civilization, several features of that civilization seem to have been at least partly shaped by competition and warfare.

Conflict, raiding, and the consequent insecurity among the rural population selected for aggregation into the more secure political centers. The resulting increases in local resource pressure, coupled with the indefensible nature of scattered swidden plots, gave further impetus to the development of intensive agricultural systems such as raised fields and terraces. Such systems were not only more productive per unit of land, they were also relatively compact, defensible, and worth defending. Once warfare became a serious threat in the Lowlands, agricultural and military strategy evolved in concert. Both, in turn, further encouraged social and economic stratification. Personnel needs for warfare, agriculture, and monumental construction may in turn have led the elites to encourage further population growth.

Monumental architecture and public art are normal characteristics of a civilization, but among the Maya they seem to have served a special purpose. Once warfare had developed throughout the region, avoiding or forestalling attack became a major consideration. The external trappings of Mayan Civilization helped to achieve this by: (a) signaling the wealth of polities and the relative population pools on which they could draw (as Mayan art and architecture still do to this day); (b) attracting unaffiliated populations by the promise of strength and security; and (c) communicating unequivocally to visitors a center's successes at warfare and its treatment of prisoners. This investment in visual display helped to compensate for the lack of significant standing military forces. It was, however, costly. While other peoples have been economically devastated when locked into an escalating campaign of military preparedness, the Maya became trapped in what may be called an 'art race.' This, and the other consequences of military competition, were as detrimental to their economy and support population as investment was for the Romans in real military power.

The Mayan peasantry supported, for a period exceeding a thousand years, an upwardly-spiraling system of interlinked responses to demographic and political pressures. These responses included monumental construction, agricultural intensification, conflict, and support of elite hierarchies, military and civil specialists, and an artisan class. This investment appears to have brought no increased subsistence security per capita, for the health and nutritional status of the population was low, and deteriorated throughout the Classic period. The Late Classic hierarchy imposed an expanded building program on a weakened, undernourished population. With such an unfavorable, and deteriorating, marginal return on investment in complexity, the collapse of the southern Classic Maya was to be expected.

The Chacoan collapse

Chacoan society of the American Southwest may, like the Romans, have attempted too much of a good thing. An early system of energy averaging made good use of the San Juan Basin's best characteristic – diversity – by means of a hierarchical network of economic linkages that was centered in Chaco Canyon. By use of this network the effects of such things as a shift in rainfall from the San Juan River (at the northern edge of the Basin) to the Red Mesa Valley (at the southern edge), an early frost near the Chuska Mountains (on the west), or a raid by one's neighbors in any area, could be distributed among all the Basin's communities. By participating in this network, each local group could insure itself against the fluctuating, unpredictable climate of this arid land, thereby increasing subsistence security, and accommodating a growing population. In effect, the scale of the production and consumption unit was raised from the local group, occupying a restricted area, to the regional population, occupying a diversified territory. Any community that linked itself to this regional pool was able to average its yearly productivity by contributing surplus produce in good years, and receiving support from the hierarchy when local productivity faltered.

For a time, when newly established, such a system can increase its effectiveness by adding new participants who increase the pool of regional diversity. The Chacoans initially pursued such a strategy, as Outlier communities were incorporated from the high diversity, high productivity Basin edge. In time, though, communities came to be added that increasingly duplicated the resource bases of existing members, that were situated in poorer, less productive areas, and that ultimately came to be located in the low diversity Basin floor itself. The result was that, as the ratio of communities/diversity deteriorated, so also did the effectiveness of the network. As proportionately fewer communities differed in their productivity cycles, the system's ability to fulfill its main purpose of buffering productivity fluctuations declined. The more densely packed communities in the productive southern Basin lands saw that opportunity and security lay elsewhere, and withdrew from the network.

This weakening and decline in effectiveness coincided with a major construction boom. The regional population, weakened in its subsistence security, was asked to support increased investments in complexity that were no longer bringing increased marginal returns. Within a few decades, construction ceased and Chacoan society collapsed.

Conclusions

A number of observations about the collapse process emerge from this chapter:

In each of the cases examined, the costliness of complexity increased over time while benefits to the population declined.

In each case, substantially increased costs occurred late, shortly before the collapse, and these were imposed on a population already weakened by the previous pattern of declining marginal returns.

For Rome and the Maya, population leveled off or declined before the collapse, and the well-being of most people deteriorated. This seems to have come about from the demands of supporting such complex systems. It is not currently known whether something similar happened in the Chacoan case, but it is noteworthy that the number of Outliers participating in this system dropped prior to the final collapse. Quite possibly Outlier communities, whose participation could not be enforced (unlike the Roman and Mayan cases), withdrew from the network before declining marginal productivity adversely affected their local populations.

For the Maya and Chacoans, subsequent abandonment of their territories, and the lack of a substantial reoccupation by agricultural peoples, suggests that there was environmental deterioration during the period of growth. This may indicate that pressures of population on resources had more to do with the Mayan and Chacoan collapses than with that of Rome. The Roman case is very different, for the later Empire was decidedly underpopulated.

In each case, peoples on the periphery (the northern European barbarians, the northern Maya, and the Western and Eastern Pueblos) rose to prominence after the older society had collapsed.

None of these cases can be completely understood by the explanations commonly advanced for them.

The fall of Rome was not due to barbarians, for the Empire was economically, organizationally, and militarily stronger than its besiegers. And it was not due to internal weaknesses, for the Empire remained essentially intact for a period of several hundred years. Rome's collapse was due to the excessive costs imposed on an agricultural population to maintain a far-flung empire in a hostile environment.

The fall of the Maya was not due to peasant revolt, for peasants supported this civilization for over 1000 years. It was not due to invasions, for which there is unclear evidence and uncertain causality, nor to agricultural deterioration, for the evidence of agricultural intensification indicates that the Maya were fully capable of increasing the productivity of their environment. The collapse of Maya Civilization was due to the burdens of an increasingly costly society borne by an increasingly weakened population. Peasant dissatisfaction, foreign pressures, internal conflict, or an agricultural crisis may have provided a final, insurmountable challenge, but such a challenge was effective only because the Maya were following a course that made them vulnerable to collapse.

The Chacoan collapse was not due to drought or to environmental deterioration, for these were factors with which the Chacoans were technically capable of dealing, and indeed had previously done so. The regional population of the San Juan Basin chose not to continue participating in the Chacoan network, nor to rise to the challenge of the final drought, because the costs of doing so had grown too high in comparison to the advantages conferred. Collapse and migration were economically preferable.

This chapter began with the observation that the framework for explaining collapse could probably not be subjected to a formal, quantitative test. The alternative was to investigate three cases in detail, asking whether the framework developed in Chapter 4 helps us to understand why these societies collapsed. The results lead us to answer the question affirmatively: the collapses of the Western Roman Empire, the Southern Lowland Maya, and Chacoan society can be understood as responses to declining marginal returns on investment in complexity.

6

Summary and implications

Every time history repeats itself
the price goes up.

Message on a popular sign

Summary
Collapse is recurrent in human history; it is global in its occurrence; and it affects the
spectrum of societies from simple foragers to great empires. Collapse is a matter of
considerable importance to every member of a complex society, and seems to be of
particular interest to many people today. Political decentralization has repercussions
in economics, art, literature, and other cultural phenomena, but these are not its
essence. Collapse is fundamentally a sudden, pronounced loss of an established level
of sociopolitical complexity.

A complex society that has collapsed is suddenly smaller, simpler, less stratified,
and less socially differentiated. Specialization decreases and there is less centralized
control. The flow of information drops, people trade and interact less, and there is
overall lower coordination among individuals and groups. Economic activity drops to
a commensurate level, while the arts and literature experience such a quantitative
decline that a dark age often ensues. Population levels tend to drop, and for those who
are left the known world shrinks.

Complex societies, such as states, are not a discrete stage in cultural evolution. Each
society represents a point along a continuum from least to most complex. Complex
forms of human organization have emerged comparatively recently, and are an
anomaly of history. Complexity and stratification are oddities when viewed from the
full perspective of our history, and where present, must be constantly reinforced.
Leaders, parties, and governments need constantly to establish and maintain legitimacy. This effort must have a genuine material basis, which means that some level of
responsiveness to a support population is necessary. Maintenance of legitimacy or
investment in coercion require constant mobilization of resources. This is an unrelenting cost that any complex society must bear.

Two major approaches to understanding the origin of the state are the conflict and
integration schools. The former sees society as an arena of class conflict. The governing institutions of the state, in this view, arose out of economic stratification, from
the need to protect the interests of propertied classes. Integration theory suggests, in
contrast, that governing institutions (and other elements of complexity) emerged out
of society-wide needs, in situations where it was necessary to centralize, coordinate,

and direct disparate subgroups. Complexity, in this view, emerged as a process of adaptation.

Both approaches have strong and weak points, and a synthesis of the two seems ultimately desirable. Integration theory is better able to account for distribution of the necessities of life, conflict theory for surpluses. There are definitely beneficial integrative advantages in the concentration of power and authority, but once established the political realm becomes an increasingly powerful influence. In both views, though, the state is a problem-solving organization, emerging because of changed circumstances (differential economic success in the conflict view; management of society-wide stresses in integration theory). In both approaches legitimacy, and the resource mobilization this requires, are constant needs.

Even though collapse has been a little understood process, that is not for lack of trying. Collapse theorists have taken to heart the Maoist dictum to let a hundred schools of thought contend. While there is a nearly incomprehensible diversity of opinions regarding collapse, these seem to boil down to a limited number of themes. These themes suffer from a number of logical failings, so that none by itself is adequate. Mystical explanations seem worst in this regard, being virtually without scientific merit. Economic explanations are logically superior. They identify characteristics of societies that make them liable to collapse, specify controlling mechanisms, and indicate causal chains between controlling mechanism and observed outcome. Yet existing economic explanations offer no general approach that would allow the understanding of collapse as a global matter. Except for the mystical theme, no existing approach is necessarily incorrect. They are, as presently formulated, simply incomplete.

Four concepts lead to understanding collapse, the first three of which are the underpinnings of the fourth. These are:

1. human societies are problem-solving organizations;
2. sociopolitical systems require energy for their maintenance;
3. increased complexity carries with it increased costs per capita; and
4. investment in sociopolitical complexity as a problem-solving response often reaches a point of declining marginal returns.

This process has been illustrated for recent history in such areas as agriculture and resource production, information processing, sociopolitical control and specialization, and overall economic productivity. In each of these spheres it has been shown that industrial societies are experiencing declining marginal returns for increased expenditures. The reasons for this are summarized below.

To the extent that information allows, rationally acting human populations first make use of sources of nutrition, energy, and raw materials that are easiest to acquire, extract, process, and distribute. When such resources are no longer sufficient, exploitation shifts to ones that are costlier to acquire, extract, process, and distribute, while yielding no higher returns.

Information processing costs tend to increase over time as a more complex society requires ever more specialized, highly trained personnel, who must be educated at greater cost. Since the benefits of specialized training are always in part attributable to the generalized training that must precede it, more technical instruction will automatically yield a declining marginal return. Research and development move from generalized knowledge that is widely applicable and obtained at little cost, to specialized topics that are more narrowly useful, are more difficult to resolve, and are resolved only at great cost. Modern medicine presents a clear example of this problem.

Sociopolitical organizations constantly encounter problems that require increased investment merely to preserve the status quo. This investment comes in such forms as increasing size of bureaucracies, increasing specialization of bureaucracies, cumulative organizational solutions, increasing costs of legitimizing activities, and increasing costs of internal control and external defense. All of these must be borne by levying greater costs on the support population, often to no increased advantage. As the number and costliness of organizational investments increases, the proportion of a society's budget available for investment in future economic growth must decline.

Thus, while initial investment by a society in growing complexity may be a rational solution to perceived needs, that happy state of affairs cannot last. As the least costly extractive, economic, information-processing, and organizational solutions are progressively exhausted, any further need for increased complexity must be met by more costly responses. As the cost of organizational solutions grows, the point is reached at which continued investment in complexity does not give a proportionate yield, and the marginal return begins to decline. The added benefits per unit of investment start to drop. Ever greater increments of investment yield ever smaller increments of return.

A society that has reached this point cannot simply rest on its accomplishments, that is, attempt to maintain its marginal return at the status quo, without further deterioration. Complexity is a problem-solving strategy. The problems with which the universe can confront any society are, for practical purposes, infinite in number and endless in variety. As stresses necessarily arise, new organizational and economic solutions must be developed, typically at increasing cost and declining marginal return. The marginal return on investment in complexity accordingly deteriorates, at first gradually, then with accelerated force. At this point, a complex society reaches the phase where it becomes increasingly vulnerable to collapse.

Two general factors can make such a society liable to collapse. First, as the marginal return on investment in complexity declines, a society invests ever more heavily in a strategy that yields proportionately less. Excess productive capacity and accumulated surpluses may be allocated to current operating needs. When major stress surges (major adversities) arise there is little or no reserve with which they may be countered. Stress surges must be dealt with out of the current operating budget. This often proves ineffectual. Where it does not, the society may be economically weakened and made more vulnerable to the next crisis.

Once a complex society enters the stage of declining marginal returns, collapse becomes a mathematical likelihood, requiring little more than sufficient passage of time to make probable an insurmountable calamity. So if Rome had not been toppled by Germanic tribes, it would have been later by Arabs or Mongols or Turks. A calamity that proves disastrous to an older, established society might have been survivable when the marginal return on investment in complexity was growing. Rome, again an excellent example, was thus able to withstand major military disasters during the Hannibalic war (late third century B.C.), but was grievously weakened by losses that were comparatively less (in regard to the size and wealth of the Roman state at these respective times) at the Battle of Hadrianople in 378 A.D. Similarly, the disastrous barbarian invasions of the first decade of the fifth century were actually smaller that those defeated by Claudius and Probus in the late third century (Dill 1899: 299).

Secondly, declining marginal returns make complexity an overall less attractive strategy, so that parts of a society perceive increasing advantage to a policy of separation or disintegration. When the marginal cost of investment in complexity becomes noticeably too high, various segments increase passive or active resistance, or overtly attempt to break away. The insurrections of the Bagaudae in late Roman Gaul are a case in point.

At some point along the declining portion of a marginal return curve, a society reaches a state where the benefits available for a level of investment are no higher than those available for some lower level (see Fig. 19). Complexity at such a point is decidedly disadvantageous, and the society is in serious danger of collapse from decomposition or external threat.

Evaluating this approach against three of the best known instances of collapse (the Western Roman Empire, the Southern Lowland Maya, and the Chacoans) yields positive results. The establishment of the Roman Empire produced an extraordinary return on investment, as the accumulated surpluses of the Mediterranean and adjacent lands were appropriated by the conquerors. Yet as the booty of new conquests ceased, Rome had to undertake administrative and garrisoning costs that lasted centuries. As the marginal return on investment in empire declined, major stress surges appeared that could scarcely be contained with yearly Imperial budgets. The Roman Empire made itself attractive to barbarian incursions merely by the fact of its existence. Dealing with stress surges required taxation and economic malfeasance so heavy that the productive capacity of the support population deteriorated. Weakening of the support base gave rise to further barbarian successes, so that very high investments in complexity yielded few benefits superior to collapse. In the later Empire the marginal return on investment in complexity was so low that the barbarian kingdoms began to seem preferable. In an economic sense they were, for the Germanic kingdoms that followed Roman rule dealt successfully with stress surges of the kind that the late Empire had found overwhelming, and did so at lower cost.

The Maya of the southern Lowlands were a demographically stressed and territorially constrained people. The requirements of management of agricultural intensification, organization for predation and defense, support of the hierarchy, and monumental construction all imposed on the Maya a costly system that brought no commensurate increase in subsistence security per capita. The health and nutritional status of the population was low, and most likely due in part to the rising cost of supporting complexity, declined throughout the Classic period. Late Classic increases in social costs came at a time of deteriorating conditions, so that the marginal return on investment in complexity left the Maya ripe for collapse.

In the American Southwest, the population of the San Juan Basin invested in hierarchy and complexity to reduce (through centralized management) the cost of a regional system of energy averaging. For a time the marginal return on this investment was favorable, but as more communities were added the diversity and effectiveness of the economic system declined. This weakening coincided with a major construction program, so that as the return on investment in complexity declined, the cost of that investment grew.

For all three cases, then, focusing on the marginal return curve of investment in complexity has clarified the collapse process, and has allowed us to see why each society was vulnerable.

Five major topics remain to be addressed. These are: (1) further observations on collapse, and on the nature of the declining productivity of complexity; (2) application and extension of the concept; (3) implications for the further study of some of the cases discussed in Chapter 1; (4) subsuming other explanatory themes under declining marginal returns; and (5) implications for contemporary times and for the future of industrial societies. As promised in the first chapter, the definition of collapse will be completed here.

Collapse and the declining productivity of complexity

We arrive in this section at one of the major implications of the study. Most of the writers whose work has been considered seem to approve of civilizations and complex societies. They see complexity as a desirable, even commendable, condition of human affairs. Civilization to them is the ultimate accomplishment of human society, far preferable to simpler, less differentiated forms of organization. An appreciation for the artistic, literary, and scientific accomplishments of civilizations clearly has much to do with this, as does the industrial world's view of itself as the culmination of human history. Toynbee is perhaps most extreme in this regard, but he is by no means atypical. Spengler, in his abhorrence of civilization and its sequelae, represents a minority view, as does Rappaport.

With such emphasis on civil society as desirable, it is almost necessary that collapse be viewed as a catastrophe. An end to the artistic and literary features of civilization, and to the umbrella of service and protection that an administration provides, are seen as fearful events, truly paradise lost. The notion that collapse is a catastrophe is rampant, not only among the public, but also throughout the scholarly professions that study it. Archaeology is as clearly implicated in this as is any other field. As a profession we have tended disproportionately to investigate urban and administrative centers, where the richest archaeological remains are commonly found. When with collapse these centers are abandoned or reduced in scale, their loss is catastrophic for our data base, our museum collections, even for our ability to secure financial backing. (Dark ages are rarely as attractive to philanthropists or funding institutions.) Archaeologists, though, are not solely at fault. Classicists and historians who rely on literary sources are also biased against dark ages, for in such times their data bases largely disappear.

A less biased approach must be not only to study elites and their creations, but also to acquire information on the producing segments of complex societies that continue, if in reduced numbers, after collapse. Archaeology, of course, has great potential to provide such information.

Complex societies, it must be emphasized again, are recent in human history. Collapse then is not a fall to some primordial chaos, but a return to the normal human condition of lower complexity. The notion that collapse is uniformly a catastrophe is contradicted, moreover, by the present theory. To the extent that collapse is due to declining marginal returns on investment in complexity, it is an *economizing* process. It occurs when it becomes necessary to restore the marginal return on organizational investment to a more favorable level. To a population that is receiving little return on the cost of supporting complexity, the loss of that complexity brings economic, and perhaps administrative, gains. Again, one is reminded of the support sometimes given by the later Roman population to the invading barbarians, and of the success of the latter at deflecting further invasions of western Europe. The attitudes of the late Maya and Chacoan populations toward their administrators cannot be known, but can easily be imagined.

Societies collapse when stress requires some organizational change. In a situation where the marginal utility of still greater complexity would be too low, collapse is an economical alternative. Thus the Chacoans did not rise to the challenge of the final drought because the cost of doing so would have been too high relative to the benefits. Although the end of the Chacoan system meant the end of some benefits (as does the end of any complex system), it also brought an increase in the marginal return on organization. The Maya, similarly, appear to have reached the point where evolution toward larger polities would have brought little return for great effort. Since the status quo was so deleterious, collapse was the most logical adjustment.

One of the explanatory themes reviewed in Chapter 3 – the 'failure to adapt' model – may now have its full weakness revealed. Proponents of this view argue, in one form or another, that complex societies end because they fail to respond to changed circumstances. This notion is clearly obviated: *under a situation of declining marginal returns collapse may be the most appropriate response.* Such societies have not failed to adapt. In an economic sense they have adapted well – perhaps not as those who value civilizations would wish, but appropriately under the circumstances.

What may be a catastrophe to administrators (and later observers) need not be to the bulk of the population (as discussed, for example, by Pfeiffer [1977: 469-71]). It may only be among those members of a society who have neither the opportunity nor the ability to produce primary food resources that the collapse of administrative hierarchies is a clear disaster. Among those less specialized, severing the ties that link local groups to a regional entity is often attractive. Collapse then is not intrinsically a catastrophe. It is a rational, economizing process that may well benefit much of the population.

One ambiguity in this view is the major loss of population that sometimes accompanies collapse. The Maya are a classic case in point. How advantageous can the Maya collapse have been if it resulted in major population loss? In fact, as the work of Sidrys and Berger (1979) shows, the relationship between Maya collapse and population loss is unclear. It is not certain that these phenomena were coeval (especially since the collapse took decades to overcome all centers), nor even that the Lowland population loss does not reflect emigration to peripheral areas. With these ambiguities unresolved, discussions of cause and effect are premature. In any event, nothing in the preceding paragraphs implies that human actions always achieve, in the long-term, a desirable outcome. Even if the Mayan collapse proved detrimental to the survival of large parts of the population in the long-run, this need not mean that in the short-term collapse was not an economizing process.

In fact, there are indications that leveling or actual decline of population may often precede collapse, even by several centuries. Such patterns have been discussed for both the Roman and Mayan cases. Recent research indicates a similar trend at the great Mississippian center of Cahokia. Population in this region apparently had peaked by ca. 1150 A.D., and declined until the final collapse 250 years later (Milner 1986).

Must every complex society endure this process? Does investment in complexity *always* come to the point where the marginal return declines? Modern economic research would not yield a clear answer to that question. The argument made here is only that, where this process is operative and continues unchecked, a society will be thereby made vulnerable to collapse. Certainly it would seem that to the extent less costly organizational solutions are chosen before more expensive ones, the need to add organizational features must regularly yield a declining marginal return. Yet among societies with the necessary capital, technological springboard, and economic and demographic incentives, obtaining a new energy subsidy (through empire-building or by exploiting a new energy source), or economic development, can for a time either reverse a declining marginal curve, or at least provide the wealth to finance it. Renfrew (1972: 36-7) makes precisely this point in regard to the evolution of complexity in Greece and the Aegean.

It must be admitted that this approach removes much of the mystery of collapse, and identifies it as a mundane economic matter. It is, as Finley would say, '...neither a dramatic nor a romantic way to look at...the great cataclysms of history. One could not make a film out of it' (1968: 161).

Further implications of declining marginal returns

It may seem from this work that archaeology is campaigning to displace economics as the 'dismal science.' Of course, the marginal product curve is nothing new. It was developed to characterize changing cost/benefit curves in resource extraction, and input/output ratios in the manufacturing sector. The idea of diminishing returns to economic activity is at least as old as the nineteenth-century classical economists: Thomas Malthus, David Ricardo, and John Stuart Mill (Barnett and Morse 1963: 2). It applies, as seen in Chapter 4, to subsistence agriculture, minerals and energy production, information processing, and to many features of sociopolitical organization. Wittfogel (1955, 1957) applied the concept of 'administrative returns' to the extension of government into economic affairs in 'Oriental Despotisms.' Lattimore (1940) accounted for the Chinese dynastic cycle in terms of increasing and declining returns. It seems that Kroeber's (1957) observations on the 'fulfillment' of art styles may refer to a situation where innovation within a style becomes increasingly difficult to achieve, leading to repetition and rearrangement of earlier work, and ultimately to a new style in which innovation is more easily attained. The phenomenon is not at all limited to the human species. Animal predators seem to follow the principle of marginal returns in their selection of environmental patches in which to forage (Charnov 1976; Krebs 1978: 45-8).

That familiar explanation of collapse – the peasant revolt (see Chapter 3) – deserves comment here. It seems insufficient to suggest that peasants revolt due to an unfair level of taxation, for cases can be presented (e.g., the Maya) where a peasantry endured exacting demands for centuries. What seems more likely to be pertinent is the marginal return on such support, and more particularly, any pattern of significant decline in this return. Peasant political action would be substantially more intelligible in this light. In modern peasant revolts, of course, other factors are involved, such as an intelligentsia adhering to an international ideology who are able to make peasantry aware of their marginal status. In any event, mere taxation level is an insufficient explanation of peasant action in this area. Some concept of cost/benefit ratios is required.

Gordon Childe had some pertinent observations on the matter:

> ...the instability of these [early] empires discloses a contradiction within them; the persistence with which the subject peoples revolted is a measure of their gratitude for the benefits [of empires], and perhaps the latter's value too. Presumably the benefits were more than outweighed by disabilities. In reality an empire of the Sargon type probably did directly destroy more wealth than it indirectly created (1951: 185).

Among his many astute observations, Polybius suggested that the triumph of Rome over Carthage was due to the fact that the former was increasing in power and the latter declining when they came into conflict. In a somewhat similar vein, Elman Service applied his 'Law of Evolutionary Potential' to suggest that older, established states become fossilized, unable to adopt innovations, and are thus outcompeted by newer, if smaller, peripheral peoples. It would be worthwhile for historians to investigate the marginal return on organizational investment that such competitors experience. An older, established state is likely to be investing in so many cumulative organizational features that its marginal return on these investments has begun to decline, leaving lower and lower reserves with which to contain stress surges. It is then understandable that such a nation is outcompeted by less complex peoples, who invest in little but warfare and experience a favorable return on that investment. Polybius' views on Rome and Carthage, seen thus, might be extended to Rome's conquest of so many older, established states and confederations about the eastern Mediterranean.

The question that logically comes next is why the pattern seen in later Roman history has not subsequently been repeated. Why has there been no sociopolitical collapse in Europe since the fall of the Western Empire? This question can be fully answered only by a major treatise, but it is profitable at this point to sketch some factors worth investigating.

There are significant differences in the evolutionary histories of societies that have emerged as isolated, dominant states, and those that have developed as interacting sets of what Renfrew (1982: 286-9) has called 'peer polities' and B. Price has labeled 'clusters' (1977). Renfrew's term is appropriately descriptive. Peer polities are those like the Mycenaean states, the later small city-states of the Aegean and the Cyclades, or the centers of the Maya Lowlands, that interact on an approximately equal level. As Renfrew and Price make clear, the evolution of such clusters of peer polities is conditioned not by some dominant neighbor, but more usually by their own mutual interaction, which may include both exchange and conflict.

In competitive, or potentially competitive, peer polity situations the option to collapse to a lower level of complexity is an invitation to be dominated by some other member of the cluster. To the extent that such domination is to be avoided, investment in organizational complexity must be maintained at a level comparable to one's competitors, *even if marginal returns become unfavorable*. Complexity must be maintained regardless of cost. Such a situation seems to have characterized the Maya, whose individual states developed as peer polities for centuries, and then collapsed within a few decades of each other (Sabloff 1986).

The post-Roman states of Europe have experienced an analogous situation, especially since the demise of the Carolingian Empire. European history of the past 1500 years is quintessentially one of peer polities interacting and competing, endlessly jockeying for advantage, and striving to either expand at a neighbor's expense or avoid having the neighbor do likewise. Collapse is simply not possible in such a situation unless all members of the cluster collapse at once. Barring this, any failure of a single polity will simply lead to expansion of another, so that no loss of complexity results. The costs of such a competitive system, as among the Maya, must be met by each polity, however unfavorable the marginal return. As Renfrew pointed out for the Cyclades, '*The specific state is legitimised in the eyes of its citizens by the existence of other states which patently do function along comparable lines*' (1982: 289 [emphasis in original]).

Peasant political action in such a situation is most logically aimed at *reformation* rather than decomposition. Where the failure of a polity would simply mean for peasants domination by some other, equivalent regime, withdrawal and apathy are meaningless. The political course followed by European peasants and other disaffected classes, under these constraints, was to increase participation, to expand their share of the decision-making process, and to secure thereby a more favorable return on organizational investment. A point worth noting for Marxists, in this regard, is that class conflict led to political evolution only when the less costly option – collapse – was removed.

While this brief discussion cannot fully explain these elements of European political history, the points made here are worth further investigation. Most likely it is no coincidence that forms of participatory government emerged in both the ancient world (Greece, Republican Rome) and the recent one under situations of peer polity competition.

The Warring States period of China, following the collapse of the Western Chou, offers an interesting contrast. Here a situation of peer polity competition (the Warring States), prior to the unification by the Ch'in, led to the development (by such thinkers as Confucius and Mo Tzu) of an ideology of good government and protection of the populace. Good rulers were thought to receive the Mandate of Heaven, and continued to enjoy this Mandate so long as they governed well. Cessation of good government, or a series of catastrophes, were signs that a dynasty had lost the Mandate of Heaven. A new dynasty would soon emerge that claimed the Mandate had devolved on it (Creel 1953; Fairbank et al. 1973: 70-3). In ancient China, then, peer polity competition evolved with an ideology of protecting the populace, rather than leading to participatory government. Perhaps participatory government was simply not possible in ancient societies that were so much larger, demographically and territorially, than the Greek city-states.

At this point we arrive at the first step toward understanding the difference between societies that slowly disintegrate and those that rapidly collapse. The Byzantine and Ottoman empires are classic examples of the former. Both gradually lost power and territory to competitors. There was in this process no collapse – no sudden loss of complexity – for each episode of weakness by these empires was simply met by expansion of their neighbors. Herein lies an important principle of collapse (and the final installment in its definition). *Collapse occurs, and can only occur, in a power vacuum.* Collapse is possible only where there is no competitor strong enough to fill the political vacuum of disintegration. Where such a competitor does exist there can be no collapse, for the competitor will expand territorially to administer the population left leaderless. Collapse is not the same thing as change of regime. Where peer polities interact collapse will affect all equally, if and when it occurs, provided that no outside competitor is powerful enough to absorb all.

Here, then, is the reason why the Mayan and Mycenaean centers collapsed simultaneously. No mysterious invaders captured each of these polities in an improbable series of fairy-tale victories. As the Mayan and Mycenaean petty states became respectively locked into competitive spirals, each had to make ever greater investments in military strength and organizational complexity. As the marginal return on these investments declined, no polity had the option to simply withdraw from the spiral, for this would have led to absorption by a neighbor. Collapse for such clusters of peer polities must be essentially simultaneous, as together they reach the point of economic exhaustion. Since in both cases no outside dominant power (in the Mesoamerican Highlands or the eastern Mediterranean) was both close enough and strong enough to take advantage of this exhaustion, collapse proceeded without external interference and lasted for centuries. (Later Greek city-states, by contrast, were confronted with powerful neighbors who would take advantage of a political vacuum, and so lacked the option of collapse.)

Here too is the final reason why, as raised in Chapter 5, the Eastern Roman Empire *could not* collapse as did that of the West. Disintegration of the Byzantine state would have simply resulted in the expansion of its peer – the Sassanian Empire (as, throughout its history, Byzantine weakness always led to expansion of its rivals). There was no possibility in the eastern Mediterranean for a drop to lower complexity commensurate to what happened in the power vacuum of western Europe in the fifth century A.D.

The occurrence of declining marginal returns, then, need not always lead to collapse: it will do so only where there is a power vacuum. In other cases it is more likely to be a source of political and military weakness, leading to slow disintegration and/or change of regime. Lewis' (1958) observations on the decline of the Ottoman Empire, and R. McC. Adams'(1978, 1981) on replacement of the Sassanian by the Islamic regime in Persia, both illustrate this process. Toynbee's account of the role of the Romano-Bulgarian War (977-1019 A.D.) in the Byzantine loss at the Battle of Manzikert (1071) (discussed in Chapter 3) shows clearly that the Byzantine conquest of the Bulgars was achieved at very high cost, for low return, and weakened the Byzantine state (Toynbee 1962 (IV): 371-2, 392, 398-402).

Suggestions for further applications

Is a pattern of declining marginal returns the sole reason for collapse? Do complex societies collapse for no other cause? Since it is not certain that all cases of collapse have yet occurred, such questions cannot be decided with finality. Nuclear war, for example, is probably capable of causing collapse, and does not fall under the category of marginal returns. At this point it can be said, on the basis of the discussion in Chapter 3, that no other existing theory can by itself account for the phenomenon, and on the basis of Chapter 5, that major instances of collapse are well clarified by the present theory. The marginal return on investment in complexity is at present the best explanation of collapse. At this point the discussion will focus on some cases of collapse that are not as well known as those discussed in Chapter 5, but for which there are presently suggestions that declining marginal returns may have been in-volved. The purpose of this discussion is to suggest directions for future research. Those cases not discussed are left out because available data are too scanty for this purpose, not because some other explanation better fits them.

Chou China. The increasing costliness of ensuring loyalty of feudal officials seems to have coincided with an upswing in barbarian incursions. There was thus a pattern of increasing costs of integration and of containing stress surges, imposed on a situation where returns for such costs may not have increased at all. Chinese dynasties have as a rule seemed to undergo deteriorating cost/benefit ratios from their founding to their demise.

Old Babylonian period. Despite the loss of dependencies during the reign of Sam-suiluna, the crown attempted nonetheless to maintain the level of administration established previously. Marginal returns decline axiomatically in an attempt to govern a smaller land area and population with an administration designed for a larger territory.

Third Dynasty of Ur/Sassanian period. As R. McC. Adams has described (1981), these were periods in Mesopotamian history when maximizing regimes attempted to increase production by expanding into marginal lands, and by intensive irrigation. This was done regardless of how returns declined relative to costs, for the purpose was to secure every last possible bit of production.

Old Kingdom Egypt. A coincidence of several factors – increasing feudal independence, declining power of the king, increasing establishment of tax-exempt funerary endowments, increased monumental construction in the Sixth Dynasty, and possible Nile unreliability – may have combined to yield a central administration that was increasingly costly while it was decreasingly wealthy and powerful. The possibility of output failure (Easton 1965b: 230), in the king's inability to secure favorable Nile floods, would have contributed to the perception of a declining marginal return.

Harappans. It is not known whether the entire Harappan territory was politically unified. If it was not, then it is possible that competitive relations among Harappan polities was a source of declining marginal returns. Current research suggests that there were indeed several independent Harappan states (Possehl 1982).

Hittites. The expansion policy that led to the establishment of the Hittite Empire achieved success only after generations of struggle. The costliness of this expansion may have left the Hittites vulnerable to the Kaska tribes, and to other less complex peoples, who seem to have been involved in toppling the empire.

Mycenaeans. As suggested previously, it is possible that the Mycenaeans, a cluster of peer polities, engaged in the same kind of competitive spiral that characterized other peer polity systems – later Greek city-states, ancient and medieval Italian city-states, post-Roman Europe, Warring States China, and the Maya. As among the Maya, the upwardly-driven costs of such a system, without any real benefits at the local level, would have induced declining marginal returns. Unlike China, where large territories and vast populations repaid conquest and unification, successful competition by any Mycenaean polity would yield little real return. The result was probably constant investment in defense, military administration, and petty warfare, with any single polity rarely experiencing a significant return on that investment.

Mauryan Empire. This empire has not been previously discussed, except for a brief reference in Chapter 3. It was established in northern India in the fourth century B.C., in response to the conquests of Alexander. By 272 B.C. it included almost the entire Indian subcontinent. Yet it lasted less than a century, and by 180 B.C. was gone. Subsequent empires never achieved the same scale. The breakup began after the death of Ashoka (232 B.C.), and one authority cites economic pressures. Vast revenues were needed to maintain the army, pay the salaries of officials, and settle newly claimed land. The Mauryans paid for this, in the later empire, by debasement of their currency (Thapar 1966: 70-91). This strategy sounds reminiscent of the Roman and Ottoman empires, both of which debased coinage to pay for declining marginal returns.

Monte Alban. Blanton (1978, 1983), as discussed in Chapter 3, argues that the population of the Valley of Oaxaca ceased to support the hierarchy at Monte Alban when it became ineffectual at dealing with disputes, and no longer necessary as a defense against Teotihuacan. If so, then the Oaxacan people acted in an expectable manner when they perceived an insufficient return on complexity.

Hohokam. As described by D. Adams (1983: 37), Fred Plog and Charles Merbs recently excavated 36 Hohokam burials dating from the fourteenth century, not long before that society's collapse. A significant amount of malnutrition was evident. This is a sparse fact indeed, but it suggests that for the Hohokam it might be worthwhile to investigate declining returns to the population for investment in complexity. Jill Neitzel has recently proposed that peripheral communities withdrew from the Hohokam system when the costs of participation exceeded the benefits (1984).

Huari. Huari appears to have invested in a major cultural transformation of the lands under its control. It imposed economic, social, and cultural changes. Major urban centers that included Huari building complexes were established in each valley. Ceramic styles were transformed. Goods and information were exchanged across the central Andes at unprecedented levels. It has been suggested that urbanism and militarism, state distribution of foodstuffs, the Andean road system, and the spread of the Quechua language began with the Huari Empire. Huari may thus have initiated the investment in these transformations, so that the later Inca had merely to reestablish the pattern and thus derive a higher marginal return. For the Huari, the set-up costs of imperial rule may have been excessively high compared to the benefits.

Less complex societies. Sahlins (1963, 1968) and Leach (1954) have argued that in simpler societies investment in political expansion, with insufficient return to the local level, engenders disaffection and collapse. Turnbull (1978) has explained the Ik collapse as abandonment of a level of complexity that, while minimal, could yield no return on investment. Hunters and gatherers, as is well known, collapse into minimal foraging units (families) when resource or social stress makes large, complex gatherings impossible.

Declining marginal returns, in general, can arise from any of the following conditions:

1. benefits constant, costs rising;
2. benefits rising, costs rising faster;
3. benefits falling, costs constant; or
4. benefits falling, costs rising.

In undertaking to study the collapse of any complex society, these conditions should be looked for.

Declining marginal returns and other theories of collapse

The extent to which a global theory is illuminating or trivial depends, in part, on its ability to clarify matters that were previously obscure, on its flexibility in application, and on its power to incorporate less general explanations. The perspective of declining marginal returns has indeed clarified the collapse process and shown itself highly flexible in application: three major, very different cases can be understood by it, and in this chapter it has been shown that a variety of other collapses are, with present information, potentially clarified.

As a very general principle, the application of this framework to specific cases cannot be automatic or mechanical. Each society that has collapsed has done so under a set of circumstances that were at least partially unique. The application of a general principle to such diversity requires different considerations in each case, including sensitivity to the peculiar circumstances of local histories.

The principle of declining marginal returns has the capacity logically to incorporate the explanatory themes discussed in Chapter 3. One exception to this may be the Mystical theme, which is difficult to incorporate in any scientific theory. Even so, some of the individual approaches of the Mystical theme may prove to be subsumable under declining marginal returns, as will be shown.

Resource depletion. The essence of depletion arguments is the gradual or rapid loss of at least part of a necessary resource base, whether due to agricultural mismanagement, environmental fluctuation, or loss of trade networks. Major weaknesses of the approach are: why steps are not taken to halt the approaching weakness; and why resource stress leads to collapse in one case and economic intensification in another. Consideration here must be given to the cost of further economic intensification projected against the marginal benefits to be gained. If the marginal utility of further economic development is too low, and/or if a society is already economically weakened by a low marginal return, then collapse in such instances would be understandable. Collapse is not understandable, under resource stress, without reference to characteristics of the society, most particularly its position on a marginal return curve. A society already experiencing a declining marginal return may not be able to capitalize the economic development that is often a response to resource stress.

New resources. The most general statement of this theme has been given by Harner (1970), who argues that new resources can alleviate shortages and inequities, ending the need for ranking and complexity. This can be squarely subsumed under declining marginal returns: when a system of ranking and complexity is no longer needed, continued support of it would yield a declining return, and so it is likely to be dropped.

Catastrophes. Catastrophe theories suffer from the same flaw as resource depletion arguments. Why, when complex social systems are designed to handle catastrophes and routinely do, would any society succumb? If any society has ever succumbed to a single-event catastrophe, it must have been a disaster of truly colossal magnitude. Otherwise, the inability of a society to recover from perturbation must be attributable to economic weakness, resulting quite plausibly from declining marginal returns.

Insufficient response to circumstances. The 'failure to adapt' model relies on a value judgement: that complex societies are preferable to simpler ones, so that their disappearance must indicate an insufficient response. It ignores the possibility that, due to declining marginal returns, collapse may be an economical and highly appropriate adjustment. One major theory under this theme, Service's 'Law of Evolutionary Potential,' has been shown earlier in this chapter to be subsumable under the principle of declining marginal returns. Conrad and Demarest's (1984) study shows how the Aztec and Inca empires reached the point of diminishing returns for expansion, and declined accordingly. Other theories grouped under this theme are not plausibly linked to collapse.

Other complex societies. Blanton's argument that Monte Alban collapsed when it was no longer necessary for some tasks (deterrence of Teotihuacan) nor efficient at others (adjudication of disputes), is fully compatible with the marginal return principle. Monte Alban collapsed, in other words, when the return it could offer became too low relative to support costs. In regard to inter-polity competition, John Hicks once suggested that '...when the ability to expand is lost, the ability to recover from disasters may go too' (1969: 59). The ability to expand may be lost due to an economic weakness, or else where the cost of expansion becomes too high relative to advantages. The latter will occur where one complex society impinges on another (e.g., Rome and Persia), and the marginal return for conquest and administration is too low.

Intruders. The scenario of tribal peoples toppling great empires presents a major explanatory puzzle. What characteristics of the less complex society and/or what weaknesses in the more complex one could lead to such a circumstance? Service, as noted, ascribed this to his Law of Evolutionary Potential, which as pointed out can be subsumed under the principle of declining marginal returns. As discussed in regard to the ideas of Polybius and Service, a more powerful state may not prevail against a weaker one if the latter is ascending a marginal return curve and the former descending. A complex society that is investing heavily in many cumulative organizational features, with low marginal return, may have little or no reserve for containing stress surges. Such a state may compete inefficiently with a population that is smaller, and on paper weaker, but that invests in little but high-return military ventures.

Conflict/contradictions/mismanagement. It was argued earlier in this chapter that peasant political action is less likely to occur under a high but static tax load than in a situation where a high tax load is yielding a perceptibly declining return to the local level. In such a situation inequity becomes obvious. Similarly, class conflict is more likely a matter of a falling than a rising marginal return. In the former situation individuals and groups, as discussed in Chapter 4, position themselves to reap maximum share of a shrinking economic pie. In a case where the marginal return is rising, class conflict may be forestalled by creating the impression that opportunity for improvement exists for all classes.

Cases where elites behave irrationally require explanation. Irrational behavior by itself explains little of history. Service made the astute observation that the success or irrationality of elite behavior is probably a function of circumstance-induced perception. Rulers simply look good during successful periods, and vice versa (Service 1975: 312).

The biologist Garrett Hardin once pointed to a disarmingly simple lesson of systems analysis that has powerful implications: '*We can never do merely one thing*' (1968: 457 [emphasis in original]). His point was that good intentions are virtually irrelevant in determining the result of altering a large, complex system. With the feedback relationships inherent in such a system, one can almost never anticipate the full consequences of any alteration. The same principle applies to misbehavior: elite mismanagement can be only partly responsible for the evolution of any complex society.

I do not wish to suggest that leadership is immaterial, only that it is of much less importance than many believe. Complex societies do not evolve on the whims of individuals. Circumstance-induced perception is likely to be of greater consequence: rulers look good when the marginal return on investment in complexity is rising, for in such a situation almost anything a leader does is overshadowed by the large payoff to society-wide investment. Conversely, when marginal returns are declining there is usually very little that leadership can do in the short term to arrest this trend, and so anything that is tried is bound to appear incompetent.

Social dysfunction. This vague theme is somewhat diverse, but its central concern seems to be with mysterious internal processes that prevent either integration or proper adaptation. Little understanding is gained by such ethereal notions. Much more would be learned by focusing on the costs and benefits of adopting complex social features.

Mystical. The mystical theme is difficult to incorporate under any scientific approach, but some of the individual studies grouped under this theme can be subsumed under the principle of declining marginal returns. David Stuart, for example, asserts that complex societies experience cyclical oscillations between more and less complex forms (which he labels 'powerful' and 'efficient'). The mystical nature of Stuart's formulation emerges when he cannot account for these oscillations, except to liken complex societies to insect swarms and to suggest that they 'burn out' (Stuart and Gauthier 1981: 10-11). Why do Stuart's 'powerful' societies revert to 'efficient' ones? The answer is most likely that they do so because, as complex societies, they experience a declining marginal return on investment in complexity, and so become liable to collapse.

Many of the scenarios under the Mystical theme rely on the growth and senescence analogy, or on such value-laden concepts as 'vigor' and 'decadence.' In one way these scenarios are like the elite mismanagement theme: societies are rated by their success at dealing with circumstances, or at expansion. Societies able to do these things are considered 'vigorous,' and those unable 'decadent.' Circumstance-induced perception is a major factor in these assessments. A society experiencing high marginal returns on investment in complexity is likely to be capable of expanding or of containing stress surges, and will appear 'vigorous' and 'growing.' A society in the phase of declining marginal returns is likely to be less capable in these matters, and so appear 'decadent.' The concepts of 'growth/senescence' and 'vigor/decadence' are vitalistic and subjective. Such value-laden terms, and related concepts, are best dropped from use. The observations on which they rely, however, can be subsumed under the principle of marginal returns. 'Moral weakness' (whatever that may be) is more likely to be ascribed to a society experiencing declining than increasing marginal returns. Moreover, as Borkenau has noted, moral crimes are committed all the time by both 'vigorous' and 'decadent' societies (1981: 51).

Chance concatenation of events. Chance concatenations cannot explain collapse, except where combinations of deleterious circumstances impinge on a society already economically weakened.

Economic explanations. The themes that unite economic explanations are declining advantages to complexity, increasing disadvantages to complexity, and/or increasing costliness of complexity. Such ideas are clearly subsumable under declining marginal returns, and indeed this principle provides the global applicability previously lacking in economic explanations.

On a more general level this principle unites both internal/external theories of change, and conflict/integration models of society. Declining marginal returns are an internal aspect of any society, following their own dynamic pattern. This pattern is based on the propensity to choose less costly organizational solutions before more costly ones. Yet changes in organizational solutions and marginal returns often result from the need to respond to changing external conditions.

Conflict and integration theories are also subsumed, for whether a people are the beneficiaries or the victims of complexity, it is necessary to take into account the cost/benefit ratio of organizational investment. Neither benign nor repressive regimes can long endure a siege of declining marginal returns (although repressive regimes may be able to endure *somewhat* longer).

The principle of declining marginal returns is indeed, then, capable of incorporating these various approaches to collapse (or at least the more worthwhile parts of these). It provides an overarching theoretical framework that unites diverse approaches, and it shows where connections exist among disparate views. It seems from this discussion that a significant range of human behavior, and a number of social theories, are clarified by this principle.

Contemporary conditions

A study of this topic must at some point discuss implications for contemporary societies, not only as a matter of social responsibility, but also because the findings point so clearly in that direction. Complex societies historically are vulnerable to collapse, and this fact alone is disturbing to many. Although collapse is an economic adjustment, it can nevertheless be devastating where much of the population does not have the opportunity or the ability to produce primary food resources. Many contemporary societies, particularly those that are highly industrialized, obviously fall into this class. Collapse for such societies would almost certainly entail vast disruptions and overwhelming loss of life, not to mention a significantly lower standard of living for the survivors.

The contemporary concern with collapse has been mentioned in Chapter 1. Surely much of the public fascination with lost civilizations derives from the vicarious threat implicit in such knowledge. 'We are aware,' wrote the noted French social philosopher Paul Valéry, 'that a civilization has the same fragility as a life' (1962: 23). Indeed this concern is sometimes extended to the very survival of the human species. Astrophysicists are currently developing a theory suggesting that the cyclic return of a distant star toward earth triggers immense comet showers that periodically wipe out multiple life forms, and will so affect the human race at the next pass (Perlman 1984).

Other scenarios for contemporary collapse include:

> nuclear war and associated climatic changes;

increasing atmospheric pollution, leading to ozone depletion, climatic changes,
  saturation of global circulation patterns, and similar disasters;
depletion of critical industrial resources;
general economic breakdown, brought on by such things as unrepayable national and international debts, disruptions in fossil fuel availability, hyperinflation, and the like.

Faced with such an array of imposing problems, and constantly bombarded with media attention to these and other dilemmas, people are naturally concerned. For reasons that are more or less rational, a respectable segment of the population of Western industrial societies fears that one or several of these factors will bring a breakdown and a new dark age. Only a veneer of complexity lies between us and the primordial chaos, it is thought, the Hobbesian war-of-all-against-all. A considerable level of political activity results from such fears, and both national priorities and international policies are to a significant degree influenced by this popular concern. Some people store food or dig fallout shelters, in expectation of the failure of a political process to resolve the situation. Others go to greater lengths, stockpiling weapons and conducting paramilitary training, even engaging in military games, in anticipation of the day when the ghost of Hobbes emerges, when we are all reduced to the conditions of the Ik.

A not inconsequential market has arisen from this, including survivalist books and magazines, and an industry that features such post-collapse necessities as weapons, survival implements, and freeze-dried food. Many of those who are less extreme have nevertheless in recent times become concerned with raising one's own food, making one's own clothing, and building shelter. Magazines that focus on such subjects as organic gardening contain articles and advertisements extolling the virtues of a lifestyle that reduces one's dependence on an ultimately unreliable industrial economy.

It is easy to overemphasize such matters, for only a small part of the population is actively preparing for collapse. On the other hand, no educated person who is aware of historical collapses can escape occasionally wondering about current conditions. I do not wish, by clinically treating such concerns as a social phenomenon, to downplay their validity. Excepting some of the more extreme views, there may indeed be reason for alarm. Certainly none can argue that industrialism will not *someday* have to deal with resource depletion and its own wastes. The major question is how far off that day is. The whole concern with collapse and self-sufficiency may itself be a significant social indicator, the expectable scanning behavior of a social system under stress, in which there is advantage to seeking lower-cost solutions. A colleague with whom I corresponded about this work inquired (facetiously I assume) whether it would be finished before our own civilization collapses.

As in the study of historical collapses, those concerned about current conditions have ignored the principle of marginal returns on investment in complexity. Whether industrial civilization will be destroyed in a nuclear war or in a cosmic collision is guesswork, and not of concern here. What can be presently addressed are matters that are known to be of importance to all societies: the costs of, and benefits from, investment in complexity.

Some of the data discussed in Chapter 4 are certainly disturbing in this regard. Patterns of declining marginal returns can be observed in at least some contemporary industrial societies in the following areas:

agriculture;
minerals and energy production;
research and development;
investment in health;
education;
government, military, and industrial management;
productivity of GNP for producing new growth; and
some elements of improved technical design.

A few caveats are in order about such trends. The examples of declining marginal returns, here and in Chapter 4, were chosen eclectically, to illustrate the contention that complex societies regularly experience such trends. These are only examples, not a rigorous examination of any modern economy. Such observations are not a full monitor of the marginal return that any particular society is experiencing *overall* on investment in complexity. There may be favorable countertrends in some spheres, perhaps such as microprocessor technology. Yet there can be no denying the disquieting nature of the statistics in Chapter 4. It is clear that at least some industrial societies are now experiencing declining marginal returns in several crucial and costly spheres of investment.

There are two opposing reactions to such trends. On the one hand there are a number of economists who, despite the reputation of their discipline for pessimism, believe that we face, not real resource shortages, only solvable economic dilemmas. They assume that with enough economic motivation, human ingenuity can overcome all obstacles. Three quotations characterize this approach.

> No society can escape the general limits of its resources, but no innovative society need accept Malthusian diminishing returns (Barnett and Morse 1963: 139).

> All observers of energy seem to agree that various energy alternatives are virtually inexhaustible (Gordon 1981: 109).

> By allocation of resources to R&D, we may deny the Malthusian hypothesis and prevent the conclusion of the doomsday models (Sato and Suzawa 1983: 81).

In the contrary view, espoused by many environmental advocates, current well-being is bought at the expense of future generations. If we do allocate more resources to R&D, and are successful at stimulating further economic growth, this will, in the environmentalist view, lead only to faster depletion, hasten the inevitable crash, and make it worse when it comes (e.g., Catton 1980). Implicit in such ideas is a call for economic *undevelopment*, for return to a simpler time of lower consumption and local self-sufficiency.

Both views are held by well-meaning persons who have intelligently studied the matter and reached opposite conclusions. Both approaches, though, suffer from the same flaw: key historical factors have been left out. The optimistic approach will be addressed first on this point, the environmental view shortly.

Economists base their beliefs on the principle of infinite substitutability. The basis of this principle is that by allocating resources to R&D, alternatives can be found to energy and raw materials in short supply. So as wood, for example, has grown expensive, it has been replaced in many uses by masonry, plastics, and other materials.

One problem with the principle of infinite substitutability is that it does not apply, in any simple fashion, to investments in organizational complexity. Sociopolitical organization, as we know, is a major arena of declining marginal returns, and one for which no substitute product can be developed. Economies of scale and advances in information-processing technology do help lower organizational costs, but ultimately these too are subject to diminishing returns.

A second problem is that the principle of infinite substitutability is, despite its title, difficult to apply indefinitely. A number of perceptive scientists, philosophers, and economists have shown that the marginal costs of research and development, as discussed in Chapter 4, have grown so high it is questionable whether technological innovation will be able to contribute as much to the solution of future problems as it has to past ones (D. Price 1963; Rescher 1978, 1980; Rifkin with Howard 1980; Scherer 1984). Consider, for example, what will be needed to solve problems of food and pollution. Meadows and her colleagues note that to increase world food production by 34 percent from 1951 to 1966 required increases in expenditures on tractors of 63 percent, on nitrate fertilizers of 146 percent, and on pesticides of 300 percent. The next 34 percent increase in food production would require even greater capital and resource inputs (Meadows et al. 1972: 53). Pollution control shows a similar pattern. Removal of all organic wastes from a sugar-processing plant costs 100 times more than removing 30 percent. Reducing sulfur dioxide in the air of a U.S. city by 9.6 times, or of particulates by 3.1 times, raises the cost of control by 520 times (Meadows et al. 1972: 134-5).

It is not that R&D cannot potentially solve the problems of industrialism. The difficulty is that to do so will require an increasing share of GNP. The principle of infinite substitutability depends on energy and technology. With diminishing returns to investment in scientific research, how can economic growth be sustained? The answer is that to sustain growth resources will have to be allocated from other sectors of the economy into science and engineering. The result will likely be at least a temporary decline in the standard of living, as people will have comparatively less to spend on food, housing, clothing, medical care, transportation, or entertainment. The allocation of greater resources to science of course is nothing new, merely the continuation of a two centuries-old trend (D. Price 1963). Such investment, unfortunately, can never yield a permanent solution, merely a respite from diminishing returns.

In past societies, as we know, declining marginal returns led to weakness, and to disintegration or collapse. If we are to escape nuclear annihilation, if we control pollution and population, and manage to circumvent resource depletion, will our fate then be sealed by the high cost and low marginal return that these things will require? Will we find, as have some past societies, that the cost of overcoming our problems is too high relative to the benefits conferred, and that not solving problems is the economical option?

In fact, there are major differences between the current and the ancient worlds that have important implications for collapse. One of these is that the world today is full. That is to say, it is filled by complex societies; these occupy every sector of the globe, except the most desolate. This is a new factor in human history. Complex societies as a whole are a recent and unusual aspect of human life. The current situation, where *all* societies are so oddly constituted, is unique. It was shown earlier in this chapter that ancient collapses occurred, and could only occur, in a power vacuum, where a complex society (or cluster of peer polities) was surrounded by less complex neighbors. There are no power vacuums left today. Every nation is linked to, and influenced by, the major powers, and most are strongly linked with one power bloc or the other. Combine this with instant global travel, and as Paul Valéry noted, '...*nothing can ever happen again without the whole world's taking a hand*' (1962: 115 [emphasis in original]).

Collapse today is neither an option nor an immediate threat. Any nation vulnerable to collapse will have to pursue one of three options: (1) absorption by a neighbor or some larger state; (2) economic support by a dominant power, or by an international financing agency; or (3) payment by the support population of whatever costs are needed to continue complexity, however detrimental the marginal return. A nation today can no longer unilaterally collapse, for if any national government disintegrates its population and territory will be absorbed by some other.

Although this is a recent development, it has analogies in past collapses, and these analogies give insight into current conditions. Past collapses, as discussed, occurred among two kinds of international political situations: isolated, dominant states, and clusters of peer polities. The isolated, dominant state went out with the advent of global travel and communication, and what remains now are competitive peer polities. Even if today there are only two major peers, with allies grouped into opposing blocs, the dynamics of the competitive relations are the same. Peer polities, such as post-Roman Europe, ancient Greece and Italy, Warring States China, and the Mayan cities, are characterized by competitive relations, jockeying for position, alliance formation and dissolution, territorial expansion and retrenchment, and continual investment in military advantage. An upward spiral of competitive investment develops, as each polity continually seeks to outmaneuver its peer(s). None can dare withdraw from this spiral, without unrealistic diplomatic guarantees, for such would be only an invitation to domination by another. In this sense, although industrial society (especially the United States) is sometimes likened in popular thought to ancient Rome, a closer analogy would be with the Mycenaeans or the Maya.

Peer polity systems tend to evolve toward greater complexity in a lockstep fashion as, driven by competition, each partner imitates new organizational, technological, and military features developed by its competitor(s). The marginal return on such developments declines, as each new military breakthrough is met by some counter-measure, and so brings no increased advantage or security on a lasting basis. A society trapped in a competitive peer polity system must invest more and more for no increased return, and is thereby economically weakened. And yet the option of withdrawal or collapse does not exist. So it is that collapse (from declining marginal returns) is not in the *immediate* future for any contemporary nation. This is not, however, due so much to anything we have accomplished as it is to the competitive spiral in which we have allowed ourselves to become trapped.

Here is the reason why proposals for economic undevelopment, for living in balance on a small planet, will not work. Given the close link between economic and military power, unilateral economic deceleration would be equivalent to, and as foolhardy as, unilateral disarmament. We simply do not have the option to return to a lower economic level, at least not a rational option. Peer polity competition drives increased complexity and resource consumption regardless of costs, human or ecological.

I do not wish to suggest by this discussion that any major power would be quickly in danger of collapse were it not for this situation. Both the primary and secondary world powers have sufficient economic strength to finance diminishing returns well into the future. As seen in the cases of the Romans and the Maya, peoples with sufficient incentives and/or economic reserves can endure declining marginal returns for centuries before their societies collapse. (This fact, however, is no reason for complacency. Modern evolutionary processes, as is well known, occur at a faster rate than those of the past.)

There are any number of smaller nations, though, that have invested quite heavily in military power out of proportion to their economic base, or in development projects with a questionable marginal payoff, that might well be vulnerable. In the world today they will not be allowed to collapse, but will be bailed out either by a dominant partner or by an international financing agency. Such instances lower the marginal return that the world as a whole experiences for its investment in complexity.

Peer polities then tend to undergo long periods of upwardly-spiraling competitive costs, and downward marginal returns. This is terminated finally by domination of one and acquisition of a new energy subsidy (as in Republican Rome and Warring States China), or by *mutual* collapse (as among the Mycenaeans and the Maya). Collapse, if and when it comes again, will this time be global. No longer can any individual nation collapse. World civilization will disintegrate as a whole. Competitors who evolve as peers collapse in like manner.

In ancient societies the solution to declining marginal returns was to capture a new energy subsidy. In economic systems activated largely by agriculture, livestock, and human labor (and ultimately by solar energy), this was accomplished by territorial expansion. Ancient Rome and the Ch'in of Warring States China adopted this course, as have countless other empire-builders. In an economy that today is activated by stored energy reserves, and especially in a world that is full, this course is not feasible (nor was it ever permanently successful). The capital and technology available must be directed instead toward some new and more abundant source of energy. Technological innovation and increasing productivity can forestall declining marginal returns only so long. A new energy subsidy will at some point be essential.

It is difficult to know whether world industrial society has yet reached the point where the marginal return for its overall pattern of investment has begun to decline. The great sociologist Pitirim Sorokin believed that Western economies had entered such a phase in the early twentieth century (1957: 530). Xenophon Zolotas, in contrast, predicts that this point will be reached soon after the year 2000 (1981: 102-3). Even if the point of diminishing returns to our present form of industrialism has not yet been reached, that point will inevitably arrive. Recent history seems to indicate that we have at least reached declining returns for our reliance on fossil fuels, and possibly for some raw materials. A new energy subsidy is necessary if a declining standard of living and a future global collapse are to be averted. A more abundant form of energy might not reverse the declining marginal return on investment in complexity, but it would make it more possible to finance that investment.

In a sense the lack of a power vacuum, and the resulting competitive spiral, have given the world a respite from what otherwise might have been an earlier confrontation with collapse. Here indeed is a paradox: a disastrous condition that all decry may force us to tolerate a situation of declining marginal returns long enough to achieve a temporary solution to it. This reprieve must be used rationally to seek for and develop the new energy source(s) that will be necessary to maintain economic well-being. This research and development must be an item of the highest priority, even if, as predicted, this requires reallocation of resources from other economic sectors. Adequate funding of this effort should be included in the budget of every industrialized nation (and the results shared by all). I will not enter the political foray by suggesting whether this be funded privately or publicly, only that funded it must be.

There are then notes of optimism and pessimism in the current situation. We are in a curious position where competitive interactions force a level of investment, and a declining marginal return, that might ultimately lead to collapse except that the competitor who collapses first will simply be dominated or absorbed by the survivor. A respite from the threat of collapse might be granted thereby, although we may find that we will not like to bear its costs. If collapse is not in the immediate future, that is not to say that the industrial standard of living is also reprieved. As marginal returns decline (a process ongoing even now), up to the point where a new energy subsidy is in place, the standard of living that industrial societies have enjoyed will not grow so rapidly, and for some groups and nations may remain static or decline. The political conflicts that this will cause, coupled with the increasingly easy availability of nuclear weapons, will create a dangerous world situation in the foreseeable future.

To a degree there is nothing new or radical in these remarks. Many others have voiced similar observations on the current scene, in greater detail and with greater eloquence. What has been accomplished here is to place contemporary societies in a historical perspective, and to apply a global principle that links the past to the present and the future. However much we like to think of ourselves as something special in world history, in fact industrial societies are subject to the same principles that caused earlier societies to collapse. If civilization collapses again, it will be from failure to take advantage of the current reprieve, a reprieve paradoxically both detrimental and essential to our anticipated future.

REFERENCES

Adams, Brooks (1896). *The Law of Civilization and Decay*. Macmillan, New York.

Adams, Daniel B. (1983). Last Ditch Archeology. *Science 83* 4(10): 28-37.

Adams, Henry (1919). *The Degradation of the Democratic Dogma*. Macmillan, New York.

Adams, Richard E. W. (1969). Maya Archaeology 1958-1968, a Review. *Latin American Research Review* 4: 3-45.

(1971). The Ceramics of Altar de Sacrificios, Guatemala. *Papers of the Peabody Museum of Archaeology and Ethnology, Harvard University* 63(1).

(1973a). The Collapse of Maya Civilization: a Review of Previous Theories. In *The Classic Maya Collapse*, edited by T. Patrick Culbert, pp. 21-34. University of New Mexico Press, Albuquerque.

(1973b). Maya Collapse: Transformation and Termination in the Ceramic Sequence at Altar de Sacrificios. In *The Classic Maya Collapse*, edited by T. Patrick Culbert, pp. 133-63. University of New Mexico Press, Albuquerque.

(1977a). Rio Bec Archaeology and the Rise of Maya Civilization. In *The Origins of Maya Civilization*, edited by Richard E. W. Adams, pp. 77-99. University of New Mexico Press, Albuquerque.

(1977b). *Prehistoric Mesoamerica*. Little, Brown, Boston.

(1980). Swamps, Canals and the Locations of Ancient Mayan Cities. *Antiquity* 54: 206-14.

(1981). Settlement Patterns of the Central Yucatan and Southern Campeche Regions. In *Lowland Maya Settlement Patterns*, edited by Wendy Ashmore, pp. 211-57. University of New Mexico Press, Albuquerque.

(1983). Ancient Land Use and Culture History in the Pasion River Region. In *Prehistoric Settlement Patterns: Essays in Honor of Gordon R. Willey*, edited by Evon Z. Vogt and Richard M. Leventhal, pp. 319-35. University of New Mexico Press and Peabody Museum of Archaeology and Ethnology, Harvard University, Albuquerque and Cambridge.

Adams, Richard E. W. and Norman Hammond (1982). Maya Archaeology, 1976-1980: a Review of Major Publications. *Journal of Field Archaeology* 9: 487-512.

Adams, Richard E. W. and Richard C. Jones (1981). Spatial Patterns and Regional Growth Among Classic Maya Cities. *American Antiquity* 46: 301-22.

Adams, Richard E. W. and Woodruff D. Smith (1981). Feudal Models for Classic Maya Civilization. In *Lowland Maya Settlement Patterns*, edited by Wendy Ashmore, pp. 335-49. University of New Mexico Press, Albuquerque.

Adams, Richard N. (1975). *Energy and Structure: a Theory of Social Power*. University of Texas Press, Austin.

Adams, Robert M. (1983). *Decadent Societies*. North Point, San Francisco.

Adams, Robert McC. (1974). Historic Patterns of Mesopotamian Irrigation Agriculture. In Irrigation's Impact on Society, edited by Theodore M. Downing and McGuire Gibson, pp. 1-6. *University of Arizona Anthropological Papers* 25.

(1978). Strategies of Maximization, Stability, and Resilience in Mesopotamian Society,

Settlement, and Agriculture. *Proceedings of the American Philosophical Society* 122: 329-35.

(1981). *Heartland of Cities*. Aldine, Chicago.

Akins, Nancy J. (1984). Temporal Variation in Faunal Assemblages from Chaco Canyon. In Recent Research on Chaco Prehistory, edited by W. James Judge and John D. Schelberg, pp. 225-40. *Reports of the Chaco Center* 8. U.S. Department of the Interior, National Park Service, Division of Cultural Research, Albuquerque.

Akins, Nancy J. and John D. Schelberg (1984). Evidence for Social Complexity as seen from the Mortuary Practices at Chaco Canyon. In Recent Research on Chaco Prehistory, edited by W. James Judge and John D. Schelberg, pp. 89-102. *Reports of the Chaco Center* 8. U.S. Department of the Interior, National Park Service, Division of Cultural Research, Albuquerque.

Akurgal, Ekrem (1962). *The Art of the Hittites* (translated by Constance McNab). Harry N. Abrams, New York.

Allchin, Bridget and Raymond Allchin (1968). *The Birth of Indian Civilization*. Penguin Books, Harmondsworth.

Altree, Wayne (1956). Toynbee's Treatment of Chinese History. In *Toynbee and History*, edited by M. F. Ashley Montagu, pp. 243-72. Porter Sargent, Boston.

Altschuler, Milton (1958). On the Environmental Limitations of Maya Cultural Development. *Southwestern Journal of Anthropology* 14: 189-98.

Ammianus Marcellinus (1939). *Ammianus Marcellinus* (translated by John C. Rolfe) (three volumes). Harvard University Press and William Heinemann, Cambridge and London.

Antoine, Pierre P., Richard L. Skarie, and Paul R. Bloom (1982). The Origin of Raised Fields Near San Antonio, Belize: an Alternative Hypothesis. In *Maya Subsistence: Studies in Memory of Dennis E. Puleston*, edited by Kent V. Flannery, pp. 227-36. Academic Press, New York.

Andrews, E. Wyllys V. and Jeremy A. Sabloff (1986). Classic to Postclassic: a Summary Discussion. In *Late Lowland Maya Civilization: Classic to Postclassic*, edited by Jeremy A. Sabloff and E. Wyllys Andrews V, pp. 433-56. University of New Mexico Press, Albuquerque.

Apter, David (1968). Government. In *International Encyclopedia of the Social Sciences*, Volume 6, edited by David L. Sills, pp. 214-30. Macmillan and Free Press, New York.

Aristotle (1984). *The Politics* (translated by Carnes Lord). University of Chicago Press, Chicago and London.

Asch, Nancy B., Richard I. Ford, and David L. Asch (1972). Paleoethnobotany of the Koster Site: the Archaic Horizons. *Illinois State Museum Reports of Investigations* 24. *Illinois Valley Archeological Program, Research Papers* 6.

Augustine, Saint (1958). *The City of God* (translated by Gerald G. Walsh, Demetrius B. Zema, Grace Monahan, and Daniel J. Honan). Image Books, Garden City.

Baker, Kenneth (1986). Treasures From the Sacred Well of the Mayas. *San Francisco Examiner Review*, Sunday, January 12.

Ball, Joseph A. (1977). The Rise of the Northern Maya Chiefdoms: a Socioprocessual Analysis. In *The Origins of Maya Civilization*, edited by Richard E. W. Adams, pp. 101-32. University of New Mexico Press, Albuquerque.

Barnett, Harold J. and Chandler Morse (1963). *Scarcity and Growth: the Economics of Natural Resource Availability*. Johns Hopkins Press, Baltimore.

Barnett, R. D. (1975a). The Sea Peoples. In *The Cambridge Ancient History* II(2) (third edition), edited by I. E. S. Edwards, C. J. Gadd, N. G. L. Hammond, and E. Sollberger, pp. 359-78. Cambridge University Press, Cambridge.

(1975b). Phrygia and the Peoples of Anatolia in the Iron Age. In *The Cambridge Ancient History* II(2) (third edition), edited by I. E. S. Edwards, C. J. Gadd, N. G. L.

Hammond, and E. Sollberger, pp. 417-42. Cambridge University Press, Cambridge.

Barreis, David A. and Reid A. Bryson (1965). Climatic Episodes and the Dating of the Mississippian Cultures. *Wisconsin Archaeologist* 46: 203-20.

Barreis, David A., Reid A. Bryson, and J. E. Kutzbach (1976). Climate and Culture in the Western Great Lakes Region. *MidContinental Journal of Archaeology* 1: 39-57.

Bateman, Fred (1969). Labor Inputs and Productivity in American Dairy Agriculture, 1850-1910. *Journal of Economic History* 29: 206-29.

Bateson, Gregory (1972). *Steps to an Ecology of Mind*. Chandler, San Francisco.

Baynes, N. H. (1943). The Decline of the Roman Empire in Western Europe: Some Modern Explanations. *Journal of Roman Studies* 33: 29-35.

Bean, Lowell John (1972). *Mukat's People: the Cahuilla Indians of Southern California*. University of California Press, Berkeley and Los Angeles.

Becatti, Giovanni (1968). *The Art of Ancient Greece and Rome*. Prentice-Hall and Harry N. Abrams, Englewood Cliffs and New York.

Becker, Marshall Joseph (1973). Archaeological Evidence for Occupational Specialization Among the Classic Period Maya at Tikal, Guatemala. *American Antiquity* 38: 396-406.

Bell, Barbara (1971). The Dark Ages in Ancient History: 1. The First Dark Age in Egypt. *American Journal of Archaeology* 75: 1-26.

Bendix, Reinhard (1956). *Work and Authority in Industry*. Wiley and Sons, New York.

Bergin, Thomas Goddard and Max Harold Fisch (translators) (1948). *The New Science of Giambattista Vico* (third edition, 1744). Cornell University Press, Ithaca.

Bernardi, Aurelio (1970). The Economic Problems of the Roman Empire at the Time of its Decline. In *The Economic Decline of Empires*, edited by Carlo M. Cipolla, pp. 16-83. Methuen, London.

Betancourt, Philip P. (1976). The End of the Greek Bronze Age. *Antiquity* 50: 40-7.

Bettinger, Robert L. and Thomas F. King (1971). Interaction and Political Organization: a Theoretical Framework for Archaeology in Owens Valley, California. *UCLA Archaeological Survey Annual Report* 13: 137-50.

Blanton, Richard E. (1978). *Monte Alban: Settlement Patterns at the Ancient Zapotec Capital*. Academic Press, New York.

    (1983). The Urban Decline at Monte Alban. In *The Cloud People: Divergent Evolution of the Zapotec and Mixtec Civilizations*, edited by Kent V. Flannery and Joyce Marcus, p. 186. Academic Press, New York.

Blanton, Richard E. and Stephen A. Kowalewski (1981). Monte Alban and After in the Valley of Oaxaca. In *Supplement to the Handbook of Middle American Indians*, Volume I: *Archaeology*, edited by Jeremy A. Sabloff, pp. 94-116. University of Texas Press, Austin.

Blau, Peter M. (1977). *Inequality and Heterogeneity: a Primitive Theory of Social Structure*. Free Press, New York.

Boak, Arthur E. R. (1955). *Manpower Shortage and the Fall of the Roman Empire in the West*. University of Michigan Press, Ann Arbor.

Boak, Arthur E. and William G. Sinnigen (1965). *A History of Rome to A.D. 565* (fifth edition). Macmillan, New York.

Boer, W. den (1956). Toynbee and Classical History. In *Toynbee and History*, edited by M. F. Ashley Montagu, pp. 221-42. Porter Sargent, Boston.

Bolin, Sture (1958). *State and Currency in the Roman Empire to 300 A.D.* Almquist and Wiksell, Stockholm.

Borkenau, Franz (1981). *End and Beginning: On the Generations of Cultures and the Origins of the West*. Columbia University Press, New York.

Boserup, Ester (1965). *The Conditions of Agricultural Growth: the Economics of Agrarian Change Under Population Pressure*. Aldine, Chicago.

(1981). *Population and Technological Change.* University of Chicago Press, Chicago and London.

Bound, John, Clint Cummins, Zvi Griliches, Bronwyn H. Hall, and Adam Jaffe (1984). Who Does R & D and Who Patents? In *R & D, Patents, and Productivity*, edited by Zvi Griliches, pp. 21-54. University of Chicago Press, Chicago and London.

Bove, Frederick J. (1981). Trend Surface Analysis and the Lowland Classic Maya Collapse. *American Antiquity* 46: 93-112.

Boxer, C. R. (1970). The Dutch Economic Decline. In *The Economic Decline of Empires*, edited by Carlo M. Cipolla, pp. 235-63. Methuen, London.

Braun, David P. (1977). *Middle Woodland – (Early) Late Woodland Social Change in the Prehistoric Central Midwestern U.S.* Ph.D. dissertation, University of Michigan. University Microfilms, Ann Arbor.

Brewbaker, James L.(1979). Diseases of Maize in the Wet Lowland Tropics and the Collapse of the Classic Maya Civilization. *Economic Botany* 33: 101-18.

Briffault, Robert (1938). *The Decline and Fall of the British Empire.* Simon and Schuster, New York.

Bronson, Bennet (1966). Roots and the Subsistence of the Ancient Maya. *Southwestern Journal of Anthropology* 22: 251-79.

Brovsky, Cindy (1985). Anasazi Flight Linked to Mass 'Ritualization.' *Durango Herald*, September 15.

Brown, Peter (1971). *The World of Late Antiquity.* Thames and Hudson, London.

Bryson, R. A., H. H. Lamb, and D. L. Donley (1974). Drought and the Decline of Mycenae. *Antiquity* 48: 46-50.

Buckley, Walter (1968). Society as a Complex Adaptive System. In *Modern Systems Research for the Behavioral Scientist*, edited by Walter Buckley, pp. 490-513. Aldine, Chicago.

Bullard, William R. (1960). Maya Settlement Patterns in Northeastern Peten, Guatemala. *American Antiquity* 25: 355-72.

(1973) Postclassic Culture in Central Peten and Adjacent British Honduras. In *The Classic Maya Collapse*, edited by T. Patrick Culbert, pp. 221-41. University of New Mexico Press, Albuquerque.

Burckhardt, Jacob (1949). *The Age of Constantine the Great* (translated by Moses Hadas). Routledge and Kegan Paul, London.

Bury, J. B. (1923). *History of the Later Roman Empire* (two volumes). Macmillan, London.

Butzer, Karl W. (1976). *Early Hydraulic Civilization in Egypt.* University of Chicago Press, Chicago.

(1980). Civilizations: Organisms or Systems? *American Scientist* 68: 517-23.

(1984). Long-term Nile Flood Variation and Political Discontinuities in Pharaonic Egypt. In *From Hunters to Farmers: The Causes and Consequences of Food Production in Africa*, edited by J. Desmond Clark and Steven A. Brandt, pp. 102-12. University of California Press, Berkeley and Los Angeles.

Cameron, Catherine J. (1984). A Regional View of Chipped Stone Raw Material Use in Chaco Canyon. In Recent Research on Chaco Prehistory, edited by W. James Judge and John D. Schelberg, pp. 137-52. *Reports of the Chaco Center* 8. U.S. Department of the Interior, National Park Service, Division of Cultural Research, Albuquerque.

Cancian, Frank (1976). Social Stratification. *Annual Review of Anthropology* 5: 227-48.

Carneiro, Robert L. (1970). A Theory of the Origin of the State. *Science* 169: 733-38.

(1978). Political Expansion as an Expression of the Principle of Competitive Exclusion. In *Origins of the State: the Anthropology of Political Evolution*, edited by Ronald Cohen and Elman R. Service, pp. 203-23. Institute for the Study of Human Issues, Philadelphia.

(1981). The Chiefdom: Precursor of the State. In *The Transition to Statehood in the New*

World, edited by Grant D. Jones and Robert R. Kautz, pp. 37-79. Cambridge University Press, Cambridge.

Carpenter, Rhys (1966). *Discontinuities in Greek Civilisation*. Cambridge University Press, Cambridge.

Carr, Edward Hallett (1961). *What is History?* Macmillan, London.

Carter, Anne P. (1966). The Economics of Technological Change. *Scientific American* 214(4): 25-31.

Casson, Stanley (1937). *Progress and Catastrophe: an Anatomy of Human Adventure*. Harper and Brothers, New York and London.

Catton, William R., Jr. (1980). *Overshoot: the Ecological Basis of Revolutionary Change*. University of Illinois Press, Urbana.

Caudwell, Christopher (1971). *Further Studies in a Dying Culture*. Monthly Review Press, New York and London.

Cépède, Michel, Françoise Houtart, and Linus Grond (1964). *Population and Food*. Sheed and Ward, New York.

Chadwick, John (1976). *The Mycenaean World*. Cambridge University Press, Cambridge.

Chagnon, Napoleon A. (1970). Ecological and Adaptive Aspects of California Shell Money. *UCLA Archaeological Survey Annual Report* 12: 1-25.

Charanis, Peter (1953). Economic Factors in the Decline of the Byzantine Empire. *The Journal of Economic History* 13: 412-24.

Charnov, Eric L. (1976). Optimal Foraging, the Marginal Value Theorem. *Theoretical Population Biology* 9: 129-36.

Childe, V. Gordon (1942). *What Happened in History*. Penguin, Baltimore.

(1951). *Man Makes Himself*. Mentor, New York.

Cipolla, Carlo M. (1970a). Editor's Introduction. In *The Economic Decline of Empires*, edited by Carlo M. Cipolla, pp. 1-15. Methuen, London.

(1970b). The Economic Decline of Italy. In *The Economic Decline of Empires*, edited by Carlo M. Cipolla, pp. 198-214. Methuen, London.

Claessen, Henri J. M. (1978). The Early State: a Structural Approach. In *The Early State*, edited by Henri J. M. Claessen and Peter Skalnik, pp. 533-96. Mouton, The Hague.

Claessen, Henri J. M. and Peter Skalnik (1978a). The Early State: Theories and Hypotheses. In *The Early State*, edited by Henri J. M. Claessen and Peter Skalnik, pp. 3-29. Mouton, The Hague.

(1978b). Limits: Beginning and End of the Early State. In *The Early State*, edited by Henri J. M. Claessen and Peter Skalnik, pp. 619-35. Mouton, The Hague.

(1978c). The Early State: Models and Reality. In *The Early State*, edited by Henri J. M. Claessen and Peter Skalnik, pp. 637-50. Mouton, the Hague.

Clark, Colin and Margaret Haswell (1966). *The Economics of Subsistence Agriculture*. Macmillan, London.

Clark, Grahame (1979). Archaeology and Human Diversity. *Annual Review of Anthropology* 8: 1-19.

Clark, Kim B. and Zvi Griliches (1984). Productivity Growth and R & D at the Business Level: Results From the PIMS Data Base. In *R & D, Patents, and Productivity*, edited by Zvi Griliches, pp. 393-416. University of Chicago Press, Chicago and London.

Clough, Shephard B. (1951). *The Rise and Fall of Civilization*. McGraw-Hill, New York.

Coe, Michael D. (1981). San Lorenzo Tenochtitlan. In *Supplement to the Handbook of Middle American Indians*, Volume I: *Archaeology*, edited by Jeremy A. Sabloff, pp. 117-46. University of Texas Press, Austin.

Cohen, Mark N. (1977). *The Food Crisis in Prehistory: Overpopulation and the Origins of Agriculture*. Yale University Press, New Haven.

Cohen, Ronald (1978). Introduction. In *Origins of the State: the Anthropology of Political*

Evolution, edited by Ronald Cohen and Elman R. Service, pp. 1-20. Institute for the Study of Human Issues, Philadelphia.

Conrad, Geoffrey and Arthur A. Demarest (1984). *Religion and Empire: the Dynamics of Aztec and Inca Expansionism*. Cambridge University Press, Cambridge.

Cook, Della C. (1981). Mortality, Age Structure and Status in the Interpretation of Stress Indicators in Prehistoric Skeletons: a Dental Example from the Lower Illinois Valley. In *The Archaeology of Death*, edited by Robert Chapman, Ian Kinnes, and Klaus Randsborg, pp. 133-44. Cambridge University Press, Cambridge.

Cook, Sherburne F. (1947). The Interrelation of Population, Food Supply and Building in Pre-Conquest Central Mexico. *American Antiquity* 13: 45-52.

Cooke, C. Wythe (1931). Why the Mayan Cities of the Peten District, Guatemala, were Abandoned. *Journal of the Washington Academy of Sciences* 21(13): 283-7.

Cordell, Linda A. (1982). The Pueblo Period in the San Juan Basin: an Overview and Some Research Problems. In *The San Juan Tomorrow: Planning for the Conservation of Cultural Resources in the San Juan Basin*, edited by Fred Plog and Walter Wait, pp. 59-83. USDI National Park Service, Southwestern Region and School of American Research, Santa Fé.

Cordy, Ross H. (1981). *A Study of Prehistoric Social Change: the Development of Complex Societies in the Hawaiian Islands*. Academic Press, New York.

Coulborn, Rushton (1954). The Rise and Fall of Civilizations. *Ethics* 64: 205-16.

(1966). Structure and Process in the Rise and Fall of Civilized Society. *Comparative Studies in Society and History* 8: 404-31.

Cowgill, George L. (1964). The End of Classic Maya Culture: a Review of Recent Evidence. *Southwestern Journal of Anthropology* 20: 145-59.

(1977). Processes of Growth and Decline at Teotihuacan: the City and the State. In *Los Procesos de Cambio: XV Mesa Redonda*, 1: 183-93. Sociedad Mexicana de Antropologia y Universidad de Guanajuato, Mexico City.

(1979). Teotihuacan, Internal Militaristic Competition, and the Fall of the Classic Maya. In *Maya Archaeology and Ethnohistory*, edited by Norman Hammond and Gordon R. Willey, pp. 51-62. University of Texas Press, Austin.

Creel, Herrlee Glessner (1953). *Chinese Thought from Confucius to Mao Tse-Tung*. University of Chicago Press, Chicago.

(1970). *The Origins of Statecraft in China*, Volume I: *The Western Chou Empire*. Aldine, Chicago.

Culbert, T. Patrick (1973a). Introduction: a Prologue to Classic Maya Culture and the Problem of its Collapse. In *The Classic Maya Collapse*, edited by T. Patrick Culbert, pp. 3-19. University of New Mexico Press, Albuquerque.

(1973b). The Mayan Downfall at Tikal. In *The Classic Maya Collapse*, edited by T. Patrick Culbert, pp. 63-92. University of New Mexico Press, Albuquerque.

(1974). *The Lost Civilization: the Story of the Classic Maya*. Harper and Row, New York.

(1977a). Early Maya Development at Tikal, Guatemala. In *The Origins of Maya Civilization*, edited by Richard E. W. Adams, pp. 27-42. University of New Mexico Press, Albuquerque.

(1977b). Maya Development and Collapse: an Economic Perspective. In *Social Process in Maya Prehistory: Studies in Honour of Sir Eric Thompson*, edited by Norman Hammond, pp. 509-30. Academic Press, London.

(n.d.). The Collapse of Classic Maya Civilization. In *The Collapse of Ancient Civilizations*, edited by N. Yoffee and G. L. Cowgill. University of Arizona Press, Tucson (in press).

Dales, George F. (1966). The Decline of the Harappans. *Scientific American* 214(5): 92-8, 100.

Davies, Nigel (1977). *The Toltecs Until the Fall of Tula*. University of Oklahoma Press, Norman.

Davis, Kingsley (1949). *Human Society*. Macmillan, New York.

Dawson, Christopher (1956). *The Dynamics of World History*. Sheed and Ward, New York.

Deevey, E. S., Don S. Rice, Prudence M. Rice, H. H. Vaughn, Mark Brenner, and M. S. Flannery (1979). Mayan Urbanism: Impact on a Tropical Karst Environment. *Science* 206: 298-306.

Demarest, Arthur A. (1979). Interregional Conflict and 'Situational Ethics' in Classic Maya Warfare. *Human Mosaic* 12: 101-11.

Denison, Edward F. (1979). *Accounting for Slower Economic Growth: the United States in the 1970s*. Brookings Institution, Washington, D.C.

Desborough, V. R. (1972). *The Greek Dark Ages*. Ernest Benn, London.
  (1975). The End of Mycenaean Civilization and the Dark Ages: (a) the Archaeological Background. In *The Cambridge Ancient History* II(2) (third edition), edited by I. E. S. Edwards, C. J. Gadd, N. G. L. Hammond, and E. Sollberger, pp. 658-77. Cambridge University Press, Cambridge.

Deutsch, Karl (1969). *Nationalism and its Alternatives*. Alfred A. Knopf, New York.

Dhavalikar, M. K. (1984). Toward an Ecological Model for Chalcolithic Cultures of Central and Western India. *Journal of Anthropological Archaeology* 3: 133-58.

Diakonoff, I. M. (1969). The Rise of the Despotic State in Ancient Mesopotamia. In *Ancient Mesopotamia: Socio-Economic History*, edited by I. M. Diakonoff, pp. 173-203. Nauka, Moscow.

Diehl, Charles (1970). The Economic Decay of Byzantium. In *The Economic Decline of Empires*, edited by Carlo M. Cipolla, pp. 92-101. Methuen, London.

Diehl, Richard A. (1981). Tula. In *Supplement to the Handbook of Middle American Indians*, Volume I: *Archaeology*, edited by Jeremy A. Sabloff, pp. 277-95. University of Texas Press, Austin.

Dill, Samuel (1899). *Roman Society in the Last Century of the Western Empire* (second edition). Macmillan, London.

DiPeso, Charles C. (1974). *Casas Grandes, a Fallen Trading Center of the Gran Chichimeca*, Volume 2: *The Medio Period*. Amerind Foundation and Northland Press, Dragoon and Flagstaff.

Doumas, Christos G. (1983). *Thera: Pompeii of the Ancient Aegean*. Thames and Hudson, London.

Doyel, David E. (1981). Late Hohokam Prehistory in Southern Arizona. *Gila Press Contributions to Archaeology* 2.

Doyel, David E., Cory D. Breternitz, and Michael P. Marshall (1984). Chacoan Community Structure: Bis sa'ani Pueblo and the Chaco Halo. In Recent Research on Chaco Prehistory, edited by W. James Judge and John D. Schelberg, pp. 37-54. *Reports of the Chaco Center* 8. U.S. Department of the Interior, National Park Service, Division of Cultural Research, Albuquerque.

Drucker, Philip, Robert F. Heizer, and Robert J. Squier (1959). Excavations at LaVenta, Tabasco, 1955. *Bureau of American Ethnology, Bulletin* 170.

Duncan-Jones, Richard (1974). *The Economy of the Roman Empire: Quantitative Studies*. Cambridge University Press, Cambridge.

Durkheim, Emile (1947). *The Division of Labor in Society* (translated by George Simpson). Free Press, Glencoe.

Easton, David (1965a). *A Systems Analysis of Political Life*. John Wiley, New York.
  (1965b). *A Framework for Political Analysis*. Prentice-Hall, Englewood Cliffs.

Eisenstadt, S. N. (1963). *The Political Systems of Empires*. Free Press, Glencoe.
  (1978). *Revolution and the Transformation of Societies*. Free Press, Glencoe.

Ekholm, Kajsa (1980). On the Limits of Civilization: the Structure and Dynamics of Global Systems. *Dialectical Anthropology* 5: 155-66.

Elliott, J. H. (1970). The Decline of Spain. In *The Economic Decline of Empires*, edited by Carlo M. Cipolla, pp. 168-95. Methuen, London.

Elster, Jon (1983). *Explaining Technical Change*. Cambridge University Press and Universitetsforlaget, Cambridge and Oslo.

Engels, Frederick (1972). *The Origin of the Family, Private Property, and the State*. International Publishers, New York.

Englert, Sebastian (1970). *Island at the Center of the World: New Light on Easter Island*. Charles Scribner's Sons, New York.

Erickson, Edwin E. (1973). The Life Cycle of Life Styles: Projecting the Course of Local Evolutionary Sequences. *Behavior Science Notes* 8: 135-60.

(1975). Growth Functions and Culture History: a Perspective on Classic Maya Cultural Development. *Behavior Science Research* 10: 37-61.

Erwin, Robert (1966). Civilization as a Phase of World History. *The American Historical Review* 71: 1181-98.

Evenson, Robert E. (1984). International Invention: Implications for Technology Market Analysis. In *R & D, Patents, and Productivity*, edited by Zvi Griliches, pp. 89-123. University of Chicago Press, Chicago and London.

Fairbank, John K., Edwin O. Reischauer, and Albert M. Craig (1973). *East Asia: Tradition and Transformation*. Houghton Mifflin, Boston.

Ferrero, Guglielmo (1914). *Ancient Rome and Modern America: a Comparative Study of Morals and Manners*. G. P. Putnam's Sons, New York and London.

Finley, Moses I. (1968). *Aspects of Antiquity: Discoveries and Controversies*. Viking Press, New York.

(1973). *The Ancient Economy*. University of California Press, Berkeley and Los Angeles.

Flannery, Kent V. (1972). The Cultural Evolution of Civilizations. *Annual Review of Ecology and Systematics* 3: 399-426.

Folan, William J., Larraine A. Fletcher, and Ellen R. Kintz (1979). Fruit, Fiber, Bark, and Resin: Social Organization of a Maya Urban Center. *Science* 204: 697-701.

Ford, Richard I. (1972). An Ecological Perspective on the Eastern Pueblos. In *New Perspectives on the Pueblos*, edited by Alfonso Ortiz, pp. 1-18. University of New Mexico Press, Albuquerque.

Fortes, M. and E. E. Evans-Pritchard (1940). Introduction. In *African Political Systems*, edited by M. Fortes and E. E. Evans-Pritchard, pp. 1-23. Oxford University Press, London.

Fowler, Melvin L. (1975). A Pre-Columbian Urban Center on the Mississippi. *Scientific American* 233(2): 92-101.

Frank, Tenney (1940). *An Economic Survey of Ancient Rome*, Volume V: *Rome and Italy of the Empire*. Johns Hopkins Press, Baltimore.

(1970). Race Mixture in the Roman Empire. In *The Fall of Rome: Can It Be Explained?* (second edition), edited by Mortimer Chambers, pp. 47-54. Holt, Rinehart and Winston, New York.

Freidel, David A. (1979). Culture Areas and Interaction Spheres: Contrasting Approaches to the Emergence of Civilization in the Maya Lowlands. *American Antiquity* 44: 36-54.

(1981). The Political Economics of Residential Dispersion Among the Lowland Maya. In *Lowland Maya Settlement Patterns*, edited by Wendy Ashmore, pp. 371-82. University of New Mexico Press, Albuquerque.

(1983). Political Systems in Lowland Yucatan: Dynamics and Structure in Maya Settlement. In *Prehistoric Settlement Patterns: Essays in Honor of Gordon R. Willey*, edited by Evon Z. Vogt and Richard M. Leventhal, pp. 375-86. University of New Mexico Press and Peabody Museum of Archaeology and Ethnology, Harvard University, Albuquerque and Cambridge.

(1985). New Light on the Dark Age: a Summary of Major Themes. In *The Lowland Maya*

Postclassic, edited by Arlen F. Chase and Prudence M. Rice, pp. 285-309. University of Texas Press, Austin.

Freidel, David A. and Vernon Scarborough (1982). Subsistence, Trade, and Development of the Coastal Maya. In *Maya Subsistence: Studies in Memory of Dennis E. Puleston*, edited by Kent V. Flannery, pp. 131-55. Academic Press, New York.

Frere, S. S. and J. K. S. St Joseph (1983). *Roman Britain From the Air*. Cambridge University Press, Cambridge.

Fried, Morton H. (1967). *The Evolution of Political Society, an Essay in Political Anthropology*. Random House, New York.

Friedman, Jonathan (1974). Marxism, Structuralism, and Vulgar Materialism. *Man* 9: 444-69.
    (1975). Tribes, States, and Transformations. In *Marxist Analyses and Social Anthropology*, edited by Maurice Bloch, pp. 161-202. Malaby Press, London.

Friedman, J. and M. J. Rowlands (1977). Notes Toward an Epigenetic Model of the Evolution of 'Civilisation.' In *The Evolution of Social Systems*, edited by J. Friedman and M. J. Rowlands, pp. 201-76. Duckworth, London.

Gauthier, Rory P., John C. Acklen, and John R. Stein (1977). An Archeological Survey of the Anaconda Company's Bluewater Mill Tailing Pond Expansion, New Mexico. Unpublished manuscript, Office of Contract Archeology, University of New Mexico, Albuquerque.

Gibbon, Edward (1776-88). *The Decline and Fall of the Roman Empire*. Modern Library, New York.

Gibson, McGuire (1974). Violation of Fallow and Engineered Disaster in Mesopotamian Civilization. In Irrigation's Impact on Society, edited by Theodore M. Downing and McGuire Gibson, pp. 7-20. *University of Arizona Anthropological Papers* 25.

Gilfallen, S. Colum (1970). Roman Culture and Dysgenic Lead Poisoning. In *The Fall of Rome: Can It Be Explained?* (second edition), edited by Mortimer Chambers, pp. 55-9. Holt, Rinehart and Winston, New York.

Gluckman, Max (1965). *Politics, Law and Ritual in Tribal Society*. Aldine, Chicago.

Godelier, M. (1977). *Perspectives in Marxist Anthropology*. Cambridge University Press, London.

Goetze, A. (1975a). The Struggle for the Domination of Syria (1400-1300 B.C.). In *The Cambridge Ancient History* II(2) (third edition), edited by I. E. S. Edwards, C. J. Gadd, N. G. L. Hammond, and E. Sollberger, pp. 1-20. Cambridge University Press, Cambridge.
    (1975b). Anatolia from Shuppiluliumash to the Egyptian War of Muwatallish. In *The Cambridge Ancient History* II(2) (third edition), edited by I. E. S. Edwards, C. J. Gadd, N. G. L. Hammond, and E. Sollberger, pp. 117-29. Cambridge University Press, Cambridge.
    (1975c). The Hittites and Syria (1300-1200 B.C.). In *The Cambridge Ancient History* II(2) (third edition), edited by I. E. S. Edwards, C. J. Gadd, N. G. L. Hammond, and E. Sollberger, pp. 252-73. Cambridge University Press, Cambridge.

Gordon, Richard L. (1981). *An Economic Analysis of World Energy Problems*. Massachusetts Institute of Technology Press, Cambridge and London.

Gould, Stephen Jay (1983). *Hen's Teeth and Horse's Toes*. W. W. Norton, New York.

Graham, John A. (1973). Aspects of Non-Classic Presences in the Inscriptions and Sculptural Art of Seibal. In *The Classic Maya Collapse*, edited by T. Patrick Culbert, pp. 207-19. University of New Mexico Press, Albuquerque.

Gray, Charles Edward (1958). The Epicyclical Evolution of Graeco-Roman Civilization. *American Anthropologist* 60: 13-31.

Griffin, James B. (1952). Culture Periods in Eastern United States Archeology. In *Archeology of Eastern United States*, edited by James B. Griffin, pp. 352-64. University of Chicago Press, Chicago.

(1960). Climatic Change: a Contributory Cause of the Growth and Decline of Northern Hopewellian Culture. *Wisconsin Archaeologist* 41: 21-33.

(1961). Some Correlations of Climatic and Cultural Change in Eastern North American Prehistory. *Annals of the New York Academy of Sciences* 95: 710-17.

(1967). Eastern North American Archaeology: a Summary. *Science* 156: 175-91.

Griliches, Zvi (1984). Introduction. In *R & D, Patents, and Productivity*, edited by Zvi Griliches, pp. 1-19. University of Chicago Press, Chicago and London.

Guha, Ashok S. (1981). *An Evolutionary View of Economic Growth.* Clarendon Press, Oxford.

Gunderson, Gerald (1976). Economic Change and the Demise of the Roman Empire. *Explorations in Economic History* 13: 43-68.

Gupta, S. P. (1982). The Late Harappans: a Study in Cultural Dynamics. In *Harappan Civilization: a Contemporary Perspective*, edited by Gregory Possehl, pp. 51-9. Oxford and IBH Publishing Co., New Delhi.

Gurney, O. R. (1973a). Anatolia, c. 1750-1600 B.C. In *The Cambridge Ancient History* II(1) (third edition), edited by I. E. S. Edwards, C. J. Gadd, N. G. L. Hammond, and E. Sollberger, pp. 228-55. Cambridge University Press, Cambridge.

(1973b). Anatolia, c. 1600-1380 B.C. In *The Cambridge Ancient History* II(1) (third edition), edited by I. E. S. Edwards, C. J. Gadd, N. G. L. Hammond, and E. Sollberger, pp. 659-85. Cambridge University Press, Cambridge

Haas, Jonathon (1982). *The Evolution of the Prehistoric State.* Columbia University Press, New York.

Hadar, Josef (1966). *Elementary Theory of Economic Behavior.* Addison-Wesley, Reading.

Hailstones, Thomas J. (1976). *Basic Economics.* South-Western Publishing Co., Cincinnati.

Hamblin, Robert L. and Brian L. Pitcher (1980). The Classic Maya Collapse: Testing Class Conflict Hypotheses. *American Antiquity* 45: 246-67.

Hammond, Mason (1946). Economic Stagnation in the Early Roman Empire. *Journal of Economic History, Supplement* 6: 63-90.

Hammond, Norman (1977). Ex Oriente Lux: a View from Belize. In *The Origins of Maya Civilization*, edited by Richard E. W. Adams, pp. 45-76. University of New Mexico Press, Albuquerque.

(1981). Settlement Patterns in Belize. In *Lowland Maya Settlement Patterns*, edited by Wendy Ashmore, pp. 157-86. University of New Mexico Press, Albuquerque.

(1982). *Ancient Maya Civilization.* Rutgers University Press, New Brunswick.

Hammond, Norman and Wendy Ashmore (1981). Lowland Maya Settlement: Geographical and Chronological Frameworks. In *Lowland Maya Settlement Patterns*, edited by Wendy Ashmore, pp. 19-36. University of New Mexico Press, Albuquerque.

Hardin, Garrett (1968). The Cybernetics of Competition: a Biologist's View of Society. In *Modern Systems Research for the Behavioral Scientist*, edited by Walter Buckley, pp. 449-59. Aldine, Chicago.

Harner, Michael J. (1970). Population Pressure and the Social Evolution of Agriculturalists. *Southwestern Journal of Anthropology* 26: 67-86.

Harris, David R. (1978). The Agricultural Foundations of Lowland Maya Civilization: a Critique. In *Pre-Hispanic Maya Agriculture*, edited by Peter D. Harrison and B. L. Turner II, pp. 301-23. University of New Mexico Press, Albuquerque.

Harrison, Peter D. (1977). The Rise of the *Bajos* and the Fall of the Maya. In *Social Process in Maya Prehistory: Studies in Honour of Sir Eric Thompson*, edited by Norman Hammond, pp. 469-508. Academic Press, London.

(1978). *Bajos* Revisited: Visual Evidence for One System of Agriculture. In *Pre-Hispanic Maya Agriculture*, edited by Peter D. Harrison and B. L. Turner II, pp. 247-53. University of New Mexico Press, Albuquerque.

(1982). Subsistence and Society in Eastern Yucatan. In *Maya Subsistence: Studies in Memory of Dennis E. Puleston*, edited by Kent V. Flannery, pp. 119-30. Academic Press, New York.

Hart, Hornell (1945). Logistic Social Trends. *American Journal of Sociology* 50: 337-52.

Haury, Emil W. (1976). *The Hohokam: Desert Farmers and Craftsmen*. University of Arizona Press, Tucson.

Haussig, H. W. (1971). *A History of Byzantine Civilization* (translated by J. M. Hussey). Praeger, New York.

Haviland, William A. (1967). Stature at Tikal, Guatemala: Implications for Classic Maya Demography and Social Organization. *American Antiquity* 32: 316-25.

(1969). A New Population Estimate for Tikal, Guatemala. *American Antiquity* 34: 429-33.

(1970). Tikal, Guatemala, and Mesoamerican Urbanism. *World Archaeology* 2: 186-97.

(1977). Dynastic Genealogies from Tikal, Guatemala: Implications for Descent and Political Organization. *American Antiquity* 42: 61-7.

Healy, Paul F. (1983). An Ancient Maya Dam in the Cayo District, Belize. *Journal of Field Archaeology* 10: 147-54.

Hegel, Georg Wilhelm Friedrich (1956). *The Philosophy of History* (translated by J. Sibree). Dover, New York.

Heichelheim, Fritz M. (1970). *An Ancient Economic History*, Volume III (translated by Joyce Stevens). A. W. Sijthoff, Leyden.

Heitland, W. E. (1962). The Roman Fate. In *Decline and Fall of the Roman Empire: Why Did It Collapse?*, edited by D. Kagen, pp. 57-70. Heath, Boston.

Herder, Johann Gottfried von (1968). *Reflections on the Philosophy of the History of Mankind* (translated by T. O. Churchhill). University of Chicago Press, Chicago and London.

Hicks, John (1969). *A Theory of Economic History*. Clarendon, Oxford.

Hirth, Kenneth G. and William Swezey (1976). The Changing Nature of the Teotihuacan Classic: a Regional Perspective from Manzanilla, Puebla. In *Las Fronteras de Mesoamerica: XIV Mesa Redonda*, 2: 11-23. Sociedad Mexicana de Antropologia, Mexico City.

Ho, Ping-Ti (1970). Economic and Institutional Factors in the Decline of the Chinese Empire. In *The Economic Decline of Empires*, edited by Carlo M. Cipolla, pp. 264-77. Methuen, London.

Hodges, Richard and David Whitehouse (1983). *Mohammed, Charlemagne and the Origins of Europe*. Cornell University Press, Ithaca.

Hogarth, D. G. (1926). The Hittites of Asia Minor. In *The Cambridge Ancient History* II, edited by J. B. Bury, S. A. Cook, and F. E. Adcock, pp. 252-74. Macmillan, New York.

Hooker, J. T. (1976). *Mycenaean Greece*. Routledge and Kegan Paul, London.

Hosler, Dorothy, Jeremy A. Sabloff, and Dale Runge (1977). Simulation Model Development: A Case Study of the Classic Maya Collapse. In *Social Process in Maya Prehistory: Studies in Honour of Sir Eric Thompson*, edited by Norman Hammond, pp. 553-90. Academic Press, London.

Hucker, Charles O. (1975). *China's Imperial Past*. Stanford University Press, Stanford.

Hughes, H. Stuart (1952). *Oswald Spengler: a Critical Estimate*. Charles Scribner's Sons, New York.

Hughes, J. Donald (1975). *Ecology in Ancient Civilizations*. University of New Mexico Press, Albuquerque.

Huntington, Ellsworth (1915). *Civilization and Climate*. Yale University Press, New Haven.

(1917). Climatic Change and Agricultural Exhaustion as Elements in the Fall of Rome. *Quarterly Journal of Economics* 31: 173-208.

Ibn Khaldun (1958). *The Muqaddimah: an Introduction to History* (three volumes) (translated by Franz Rosenthal). Pantheon, New York.

Isaac, James Paton (1971). *Factors in the Ruin of Antiquity: a Criticism of Ancient Civilization*. Bryant Press, Toronto.

Isbell, William H. (1978). Environmental Perturbations and the Origin of the Andean State. In *Social Archeology: Beyond Subsistence and Dating*, edited by Charles L. Redman, Mary Jane Berman, Edward V. Curtin, William T. Langhorne, Jr., Nina M. Versaggi, and Jeffrey C. Wanser, pp. 303-13. Academic Press, New York.

Jacobsen, Thorkild and Robert McC. Adams (1958). Salt and Silt in Ancient Mesopotamian Agriculture. *Science* 128: 1251-8.

Jankowska, N. B. (1969). Some Problems in the Economy of the Assyrian Empire. In *Ancient Mesopotamia: Socio-Economic History*, edited by I. M. Diakonoff, pp. 253-76. Nauka, Moscow.

Jelinek, Arthur (1967). A Prehistoric Sequence in the Middle Pecos Valley, New Mexico. *Museum of Anthropology, University of Michigan, Anthropological Papers* 31.

Johnson, Gregory J. (1973). Local Exchange and Early State Development in Southwestern Iran. *Museum of Anthropology, University of Michigan, Anthropological Papers* 51.

(1978). Information Sources and the Development of Decision-Making Organizations. In *Social Archeology: Beyond Subsistence and Dating*, edited by Charles L. Redman, Mary Jane Berman, Edward V. Curtin, William T. Langhorne, Jr., Nina M. Versaggi, and Jeffrey C. Wansner, pp. 87-112. Academic Press, New York.

(1982). Organization Structure and Scalar Stress. In *Theory and Explanation in Archaeology: the Southampton Conference*, edited by C. Renfrew, M. J. Rowlands, and B. A. Segraves, pp. 389-421. Academic Press, New York.

Jones, A. H. M. (1964). *The Later Roman Empire, 284-602: a Social, Economic and Administrative Survey*. University of Oklahoma Press, Norman.

(1974). *The Roman Economy: Studies in Ancient Economic and Administrative History*. Basil Blackwell, Oxford.

Jones, C. (1977). Inauguration Dates of Three Late Classic Rulers of Tikal, Guatemala. *American Antiquity* 42: 28-60.

Jones, W. H. S. (1907). *Malaria: a Neglected Factor in the History of Greece and Rome*. Macmillan and Bowes, Cambridge.

Judge, W. James (1979). The Development of a Complex Cultural Ecosystem in the Chaco Basin, New Mexico. In Proceedings of the First Conference on Scientific Research in the National Parks, Volume II, edited by Robert M. Linn, pp. 901-905. *National Park Service Transactions and Proceedings Series* 5.

(1982). The Paleo-Indian and Basketmaker Periods: an Overview and Some Research Problems. In *The San Juan Tomorrow: Planning for the Conservation of Cultural Resources in the San Juan Basin*, edited by Fred Plog and Walter Wait, pp. 5-57. USDI National Park Service, Southwest Region and School of American Research, Santa Fé.

Judge, W. J., W. B. Gillespie, S. H. Lekson, and H. W. Toll (1981). Tenth Century Developments in Chaco Canyon. In Collected Papers in Honor of Erik Kellerman Reed, edited by Albert H. Schroeder, pp. 65-98. *Archaeological Society of New Mexico Anthropological Papers* 6.

Kann, Robert A. (1968). *The Problem of Restoration*. University of California Press, Berkeley and Los Angeles.

Katz, Friedrich (1972). *The Ancient American Civilizations*. Praeger, New York.

Kelley, J. Charles (1952). Factors Involved in the Abandonment of Certain Peripheral Southwestern Settlements. *American Anthropologist* 54: 356-87.

Kincaid, Chris, John R. Stein, and Daisy F. Levine (1983). Road Verification Summary. In *Chacoan Roads Project, Phase 1: a Reappraisal of Prehistoric Roads in the San Juan Basin*, edited by Chris Kincaid, pp. 9-1 to 9-78. USDI Bureau of Land Management, New Mexico State Office and Albuquerque District Office, Santa Fé and Albuquerque.

King, Thomas F. (1981). The NART: a Plan to Direct Archeology Toward More Relevant Goals in Modern Life. *Early Man* 3(4): 35-7.

Kolata, Alan L. (1986). The Agricultural Foundations of the Tiwanaku State: a View from the Heartland. *American Antiquity* 51: 748-62.

Krader, Lawrence (1978). The Origin of the State among the Nomads of Asia. In *The Early State*, edited by Henri J. M. Claessen and Peter Skalnik, pp. 93-107. Mouton, The Hague.

Krebs, John R. (1978). Optimal Foraging: Decision Rules for Predators. In *Behavioural Ecology: an Evolutionary Approach*, edited by J. R. Krebs and N. B. Davies, pp. 23-63. Blackwell Scientific Publications, Oxford.

Kristensen, Thorkil (1974). *Development in Rich and Poor Countries*. Praeger, New York.

Kroeber, Alfred L. (1944). *Configurations of Culture Growth*. University of California Press, Berkeley and Los Angeles.

(1957). *Style and Civilizations*. Cornell University Press, Ithaca.

(1958). Gray's Epicyclical Evolution. *American Anthropologist* 60: 31-8.

Kuhn, Thomas S. (1962). *The Structure of Scientific Revolutions*. University of Chicago Press, Chicago.

Kurjack, Edward B. (1974). Prehistoric Lowland Maya Community and Social Organization. *Middle American Research Institute Publication* 38.

Kurtz, Donald V. (1978). The Legitimation of the Aztec State. In *The Early State*, edited by Henri J. M. Claessen and Peter Skalnik, pp. 169-89. Mouton, The Hague.

Kus, James S. (1984). The Chicama-Moche Canal: Failure or Success? An Alternative Explanation for an Incomplete Canal. *American Antiquity* 49: 408-15.

Lanning, Edward P. (1967). *Peru Before the Incas*. Prentice-Hall, Englewood Cliffs.

Lattimore, Owen (1940). *Inner Asian Frontiers of China*. Beacon Press, Boston.

Laughlin, Charles D., Jr. and Ivan A. Brady (1978). Introduction: Diaphysis and Change in Human Populations. In *Extinction and Survival in Human Populations*, edited by Charles D. Laughlin, Jr. and Ivan A. Brady, pp. 1-48. Columbia University Press, New York.

Lawler, James H. L. (1970). *Socio-Mathematics and Cyclic History*. J. Grant Stevenson, Provo.

Leach, Edmund R. (1954). *Political Systems of Highland Burma*. Beacon Press, Boston.

Lee, Richard B. (1969). Eating Christmas in the Kalahari. *Natural History* 78(10): 14, 16, 18, 21-2, 60-3.

Lekson, Stephen (1984). Standing Architecture at Chaco Canyon and the Interpretation of Local and Regional Organization. In Recent Research on Chaco Prehistory, edited by W. James Judge and John D. Schelberg, pp. 55-73. *Reports of the Chaco Center* 8. U.S. Department of the Interior, National Park Service, Division of Cultural Research, Albuquerque.

Lenski, Gerhard E. (1966). *Power and Privilege: a Theory of Social Stratification*. McGraw-Hill, New York.

Lester, Curtis and Earl Neller (1978). Casamero Site – Phase III. USDI Bureau of Land Management, New Mexico State Office, Physical Protection Workbook, Santa Fé.

Levenson, Joseph R. and Franz Schurman (1969). *China: an Interpretive History*. University of California Press, Berkeley and Los Angeles.

Levy, Jean-Philippe (1967). *The Economic Life of the Ancient World* (translated by John G. Biram). University of Chicago Press, Chicago.

Lewis, Bernard (1958). Some Reflections on the Decline of the Ottoman Empire. *Studia Islamica* 9: 111-27.

Lowe, John W. G. (1985). *The Dynamics of Apocalypse: a Systems Simulation of the Classic Maya Collapse*. University of New Mexico Press, Albuquerque.

Lumbreras, Luis Guillermo (1974). *The Peoples and Cultures of Ancient Peru* (translated by Betty J. Meggers). Smithsonian Institute Press, Washington, D.C.

Lyons, Thomas R. and Robert K. Hitchcock (1977). Remote Sensing Interpretation of an Anasazi Land Route System. In Aerial Remote Sensing Techniques in Archeology, edited by Thomas R. Lyons and Robert K. Hitchcock, pp. 111-34. *Reports of the Chaco Center* 2.

MacArthur, Robert H. (1972). *Geographical Ecology: Patterns in the Distribution of Species.* Harper and Row, New York.

Machlup, Fritz (1962). *The Production and Distribution of Knowledge in the United States.* Princeton University Press, Princeton.

Mackie, Euan W. (1961). New Light on the End of Classic Maya Culture at Benque Viejo, British Honduras. *American Antiquity* 27: 216-24.

MacMullen, Ramsey (1976). *Roman Government's Response to Crisis, A.D. 235-337.* Yale University Press, New Haven and London.

Magnusson, Magnus (1980). *Vikings!* Dutton, New York.

Mansfield, Edwin (1968). *The Economics of Technological Change.* Norton, New York.

(1971). *Technological Change.* Norton, New York.

Mansfield, Harvey C., Jr. (1979). *Machiavelli's New Modes and Orders: a Study of the 'Discourses on Livy.'* Cornell University Press, Ithaca and London.

Marcus, Joyce (1976). *Emblem and State in the Classic Maya Lowlands: an Epigraphic Approach to Territorial Organization.* Dumbarton Oaks Research Library and Collection, Washington, D.C.

(1983). Lowland Maya Archaeology at the Crossroads. *American Antiquity* 48: 454-88.

Marinatos, S. (1939). The Volcanic Destruction of Minoan Crete. *Antiquity* 13: 425-39.

Marshall, Michael P., John R. Stein, Richard W. Loose, and Judith E. Novotny (1979). *Anasazi Communities of the San Juan Basin.* Public Service Company of New Mexico and New Mexico Historic Preservation Bureau, Albuquerque and Santa Fé.

Martin, M. Kay (1969). South American Foragers: a Case Study of Cultural Devolution. *American Anthropologist* 71: 243-60.

Martin, Paul S. and Fred Plog (1973). *The Archaeology of Arizona: a Prehistory of the Southwest Region.* Doubleday/Natural History Press, New York.

Martin, P. S., G. I. Quimby, and D. Collier (1947). *Indians Before Columbus.* University of Chicago Press, Chicago.

Matheny, Ray T. (1976). Maya Lowland Hydraulic Systems. *Science* 193: 639-46.

(1978). Northern Maya Lowland Water-Control Systems. In *Pre-Hispanic Maya Agriculture,* edited by Peter D. Harrison and B. L. Turner II, pp. 185-210. University of New Mexico Press, Albuquerque.

(1982). Ancient Lowland and Highland Maya Water and Soil Conservation Strategies. In *Maya Subsistence: Studies in Memory of Dennis E. Puleston,* edited by Kent V. Flannery, pp. 157-78. Academic Press, New York.

Mathewson, Kent (1977). Maya Urban Genesis Reconsidered: Trade and Intensive Agriculture as Primary Factors. *Journal of Historical Geography* 3: 203-15.

Mathien, Frances Joan (1984). Social and Economic Implications of Jewelry Items of the Chaco Anasazi. In Recent Research on Chaco Prehistory, edited by W. James Judge and John D. Schelberg, pp. 173-86. *Reports of the Chaco Center* 8. U.S. Department of the Interior, National Park Service, Division of Cultural Research, Albuquerque.

Mattingly, Harold (1960). *Roman Coins* (second edition). Quadrangle, Chicago.

Matz, F. (1973a). The Maturity of Minoan Civilization. In *The Cambridge Ancient History* II(1) (third edition), edited by I. E. S. Edwards, C. J. Gadd, N. G. L. Hammond, and E. Sollberger, pp. 141-64. Cambridge University Press, Cambridge.

(1973b). The Zenith of Minoan Civilization. In *The Cambridge Ancient History* II(1) (third edition), edited by I. E. S. Edwards, C. J. Gadd, N. G. L. Hammond, and E. Sollberger, pp. 557-81. Cambridge University Press, Cambridge.

Mazzarino, Santo (1966). *The End of the Ancient World* (translated by George Holmes). Faber and Faber, London.

McCain, Garvin and Erwin M. Segal (1973). *The Game of Science* (second edition). Brooks/Cole, Monterey.

McGuire, Randall H. (1982). Problems in Culture History. In *Hohokam and Patayan: Prehistory of Southwestern Arizona*, edited by Randall H. McGuire and Michael B. Schiffer, pp. 153-222. Academic Press, New York.

  (1983). Breaking Down Cultural Complexity: Inequality and Heterogeneity. In *Advances in Archaeological Method and Theory*, Volume 6, edited by Michael B. Schiffer, pp. 91-142. Academic Press, New York.

McNeill, William H. (1976). *Plagues and Peoples*. Anchor/Doubleday, Garden City.

Meadows, Donella H., Dennis L. Meadows, Jorgen Randers, and William W. Behrens III (1972). *The Limits to Growth*. Universe Books, New York.

Meggers, Betty J. (1954). Environmental Limitation on the Development of Culture. *American Anthropologist* 56: 801-24.

Melikishvili, G. A. (1976-7). The Character of the Socioeconomic Structure in the Ancient East. *Soviet Anthropology and Archeology* 15(2-3): 29-49.

Melko, Matthew (1969). *The Nature of Civilizations*. Porter Sargent, Boston.

Mensch, Gerhard (1979). *Stalemate in Technology: Innovations Overcome the Depression*. Ballinger, Cambridge.

Miller, Daniel (1985). Ideology and the Harappan Civilization. *Journal of Anthropological Archaeology* 4: 34-71.

Millon, Rene (1981). Teotihuacan: City, State, and Civilization. In *Supplement to the Handbook of Middle American Indians*, Volume I: *Archaeology*, edited by Jeremy A. Sabloff, pp. 198-243. University of Texas Press, Austin.

Mills, Elliot (1905). *The Decline and Fall of the British Empire*. Alden and Co., Bocardo Press, and Simkin, Marshall, Hamilton, Kent and Co., Oxford and London.

Milner, George R. (1986). Mississippian Period Population Density in a Segment of the Central Mississippi River Valley. *American Antiquity* 51: 227-38.

Minnis, Paul E. (1985). *Social Adaptation to Food Stress: a Prehistoric Southwestern Example*. University of Chicago Press, Chicago and London.

Mishan, Ezra J. (1977). *The Economic Growth Debate*. George Allen and Unwin, London.

Mohring, Herbert (1965). Urban Highway Investments. In *Measuring Benefits of Government Investments*, edited by Robert Dorfman, pp. 231-91. Brookings Institution, Washington, D.C.

Molloy, John P. and William L. Rathje (1974). Sexploitation among the Late Classic Maya. In *Mesoamerican Archaeology: New Approaches*, edited by Norman Hammond, pp. 431-44. Duckworth, London.

Montagu, M. F. Ashley (editor) (1956). *Toynbee and History*. Porter Sargent, Boston.

Montesquieu, Charles Louis (1968). *Considerations on the Causes of the Greatness of the Romans and Their Decline* (translated by David Lowenthal). Cornell University Press, Ithaca.

Moore, James A. (1981). The Effects of Information Networks in Hunter-Gatherer Societies. In *Hunter-Gatherer Foraging Strategies: Ethnographic and Archeological Analyses*, edited by Bruce Winterhalder and Eric Alden Smith, pp. 194-217. University of Chicago Press, Chicago.

Morley, Sylvanus G. (1956). *The Ancient Maya* (third edition). Stanford University Press, Stanford.

Moseley, Michael E. (1983). The Good Old Days *were* Better: Agrarian Collapse and Tectonics. *American Anthropologist* 85: 773-99.

Mylonas, George E. (1966). *Mycenae and the Mycenaean Age*. Princeton University Press, Princeton.

Needham, Joseph (1965). *Science and Civilisation in China*, Volume 1: *Introductory Orientation*. Cambridge University Press, Cambridge.

Nehru, Jawaharlal (1959). *The Discovery of India*. Doubleday, New York.

Neitzel, Jill E. (1984). The Organization of the Hohokam Regional System. *American Archaeology* 4: 207-16.

Netting, Robert M. (1972). Sacred Power and Centralization: Aspects of Political Adaptation in Africa. In *Population Growth: Anthropological Implications*, edited by Brian Spooner, pp. 219-44. Massachusetts Institute of Technology Press, Cambridge.

(1977). Maya Subsistence: Mythologies, Analogies, Possibilities. In *The Origins of Maya Civilization*, edited by Richard E. W. Adams, pp. 299-333. University of New Mexico Press, Albuquerque.

Nials, Fred L. (1983). Physical Characteristics of Chacoan Roads. In *Chacoan Roads Project, Phase I: a Reappraisal of Prehistoric Roads in the San Juan Basin*, edited by Chris Kincaid, pp. 6-1 to 6-51. USDI Bureau of Land Management, New Mexico State Office and Albuquerque District Office, Santa Fé and Albuquerque.

Nordhaus, William D. (1969). *Invention, Growth, and Welfare: a Theoretical Treatment of Technological Change*. Massachusetts Institute of Technology Press, Cambridge.

North, Douglass C. and Robert Paul Thomas (1973). *The Rise of the Western World: a New Economic History*. Cambridge University Press, Cambridge.

Oates, Joan (1979). *Babylon*. Thames and Hudson, London.

O'Connor, David (1974). Political Systems and Archaeological Data in Egypt: 2600-1780 B.C. *World Archaeology* 6: 15-38.

O'Laughlin, Bridget (1975). Marxist Approaches in Anthropology. *Annual Review of Anthropology* 4: 341-70.

Olson, Mancur (1982). *The Rise and Decline of Nations*. Yale University Press, New Haven.

Ormsby-Gore, David (1966). *Must the West Decline?* Columbia University Press, New York.

Pakes, Ariel and Zvi Griliches (1984). Patents and R & D at the Firm Level: a First Look. In *R & D, Patents, and Productivity*, edited by Zvi Griliches, pp. 55-72. University of Chicago Press, Chicago and London.

Parkinson, C. Northcote (1957). *Parkinson's Law, and Other Studies in Administration*. Houghton Mifflin, Boston.

(1960). *The Law and the Profits*. John Murray, London.

(1963). *East and West*. Mentor, New York.

(1971). *The Law of Delay*. Houghton Mifflin, Boston.

Parsons, Jeffrey R. (1968). Teotihuacan, Mexico, and Its Impact on Regional Demography. *Science* 162: 872-7.

Pearson, Michael Parker (1984). Economic and Ideological Change: Cyclic Growth in the Pre-State Societies of Jutland. In *Ideology, Power and Prehistory*, edited by Daniel Miller and Christopher Tilley, pp. 69-92. Cambridge University Press, Cambridge.

Pendergast, David M. (1985). Lamanai, Belize: an Updated View. In *The Lowland Maya Postclassic*, edited by Arlen F. Chase and Prudence M. Rice, pp. 91-103. University of Texas Press, Austin.

(1986). Stability through Change: Lamanai, Belize, from the Ninth to the Seventeenth Century. In *Late Lowland Maya Civilization: Classic to Postclassic*, edited by Jeremy A. Sabloff and E. Wyllys Andrews V, pp. 223-49. University of New Mexico Press, Albuquerque.

Perlman, David (1984). Faraway Star That May Rain Death on Earth. *San Francisco Chronicle*, February 26.

Perrow, Charles (1984). *Normal Accidents: Living With High-Risk Technologies*. Basic Books, New York.

Petrie, Sir William Matthew Flinders (1911). *The Revolutions of Civilisation*. Harper, London and New York.

Pfeiffer, John E. (1974). America's First City. *Horizon* 16(2): 58-63.

(1975). The Life and Death of a Great City. *Horizon* 17(1): 82-95.

(1977). *The Emergence of Society: a Prehistory of the Establishment*. McGraw-Hill, New York.

Phillips, David A. (1979). The Growth and Decline of States in Mesoamerica. *Journal of the Steward Anthropological Society* 10: 137-59.

Piganiol, André (1962). The Causes of the Ruin of the Roman Empire. In *Decline and Fall of the Roman Empire: Why Did It Collapse?*, edited by D. Kagen, pp. 86-91. Heath, Boston.

Piggott, Stuart (1950). *Prehistoric India to 1000 B.C.* Penguin, Harmondsworth.

Plato (1926). *Laws* (translated by R. G. Bury). William Heinemann and Harvard University Press, London and Cambridge.

   (1929). *Timaeus, Critias, Cleitophon, Menexenus, Epistles* (translated by R. G. Bury). Harvard University Press and William Heinemann, Cambridge and London.

   (1955). *The Republic* (translated by H. D. P. Lee). Penguin, Baltimore.

Plog, Fred (1983). Political and Economic Alliances on the Colorado Plateaus, A.D. 400-1450. In *Advances in World Archaeology*, Volume 2, edited by Fred Wendorf and Angela Close, pp. 289-330. Academic Press, New York.

Polybius (1979). *The Rise of the Roman Empire* (translation by Ian Scott-Kilvert of *The Histories*). Penguin, Harmondsworth.

Pomerance, Leon (1970). The Final Collapse of Santorini (Thera): 1400 or 1200 B.C.? *Studies in Mediterranean Archaeology* XXVI. Paul Aströms Förlag, Göteborg.

Possehl, Gregory L. (1982). The Harappan Civilization: a Contemporary Perspective. In *Harappan Civilization: a Contemporary Perspective*, edited by Gregory Possehl, pp. 15-28. Oxford and IBH Publishing Co., New Delhi.

Powers, Robert P. (1984). Regional Interaction in the San Juan Basin: the Chacoan Outlier System. In Recent Research on Chaco Prehistory, edited by W. James Judge and John D. Schelberg, pp. 23-36. *Reports of the Chaco Center* 8. U.S. Department of the Interior, National Park Service, Division of Cultural Research, Albuquerque.

Powers, Robert P., William B. Gillespie, and Stephen H. Lekson (1983). The Outlier Survey: a Regional View of Settlement in the San Juan Basin. *Reports of the Chaco Center* 3. USDI National Park Service, Division of Cultural Research, Albuquerque.

Price, Barbara (1977). Shifts of Production and Organization: a Cluster Interaction Model. *Current Anthropology* 18: 209-34.

Price, Derek de Solla (1963). *Little Science, Big Science*. Columbia University Press, New York.

Proskouriakoff, Tatiana (1960). Historical Implications of a Pattern of Dates at Piedras Negras, Guatemala. *American Antiquity* 25: 454-75.

   (1963). Historical Data in the Inscriptions of Yaxchilan, Part I. *Estudios de Cultura Maya* 3: 149-66.

   (1964). Historical Data in the Inscriptions of Yaxchilan, Part II. *Estudios de Cultura Maya* 4: 177-201.

Puleston, Dennis E. (1974). Intersite Areas in the Vicinity of Tikal and Uaxactun. In *Mesoamerican Archaeology: New Approaches*, edited by Norman Hammond, pp. 303-11. Duckworth, London.

   (1977). The Art and Archaeology of Hydraulic Agriculture in the Maya Lowlands. In *Social Process in Maya Prehistory: Studies in Honour of Sir Eric Thompson*, edited by Norman Hammond, pp. 449-67. Academic Press, London.

   (1978). Terracing, Raised Fields, and Tree Cropping in the Maya Lowlands: a New Perspective on the Geography of Power. In *Pre-Hispanic Maya Agriculture*, edited by Peter D. Harrison and B. L. Turner II, pp. 225-45. University of New Mexico Press, Albuquerque.

   (1979). An Epistemological Pathology and the Collapse, or Why the Maya Kept the Short Count. In *Maya Archaeology and Ethnohistory*, edited by Norman Hammond and Gordon R. Willey, pp. 63-71. University of Texas Press, Austin.

Raikes, R. L. (1964). The End of the Ancient Cities of the Indus. *American Anthropologist* 66: 284-99.

Rands, Robert L. (1973). The Classic Maya Collapse: Usumacinta Zone and the Northwestern Periphery. In *The Classic Maya Collapse*, edited by T. Patrick Culbert, pp. 165-205. University of New Mexico Press, Albuquerque.

Rappaport, Roy A. (1977). Maladaptation in Social Systems. In *The Evolution of Social Systems*, edited by J. Friedman and M. J. Rowlands, pp. 49-71. Duckworth, London.

Rathje, William L. (1970). Socio-Political Implications of Lowland Maya Burials: Methodology and Tentative Hypotheses. *World Archaeology* 1: 359-74.

(1971). The Origin and Development of Lowland Classic Maya Civilization. *American Antiquity* 36: 275-85.

(1973). Classic Maya Development and Denouement: a Research Design. In *The Classic Maya Collapse*, edited by T. Patrick Culbert, pp. 405-54. University of New Mexico Press, Albuquerque.

Reed, Erik K. (1944). The Abandonment of the San Juan Basin. *El Palacio* 51: 61-74.

Reina, Ruben E. (1967). Milpas and Milperos: Implications for Prehistoric Times. *American Anthropologist* 69: 1-20.

Renfrew, Colin (1972). *The Emergence of Civilisation: the Cyclades and the Aegean in the Third Millennium B.C.* Methuen, London.

(1979). Systems Collapse as Social Transformation: Catastrophe and Anastrophe in Early State Societies. In *Transformations: Mathematical Approaches to Culture Change*, edited by Colin Renfrew and Kenneth L. Cooke, pp. 481-506. Academic Press, New York.

(1982). Polity and Power: Interaction, Intensification and Exploitation. In *An Island Polity: the Archaeology of Exploitation on Melos*, edited by Colin Renfrew and Malcolm Wagstaff, pp. 264-90. Cambridge University Press, Cambridge.

Rescher, Nicholas (1978). *Scientific Progress: a Philosophical Essay on the Economics of Research in Natural Science*. University of Pittsburgh Press, Pittsburgh.

(1980). *Unpopular Essays on Technological Progress*. University of Pittsburgh Press, Pittsburgh.

Rice, Don S. (1976). Middle Preclassic Maya Settlement in the Central Maya Lowlands. *Journal of Field Archaeology* 3: 425-45.

(1978). Population Growth and Subsistence Alternatives in a Tropical Lacustrine Environment. In *Pre-Hispanic Maya Agriculture*, edited by Peter D. Harrison and B. L. Turner II, pp. 63-115. University of New Mexico Press, Albuquerque.

(1986). The Peten Postclassic: a Settlement Perspective. In *Late Lowland Maya Civilization: Classic to Postclassic*, edited by Jeremy A. Sabloff and E. Wyllys Andrews V, pp. 301-44. University of New Mexico Press, Albuquerque.

Rice, Don S. and Dennis E. Puleston (1981). Ancient Maya Settlement Patterns in the Peten, Guatemala. In *Lowland Maya Settlement Patterns*, edited by Wendy Ashmore, pp. 121-156. University of New Mexico Press, Albuquerque.

Rice, Prudence M. (1986). The Peten Postclassic: Perspectives from the Central Peten Lakes. In *Late Lowland Maya Civilization: Classic to Postclassic*, edited by Jeremy A. Sabloff and E. Wyllys Andrews V, pp. 251-99. University of New Mexico Press, Albuquerque.

Rice, Prudence M. and Don S. Rice (1985). Topoxte, Macanche, and the Central Peten Postclassic. In *The Lowland Maya Postclassic*, edited by Arlen F. Chase and Prudence M. Rice, pp. 166-83. University of Texas Press, Austin.

Rifkin, Jeremy with Ted Howard (1980). *Entropy*. Viking Press, New York.

Ross, Ronald (1907). Introduction. In *Malaria: a Neglected Factor in the History of Greece and Rome*, by W. H. S. Jones, pp. 1-14. Macmillan and Bowes, Cambridge.

Rostovtzeff, M. (1926). *The Social and Economic History of the Roman Empire*. Oxford University Press, Oxford.

Rostow, W. W. (1960). *The Stages of Economic Growth*. Cambridge University Press, Cambridge.

(1980). *Why the Poor Get Richer and the Rich Slow Down*. University of Texas Press, Austin.

Rostow, W. W. with Frederick E. Fordyce (1978). Growth Rates at Different Levels of Income and Stage of Growth: Reflections on Why the Poor Get Richer and the Rich Slow Down. *Research in Economic History* 3: 47-86.

Russell, J. C. (1958). Late Ancient and Medieval Population. *Transactions of the American Philosophical Society* 48(3).

Sabloff, Jeremy A. (1971). The Collapse of Classic Maya Civilization. In *Patient Earth*, edited by J. Harte and R. Socolow, pp. 16-27. Holt, Rinehart and Winston, New York.

(1973a). Major Themes in the Past Hypotheses of the Maya Collapse. In *The Classic Maya Collapse*, edited by T. Patrick Culbert., pp. 35-40. University of New Mexico Press, Albuquerque.

(1973b). Continuity and Disruption During Terminal Late Classic Times at Seibal: Ceramic and Other Evidence. In *The Classic Maya Collapse*, edited by T. Patrick Culbert. pp. 107-31. University of New Mexico Press, Albuquerque.

(1986). Interaction Among Classic Maya Polities: a Preliminary Examination. In *Peer Polity Interaction and Socio-Political Change*, edited by Colin Renfrew and John F. Cherry, pp. 109-16. Cambridge University Press, Cambridge.

Sabloff, Jeremy A. and Gordon R. Willey (1967). The Collapse of Maya Civilization in the Southern Lowlands: a Consideration of History and Process. *Southwestern Journal of Anthropology* 23: 311-36.

Sahlins, Marshall D. (1958). *Social Stratification in Polynesia*. University of Washington Press, Seattle.

(1963). Poor Man, Rich Man, Big Man, Chief: Political Types in Melanesia and Polynesia. *Comparative Studies in Society and History* 5: 285-303.

(1968). *Tribesmen*. Prentice-Hall, Englewood Cliffs.

(1971). The Intensity of Domestic Production in Primitive Societies: Social Inflections of the Chayanov Slope. In Studies in Economic Anthropology, edited by George Dalton, pp. 30-51. *American Anthropological Association Anthropological Papers* 7.

Salmon, Edward T. (1970). The Roman Army and the Disintegration of the Roman Empire. In *The Fall of Rome: Can It Be Explained?* (second edition), edited by Mortimer Chambers, pp. 37-46. Holt, Rinehart and Winston, New York.

Sanders, William T. (1962). Cultural Ecology of the Maya Lowlands, Part I. *Estudios de Cultura Maya* 2: 79-121.

(1963). Cultural Ecology of the Maya Lowlands, Part II. *Estudios de Cultura Maya* 3: 203-41.

(1973). The Cultural Ecology of the Lowland Maya: a Reevaluation. In *The Classic Maya Collapse*, edited by T. Patrick Culbert. pp. 325-65. University of New Mexico Press, Albuquerque.

(1977). Environmental Heterogeneity and the Evolution of Lowland Maya Civilization. In *The Origins of Maya Civilization*, edited by Richard E. W. Adams, pp. 287-97. University of New Mexico Press, Albuquerque.

(1981a). Classic Maya Settlement Patterns and Ethnographic Analogy. In *Lowland Maya Settlement Patterns*, edited by Wendy Ashmore, pp. 351-69. University of New Mexico Press, Albuquerque.

(1981b). Ecological Adaptation in the Basin of Mexico: 23,000 B.C. to the Present. In *Supplement to the Handbook of Middle American Indians*, Volume I: *Archaeology*, edited by Jeremy A. Sabloff, pp. 147-97. University of Texas Press, Austin.

Sanders, William T., Jeffrey R. Parsons, and Robert S. Santley (1979). *The Basin of Mexico: Ecological Processes in the Evolution of a Civilization*. Academic Press, New York.

Sanders, William T. and Barbara J. Price (1968). *Mesoamerica: the Evolution of a Civilization*. Random House, New York.

Sanders, William T. and David Webster (1978). Unilinealism, Multilinealism, and the Evolution of Complex Societies. In *Social Archeology: Beyond Subsistence and Dating*, edited by Charles L. Redman, Mary Jane Berman, Edward V. Curtin, William T. Langhorne, Jr., Nina M. Versaggi, and Jeffrey C. Wanser, pp. 249-302. Academic Press, New York.

Sato, Ryuzo and Gilbert S. Suzawa (1983). *Research and Productivity: Endogenous Technical Change*. Auburn House, Boston.

Saul, Frank P. (1972). The Human Skeletal Remains of Altar de Sacrificios: an Osteobiographic Analysis. *Papers of the Peabody Museum of Archaeology and Ethnology, Harvard University* 63 (2).

(1973). Disease in the Maya Area: the Pre-Columbian Evidence. In *The Classic Maya Collapse*, edited by T. Patrick Culbert., pp. 301-24. University of New Mexico Press, Albuquerque.

Scarborough, Vernon L. (1983). A Preclassic Maya Water System. *American Antiquity* 48: 720-44.

Schelberg, John D. (1982). *Economic and Social Development as an Adaptation to a Marginal Environment in Chaco Canyon, New Mexico*. Ph.D. dissertation, Northwestern University. University Microfilms, Ann Arbor.

(1984). Analogy, Complexity, and Regionally-Based Perspectives. In Recent Research on Chaco Prehistory, edited by W. James Judge and John D. Schelberg, pp. 5-21. *Reports of the Chaco Center* 8. U.S. Department of the Interior, National Park Service, Division of Cultural Research, Albuquerque.

Scherer, Frederic M. (1984). *Innovation and Growth: Schumpeterian Perspectives*. Massachusetts Institute of Technology Press, Cambridge and London.

Schmookler, Jacob (1962). Economic Sources of Inventive Activity. *The Journal of Economic History* 22: 1-20.

(1966). *Invention and Economic Growth*. Harvard University Press, Cambridge.

Schwartz, Eugene S. (1971). *Overkill: the Decline of Technology in Modern Civilization*. Quadrangle, New York.

Schweitzer, Albert (1923). *The Philosophy of Civilization, Part I: the Decay and the Restoration of Civilizations* (translated by C. T. Campion). Black, London.

Segraves, B. Abbott (1974). Ecological Generalization and Structural Transformation of Sociocultural Systems. *American Anthropologist* 76: 530-52.

Service, Elman R. (1960). The Law of Evolutionary Potential. In *Evolution and Culture*, edited by Marshall D. Sahlins and Elman R. Service, pp. 93-122. University of Michigan Press, Ann Arbor.

(1962). *Primitive Social Organization, an Evolutionary Perspective*. Random House, New York.

(1975). *Origins of the State and Civilization: the Process of Cultural Evolution*. Norton, New York.

(1978). Classical and Modern Theories of the Origins of Government. In *Origins of the State: the Anthropology of Political Evolution*, edited by Ronald Cohen and Elman R. Service, pp. 21-34. Institute for the Study of Human Issues, Philadelphia.

Sharer, Robert J. (1977). The Maya Collapse Revisited: Internal and External Perspectives. In *Social Process in Maya Prehistory: Studies in Honour of Sir Eric Thompson*, edited by Norman Hammond, pp. 531-52. Academic Press, London.

(1982). Did the Maya Collapse? A New World Perspective on the Demise of the Harappan Civilization. In *Harappan Civilization: a Contemporary Perspective*, edited by Gregory Possehl, pp. 367-83. Oxford and IBH Publishing Co., New Delhi.

(1985). Terminal Events in the Southeastern Lowlands: a View from Quirigua. In *The*

Lowland Maya Postclassic, edited by Arlen F. Chase and Prudence M. Rice, pp. 245-53. University of Texas Press, Austin.

Shils, Edward A. (1975). *Center and Periphery: Essays in Macrosociology*. University of Chicago Press, Chicago.

Shimkin, Demitri B. (1973). Models for the Downfall: Some Ecological and Culture-Historical Considerations. In *The Classic Maya Collapse*, edited by T. Patrick Culbert, pp. 269-99. University of New Mexico Press, Albuquerque.

Shockley, William (1972). Dysgenics, Geneticity, Raceology: a Challenge to the Intellectual Responsibility of Educators. *Phi Delta Kappan* 53: 297-307.

Sidrys, Raymond and Rainer Berger (1979). Lowland Maya Radiocarbon Dates and the Classic Maya Collapse. *Nature* 277: 269-74.

Siemens, Alfred H. (1978). Karst and the Pre-Hispanic Maya in the Southern Lowlands. In *Pre-Hispanic Maya Agriculture*, edited by Peter D. Harrison and B. L. Turner II, pp. 117-43. University of New Mexico Press, Albuquerque.

  (1982). Prehispanic Agricultural Use of the Wetlands of Northern Belize. In *Maya Subsistence: Studies in Memory of Dennis E. Puleston*, edited by Kent V. Flannery, pp. 205-25. Academic Press, New York.

Siemens, Alfred E. and Dennis E. Puleston (1972). Ridged Fields and Associated Features in Southern Campeche: New Perspectives on the Lowland Maya. *American Antiquity* 37: 228-39.

Simkhovitch, Vladimir G. (1916). Rome's Fall Reconsidered. *Political Science Quarterly* 31: 201-43.

Simon, H. (1965). The Architecture of Complexity. *General Systems* 10: 63-76.

Skalnik, Peter (1978). The Early State as a Process. In *The Early State*, edited by Henri J. M. Claessen and Peter Skalnik, pp. 597-618. Mouton, The Hague.

Smith, William Stevenson (1971). The Old Kingdom in Egypt and the Beginning of the First Intermediate Period. In *The Cambridge Ancient History* I(2) (third edition), edited by I. E. S. Edwards, C. J. Gadd, and N. G. L. Hammond, pp. 145-207. Cambridge University Press, Cambridge.

Snodgrass, Anthony M. (1971). *The Dark Age of Greece*. Edinburgh University Press, Edinburgh.

Sorokin, Pitirim A. (1950). *Social Philosophies of an Age of Crisis*. Beacon Press, Boston.

  (1957). *Social and Cultural Dynamics*. Porter Sargent, Boston.

Soustelle, Jacques (1984). *The Olmecs: the Oldest Civilization in Mexico* (translated by Helen R. Lane). Doubleday, Garden City.

Spengler, Oswald (1962). *The Decline of the West* (translated by Charles Francis Atkinson). Modern Library, New York.

Spinden, Herbert J. (1928). The Ancient Civilizations of Mexico and Central America. *American Museum of Natural History, Handbook Series* 3.

Ste. Croix, G. E. M. de (1981). *The Class Struggle in the Ancient Greek World*. Duckworth, London.

Stephens, John Lloyd (1850). *Incidents of Travel in Central America, Chiapas, and Yucatan*. Harper and Brothers, New York.

Steward, Julian H. (1955). *Theory of Culture Change*. University of Illinois Press, Urbana.

Stone, Lawrence (1956). Historical Consequences and Happy Families. In *Toynbee and History*, edited by M. F. Ashley Montagu, pp. 111-14. Porter Sargent, Boston.

Struever, Stuart (1964). The Hopewell Interaction Sphere in Riverine-Western Great Lakes Culture History. In Hopewellian Studies, edited by Joseph R. Caldwell and Robert L. Hall, pp. 85-106. *Illinois State Museum Scientific Papers* 12.

Struever, Stuart and Gail L. Houart (1972). An Analysis of the Hopewell Interaction Sphere. In

Social Exchange and Interaction, edited by Edwin N. Wilmsen, pp. 47-79. *Museum of Anthropology, University of Michigan, Anthropological Papers* 46.

Struve, V. V. (1969). The Problem of the Genesis, Development, and Disintegration of the Slave Societies in the Ancient Orient. In *Ancient Mesopotamia: Socio-Economic History*, edited by I. M. Diakonoff, pp. 17-69. Nauka, Moscow.

Stuart, David E. and Rory P. Gauthier (1981). *Prehistoric New Mexico: Background for Survey.* New Mexico Historic Preservation Bureau, Santa Fé.

Stubbings, Frank H. (1975a). The Expansion of the Mycenaean Civilization. In *The Cambridge Ancient History* II(2) (third edition), edited by I. E. S. Edwards, C. J. Gadd, N. G. L. Hammond, and E. Sollberger, pp. 165-87. Cambridge University Press, Cambridge.

  (1975b). The Recession of Mycenaean Civilization. In *The Cambridge Ancient History* II(2) (third edition), edited by I. E. S. Edwards, C. J. Gadd, N. G. L. Hammond, and E. Sollberger, pp. 338-58. Cambridge University Press, Cambridge.

Suttles, Wayne (1960). Affinal Ties, Subsistence, and Prestige Among the Coast Salish. *American Anthropologist* 62: 296-305.

Taagepera, Rain (1968). Growth Curves of Empires. *General Systems* 13: 171-75.

Tainter, Joseph A. (1977). Modeling Change in Prehistoric Social Systems. In *For Theory Building in Archaeology*, edited by Lewis R. Binford, pp. 327-51. Academic Press, New York.

  (1978). Mortuary Practices and the Study of Prehistoric Social Systems. In *Advances in Archaeological Method and Theory*, Volume I, edited by Michael B. Schiffer, pp. 105-41. Academic Press, New York.

  (1980). Behavior and Status in a Middle Woodland Mortuary Population from the Illinois Valley. *American Antiquity* 45: 308-13.

  (1983). Woodland Social Change in the Central Midwest: a Review and Evaluation of Interpretive Trends. *North American Archaeologist* 4: 141-61.

Tainter, Joseph A. and David 'A' Gillio (1980). *Cultural Resources Overview, Mt. Taylor Area, New Mexico.* USDA Forest Service, Southwestern Regional Office and USDI Bureau of Land Management, New Mexico State Office, Albuquerque and Santa Fé.

Taylour, William (1964). *The Mycenaeans.* Praeger, New York.

Thapar, B. K. (1982). The Harappan Civilization: Some Reflections On Its Environment and Resources and Their Exploitation. In *Harappan Civilization: a Contemporary Perspective*, edited by Gregory Possehl, pp. 3-13. Oxford and IBH Publishing Co., New Delhi.

Thapar, Romila (1966). *A History of India*, Volume 1. Penguin, Harmondsworth.

Thomas, Prentice M., Jr. (1981). Prehistoric Maya Settlement Patterns at Becan, Campeche, Mexico. *Middle American Research Institute Publication* 45.

Thompson, J. Eric S. (1966). *The Rise and Fall of Maya Civilization* (second edition). University of Oklahoma Press, Norman.

Thompson, Kenneth W. (1956). Toynbee's Approach to History Reviewed. In *Toynbee and History*, edited by M. F. Ashley Montagu, pp. 200-20. Porter Sargent, Boston.

Toll, H. Wolcott (1984). Trends in Ceramic Import and Distribution in Chaco Canyon. In *Recent Research on Chaco Prehistory*, edited by W. James Judge and John D. Schelberg, pp. 115-35. *Reports of the Chaco Center* 8. U.S. Department of the Interior, National Park Service, Division of Cultural Research, Albuquerque.

Toll, Mollie S. (1984). Taxonomic Diversity in Flotation and Macrobotanical Assemblages from Chaco Canyon. In *Recent Research on Chaco Prehistory*, edited by W. James Judge and John D. Schelberg, pp. 241-9. *Reports of the Chaco Center* 8. U.S. Department of the Interior, National Park Service, Division of Cultural Research, Albuquerque.

Tourtellot, Gair and Jeremy A. Sabloff (1972). Exchange Systems Among the Ancient Maya. *American Antiquity* 37: 126-35.

Toutain, Jules (1968). *The Economic Life of the Ancient World.* Barnes and Noble, New York.

Towner, R. H. (1923). *The Philosophy of Civilization* (two volumes). G. P. Putnam's Sons, New York and London.

Toynbee, Arnold J. (1962). *A Study of History* (twelve volumes). Oxford University Press, Oxford.

   (1965). *Hannibal's Legacy* (two volumes). Oxford University Press, Oxford.

Trevor-Roper, Hugh (1956). Testing the Toynbee System. In *Toynbee and History*, edited by M. F. Ashley Montagu, pp. 122-4. Porter Sargent, Boston.

Tuchman, Barbara (1984). *The March of Folly*. Alfred A. Knopf, New York.

Tul'chinskii, L. I. (1967). Problems in the Profitability of Investments in Public Education. *Soviet Review* 8(1): 46-54.

Turco, Richard P., Owen B. Toon, Thomas P. Ackerman, James B. Pollack, and Carl Sagan (1984). The Climatic Effects of Nuclear War. *Scientific American* 251(2): 33-43.

Turnbull, Colin M. (1978). Rethinking the Ik: a Functional Non-Social System. *In Extinction and Survival in Human Populations*, edited by Charles D. Laughlin, Jr., and Ivan A. Brady, pp. 49-75. Columbia University Press, New York.

Turner, B. L. II (1974). Prehistoric Intensive Agriculture in the Mayan Lowlands. *Science* 185: 118-24.

   (1978). Ancient Agricultural Land Use in the Central Maya Lowlands. In *Pre-Hispanic Maya Agriculture*, edited by Peter D. Harrison and B. L. Turner II, pp. 163-83. University of New Mexico Press, Albuquerque.

   (1979). Prehispanic Terracing in the Central Maya Lowlands: Problems of Agricultural Intensification. In *Maya Archaeology and Ethnohistory*, edited by Norman Hammond and Gordon R. Willey, pp. 103-15. University of Texas Press, Austin.

Turner, B. L. II and Peter D. Harrison (1978). Implications from Agriculture for Maya Prehistory. In *Pre-Hispanic Maya Agriculture*, edited by Peter D. Harrison and B. L. Turner II, pp. 337-73. University of New Mexico Press, Albuquerque.

Tyumenev, A. I. (1969). The State Economy of Ancient Sumer. In *Ancient Mesopotamia: Socio-Economic History*, edited by I. M. Diakonoff, pp. 70-87. Nauka, Moscow.

Upham, Steadman (1982). *Polities and Power: an Economic and Political History of the Western Pueblo*. Academic Press, New York.

   (1984). Adaptive Diversity and Southwestern Abandonments. *Journal of Anthropological Research* 40: 235-56.

U.S. Bureau of the Census (1983). *Statistical Abstract of the United States: 1984* (104th edition). U.S. Government Printing Office, Washington, D.C.

Valéry, Paul (1962). *History and Politics* (translated by Denise Folliot and Jackson Mathews). Bollingen, New York.

Vayda, Andrew P. (1961a). Expansion and Warfare among Swidden Agriculturalists. *American Anthropologist* 63: 346-58.

   (1961b). A Re-examination of Northwest Coast Economic Systems. *Transactions of the New York Academy of Sciences II*, 23: 618-24.

   (1967). Pomo Trade Feasts. *In Tribal and Peasant Economies*, edited by George Dalton, pp. 494-500. Natural History Press, Garden City.

Vermeule, Emily T. (1964). *Greece in the Bronze Age*. University of Chicago Press, Chicago.

Vickery, Kent (1970). Evidence Supporting the Theory of Climatic Change and the Decline of Hopewell. *Wisconsin Archaeologist* 51: 57-76.

Vita-Finzi, Claudio (1969). *The Mediterranean Valleys*. Cambridge University Press, Cambridge.

Vives, Jaime Viceas (1970). The Decline of Spain in the Seventeenth Century. In *The Economic Decline of Empires*, edited by Carlo M. Cipolla, pp. 121-67. Methuen, London.

Vivian, R. Gwinn (1970). An Inquiry into Prehistoric Social Organization in Chaco Canyon,

New Mexico. In *Reconstructing Prehistoric Pueblo Societies*, edited by William Longacre, pp. 59-83. University of New Mexico Press, Albuquerque.

Vivo Escoto, Jorge A. (1964). Weather and Climate of Mexico and Central America. In *Handbook of Middle American Indians*, Volume I: *Natural Environment and Early Cultures*, edited by R. C. West, pp. 187-215. University of Texas Press, Austin.

Volney, C. F. (1793). *The Ruins; or Meditations on the Revolutions of Empires*. Calvin Blanchard, New York.

Waateringe, W. Groenman van (1983). The Disastrous Effects of the Roman Occupation. In Roman and Native in the Low Countries: Spheres of Interaction, edited by Roel Brandt and Jan Slofstra, pp. 147-57. *British Archaeological Reports International Series* 184.

Wailes, Bernard (1972). Plow and Population in Temperate Europe. In *Population Growth: Anthropological Implications*, edited by Brian Spooner, pp. 154-79. Massachusetts Institute of Technology Press, Cambridge.

Waines, David (1977). The Third Century Internal Crisis of the Abbasids. *Journal of the Economic and Social History of the Orient* 20: 282-306.

Walbank, F. W. (1967). Social Structure and Economy in the Roman Empire. In *The Decline of Empires*, edited by S. N. Eisenstadt, pp.75-83. Prentice-Hall, Englewood Cliffs.

(1969). *The Awful Revolution: the Decline of the Roman Empire in the West*. University of Toronto Press, Toronto.

(1970). Shrinkage, Crisis, and the Corporative State. In *The Fall of Rome: Can It Be Explained?* (second edition), edited by Mortimer Chambers, pp. 83-90. Holt, Rinehart and Winston, New York.

Wallen, C. C. (1956). Fluctuations and Variability in Mexican Rainfall. In The Future of Arid Lands, edited by Gilbert F. White, pp. 141-55. *American Association for the Advancement of Science Publication* 43.

Wason, Margaret Ogilvie (1973). *Class Struggles in Ancient Greece*. H. Fertig, New York.

Weaver, Donald E. (1972). A Cultural-Ecological Model for the Classic Hohokam Period in the Lower Salt River Valley, Arizona. *The Kiva* 38: 43-52.

Weaver, Muriel Porter (1972). *The Aztecs, the Maya, and Their Predecessors*. Seminar Press, New York.

Webb, Malcolm C. (1965). The Abolition of the Taboo System in Hawaii. *Journal of the Polynesian Society* 74: 21-39.

(1973). The Peten Maya Decline Viewed in the Perspective of State Formation. In *The Classic Maya Collapse*, edited by T. Patrick Culbert, pp. 367-404. University of New Mexico Press, Albuquerque.

(1975). The Flag Follows Trade: an Essay on the Necessary Interaction of Military and Commercial Factors in State Formation. In *Ancient Civilization and Trade*, edited by C. C. Lamberg-Karlovsky and Jeremy A. Sabloff, pp. 155-209. University of New Mexico Press, Albuquerque.

Weber, Max (1976). *The Agrarian Sociology of Ancient Civilizations* (translated by R. I. Frank). NLB, London.

Webster, David (1975). Warfare and the Evolution of the State: a Reconsideration. *American Antiquity* 40: 464-70.

(1976a). Defensive Earthworks at Becan, Campeche, Mexico. *Middle American Research Institute Publication* 44.

(1976b). On Theocracies. *American Anthropologist* 78: 812-28.

(1977). Warfare and the Evolution of Maya Civilization. In *The Origins of Maya Civilization*, edited by Richard E. W. Adams, pp. 335-72. University of New Mexico Press, Albuquerque.

Wenke, Robert J. (1981). Explaining the Evolution of Cultural Complexity: a Review. In

Advances in Archaeological Method and Theory, Volume 4, edited by Michael B. Schiffer, pp. 79-127. Academic Press, New York.

West, Louis C. (1933). The Economic Collapse of the Roman Empire. *The Classics Journal* 28: 96-106.

Westermann, W. L. (1915). The Economic Basis of the Decline of Ancient Culture. *American Historical Review* 20: 723-43.

Wheeler, Sir Robert Eric Mortimer (1966). *Civilizations of the Indus Valley and Beyond*. Thames and Hudson, London.

    (1968). *The Indus Civilization* (third edition). Cambridge University Press, Cambridge.

White, Chris (1974). Lower Colorado River Area Aboriginal Warfare and Alliance Dynamics. In ?ANTAP: California Indian Political and Economic Organization, edited by Lowell John Bean and Thomas F. King, pp. 113-35. *Ballena Press Anthropological Papers* 2.

White, Leslie A. (1949). *The Science of Culture*. Farrar, Straus and Giroux, New York.

    (1959). *The Evolution of Culture*. McGraw-Hill, New York.

Whittington, Stephen L. (1986). Disease Stress in the Lower Classes of Late Classic Copan. Paper Presented at the Fifty-First Annual Meeting of the Society for American Archaeology, New Orleans.

Widney, Joseph (1937). *Civilizations and their Diseases*. Pacific Publishing Co., Los Angeles.

Wilken, Gene C. (1971). Food-Producing Systems Available to the Ancient Maya. *American Antiquity* 36: 432-48.

Wilkinson, Richard G. (1973). *Poverty and Progress: an Ecological Model of Economic Development*. Methuen, London.

Willetts, R. F. (1977). *The Civilization of Ancient Crete*. B. T. Batsford, London.

Willey, Gordon R. (1966). *An Introduction to American Archaeology*, Volume 1: *North and Middle America*. Prentice-Hall, Englewood Cliffs.

    (1971). *An Introduction to American Archaeology*, Volume 2: *South America*. Prentice-Hall, Englewood Cliffs.

    (1973). Certain Aspects of the Late Classic to Postclassic Periods in the Belize Valley. In *The Classic Maya Collapse*, edited by T. Patrick Culbert, pp. 93-106. University of New Mexico Press, Albuquerque.

    (1974). The Classic Maya Hiatus: a 'Rehearsal' for the Collapse? In *Mesoamerican Archaeology: New Approaches*, edited by Norman Hammond, pp. 417-30. Duckworth, London.

    (1977a). The Rise of Classic Maya Civilization: a Pasion Valley Perspective. In *The Origins of Maya Civilization*, edited by Richard E. W. Adams, pp. 133-57. University of New Mexico Press, Albuquerque.

    (1977b). The Rise of Maya Civilization: a Summary View. In *The Origins of Maya Civilization*, edited by Richard E. W. Adams, pp. 383-423. University of New Mexico Press, Albuquerque.

    (1978). Pre-Hispanic Maya Agriculture: a Contemporary Summation. In *Pre-Hispanic Maya Agriculture*, edited by Peter D. Harrison and B. L. Turner II, pp. 325-35. University of New Mexico Press, Albuquerque.

    (1980). Towards an Holistic View of Ancient Maya Civilisation. *Man* 15: 249-66.

    (1981). Maya Lowland Settlement Patterns: a Summary View. In *Lowland Maya Settlement Patterns*, edited by Wendy Ashmore, pp. 385-415. University of New Mexico Press, Albuquerque.

    (1982). Maya Archeology. *Science* 215: 260-67.

Willey, Gordon R., William R. Bullard, Jr., John B. Glass, and James C. Gifford (1965). Prehistoric Maya Settlements in the Belize Valley. *Papers of the Peabody Museum of Archaeology and Ethnology* 54.

Willey, Gordon R. and Demitri B. Shimkin (1971a). The Collapse of Classic Maya Civilization in the Southern Lowlands: a Symposium Summary Statement. *Southwestern Journal of Anthropology* 27: 1-18.

(1971b). Why did the Pre-Columbian Maya Civilization Collapse? *Science* 173: 656-8.

(1973). The Maya Collapse: a Summary View. In *The Classic Maya Collapse*, edited by T. Patrick Culbert, pp. 457-501. University of New Mexico Press, Albuquerque.

Wilson, Charles (1969). *Economic History and the Historian*. Praeger, New York.

Winkless, Nels and Iben Browning (1975). *Climate and the Affairs of Men*. Harper's Magazine Press, New York.

Wiseman, Frederick W. (1978). Agricultural and Historical Ecology of the Maya Lowlands. In *Pre-Hispanic Maya Agriculture*, edited by Peter D. Harrison and B. L. Turner II, pp. 35-61. University of New Mexico Press, Albuquerque.

(1983). Subsistence and Complex Societies: the Case of the Maya. In *Advances in Archaeological Method and Theory*, Volume 6, edited by Michael B. Schiffer, pp. 141-89. Academic Press, New York.

Wittfogel, Karl (1955). Developmental Aspects of Hydraulic Societies. In *Irrigation Civilizations: a Comparative Study*, edited by Julian H. Steward, pp. 43-57. Pan American Union, Washington, D.C.

(1957). *Oriental Despotism: a Comparative Study of Total Power*. Yale University Press, New Haven.

Wolf, Eric R. (1969). *Peasant Wars of the Twentieth Century*. Harper and Row, New York.

Wolfle, Dael (1960). How Much Research for a Dollar? *Science* 132: 517.

Woodburn, James (1982). Egalitarian Societies. *Man* 17: 431-51.

Woodward, Ernest L. (1916). *Christianity and Nationalism in the Later Roman Empire*. Longman's Green, London.

Worthington, Nancy L. (1975). National Health Expenditures, 1929-74. *Social Security Bulletin* 38(2): 3-20.

Wright, Henry T. (1969). The Administration of Rural Production in an Early Mesopotamian Town. *Museum of Anthropology, University of Michigan, Anthropological Papers* 38.

(1977a). Recent Research on the Origin of the State. *Annual Review of Anthropology* 6: 379-97.

(1977b). Toward an Explanation of the Origin of the State. In *Explanation of Prehistoric Change*, edited by James N. Hill, pp. 215-30. University of New Mexico Press, Albuquerque.

Yoffee, Norman (1977). The Economic Role of the Crown in the Old Babylonian Period. *Bibliotheca Mesopotamica* 5. Undena, Los Angeles.

(1979). The Decline and Rise of Mesopotamian Civilization. *American Antiquity* 44: 5-35.

(1982). The Collapse of Civilization in Ancient Mesopotamia. Paper presented at the Collapse of Ancient Civilizations Symposium, School of American Research, Santa Fé.

Zolotas, Xenophon (1981). *Economic Growth and Declining Social Welfare*. New York University Press, New York and London.